Action Ascription in Interaction

Bringing together a team of global experts, this is the first volume to focus on the ways in which meanings are ascribed to actions in social interaction. It builds on the research traditions of Conversation Analysis and Pragmatics, and highlights the role of interactional, social, linguistic, multimodal, and epistemic factors in the formation and ascription of action-meanings. It shows how inference and intention ascription are displayed and drawn upon by participants in social interaction. Each chapter reveals practices, processes, and uses of action ascription, based on the analysis of audio and video recordings from nine different languages. Action ascription is conceptualised in this volume as not merely a cognitive process, but a social action in its own right that is used for managing interactional concerns and guiding the subsequent course of social interaction. It will be essential reading for academic researchers and advanced students interested in the relationship between language, behaviour, and social interaction.

ARNULF DEPPERMANN is Professor of German Linguistics, Leibniz-Institut für Deutsche Sprache, Mannheim, Germany. He studies language use in multimodal interaction, and his research interests focus on grammar, semantics, and understanding in interaction, action formation and ascription, interactional histories, and the coordination of language and body. He is founding editor of the open access journal *Gesprächsforschung* and associate editor of the *Journal of Pragmatics*.

MICHAEL HAUGH is Professor of Linguistics, School of Languages and Cultures, University of Queensland, Australia. His research interests centre on the role of language in social interaction, (im)politeness, teasing, and speaker meaning. He is an elected Fellow of the Australian Academy of Humanities, was co-editor in chief of the *Journal of Pragmatics* from 2015 to 2020, and is currently co-editor of the Cambridge Elements in Pragmatics series.

Studies in Interactional Sociolinguistics

FOUNDING EDITOR
John J. Gumperz (1922–2013)

EDITORS
Paul Drew, Rebecca Clift, Lorenza Mondada, Marja-Leena Sorjonen

1 *Discourse Strategies* John J. Gumperz
2 *Language and Social Identity* edited by John J. Gumperz
3 *The Social Construction of Literacy* Jenny Cook-Gumperz
4 *Politeness: Some Universals in Language Usage* Penelope Brown and Stephen C. Levinson
5 *Discourse Markers* Deborah Schiffrin
6 *Talking Voices: Repetition, Dialogue, and Imagery in Conversational Discourse* Deborah Tannen
7 *Conducting Interaction: Patterns of Behaviour in Focused Encounters* Adam Kendon
8 *Talk at Work: Interaction in Institutional Settings* edited by Paul Drew and John Heritage
9 *Grammar in Interaction: Adverbial Clauses in American English Conversations* Cecilia E. Ford
10 *Crosstalk and Culture in Sino-American Communication* Linda W. L. Young (with foreword by John J. Gumperz)
11 *AIDS Counselling: Institutional Interaction and Clinical Practice* Anssi Perakyla
12 *Prosody in Conversation: Interactional Studies* edited by Elizabeth Couper-Kuhlen and Margret Selting
13 *Interaction and Grammar* edited by Elinor Ochs, Emanuel A. Schegloff and Sandra A. Thompson
14 *Credibility in Court: Communicative Practices in the Camorra Trials* Marco Jacquemet
15 *Interaction and the Development of Mind* A. J. Wootton
16 *The News Interview: Journalists and Public Figures on the Air* Steven Clayman and John Heritage
17 *Gender and Politeness* Sara Mills
18 *Laughter in Interaction* Philip Glenn
19 *Matters of Opinion: Talking about Public Issues* Greg Myers
20 *Communication in Medical Care: Interaction between Primary Care Physicians and Patients* edited by John Heritage and Douglas Maynard
21 *In Other Words: Variation in Reference and Narrative* Deborah Schiffrin
22 *Language in Late Modernity: Interaction in an Urban School* Ben Rampton
23 *Discourse and Identity* edited by Anna De Fina, Deborah Schiffrin and Michael Bamberg

24 *Reporting Talk: Reported Speech in Interaction* edited by Elizabeth Holt and Rebecca Clift
25 *The Social Construction of Literacy*, 2nd Edition edited by Jenny Cook-Gumperz
26 *Talking Voices*, 2nd Edition Deborah Tannen
27 *Conversation Analysis*: Comparative Perspectives edited by Jack Sidnell
28 *Impoliteness: Using Language to Cause Offence* Jonathan Culpeper
29 *The Morality of Knowledge in Conversation* edited by Tanya Stivers, Lorenza Mondada and Jakob Steensig
30 *Conversational Repair and Human Understanding* edited by Makoto Hayashi, Geoffrey Raymond, and Jack Sidnell
31 *Grammar in Everyday Talk: Building Responsive Actions* Sandra A. Thompson, Barbara A. Fox, and Elizabeth Couper-Kuhlen
32 *Multimodal Conduct in the Law: Language, Gesture and Materiality in Legal Interaction* Gregory Matoesian and Kristin Enola Gilbert
33 *The Suspect's Statement: Talk and Text in the Criminal Process* Martha Komter
34 *How Mediation Works: Resolving Conflict Through Talk* Angela Cora Garcia
35 *Action Ascription in Interaction* edited by Arnulf Deppermann and Michael Haugh

Action Ascription in Interaction

Edited by

Arnulf Deppermann

Leibniz-Institut für Deutsche Sprache, Mannheim, Germany

Michael Haugh

University of Queensland, Australia

Shaftesbury Road, Cambridge CB2 8EA, United Kingdom

One Liberty Plaza, 20th Floor, New York, NY 10006, USA

477 Williamstown Road, Port Melbourne, VIC 3207, Australia

314–321, 3rd Floor, Plot 3, Splendor Forum, Jasola District Centre, New Delhi – 110025, India

103 Penang Road, #05–06/07, Visioncrest Commercial, Singapore 238467

Cambridge University Press is part of Cambridge University Press & Assessment, a department of the University of Cambridge.

We share the University's mission to contribute to society through the pursuit of education, learning and research at the highest international levels of excellence.

www.cambridge.org
Information on this title: www.cambridge.org/9781108465076

DOI: 10.1017/9781108673419

First published 2022
First paperback edition 2024

A catalogue record for this publication is available from the British Library

Library of Congress Cataloging-in-Publication data
Names: Depperman, Arnulf, editor. | Haugh, Michael, editor.
Title: Action ascription in interaction / edited by Arnulf Depperman, Michael Haugh.
Description: Cambridge ; New York, NY : Cambridge University Press, 2022. |
Series: Studies in interactional sociolinguistics ; 35 | Includes bibliographical references and index.
Identifiers: LCCN 2021037829 (print) | LCCN 2021037830 (ebook) |
ISBN 9781108474627 (hardback) | ISBN 9781108465076 (paperback) |
ISBN 9781108673419 (epub)
Subjects: LCSH: Speech acts (Linguistics) | Social interaction. | Conversation analysis. |
Pragmatics. | Semantics. | BISAC: LANGUAGE ARTS & DISCIPLINES /
Linguistics / Sociolinguistics
Classification: LCC P95.55 .A29 2022 (print) | LCC P95.55 (ebook) |
DDC 401/.452–dc23/eng/20211102
LC record available at https://lccn.loc.gov/2021037829
LC ebook record available at https://lccn.loc.gov/2021037830

ISBN 978-1-108-47462-7 Hardback
ISBN 978-1-108-46507-6 Paperback

Contents

Figures

Tables

Contributors

ROBERT B. ARUNDALE (University of Alaska Fairbanks, USA)

LOTTE VAN BURGSTEDEN (Vrije Universiteit Amsterdam, The Netherlands)

ELIZABETH COUPER-KUHLEN (University of Helsinki, Finland)

ARNULF DEPPERMANN (Leibniz-Institut für Deutsche Sprache, Mannheim, Germany)

PAUL DREW (University of York, UK)

N. J. ENFIELD (University of Sydney, Australia)

MICHAEL HAUGH (University of Queensland, Australia)

MAKOTO HAYASHI (Nagoya University, Japan)

HENRIKE HELMER (Leibniz-Institut für Deutsche Sprache, Mannheim, Germany)

JOHN HERITAGE (University of California at Los Angeles, USA)

TAKESHI HIRAMOTO (Kyoto Prefectural University, Japan)

JULIA KAISER (Leibniz-Institut für Deutsche Sprache, Mannheim, Germany)

TOM KOOLE (University of Groningen, The Netherlands)

LORENZA MONDADA (University of Basel, Switzerland)

JACK SIDNELL (University of Toronto, Canada)

SANDRA A. THOMPSON (University of California at Santa Barbara, USA)

YAXIN WU (Ocean University of China, China)

GUODONG YU (Ocean University of China, China)

Introduction

1 Action Ascription in Social Interaction

Arnulf Deppermann and Michael Haugh

1.1 Introduction: Action and Action Ascription

There is a long-standing tradition of theorizing 'action' in philosophy and linguistic pragmatics. Speech act theory claims that individual actions are instantiations of abstract types of speech acts, which are seen as conventional, "institutional" facts (Searle 1969). Their production and understanding is said to rely on rules, importantly including illocutionary force indicating devices (IFIDs), which index the kind of speech act an utterance is held to implement (Searle & Vanderveken 1985). Gricean pragmatics (Grice 1989), neo-Gricean pragmatics (Levinson 2006), and relevance theory (Sperber & Wilson 1995), however, point out that such rules are not able to properly account for indirect speech acts. They instead insist on the primary role of intentions and inferential processes in understanding speech acts (see also Brandom 1994, 2014). These approaches, however, lack empirical foundations for the most part. Among other problems, the issues of segmentation, identification, and interpretation of actions in context have not yet been settled to a satisfying degree in the context of those traditional approaches in the philosophy of language and linguistic pragmatics (Drew & Couper-Kuhlen 2014a; Levinson 2013). Indeed, Levinson (2017) has recently argued that

> despite the fact that speech acts are clearly central to an understanding of language use, they have been largely off the linguistics agenda since the 1980s . . . research on speech acts boomed for a little over a decade (in the 1970s and 1980s) and then went out of fashion without the most fundamental issues being resolved at all. (2017: 199–200)

Conversation analysis offers, in contrast, an alternative approach, which has continued to develop since the late 1960s, by studying actions in the broader sequential environments in which they are invariably situated. Actions here are conceived of as sequentially positioned and contextually sensitive (Sacks 1992; Sacks, Schegloff & Jefferson 1974; Schegloff 2007). Conversation analysis has an extensive tradition of research into the way actions are responsive to prior talk, showing the subtle nature of the relationships between first and second actions (e.g., Raymond 2003; Thompson, Fox & Couper-Kuhlen 2015).

Responses have been shown to be major constituents for understanding actions in context. In a seminal paper, Sacks, Schegloff and Jefferson (1974) argued that "it is a systematic consequence of the turn-taking organization of conversation that it obliges its participants to display to each other, in a turn's talk, their understanding of other turns' talk" (1974: 728). For instance, they claimed:

> when A addresses a first pair-part such as a 'question' or a 'complaint' to B, we have noted, A selects B as next speaker, and selects for B that he next perform a second part for the 'adjacency pair' A has started, i.e. an 'answer' or an 'apology' (among other possibilities) respectively. B, in so doing, not only performs that utterance-type, but thereby displays (in the first place to his co-participants) his understanding of the prior turn's talk as a first part, as a 'question' or 'complaint'. (Sacks, Schegloff & Jefferson 1974: 728)

The observation that a participant's understanding of a prior turn can be inferred from their response to it by analysts gave rise to what has become known as the 'next-turn proof procedure':

> while understandings of other turns' talk are displayed to co-participants, they are available as well to professional analysts, who are thereby afforded a proof criterion (and a search procedure) for the analysis of what a turn's talk is occupied with. Since it is the parties' understandings of prior turns' talk that is relevant to their construction of next turns, it is their understandings that are wanted for analysis. The display of those understandings in the talk of subsequent turns affords both a resource for the analysis of prior turns and a proof procedure for professional analyses of prior turns – resources intrinsic to the data themselves. (Sacks, Schegloff & Jefferson 1974: 729)

Response has thus been formulated as critical to the analysis of social action from the very beginnings of the field. Yet, the response in the next turn, i.e. in second position to the action at issue, may not display an action ascription that is sufficient for all practical purposes. One reason is that there may be many different and even competing possible action ascriptions that can be inferred from the response (we will deal with this issue of implicit versus explicit action ascriptions and possible ambiguities below). A second, more fundamental point concerning the social reality of action ascription is that the next turn can only convey the *recipient's understanding* of the prior action, but does not yet provide an analytical warrant for an *intersubjective action ascription.* Intersubjectivity can only be taken to be accomplished sequentially if the producer of the original, first-positioned action produces a turn in third position that confirms the action ascription that the recipient's turn in second position has indexed or formulated (Arundale 1999; Deppermann 2015; Schegloff 1991; Sidnell 2014). Without a third-turn confirmation, the intersubjective status of the action ascription in second position remains unsettled, and so the actual understandings of the participants may remain unreconciled

(Coulter 1983). The third turn is, therefore, a key sequential occasion for restoring intersubjectivity (e.g., Heritage 1984; Schegloff 1992; Seuren 2018), in particular, through repair, in cases where the producer of the original turn finds they have not been 'correctly' understood (Schegloff 1992). Of course, it can turn out even later than in third position that participants' understandings have been at odds, thus calling for efforts to secure understandings which are sufficiently shared (e.g., Deppermann 2018). An intersubjectively shared and socially valid action ascription thus is warranted neither by the agent's intention nor by the recipient's response, but rather is the outcome of an interactional process of mutual displays, and possibly negotiation, of participants' understandings of prior actions. The three-position sequential architecture of intersubjectivity (Heritage 1984) thus systematically affords action ascription as "a temporally extended work-in-progress that is managed through the serial interlocking of actions in a process of successive confirmation and specification" (Clayman & Heritage 2014: 57). Of course, in the course of this emergent interactional process, action ascriptions may also be revised, left open, or even become an object of enduring dissent.

However, while the claim that how a prior action is understood by participants can be inferred from the way in which it is responded to and possibly negotiated afterwards is critical to the analysis of action, it does not on its own provide sufficient grounds for a comprehensive theory of action. It leaves open, for instance, the question of how participants recognize actions in the first place, a point which Schegloff (2007) framed as the 'action formation' problem:

> how are the resources of the language, the body, the environment of the interaction, and the position *in* the interaction fashioned into conformations designed to be, and to be recognized by recipients as, particular actions – actions like requesting, inviting, granting, complaining, agreeing, telling, noticing, rejecting, and so on – in a class of unknown size? (Schegloff 2007: xiv)

It was subsequently observed by Stivers and Rossano (2010b) that the design and recognition of actions also involves the "action ascription" problem:

> despite a heavy emphasis on action within the CA literature, we still lack a theory of action ascription. The bread and butter of CA has been identifying practices for varying the social-relational aspects of actions; however, we know relatively little about how people design and recognize the actions themselves in the first instance. (Stivers & Rossano 2010b: 53–4)

Recent research in conversation analysis and interactional linguistics has considerably broadened our knowledge of the role of linguistic formats and turn design in action formation (under the heading 'social action formats', see Section 1.3) and the interactional organization of various kinds of actions, with requests and related actions being a major focus of such research (Drew & Couper-Kuhlen 2014b; Kendrick & Drew 2016; Rossi 2015; Sorjonen, Raevaara & Couper-Kuhlen 2017; Zinken 2016). There has also been a growing body of work on the role of epistemics (Heritage 2012a, 2012b) and deontics (Stevanovic & Peräkylä 2012, 2014) in action formation and response (Thompson, Fox & Couper-Kuhlen 2015). Yet despite the insights this growing body of work has offered, an elaborate conversation-analytic concept of 'action' has not yet emerged, and the relationship between the position of an action (i.e. the relevance of sequential organization, Schegloff 1984), its composition (i.e. the relevance of linguistic turn design, Couper-Kuhlen 2014), and other contextual features for the situated understanding of actions has remained the subject of dispute. A key point of departure for clarifying this is arguably the notion of action ascription (Levinson 2013).

Action ascription can be understood from two broad perspectives. On one view, it refers to the ways in which actions constitute categories by which members make sense of their world, and forms a key foundation for holding others (morally) accountable for their conduct (Jayyusi 1991). On another view, it refers to the ways in which we accountably respond to the actions of others, thereby accomplishing sequential versions of meaningful social experience (Sacks 1985). According to the latter view, the response of participants to prior actions relies on some form of action ascription, which is indexed by the design of the response, although the ascription is more or less implicit, and can be rather indeterminate at times. In short, action ascription can be understood as a matter of categorization of prior actions or responding in ways that are sequentially fitted to prior actions, or both. On both views, however, action ascription involves attributing action(s) to (just) prior conduct. Where these views differ is the extent to which this attribution is assumed to be explicit or tacit, whether or not action ascription is understood to be primarily inferential in nature or a social action in its own right, and whether action ascription is necessary for response generation or not. These views do not necessarily exclude each other; they can also be seen as descriptions of different ways in which action ascription can play a role and become manifest in social interaction.

The aim of this volume is to further our understanding of action ascription and to better elucidate the role it might play in an empirically grounded theory of action in social interaction. It takes close scrutiny of situated action ascription in turns that are responsive to prior turns (frequently but not always in second position) in their sequential and multimodal contexts as its point of departure for studying action from the participants' point of view. The aim is to enable us to move forward in addressing complex questions around how linguistic practice, bodily conduct, rules/conventions, inferential reasoning, and indexical interpretation enter into the interpretation of situated action.

We begin this introductory chapter by moving in Section 1.2 to frame action ascription as a members' concern and to consider the issues that doing so raises. We next move, in Section 1.3, to briefly summarize the different approaches to action ascription that have developed in the field, and some key points of theoretical contention that have emerged. This is followed, in Section 1.4, by an overview of the key constituents and resources of action ascription that have been identified in conversation-analytic research, before going on in Section 1.5 to discuss how action ascription can itself be considered a form of social action. We conclude in Section 1.6 with an overview of the remaining chapters in this volume.

1.2 Action Ascription as a Members' Concern

What counts as social action is a much more complex question than might first appear. A naive view of interaction might hold that it can be readily parsed into discrete sequences of actions, such as 'questions' (and 'answers'), 'complaints' (and 'apologies'), 'requests' (and 'offers'), 'invitations (and 'acceptances' or 'refusals'), and so on. In reality things are somewhat more complex. For a start, these kinds of action categories are far too gross to capture the kinds of things that concern participants themselves. They are also inherently normative categories and so defeasible (that is, their applicability can be contested by participants). Yet to conclude that action ascription is not of practical importance would be to ignore empirical evidence that participants themselves are concerned with action ascription, not just in the sense of explicitly holding others accountable for particular actions as discussed by Jayyusi (1991), and more recently by Sidnell (2017), but arguably in a more fundamental sense of figuring out just what it is the other party is doing and how to respond. This process of figuring out may not be readily describable by participants, but it arguably lies at the heart of what drives social interaction.

Consider the following two extracts from a telephone call between two friends. The first comes from earlier in the conversation when Edna has 'invited' Margy and her mother up to Cocos "someday" for lunch. It turns out Edna intends to pay for the lunch, a 'proposal' that Margy rejects with a 'counter-proposal' that they split the bill (see Drew 1984: 149; cf. Clayman & Heritage 2014: 61–2; Couper-Kuhlen 2014: 626; Kendrick & Drew 2014: 105).

Excerpt 1.1 NB:VII: 1:46

EDN: wul why don't we: uh-m: why don't i take you'n mo:m
up there tuh: coco's. someday fer lu:nch.

03 we'll go, bkuzz up there tu[h,
04 MAR: [k goo:d.
05 EDN: ha:h?
06 MAR: that's a good deal. .hh-.hh=
07 EDN: =eh i'll take you bo:th[up
08 MAR: [no:::: wil all go dutch.=
09 =b't[let's do that.]
10 EDN: [n o : we wo:n'] t.

The matter remains unresolved as they then move on to talk about other things.

Later in the call, in response to a pre-closing, Margy launches a more specific ‘proposal’ that they go up to Coco’s for lunch next week when her mother comes down. Jefferson, Sacks and Schegloff (1977: 27–69) develop a finely nuanced analysis of this ‘offence-remedial’ sequence, which is instructive with respect to how far we might take the analysis of action. Our point here, however, is rather more simple. In advocating why they should go to Coco’s for lunch, Edna proffers a three-part list (Jefferson 1990), which includes claiming Coco’s is “fun” (line 7), “pretty” (line 9), and “cheap” (line 12). It is the latter that appears to subsequently occasion the extended ‘offence-remedial’ sequence in which Edna repeatedly claims she “didn’t mean that” (lines 19, 21, 29, 38; also lines 34–5)

Excerpt 1.2 NB:VII: 7:09

01 EDN: .t.hhhhhhhhhhhh well honey li:sten ah'll thhalk with yeh:: uh:
02 wil[git tih] ge[ther::[e]
03 MAR: [.hhhhhh] [eH e y[w] 'l edna maybe next week el-e-you:ll
04 li:ke e:lss she's a lotta fun. she's comin down, .t.h-.h-.h
05 yihknow,.h-.h and uh m- why don't we all do that. w'l go up
06 en eat et coco's? er will go someplace e:lse.=
07 EDN: =oh vco[co's is FUN UP] THERE ON THE HILL=
08 MAR: [(oh figgy neh)]
09 EDN: ='n yuh look do[wn it's so p] retty,
10 MAR: [y:::: ye:ah.]
11 yeah. let's do it.
12 EDN: -> AN IT'S chea:p, hu
13 MAR: yehh[hahh]
14 EDN: [hihh] #h:::::(h)i'm O::n ah:.ehhh=
15 =I'M ON [RETI[:RE[MENT.] .hhh
16 MAR: [.hhh[hey[w'l y] :yer not takin' us edna=
17 =b't i[: thin[k'd be f u n [tih go:.]
18 EDN: [.hhhhh[O H : DON'T [be s::uh] hh=
19 -> =u-i[: did] 'n mean that ruh-ah::=.
20 MAR: [n o-]
21 EDN: -> =i:hh didn't m:mean[that[et].

```
MAR:                          [.hhh[we] ll n[o i:'m no:t-] gon] na invite=
EDN:                                   [a : : : : :] ll.]
MAR:      =all'v us:: up there en'n then i-have you pay the bi:ll.hhh
          i[: j's] think id be f:fundee a[ll have all] of us go:.=
EDN:      [ehhh!]                        [°(           )]
MAR:      =en i want elss tuh seeyuh.hh[hh
EDN:                                   [.hhh=
       -> =oh[:  h o n e y   i]  didn'] mean that=
MAR:         [(yihknow I mean)] she's-]
EDN:      =[et a-] ah::::::::ll.]
MAR:      =[she's] j's the kind'v] a person thet yihknow it dezn't
          make any di[ffrence  ( )
EDN: ->              [BUD SAYS IT SURE SOUNDED LIKE I MEANT IT=
       -> =B'T[I DIDN'T,]
MAR:      [ U:A::hhhh] haahhaah[haa]
EDN:      [i d] on't have a di:ner's-.hh=
       -> =no-u-honey i: r:rilly didn'mean[ tha:[t but BU] D'n[ i]=
MAR:                                      [ .hh-[ I : : :]    [ oo]=
EDN:      =ATE UP THERE the other night it ws:: really good foo:d
          very reas'na[ ble.]
MAR:      [(h)i] - edna you know i dih-y[ouknow]=
```

The question, then, is what did Edna *do* by saying “AN IT’S chea:p, hu” in line 12, such that it can cause this evident consternation? While a detailed analysis of this lies beyond the scope of this introductory chapter, the data extract nicely illustrates the way in which account-ability as intelligibility and accountability as responsibility (Robinson 2016) are intertwined. In short, what Edna is holding herself accountable for through these repeated denials is that her claim that Coco’s is “cheap” is hearable – that is, account-able – as a reason for why she prefers it over another place, *presuming that she will be paying for that lunch*. This inference makes account-able a range of other inferences, the exact nature of which were perhaps best known to those participants. However, they are clearly treated as undesirable by Edna. In any case, the point is made well enough, we think, that ascribing action(s) is evidently a member’s concern.

A turn to action ascription thus means adopting a members’ perspective. Indeed, the aim of this volume is to focus on understandings of ‘action’ from a participants’ point of view, and to ask how this impinges on the scientific understanding of action to arrive at an empirically warranted conceptualization of ‘action’ from the members’ point of view, as attested by their conversational behavior. This leads us to consider the following issues: How do members themselves conceive of actions and how do they ascribe actions to behavior? Which interpretive constituents enter into ascriptions of actions? How is action ascription displayed in social interaction and how is it consequential to the interactional process?

In attempting to address such questions in the course of this volume, it is important to bear in mind a number of key parameters relating to action ascription for members. These include the scope of 'action', granularity in their description, and the inevitable multifunctionality of 'action' (cf. Sidnell 2017: 326).

(a) *The scope of action ascription.* Social actions must be addressed to particular others (see already Weber [1968/1922], who claimed that actions are addressed to others and oriented to them in their trajectory, i.e. they are responsive). Actions in CA are generally taken to be the "main business" of a turn (Levinson 2013: 107). On some accounts this is whatever is (taken as) intended as the purpose/goal of that turn by the speaker, and distinguished from "collateral effects" (Sidnell & Enfield 2014: 426), such as referring, positioning and identity claims, indexing relationships and roles, epistemic claims, and emotion displays, which are not classically regarded as actions. On other accounts, advocated, for instance, by Schegloff (1996: 165), the main or primary action is "what the response must deal with in order to count as an adequate next turn" (Levinson 2013: 107; cf. Rossi 2018: 379). Levinson (2013) draws a further distinction between "primary actions" and "secondary actions." The latter include display of expertise, emotions, "off-record actions," and the like, which may well be "intended," but "do not change the nature of the sequential action type now due" (2013: 107).

Actions for members, however, can go beyond what is traditionally understood in scientific accounts of action, as notions such as 'intention' or 'purpose' vary in their scope just as much as the notion of action itself (Duranti 2015; Gibbs 1999; Haugh & Jaszczolt 2012). For members, then, action ascription is fundamentally tied to the issue of the segmentation of the flow of acting into discrete actions (see Schütz 1976). This raises the question of which stretch of behavior members are responding to and treating as 'a single action' (cf. Szczepek-Reed & Raymond 2013). These units may well be different from the prototypical actions discussed in the literature: people may respond selectively to prior talk and respond to units much larger than basic actions, for example, when responding to a multi-unit turn.

(b) *The granularity of action ascription.* Action ascription means categorizing some stretch of behavior as something, that is, it is always aspectual. This categorization is overwhelmingly done tacitly – we don't normally talk about what it is we are doing – but invariably presupposes some kind of ontology of action (Sidnell & Enfield 2014). The nature of this ontology of action is complex in the case of social interaction, as there is considerable variation in action labels across different languages (e.g., Duranti 1988; Hakulinen & Sorjonen 2012; Rosaldo 1982), and among researchers (i.e. scientific use) and participants (i.e. everyday use) (Levinson 2013; Pillet-Shore 2021;

Schegloff 2007), so establishing a definitive typology seems an impossible task. The elusiveness of any such typology is due, however, to an even more fundamental issue for members, namely that categories and descriptions can vary in their degree of granularity (Schegloff 1988, 2000), or what Sacks (1963) earlier referred to as the "etcetera problem." The very same utterance can thus be described in a multitude of different ways. *Can you pass the salt?*, for instance, can be glossed as 'A wants me to do something', 'A has requested me to do something', 'A has requested me in an unobtrusive way to do something', and so on. What is important to note here is that for members, action ascription does not just mean ascribing a type, but ascribing who (in which role, etc.) has done what (object of the action) to whom under what conditions (circumstances, with regard to expectations) in which ways (politeness, emotional tone, recipient design, etc.). As Clayman and Heritage (2014) note, for instance, in relation to the ascription of 'requests', 'offers', and 'invitations', "action formulations can be *compacted*, glossing over the details of what will transpire and thereby obscuring any service-related characteristics and the benefactive configuration they would implicate; or they can be *expanded*, with benefactive details specified, elaborated, and thus foregrounded" (2014: 61, original emphasis). In other words, action ascription always means a situated interpretation of a prior turn concerning (some of) its (potential) indexical facets. The level of granularity which is characteristic of action types generally used in the literature, such as commands, requests, and instructions, may not, of course, matter to members in particular circumstances. Instead, what is required by those members may indeed only be a coarser attribution (e.g., a deontic expectation). As Enfield and Sidnell (2017a, 2017b) argue, one does not need to be able to describe a prior action in order to be able to respond to it. However, at other times much more fine-grained distinctions can matter, many of which have not yet been captured by action types and labels discussed in the literature (Schegloff 1996). Yet while ascriptions of action can vary in their degree of granularity, the interactional reality of action types for response generation, and thus for members, is strongly supported by observable regularities and expectancies concerning sequential organization (Kendrick et al. 2020; Kevoe-Feldman & Robinson 2012; Schegloff 2007; Thompson, Fox & Couper-Kuhlen 2015).

(c) *The multifunctionality of 'action'*. The multi-layering and equivocality of actions is a pervasive feature of them in social interaction, a point noted some decades ago in linguistic pragmatics (Levinson 1981; Thomas 1995), although it has only been the subject of concerted conversation-analytic studies in recent years (e.g., Rossi 2018). However, while a single 'action unit' can give rise to multiple actions (Levinson 2013), and even to some degree of equivocality with respect to how one responds to that utterance, turn, etc. (e.g., Drew 2018), this is not to say that action ascription does not matter for response generation.

People can be seen to respond to different layers of action-meaning at the same time in their responses (e.g., making an assertion, thereby making an assessment, thereby disagreeing, thereby rejecting an identity-claim of the interlocutor). The multi-layering of 'action units' is also related to the temporality of actions (Deppermann 2015): every action potentially has a retrospective meaning (interpreting prior actions), a prospective aspect (projecting next actions), and a meaning in and of itself. Consequently, ascription can focus, possibly selectively, on one or more of these three temporal facets of any 'action unit'.

1.3 Approaches to Action Ascription

Recent research on action formation has demonstrated the central role played by social action formats in action formation and recognition (Couper-Kuhlen 2014; Fox 2007; Thompson, Fox & Couper-Kuhlen 2015). However, as those working on social action formats acknowledge, the meaning of actions is not straightforwardly coded in these formats, but is positionally sensitive to prior context, and is even sometimes equivocal. Actions often cannot simply be recognized from talk or conduct, and participants have to figure out and negotiate which action(s) some stretch of behavior has been implementing. Inference is thus central to action ascription, especially as not every action comes with a straightforward social action format. However, it is one thing to assert that action ascription is critically dependent on inferences made by participants (and inferences about those inferences made by analysts). It is another thing to provide a systematic account of the account-able grounds for making those inferences. As action ascription has become the focus of attention over the past decade a number of different approaches to it have emerged. In this section, we briefly review three of the most important ones: the "assemblages approach" (Schegloff 1996, 1997, 2006; see also Garfinkel & Sacks 1970), the "inferential approach" (Levinson 2013, 2017), and the "semiotic approach" (Enfield & Sidnell 2017a, 2017b; Sidnell 2017; Sidnell & Enfield 2014).

The "assemblages approach" to action ascription builds on the ethnomethodological notion of practices (or procedures or methods) by which members make sense of their world (Garfinkel 1967; Garfinkel & Sacks 1970). A practice is a recurrent assemblage of particular features of the composition (both linguistic and non-linguistic) and the position (within a TCU, turn, sequence, and overall structural organization) of an element of conduct destined to accomplish a certain action (Heritage 2010; Schegloff 1996, 2007). While this might seem to privilege action formation, on an ethnomethodological view, "the activities whereby members produce and manage settings of organised everyday affairs are identical with members' procedures for making those settings 'account-able'" (Garfinkel 1967: 1). In other words, elements of conduct are intelligible (i.e. recognizable, understandable) as implementing actions on the basis of the practices by which they are implemented, and actions are thus "done as assemblages of practices" (Garfinkel & Sacks 1970: 340). The view that defined practices can be mapped to particular actions is termed the "practions approach" and attributed to Schegloff by Enfield (2013: 100; see also Enfield & Sidnell 2017a: 105–6; Sidnell & Enfield 2014: 430). However, there are reasons to resist the seemingly seductive idea that practices determine actions, and that action ascription is therefore simply a matter of recognizing these practices (Schegloff 1997: 539).

The "inferential approach" to action ascription developed by Levinson (2013, 2017) locates action ascription at the intersection of cognition-for-interaction and sequentially ordered interaction. On this view, action ascription involves parsing linguistic, gaze, and prosodic features of the design of the prior turn, features of the interactional context, including epistemic (a)symmetry, sequential position, and the attribution of projects and tiered action plans (Levinson 2013: 127, 2017: 208–11). Most of these features are now widely accepted as important resources for action ascription, a point which we will move to discuss in further detail in the following section. What distinguishes Levinson's approach to action ascription from the "assemblages approach," then, is the emphasis he places on the need for participants to rapidly merge different sources of information through both bottom-up and top-down inferential processes. Levinson argues the former are likely probabilistic (i.e. Bayesian) forms of inference, as it has been repeatedly demonstrated that linguistic formats cannot be reliably mapped to actions, although he points out that this may be, in part, a function of the fact that "where multiple forms are available, they may each carry subtly different presuppositions about background conditions" (Levinson 2017: 209). Top-down inferential processes rely on abductive reasoning and other forms of practical reasoning, of which the classic question in conversation-analytic research, "Why that now?" (Schegloff & Sacks 1973: 299), is an instance.[1] Pomerantz (2017) argues this means that "recognizing an action is fundamentally indexical, that is, its meaning is dependent on the context in which it occurs" (2017: 74). Levinson (2013, 2017) takes this further, however, in proposing that action ascription also involves inferences about the "the likely goal structure or plans of the speaker . . . the inference schema we use to understand any sequence of actions" (Levinson 2017: 211). However, while such schema can indeed be convincingly applied to action sequences post facto, and underlying plans of speakers seemingly reconstructed, it remains to be seen the extent to which these putative inferential schema are drawn upon *in situ* when participants do

[1] Schegloff (1998) subsequently claimed that "why that now" is fundamentally indexical with respect to both the referent of the 'that' and the 'now'.

not have access to what comes next (Drew 2011). Indeed, Levinson (2017) cautions that there is still as yet "no complete model of how these various kinds of information come together in action attribution" (2017: 214).

The "semiotic approach" to action ascription has been developed by Enfield and Sidnell (2017a, 2017b; see also Sidnell & Enfield 2014; Sidnell 2017). They draw an important distinction between *responding* to an action and *describing* an action. Similar to the other two approaches to action ascription, Enfield and Sidnell (2017a, 2017b) argue that participants draw on combinations of features of the composition and position of prior moves, which on a semiotic view constitute "signs," in responding to a prior action. They also echo Levinson (2013, 2017) in arguing that "action is subject to multiple possible descriptions simultaneously" (Enfield & Sidnell 2017b: 523), as well as Schegloff (2006) in arguing that because of the inherent temporality of composition and position, "action is [also] subject to multiple, successive interpretations or understandings or drafts" (Enfield & Sidnell 2017b: 523). Where they differ is in the central importance they place on inferences about the speaker's goals that are motivated by combinations of "signs" in guiding participants in how to respond appropriately to prior moves (Enfield & Sidnell 2017b: 517), and in their assumption that participants build "a token understanding of what a person is doing by what they are saying" (2017b: 524). They argue that understanding action does not require typing or categorizing prior conduct by participants, but consists entirely in responding appropriately to that prior move. Sidnell (2017) argues, however, that there is still a place for ascribing action types with respect to their accountability. He claims action types are fundamental to assigning responsibility for action through explicit attributions of actions, and contestation of those attributions by members. Enfield and Sidnell (2017b) go on to conclude that

> an interactant is able to produce an appropriate response to another's move in interaction by building a token understanding of what a person is doing by what they are saying, based on features of the move's design and positioning ... there is no analytical need to propose that interactants categorize actions by binning token moves as this or that action type. (Enfield & Sidnell 2017b: 524)

The "semiotic approach" treats types of actions as useful heuristics for analysts, but argues that for members there are only situated tokens. However, as they earlier pointed out, "any account of social action presupposes an ontology of action whether this is made explicit or not" (Sidnell & Enfield 2014: 423). They advocate an ontology of action that consists of highly generalized categories of action. One example of a generalized ontology of action is that of Tomasello (2008), who proposes a three-way distinction between "requesting: to secure another's help for meeting your own goals," "helping: to provide help for meeting another's goals," and "sharing: for meeting common goals, and for the cohesion of social relationships" grounded in phylogeny (Enfield & Sidnell 2017b: 528). An alternative is Searle's (1969) four-way distinction between assertives (corresponding to *beliefs*), directives (corresponding to *desires*), commissives (corresponding to *intentions*), and expressives (corresponding to *feelings*), which is grounded in a theory of intentionality (i.e. directed mental acts/processes). In advocating such an ontology, they relegate technical categories of action developed in CA to the status of "convenient heuristics" that play "a useful role in analysis, and in scholarly communication" but do not in themselves "provide a general account for action in interaction" (Enfield & Sidnell 2017b: 529).

One challenge facing all accounts of action ascription is how to accommodate actions to which there is not a clear response. Stivers and Rossano (2010a) have argued that some actions, such as assessments or noticings, do not always receive clear uptake (although cf. Schegloff [2010] for a counteranalysis). They go on to suggest that this has implications for accounts of action ascription that rely on "the responsive turn in action analysis" (Stivers & Rossano 2010b: 54), and ask that if there is no uptake, "how are we to ascertain what action the speaker designed or what action the recipient understood him/her to be implementing?" (2010b: 54). However, while responsive turns are critical to analyzing action ascription as a form of social action, there are other resources by which members ascribe actions in a more general sense. It is to a consideration of the constituents of and resources for action ascription that we now turn.

1.4 Constituents and Resources of Action Ascription

What resources do members draw on in order to ascribe actions? Of course, the most obvious source is action formation. Yet, it is still up for debate to what degree features of turn design determine action ascription (Couper-Kuhlen 2014). Social action formats are conventional ways of delivering an action (Fox 2007). Still, they are themselves context-dependent, and so action ascriptions based on formats are invariably defeasible. In addition, turns at talk often do not draw on definite social action formats, or they may be designed to be ambiguous or equivocal as to which action(s) are being implemented (Drew 2018). The question is thus: How and when are the action implications of a turn open to dispute, negotiation, misunderstanding, or being overridden by other sources of meaning? An answer to this question includes identifying which interpretive resources enter into action ascription by participants, and how these relate to the composition of an action and its position within an interactional sequence. Resources which have to be considered include:

(1) syntactic and prosodic format of turns (Couper-Kuhlen 2014; Couper-Kuhlen & Selting 2018; Thompson, Fox & Couper-Kuhlen 2015);

(2) multimodal aspects of action formation other than linguistic turn design (Goodwin 2000, 2013, 2017; Holler, Kendrick & Levinson 2018; Hömke, Holler and Levinson 2018; Mondada 2014);
(3) the sequential position of the turn, including within TCUs, turns, and sequences (Schegloff 1984, 1995, 1996, 2007);
(4) the larger interaction type and joint projects therein (Clark 1996; Goodwin 2000, 2017; Levinson 2013; Linell 1998; Schegloff 2007);
(5) participants' identities and associated epistemic (Heritage 2012a, 2012b) and deontic (Stevanovic & Peräkylä 2012, 2014) (a)symmetries;
(6) elements of preference organization and (dis)preferred formats (Clift 2016; Pillet-Shore 2016, 2021);
(7) cognitive ascriptions (Deppermann 2012), including the attribution of (culture-specific) concepts of intentionality and what it means to be an actor (Duranti 1988, 2015); and
(8) attributions of accountability (Haugh 2013; Robinson 2016).

The contributions in this volume ask how participants index these (and potentially still other) aspects as being relevant for action ascription, when they matter, and how they are related to each other (in potentially disputed ways). These considerations will be related to properties of the turn-to-be-understood (e.g., vagueness, indirectness), to situated interactional concerns (e.g., dealing with sensitive matters, strategic interaction, specifics of activity type, genre, identities, and participation framework), and to the larger interactional projects which a turn may serve and which themselves may be negotiated through action ascription.

A major issue which is yet to be adequately addressed is the role of cognition in action ascription. The ascription of intentions, strategies, plans, and projects has been argued to be crucial for action ascription (Levinson 2013, 2017). Indeed, there is an increasing body of work that demonstrates the role cognitive processing plays in action ascription (e.g., Bögels, Kendrick & Levinson 2020; Gisladottir, Bögels & Levinson 2018; Gisladottir, Chwilla & Levinson 2015). Actions can be understood as being instrumental or metonymically related to higher-order goals or projects, indexing larger beliefs, and purposes (Brandom 1994, 2014; Clark 1996; Gibbs 1999; Levinson 1981, 2013, 2017). However, the overt ascription of cognitive states to interpret actions is rare; explicit intention-ascription sometimes happens, but this is tied to specific pragmatic problems and uses (Edwards 2008; Haugh 2008, 2013). Moreover, while the goal-directedness of social behavior is certainly a major constituent of action ascription (Enfield & Sidnell 2017a, 2017b; Levinson 2013, 2017), not all instances of action ascription can be readily reduced to particular goals. Indeed, reference to goals alone may only be sufficient for very basic actions, such as object transfer. In most cases, many other factors enter into action ascription: how something was done, by whom to whom, with which emotional stance, attending (or not) to which side conditions, and how the action affects the ascriber (emotionally, morally, regarding their social position, in front of others, and so on).

The relative importance of cognitive factors, such as goals and intentions (Enfield & Sidnell 2017a, 2017b; Levinson 2013, 2017), on the one hand, and social factors, such as relevance rules and normative structures (Haugh 2013; Robinson 2016), on the other hand, for action ascription is also an important issue needing further careful debate. The normative accountability of action is calculated with respect to situated expectations about appropriate and rational behavior that are immanent to the moral order of interaction (Haugh 2013, 2017). This can converge with intention ascriptions (e.g., in the case of attributions of rational action), but does not necessarily need or imply them. Expectations of social accountability concerning which kind of action is due in an interactional environment and the relationship between them and the actual behavior like fulfillment, marked contrast, exaggerated compliance, ironicization, role distance, and so on may lead to ascriptions based on convention and accountability, which do not have to rely on the attribution of intentions. On the contrary, if action ascription were entirely normative, the issue of action ascription could be subsumed under action formation, because the latter would entail the first, reducing action ascription to being simply a matter of action recognition. However, action ascriptions can be calibrated and modulated through reference to the actor's intentions and their knowledge, their biographies, motives, preferences, and so on (as earlier noted by Garfinkel 1967). The inherent reflexivity of action by virtue of recipient design also means that the accountability of action crucially includes a consideration of how a turn can be heard given the presence of just these recipients, their knowledge, their normative expectations, and personal preferences. This becomes particularly clear if turns are addressed to multiple recipients (Clark & Carlson 1982; Deppermann 2014; Hindmarsh & Pilnick 2002; Mondada 2014). Accountability, of course, can be negotiated and disputed, because construals of action are flexible, albeit to varying degrees (Haugh 2008, 2013). Rhetorical skills can matter here too, because the degree of flexibility in ascribing accountable conduct is directly related to inferential work and the ways in which a participant is able to account for it verbally.

Since action ascription for the most part is not simply a matter of the recognition or decoding of fully conventional, context-free interpretations of prior actions, inference is an important, inevitable part of action ascription. Inference is necessary in order to relate behavior to both the immediately prior and the global context, taking into account both its composition and its position in an action sequence. Scholars in discursive psychology have eschewed discussion of inferences and other cognitive operations (e.g., Antaki 2004; Edwards 2006; Potter & Edwards 2013). Yet, the fact remains that inferences are implicitly made and used in action analysis (Deppermann 2012), and are inevitable for even the most basic understandings of reference, coherence, and action in sequences of interaction (Deppermann 2018) – a tradition that goes back to the earliest work in CA (e.g., Sacks' [1992] lectures on the "inference-making machine"). CA scholars arguably need to be more explicit about what inferences enter into their analyses of action and from what sources such inferences are derived (Deppermann 2012; Pomerantz 2017).

1.5 Action Ascription as Social Action

Responding to an action is itself a form of social action (Drew 2011). Action ascription is not simply a cognitive process, which is a prerequisite for response generation, but is itself an action with its own distinct features of interactional design and use. The observability of action ascription ranges from more tacit forms to overt formats of action ascription that are explicitly formulated as such, as in some kinds of formulations or candidate understandings. Certain kinds of responses systematically construe prior talk as having been implementing a certain action by presupposing a kind of action as a condition under which the response makes sense (e.g., by construing a prior turn as advice-seeking through responding with advice). Such implicit practices may themselves be conventional or highly indexical. The uses of action ascription itself matter to participants, including the different kinds of actions which are implemented through action ascriptions (e.g., confirmation checks, reproaches), and their importance for the interactional business at hand. This pragmatic perspective on action ascription as being itself a form of social action, which, reflexively, is also an object of temporal, interactional negotiation, means attending to its consequences in interaction: How are ascriptions taken up by the producer of the action in first position, and how are they instrumental to paving the way for future action sequences to unfold? Action ascription often reveals itself not by a single next-positioned action, but an extended process of interactional negotiation, in which ascriptions are enriched, repaired, or stabilized. In fact, action ascription may even be argued to work reciprocally, as Goffman (1976), for instance, has argued with reference to the definition of first pair parts (FPP) and second pair parts (SPP). Goffman (1976) points out that you only know what an SPP does (e.g., that it is an answer) if you know what came before (e.g., a question), but the nature of that very FPP is only defined by the response to it – it could as well have been regarded as a rhetorical question, an announcement, a reproach, and so on, if a different kind of response had occurred. The study of action ascription as itself being a form of action offers yet another window on the utility of concepts of 'action' from a members' point of view, drawing out how "successive actions interlock to function as ways of validating, adjusting or invalidating the actions to which they respond in the conversational flow" (Clayman & Heritage 2014: 56; see also Schegloff 1995).

1.6 Overview of the Volume

This volume aims to complement recent research in action formation, which deals with the production side of actions, by focusing on the reception side. Focusing on turns that are responsive to prior turns – often but not always in second position – as a common point of departure, the volume shows how, in addition to the turn design of actions, the work of recipients is crucial to an intersubjective understanding of actions. The contributions elucidate contexts and kinds of conversational behaviors which make additional interpretive efforts critical for the accomplishment of intersubjective action. Complementing prior work on action formation, the action ascription approach is a second major constituent for building a comprehensive theory of conversational action in context. The contributions in this volume consider three main aspects of action ascription:

- How do participants conceive of 'actions'? This question concerns the units that are treated as the basis for action ascription, the varying degrees of granularity in understandings of an action, the various aspects taken to be relevant for its interpretation, and the ways in which participants deal with actions that are multilayered or equivocal.
- Which resources do participants draw on to ascribe an action to another party's behavior? These include the various linguistic, bodily, inferential, sequential, and broader contextual resources that participants draw upon in action ascription.
- Which (implicit and explicit) practices of action ascription do participants use, and how are these responded to in turn? This builds on Drew's (2011) fundamental insight that action ascription is itself an action, as recipients can shape the current action-in-progress through the ways in which they construe it in next (or subsequent) turns.

While all the chapters in this volume touch upon all three of these questions, the book itself is organized into three parts: Part I, Constituents of Action Ascription; Part II, Practices of Action Ascription; and Part III, Revisiting Action Ascription.

Part I deals with the underlying constituents of action ascription, describing the discursive and sequential resources participants use in ascribing an action.

In Chapter 2, Robert B. Arundale, building on his Conjoint Co-constituting Model of Communicating (Arundale 2010, 2020), makes a case for the need for an understanding of action ascription in interaction grounded in a temporal order that is intertwined with but distinct from the sequential order. A key claim made in this chapter is that action ascription is necessarily tied to interleaving three-position sequences through which speaker's and recipient's provisional action ascriptions become operative.

Paul Drew, who has been one of the leading figures in conversation analysis for decades, follows, in Chapter 3, with a detailed, highly nuanced account of what he calls the micro-politics of action, building on his claim that action ascription is itself a form of social action. He astutely describes how participants work to avoid or disguise particular action ascriptions, and argues this is due to the different 'values' that may be attached to different actions.

Chapter 4, by Michael Haugh, a proponent of an approach to pragmatics grounded in conversation analysis, discusses two interrelated implications of a treatment of action ascription as accountable social action for our understanding of the role of inference in action ascription. The first is that the underlying procedural infrastructure of social action is necessarily premised on three basic positions, not two, for displaying inferences about action ascription. The second is that an analysis of action ascription as social action provides an analytical window into practical reasoning by participants and the inferences that are made procedurally available, as well as suppressed or avoided, in the course of ascribing action.

Lorenza Mondada, one of the most prominent researchers on multimodal interaction worldwide, considers in Chapter 5 how multimodal conduct, that is, bodily aspects of action formation, and the overall structure of an interaction type together with the sequential position of an action account for the ascription of actions, as well as drawing attention to the way in which action ascription lies on a continuum from more explicit or overt through to more implicit or tacit. Collectively, the contributions in Part I elucidate what enters into a vernacular understanding of 'action': the constituents, their interrelations, and how they are put to use in order to arrive at situated action ascriptions.

Part II focuses on different practices of action ascription, ranging from environments in which action ascription is accomplished more explicitly through to more tacit forms of action ascription and the interactional consequences of these different action ascription practices.

The first two chapters in this section focus on overt action ascription. In Chapter 6, Arnulf Deppermann, another key proponent of an approach to pragmatics grounded in conversation analysis who has been working on the role of cognition in displaying understanding in interaction, and Julia Kaiser describe how explicit ascriptions of intentions are used to not only clarify but also criticize the action in a prior turn with an eye to its import for future cooperation.

Henrike Helmer, who did her PhD on the understanding of implicit topics in interaction, deals with the ascription of strategic action and the exposure of (alleged) "real" intentions in political conflict talk in Chapter 7. These first two chapters demonstrate not only that overt or explicit action ascription figures importantly in the understanding of actions, but that explicitly invoking intention(ality) and other cognitive processes in interaction is itself a powerful means for construing social action in warranting or denying the accountability of participants for those actions.

The focus then shifts to action ascription practices that are more implicit or indexical, but are nevertheless systematically used to ascribe a certain action to another participant's prior talk. Elizabeth Couper-Kuhlen and Sandra A. Thompson, both leading protagonists of interactional linguistics, examine in Chapter 8 how prior talk is implicitly portrayed as advice-seeking in terms of format and sequence, and how advice-giving turns are responded to.

Takeshi Hiramoto and Makoto Hayashi, who are leading researchers on conversational interaction in Japanese, focus in Chapter 9 on the role that the deontic status of an actor within a local network of relationships has for the ascription of action(s) in indirect talk.

In Chapter 10, Yaxin Wu and Guodong Yu, who are experts on conversation in Mandarin Chinese, discuss a turn-constructional format of answering which indexes that the question being answered is considered to be inapposite. They demonstrate that a particular linguistic format is here specialized to address aspects of the accountability of others' actions.

In Chapter 11, Tom Koole, who has done important research on understanding in interaction, and Lotte van Burgsteden discuss action ascription in the case of thanking in emergency calls. They show that thanking can portray the caller's action either as requesting a service or as offering help. Their work shows how action ascriptions can extend beyond single actions to larger stretches of discursive action.

Part III of this volume presents two critical perspectives on action ascription. In Chapter 12, N. J. Enfield and Jack Sidnell, two leading protagonists of conversation analysis in linguistic anthropology, distinguish between action ascription as response and action ascription as describing, and argue that the 'binning' approach to social action conflates the two.

Finally, in Chapter 13, John Heritage, another central figure in conversation analysis for more than four decades, masterfully overviews what we have learned to date, and highlights some of the outstanding questions that remain in our attempts to unravel action ascription.

In sum, the chapters in this volume are some of the first to systematically address the receptive side of action – action ascription – and thus the interactional processes by which actions are negotiated and defined as interactional realities for participants in various forms of interaction. We hope the volume will thus be seen as making a useful contribution to current debates about social action in the fields of conversation analysis and pragmatics.

REFERENCES

Antaki, C. (2004). Reading minds or dealing with interactional implications? *Theory and Psychology*, 14, 667–83.

Arundale, R. B. (1999). An alternative model and ideology of communication for an alternative to politeness theory. *Pragmatics*, 9(1), 119–53.

(2010). Constituting face in conversation: Face, facework and interactional achievement. *Journal of Pragmatics*, 42, 2078–105.

(2020). *Communicating and Relating: Constituting Face in Everyday Interacting*. Oxford: Oxford University Press.

Bögels, S., Kendrick, K. & Levinson, S. C. (2020). Conversational expectations get revised as response latencies unfold. *Language, Cognition and Neuroscience*, 35 (6), 766–99.

Brandom, R. B. (1994). *Making It Explicit*. Cambridge, MA: Harvard University Press.

(2014). Intentionality and language. In N. Enfield, P. Kockelman & J. Sidnell, eds., *Cambridge Handbook of Linguistic Anthropology*. Cambridge: Cambridge University Press, pp. 347–63.

Clark, H. (1996). *Using Language*. Cambridge: Cambridge University Press.

Clark, H. & Carlson, T. (1982). Hearers and speech acts. *Language*, 58, 332–73.

Clayman, S. & Heritage, J. (2014). Benefactors and beneficiaries: Benefactive status and stance in the management of offers and requests. In P. Drew & E. Couper-Kuhlen, eds., *Requesting in Social Interaction*. Amsterdam: John Benjamins, pp. 55–86.

Clift, R. (2016). *Conversation Analysis*. Cambridge: Cambridge University Press.

Coulter, J. (1983). Contingent and a priori structures in sequential analysis. *Human Studies*, 6(1), 361–74.

Couper-Kuhlen, E. (2014). What does grammar tell us about social action? *Pragmatics*, 24(3), 623–47.

Couper-Kuhlen, E. & Selting, M. (2018). *Interactional Linguistics*. Cambridge: Cambridge University Press.

Deppermann, A. (2012). How does 'cognition' matter to the analysis of talk-in-interaction? *Language Sciences*, 34(6), 746–67.

(2014). Multimodal participation in simultaneous joint projects: Interpersonal and intrapersonal coordination in paramedic emergency drills. In P. Haddington, T. Keisanen, L. Mondada & M. Nevile, eds., *Multiactivity in Social Interaction: Beyond Multitasking*. Amsterdam: John Benjamins, pp. 247–82.

(2015). Retrospection and understanding in interaction. In A. Deppermann & S. Günthner, eds., *Temporality in Interaction*. Amsterdam: John Benjamins, pp. 57–94.

(2018). Inferential practices in social interaction: A conversation-analytic account. *Open Linguistics*, 4(1), 35–55.

Drew, P. (1984). Speakers' reportings in invitation sequences. In J. M. Atkinson & J. Heritage, eds., *Structures of Social Action: Studies in Conversation Analysis*. Cambridge: Cambridge University Press, pp. 129–51.

(2011). Reflections on the micro-politics of social action, in interaction. Paper presented at the 12th International Pragmatics Association Conference, University of Manchester.

(2018). Inferences and indirectness in interaction. *Open Linguistics*, 4(1), 241–59.

Drew, P. & Couper-Kuhlen, E. (2014a). Requesting – from speech act to recruitment. In P. Drew & E. Couper-Kuhlen, eds., *Requesting in Social Interaction.* Amsterdam: John Benjamins, pp. 1–34.

Drew, P. & Couper-Kuhlen, E., eds. (2014b). *Requesting in Social Interaction.* Amsterdam: John Benjamins.

Duranti, A. (1988). Intentions, language, and social action in a Samoan context. *Journal of Pragmatics*, 12(1), 13–33.

(2015). *The Anthropology of Intentions.* Cambridge: Cambridge University Press.

Edwards, D. (2006). *Discourse and Cognition*. London: Sage.

(2008). Intentionality and mens rea in police interrogations: The production of actions as crimes. *Intercultural Pragmatics*, 5(2), 177–99.

Enfield, N. J. (2013). *Relationship Thinking*. Oxford: Oxford University Press.

Enfield, N. J. & Sidnell, J. (2017a). *The Concept of Action.* Cambridge: Cambridge University Press.

(2017b). On the concept of action in the study of interaction. *Discourse Studies*, 19, 515–35.

Fox, B. (2007). Principles shaping grammatical practices: An exploration. *Discourse Studies,* 9(3), 299–318.

Garfinkel, H. (1967). *Studies in Ethnomethodology*. Englewood Cliffs, NJ: Prentice Hall.

Garfinkel, H. & Sacks, H. (1970). On formal structures of practical action. In J. C. McKinney & E. A. Tiryakian, eds., *Theoretical Sociology: Perspectives and Developments.* New York, NY: Appleton-Century-Crofts, pp. 338–66.

Gibbs, R. W. Jr (1999). *Intentions in the Experience of Meaning*. Cambridge: Cambridge University Press.

Gisladottir, R., Bögels, S. & Levinson, S. C. (2018). Oscillatory brain responses reflect anticipation during comprehension of speech acts in spoken dialogue. *Frontiers in Human Neuroscience*, 12, 34, doi:10.3389/ fnhum.2018.00034.

Gisladottir, R., Chwilla, D. & Levinson, S. C. (2015). Conversation electrified: ERP correlates of speech act recognition in underspecified utterances. *PLoS One*, 10(3): e0120068.

Goffman, E. (1976). Replies and responses. *Language in Society*, 5(3), 257–313.

Goodwin, C. (2000). Action and embodiment within situated human interaction. *Journal of Pragmatics*, 32, 1489–522.

(2013) The co-operative, transformative organisation of human action and knowledge. *Journal of Pragmatics*, 46(1), 8–23.

(2017). *Co-operative Action*. Cambridge: Cambridge University Press.

Grice, H. P. (1989). *Studies in the Ways of Words*. Cambridge, MA: Harvard University Press.

Hakulinen, A. & Sorjonen, M.-L. (2012). Being equivocal: Affective responses left unspecified. In A. Peräkylä & M.-L. Sorjonen, eds., *Emotion in Interaction.* Oxford: Oxford University Press, pp. 147–73.

Haugh, M. (2008). The place of intention in the interactional achievement of implicature. In I. Kecskes & J. Mey, eds., *Intention, Common Ground and the Egocentric Speaker-Hearer.* Berlin: Mouton de Gruyter, pp. 45–85.

(2013). Speaker meaning and accountability in interaction. *Journal of Pragmatics*, 48 (1), 41–56.

(2017). Implicatures and the inferential substrate. In P. Cap & M. Dynel, eds., *Implicitness: From Lexis to Discourse*. Amsterdam: John Benjamins, pp. 281–304.

Haugh, M. & Jaszczolt, K. M. (2012). Speaker intentions and intentionality. In K. Allan & K. M. Jaszczolt, eds., *Cambridge Handbook of Pragmatics*. Cambridge: Cambridge University Press, pp. 87–112.

Heritage, J. (1984). *Garfinkel and Ethnomethodology*. Cambridge: Polity Press.

(2010). Conversation analysis: Practices and methods. In D. Silverman, ed., *Qualitative Sociology*, 3rd ed. London: Sage, pp. 208–30.

(2012a). Epistemics in action: Action formation and territories of knowledge. *Research on Language and Social Interaction*, 45(1), 1–29.

(2012b). The epistemic engine: Sequence organization and territories of knowledge. *Research on Language and Social Interaction*, 45(1), 30–52.

Hindmarsh, J. & Pilnick, A. (2002). The tacit order of teamwork: Collaboration and embodied conduct in anaesthesia. *The Sociological Quarterly*, 43(2), 139–64.

Holler, J., Kendrick, K. & Levinson, S. C. (2018). Processing language in face-to-face conversation: Questions with gestures get faster responses. *Psychonomic Bulletin & Review*, 25(5), 1900–8.

Hömke, P., Holler, J. & Levinson, S. C. (2018). Eye blinks are perceived as communicative signals in human face-to-face interaction. *PLoS One*, 13(12): e0208030.

Jayyusi, L. (1991). Values and moral judgement: Communicative praxis as moral order. In G. Button, ed., *Ethnomethodology and the Human Sciences*. Cambridge: Cambridge University Press, pp. 227–51.

Jefferson, G. (1990). List-construction as a task and a resource. In G. Psathas, ed., *Interaction Competence*. Washington, DC: University Press of America, pp. 63–92.

Jefferson, G., Sacks, H. & Schegloff, E. (1977). Preliminary notes on the sequential organization of laughter. Pragmatics microfiche. Cambridge University.

Kendrick, K. & Drew, P. (2014). The putative preference for offers over requests. In P. Drew & E. Couper-Kuhlen, eds., *Requesting in Social Interaction*. Amsterdam: John Benjamins, pp. 87–114.

(2016). Recruitment: Offers, requests, and the organization of assistance in interaction. *Research on Language and Social Interaction*, 49(1), 1–19.

Kendrick, K., Brown, P., Dingemanse, M. et al. (2020). Sequence organisation: A universal infrastructure for social action. *Journal of Pragmatics*, 168, 119–38.

Kevoe-Feldman, H. & Robinson, J. D. (2012). Exploring essentially three-turn courses of action: An institutional case study with implications for ordinary talk. *Discourse Studies*, 14(2), 217–41.

Levinson, S. C. (1981). The essential inadequacies of speech act models of dialogue. In H. Parret, M. Sbisà & J. Verscheuren, eds., *Possibilities and Limitations of Pragmatics: Proceedings of the Conference on Pragmatics, Urbino, July 8–14, 1979*. Amsterdam: John Benjamins, pp. 473–92.

(2006). On the human "interaction engine." In N. J. Enfield & S. C. Levinson, eds., *Roots of Human Sociality*. Oxford: Berg, pp. 39–69.

(2013). Action formation and ascription. In J. Sidnell & T. Stivers, eds., *The Handbook of Conversation Analysis*. Chichester: Wiley Blackwell, pp. 103–30.

(2017). Speech acts. In Y. Huang, ed., *Oxford Handbook of Pragmatics*. Oxford: Oxford University Press, pp. 199–216.

Linell, P. (1998). *Approaching Dialogue*. Amsterdam: John Benjamins.
Mondada, L. (2014). The local constitution of multimodal resources for social interaction. *Journal of Pragmatics*, 65, 137–56.
Pillet-Shore, D. (2016). Criticizing another's child: How teachers evaluate students during parent–teacher conferences. *Language in Society*, 45(1), 33–58.
(2021). When to make the sensory social: Registering in face-to-face openings. *Symbolic Interaction*, 44(1), 10–39, doi:10.1002/symb.481.
Pomerantz, A. (2017). Inferring the purpose of a prior query and responding accordingly. In G. Raymond, G. Lerner & J. Heritage, eds., *Enabling Human Conduct: Studies of Talk-in-Interaction in Honour of Emanuel A. Schegloff*. Amsterdam: John Benjamins, pp. 61–76.
Potter, J. & Edwards, D. (2013). Conversation analysis and psychology. In J. Sidnell & T. Stivers, eds., *Handbook of Conversation Analysis*. Malden, MA: Wiley Blackwell, pp. 701–25.
Raymond, G. (2003). Grammar and social organization: Yes/no interrogatives and the structure of responding. *American Sociological Review*, 68(6), 939–67.
Robinson, J. D. (ed.) (2016). *Accountability in Social Interaction*. Oxford: Oxford University Press.
Rosaldo, M. (1982). The things we do with words: Ilongot speech acts and speech act theory in philosophy. *Language in Society*, 11(2), 203–37.
Rossi, G. (2015). *The request system in Italian interaction* (Ph.D. dissertation). Nijmegen: Radboud University.
(2018). Composite social actions: The case of factual declaratives in everyday interaction. *Research on Language and Social Interaction*, 51(4), 379–97.
Sacks, H. (1963). Sociological description. *Berkeley Journal of Sociology*, 8, 1–16.
(1985). The inference-making machine. In T. van Dijk, ed., *Handbook of Discourse Analysis*. London: Academic Press, pp. 13–23.
(1992). *Lectures on Conversation*. 2 vols. Oxford: Blackwell.
Sacks, H., Schegloff, E. A. & Jefferson, G. (1974). A simplest systematics for the organisation of turn-taking in conversation. *Language*, 50(4), 696–735.
Schegloff, E. A. (1984). On some questions and ambiguities in conversation. In J. M. Atkinson & J. Heritage, eds., *Structures of Social Action: Studies in Conversation Analysis*. Cambridge: Cambridge University Press, pp. 28–52.
(1988). Description in the social sciences I: Talk-in-interaction. *IPrA Papers in Pragmatics*, 2(1–2), 1–24.
(1991). Reflections on talk and social structure. In D. Boden & D. Zimmerman, eds., *Talk and Social Structure*. Cambridge: Cambridge University Press, pp. 44–70.
(1992). Repair after next turn: The last structurally provided defense of intersubjectivity in conversation. *American Journal of Sociology*, 97(5), 1295–345.
(1995). Discourse as an interactional achievement III: The omnirelevance of action. *Research on Language and Social Interaction*, 28(3), 185–211.
(1996). Confirming allusions: Toward an empirical account of action. *American Journal of Sociology*, 104(1), 161–216.
(1997). Practices and actions: Boundary cases of other-initiated repair. *Discourse Processes*, 23(3), 499–545.

(1998). Reply to Wetherell. *Discourse & Society*, 9(3), 413–16.
(2000). On granularity. *Annual Review of Sociology*, 26, 715–20.
(2006). On possibles. *Discourse Studies*, 8(1), 141–57.
(2007). *Sequence Organization in Interaction: A Primer in Conversation Analysis*. Cambridge: Cambridge University Press.
(2010). Commentary on Stivers and Rossano: Mobilizing response. *Research on Language and Social Interaction*, 43(1), 38–48.
Schegloff, E. A. & Sacks, H. (1973). Opening up closings. *Semiotica*, 8(4), 289–327.
Schütz, A. (1976). The social world and the theory of social action. In A. Brodersen, ed., *A. Schütz, Collected Papers Volume 3: Studies in Social Theory*. Berlin: Springer, pp. 3–19.
Searle, J. (1969). *Speech Acts: An Essay in the Philosophy of Language*. Cambridge: Cambridge University Press.
Searle, J. & Vanderveken, D. (1985). *Foundations of Illocutionary Logic*. Cambridge: Cambridge University Press.
Seuren, L. M. (2018). Assessing answers: Action ascription in third position. *Research on Language and Social Interaction*, 51(1), 33–51.
Sidnell, J. (2014). The architecture of intersubjectivity revisited. In N. J. Enfield, P. Kockelman & J. Sidnell, eds., *Cambridge Handbook of Linguistic Anthropology*. Cambridge: Cambridge University Press, pp. 364–99.
(2017). Action in interaction is conduct under a description. *Language in Society*, 46 (3), 313–37.
Sidnell, J. & Enfield, N. J. (2014). The ontology of action, in interaction. In N. Enfield, P. Kockelman & J. Sidnell, eds., *Cambridge Handbook of Linguistic Anthropology*. Cambridge: Cambridge University Press, pp. 423–46.
Sorjonen, M.-L., Raevaara, L. & Couper-Kuhlen, E., eds. (2017). *Imperative Turns at Talk: The Design of Directives in Action*. Amsterdam: John Benjamins.
Sperber, D. & Wilson, D. (1995). *Relevance: Communication and Cognition*, 2nd ed. Oxford: Blackwell.
Stevanovic, M. & Peräkylä, A. (2012). Deontic authority in interaction: The right to announce, propose, and decide. *Research on Language and Social Interaction*, 45 (4), 297–321.
(2014). Three orders in the organization of human action: On the interface between knowledge, power, and emotion in interaction and social relations. *Language in Society*, 43(2), 185–207.
Stivers, T. & Rossano, F. (2010a). Mobilizing response. *Research on Language and Social Interaction*, 43(1), 3–31.
(2010b). A scalar view of response relevance. *Research on Language and Social Interaction*, 43(1), 49–56.
Szczepek-Reed, B. & Raymond, G., eds. (2013). *Units of Talk – Units of Action*. Amsterdam: John Benjamins.
Thomas, J. (1995). *Meaning in Interaction: An Introduction to Pragmatics*. London: Longman.
Thompson, S., Fox, B. & Couper-Kuhlen, E. (2015). *Grammar in Everyday Talk: Building Responsive Actions*. Cambridge: Cambridge University Press.

Tomasello, M. (2008). *Origins of Human Communication*. Cambridge, MA: MIT Press.

Weber, M. (1968[1922]). *Economy and Society: An Outline of Interpretive Sociology*. New York, NY: Bedminster.

Zinken, J. (2016). *Requesting Responsibility: The Morality of Grammar in Polish and English Family Interaction*. Oxford: Oxford University Press.

Part I

Constituents of Action Ascription

2 Temporal Organization and Procedure in Ascribing Action

Robert B. Arundale

2.1 Introduction

Human interaction is organized in time, but that organization is neither automatic nor externally imposed. It is an effortful creation internal to everyday interaction as participants produce next utterances and place them adjacent to their own or other's prior utterances (Arundale & Good 2002: 144; Rawls 2006: 7). The temporal organization of interaction is at minimum a dyadic phenomenon, because even though single individuals can do things in temporal order, no single individual can unilaterally create the temporal order of interaction (Rawls 2005: 172–3). Participants produce utterances in sequence using their respective knowledges of the normative sequential organizations of a wide range of elements of interaction, key among those elements being turns in a sequence of turns, actions in a sequence of actions, and repair initiations in a sequence of utterances. These and other sequential organizations are omnirelevant and coincident in interaction, but distinct from one another in that each rests on a different normative order (Lerner 2019: 389). I argue in Section 2.2 that these sequential organizations are distinct, although inseparable from, the temporal organization of adjacency, nextness, and progressivity of elements in sequence: an organization that has been widely acknowledged, but less closely examined than the sequential organizations surveyed in Sidnell and Stivers (2013) and Robinson (2016: 6–7). Examining the temporal organization of interaction more closely in Section 2.3 has implications for examining the sequence organization of action in Section 2.4, and more specifically for examining how participants ascribe actions to utterances, as in Section 2.5. Those insights make apparent the importance of third position utterances in action ascription, as in Section 2.6.

2.2 The Temporal Organization of Adjacency, Nextness, and Progressivity

Schegloff (2007: 14–15) indicates the centrality of next adjacency or of contiguity in human interacting:

> Among the most pervasively relevant features in the organization of talk-and-other-conduct-in-interaction is the relationship of adjacency or "nextness." The default relationship between components of most kinds of organization is that each should come next after the prior. In articulating a turn-constructional unit, each element – each word, for example – should come next after the one before; in fact at a smaller level of granularity, each syllable – indeed, each sound – should come next after the one before it. So also with the several turn-constructional units that compose a multi-unit turn; so also with the consecutive turns that compose a spate of talk; so also with the turns that compose a sequence, etc. Moving from some element to a hearably-next-one with nothing intervening is the embodiment of, and the measure of progressivity.

In more general terms, relationships of adjacency are expectations that for some particular element that has taken or is taking place, there is some limited range of elements that should follow next in sequence. Such expectations are invoked in the moment of interaction by the presence of a prior element, whose final form cannot be known until that element is complete. These expectations are forward-oriented or proactive in that each element in turn brings into play expectations for a next element or elements to follow. But they are also backward-oriented or retroactive, because the expectation for what is to appear next was invoked by the occurrence of the prior element (Schegloff 2007: 15–16), and has implications for interpreting that element. Relationships of adjacency may extend well backward (Schegloff 1992: 1319) and forward from the current element, although relationships between the immediately anterior and posterior elements are the most salient. Such expectations may be characteristic of a particular dyad, small group, community, or larger social group, expectations in the latter cases having the status of normative expectations. The generic, default expectation is for a next element that falls within the expected range, and so confirms the expectation such that the new next element is "seen, but unnoticed" (Heritage 1984: 118) and the sequence is understood as routine. A next element that falls outside the range violates the expectation and is quite likely to be "seen and noticed" as a departure from what is routine (1984: 253). Schegloff (2007: 15) points directly to such departures from expectations in adding that:

> Should something intervene between some element and what is hearable as a/the next one due – should something violate or intervene with their contiguity, whether next sound, next word, or next turn – it will be heard as qualifying the progressivity of talk, and will be examined for its import, for what understanding should be accorded it. Each next element of such a progression can be inspected to find how it reaffirms the

understanding-so-far of what has preceded, or favors one or more of several such understandings that are being entertained, or how it requires reconfiguration of that understanding.

Note two important features of Schegloff's characterizations. First, nextness, adjacency, and progressivity are generic characterizations in that they apply to sequences of elements at all levels of granularity, including but not limited to sounds within syllables, syllables within words, words within turns, turns within sequences of turns, actions within sequences of actions, and sequences of actions within overall sequential organizations of action (e.g., Robinson 2013). In other words, nextness, adjacency, and progressivity are generic, *context-free* characteristics of the temporal organization of all sequences of elements in interaction, with the default relationship between the elements in such sequences being that each "should come next after the prior," or should fall within the range of expected next elements. Second, granting that nextness, adjacency, and progressivity are generic characteristics of interaction, it is nevertheless the case that participants cannot assess whether a given next element should or should not come next after a given prior element apart from the expectations entailed in at least one normative sequential organization of elements: specific normative expectations for what sounds, words, turns, actions, sequences of actions, and more, should come next in the sequence of such elements the participants are generating in their particular, *context-bound* situation.

In other words, the temporal organization, or the serial contiguity, nextness, adjacency, and progressivity of elements in interaction is a generic organization distinct from but at the same time dependent upon and generated in view of one or more specific normative sequential organizations. My focus in this chapter is on the nextness, adjacency, and progressivity of elements at the level of turn-constructional units (TCUs) and above in everyday direct sequential interaction (Arundale 2020: 54). That the temporal organization of TCUs/turns is foundational in interaction is apparent in Sacks's 1972 (1992: 554) forwarding of what Heritage (1984: 261) identifies as a "fundamental ordering principle for conversation," namely that "a turn's talk will be heard as directed to a prior turn's talk, unless special techniques are used to locate some other talk to which it is directed" (Sacks, Schegloff & Jefferson 1974: 728; cf. Garfinkel 1961: 63; Rawls 2005: 174). The principle is fundamental because as Sacks (1992: 559) argued, the talk and conduct in any next adjacent position is privileged because "there is only one generic place where you need not include information as to which utterance you're intending to relate an utterance to, and that is if you are in *next position* to an [immediately prior] utterance." Put somewhat differently, the utterance in *next adjacent position* is in all cases privileged by the default presumption that whatever utterance appears in that position is linked in some way with whatever utterance appears in the immediately prior position.

One direct consequence of that default presumption is that as participants interpret utterances in everyday interaction, they are continually engaged both in inspecting each and every next adjacent utterance, and in assessing whether that next adjacent utterance *should or should not come next after the prior*, in view of the specific, coincident, normative adjacency relationships invoked at that point in the current sequence-in-progress. Assessing whether the next adjacent utterance should or should not come next after the immediately prior utterance is an essential component not only in a participant's interpreting of the immediately prior utterance, but also in his or her designing and delivering an utterance to follow that next adjacent utterance. The process of assessing whether the next adjacent utterance is or is not a hearably-next-one – whether it should or should not come next after the immediately prior utterance – is what I will refer to here as the process of "assessing nextness" in inspecting each new next adjacent utterance. Assessing nextness is central to participants in creating the temporal order of their particular interaction, and in Section 2.3 I adopt the perspective of the participant in examining how individuals conjointly co-constitute that order as they assess nextness. Before doing so let me clarify what I refer to here as an "utterance" and as a "position."

Human sequential interaction is turn-organized, as apparent above in Sacks, Schegloff, and Jefferson's (1974: 728) discussion of the fundamental ordering principle. But note that in pointing to the default presumption underlying that principle, Sacks (1992: 559) used the terms "an utterance" where Sacks, Schegloff, and Jefferson use the terms "a turn's talk." Although it is by no means an ideal alternative to the terms "turn" and "TCU," I will follow Sacks's lead in employing the term "utterance" as more inclusive than "turn" (Arundale 2020: 50–2). I do so because "turn" and "TCU" have regularly been employed with reference to vocal and verbal utterances, seemingly to the exclusion of nonvocal and nonverbal activities, and of the occasioned absence of activity (Drew 2013: 132; Schegloff 1995: 198), that participants orient to and that are procedurally consequential in interaction in the same ways as vocal and verbal activities. Note second that Sacks (1992: 559) used the term "position" to identify the location of an utterance placed next adjacent to a prior utterance in a sequence of utterances. I will follow his lead here, as well. Specifically, in examining the temporal organization of adjacency, nextness, and progressivity I will employ the term "position" in referring to the location of a recognizable and interpretable next adjacent utterance by a different participant (Arundale 2020: 52–3). This level of specificity is necessary because what defines a "position" varies depending on its use with regard to different sequential organizations in interaction (Mazeland 2013: 475–6). Positions in the sequence organization of paired conversational actions need not be next adjacent, and in the organization of repair (Section 2.4), positions are locations in the repair initiation opportunity space (Schegloff 1992: 1326–7).

2.3 The Temporal Organization of Interaction: A Procedural Perspective

One implication of Sacks, Schegloff, and Jefferson's (1974: 728) observation that "a turn's talk will be heard as directed to a prior turn's talk, unless special techniques are used" is that "a turn's talk will display its speaker's understanding of a prior turn's talk, and whatever other talk it marks itself as directed to." They add that "[i]n the first place, of course, such understandings are displayed to co-participants," so that a prior speaker may "self-select as next speaker if he [*sic*] finds the understanding of his prior utterance, displayed by current speaker in current turn, unacceptable" (1974: 728–9). Sacks, Schegloff, and Jefferson (1974: 729) add a further key implication:

> ... while understandings of other turn's talk are displayed to co-participants, they are available as well to professional analysts, who are thereby afforded a proof criterion ... for the analysis of what a turn's talk is occupied with. Since it is the parties' understandings of prior turns' talk that is relevant to their construction of next turns, it is THEIR understandings that are wanted for analysis. The display of those understandings in the talk of subsequent turns affords both a resource for the analysis of prior turns and a proof procedure for professional analyses of prior turns – resources intrinsic to the data themselves.

Conversation analysis is distinct from other approaches to discourse analysis in its insistence that in coming to an interpreting of a what a prior turn's talk "is occupied with," analysts utilize the very same, next turn resources that the participants utilize. In other words, the proof procedure that a conversation analyst engages in his or her interpretive work rests on the very same conversation-intrinsic data that the participants employ in their interpretive work. Note importantly, however, that because analysts and participants utilize the same next turn resource as data does not imply that the procedure that analysts employ in forming an interpreting of a participant's prior utterance is the same as the procedure that the participants themselves employ. A conversation analyst is not an engaged, situated participant, and forms his or her interpreting of an utterance in interaction only *post hoc*, knowing how the entire interaction unfolded, how each utterance eventually came to be interpreted over the time course of the interaction, and employing an external conceptual apparatus in his or her interpreting (Arundale 2020: 222). In contrast, a participant is a directly engaged, situated individual, who creates an interpreting of a given utterance *in tempore* or within the emerging time course of the interaction, not knowing how the entire interaction will unfold, not knowing how any utterance beyond the prior utterance will come to be interpreted over the time course of the interaction, and employing the "attitude of daily life" in his or her interpreting (Heritage 1984: 101).

The participant's procedure for interpreting utterances in interaction is distinct from the analyst's procedure, and paraphrasing Sacks, Schegloff, and Jefferson's (1974: 729) argument above, "since it is the parties' interpretings of prior utterances that is relevant to their construction of next utterances, it is THEIR interpretings that are wanted for analysis." It follows that the procedure a conversation analyst engages in examining participant's interpretings needs to be informed by a detailed understanding of the procedure the participants engage in creating THEIR interpretings. Indeed, knowing the participant's procedure for interpreting would appear to be essential in adopting the participant's perspective on his or her interpreting. Examining the participant's procedure in this section indicates both how it is distinct from the analyst's procedure, and how, in engaging the procedure in assessing the nextness of utterances, the participants create the temporal order of their particular, situated interaction. Note that in paraphrasing Sacks, Schegloff, and Jefferson (1974) above I use the term "interpreting" where they use the term "understanding." That is a deliberate choice so as to avoid intimating that in using the display of interpreting provided in a next adjacent utterance, either (a) the analyst comes to "understand" the prior participant's utterance in the same way as that participant, or (b) the prior and the next participant come to "understand" the prior participant's utterance in the same way (cf. Arundale 2020: 97–9).

From the participant's perspective, interpreting utterances in interaction is a process carried out by separate individuals in one another's presence, those individuals having direct access to their own interpretings, but only indirect access to any other individual's interpretings (Arundale 2020: 114–17, 120–30). But although the process of interpreting is carried out by individuals, the procedure involved requires two or more participants mutually engaged in assessing the nextness of each and every utterance as it is placed next adjacent to the immediately prior utterance. Central to examining the participant's procedure is distinguishing between two types of interpreting that arise in the time course of interacting as the participants alternate between being speaker and recipient in assessing the nextness of each successive utterance. Consider Marty and Loes's conversation in Excerpt 2.1. Their interaction occurred in the mid-1980s "in a research organization, just after the beginning of the year. Loes is the receptionist and keeper of supplies; Marty is a visiting researcher" (Schegloff 1992: 1321).[1]

[1] Schegloff observed Marty and Loes's conversation in English, in the 1980s in the Netherlands, and transcribed it as a field note (1992: 1321). Important details such as pause lengths, body posture, and gaze are therefore not available. The transcript is sufficient, however, for the present purpose of examining the participant's procedure.

Excerpt 2.1

```
01 MAR:    loes, do you have a calendar,
02 LOE:    yeah ((reaches for her desk calendar))
03 MAR:    do you have one that hangs on the wall?
04 LOE:    oh, you want one.
05 MAR:    yeah
```

Marty creates his interpreting of his utterance 1 as he designs it for Loes to interpret. As he delivers his utterance he both anticipates how Loes will interpret it, and how she might respond, with regard to the normative organizations of action, and of yes/no interrogatives (YNIs), as Raymond (2003). At the point Marty delivers his utterance, and before Loes places her utterance 2 next adjacent to it, Marty has no evidence regarding Loes's interpreting of utterance 1. His own interpreting utterance 1 is at this point what I identify as a "provisional" interpreting, *not in the sense that he is somehow unsure of his own interpreting of it, but in the sense that prior to Loes's utterance 2, he has no evidence regarding how Loes will interpret his utterance 1 in their particular, situated interaction*. More specifically, Marty's interpreting is his "*speaker* provisional interpreting" of his utterance 1. As Loes interprets Marty's utterance 1 she creates her "*recipient* provisional interpreting" of it, in the parallel sense that prior to Marty's utterance 3, she has *no evidence regarding how Marty has interpreted his own utterance in their particular, situated interaction*. If she is to continue in the conversation she has no option other than to ascribe her recipient provisional interpreting to Marty as his interpreting of his utterance 1, and on that basis to design and deliver her utterance 2 next adjacent to it. As she does so, Loes not only anticipates his interpreting of her utterance, which is her speaker provisional interpreting of her utterance 2, but also creates expectations regarding his uptake in utterance 3.

As Marty interprets Loes's utterance 2 he first creates his recipient provisional interpreting of it, and then employs that interpreting in assessing nextness with regard to his speaker provisional interpreting of his own utterance 1. The evidence available to analysts from the conversation as a whole indicates that Loes's utterance 2 is consistent with the normative sequential expectations for the action of granting a request, as well as for a response to a YNI, but that Loes has interpreted Marty's utterance as a request to use her desk calendar, rather than to obtain a wall calendar as he had anticipated. As Marty assesses nextness, he confirms his speaker provisional interpreting of utterance 1 with regard to action and to YNIs, but he must reconfigure that interpreting with regard to the type of calendar referenced (Schegloff 2007: 15). In other words, Loes's utterance 2 is not in all respects what should follow next from his utterance: there is progressivity with regard to action and YNIs, but her utterance qualifies progressivity with regard to object reference. As Marty assesses nextness with regard to Loes's utterance 2, what has until now been his speaker *provisional* interpreting of his utterance 1 becomes his speaker *operative* interpreting of it. It is an "operative" interpreting, *not in the sense that his interpreting is determinate or final, or that his new interpreting of his utterance is the same as her interpreting of it, but in the sense that he now has some evidence regarding how Loes has interpreted his utterance 1 in their particular, situated interaction*: evidence that he can use in designing and delivering his next utterance in their sequence-in-progress.

In short, a *provisional interpreting* is one that has not yet been assessed in view of another participant's subsequent utterance, even though one may be quite certain about that initial interpreting, and an *operative interpreting* is a provisional interpreting that has been assessed in view another participant's subsequent utterance, even though one might later change that interpreting (Arundale 2020: 58–66).

Note then that this two-position organization of a speaker's given first position utterance, together with a recipient's next adjacent second position utterance, provides *the speaker of the given utterance* with working evidence of the recipient's interpreting of that first position utterance. That evidence is essential to the speaker in continuing on in the interaction, but by itself the two-position organization leaves the recipient of the given utterance with no more than his or her recipient provisional interpreting of that first position utterance. This is the two-position temporal organization of next adjacency characterized by Sacks (1992: 554) and by Schegloff (2007: 14), and long identified as the "interactional achievement" of turns at talk and conduct, and of conversational action (Schegloff 1981: 7, 1988, 1995; see Arundale 2020: 72–9).

Consider what takes place next as Marty and Loes's sequence of utterances continues to unfold. Using his speaker operative interpreting of his utterance 1, together with his recipient provisional interpreting of her utterance 2, Marty designs his utterance 3 and places it next adjacent to her utterance. In this case Marty departs from the normative sequential expectations for initiating repair in utterance 3 (Schegloff 1992: 1304–17), and instead designs another YNI that reworks his utterance 1, but now with specific reference to a wall calendar. As Marty delivers utterance 3 he both anticipates Loes's interpreting of it (his speaker provisional interpreting of utterance 3), and creates expectations regarding her uptake in utterance 4 with regard to action and YNIs, very likely anticipating that Loes will in some way address the difference in their respective initial interpretings of utterance 1 that his reworking makes evident.

As Loes interprets Marty's utterance 3 she first creates her recipient provisional interpreting of it, then employs that interpreting in assessing nextness with regard to her speaker provisional interpreting of her own utterance 2. The conversation as whole provides evidence that for Loes, Marty's utterance 3 is not what should come next after her utterance 2: it qualifies progressivity in that it is not an action that would normatively be expected to follow her granting of his request. Loes must examine the qualification "for its import, for what understanding should be accorded it" (Schegloff 2007: 15). Because Marty's utterance 3 renews his request in utterance 1, but references a wall calendar rather than a desk calendar, his reworking provides Loes with evidence that what should have come next in her utterance 2 was her granting of a wall calendar. That evidence entails that Loes must reconfigure her interpreting of her utterance 2 as granting a different type of calendar than he had initially requested. As Loes assesses the nextness of Marty's utterance 3 with regard to her utterance 2, what has until now been her speaker *provisional* interpreting of her utterance 2 becomes her speaker *operative* interpreting of it.

But that is not all that happens. What has been regularly overlooked is that the evidence of Marty's interpreting of her utterance 2 that Loes gains in creating her speaker operative interpreting of it has direct implications for her interpreting of Marty's utterance 1. That is the case because she had designed and delivered her utterance 2 in uptake to his utterance 1: if she has reconfigured her interpreting of her utterance 2, she must reconfigure her interpreting of his utterance 1. Specifically, if what should have come next in her utterance 2 was her granting of a wall calendar, then by inference Marty's utterance 1 was a request for a wall calendar, not a request for her desk calendar. The evidence Loes gains in assessing nextness in light of Marty's utterance 3 enables her to create not only her speaker operative interpreting of her own utterance 2, as above, but also her recipient *operative* interpreting of Marty's utterance 1, which until the point of his utterance 3 has remained her recipient *provisional* interpreting of it. The remainder of their conversation provides evidence. Loes's utterance 4 is a fourth position repair that explicitly identifies her newly created recipient operative interpreting of Marty's utterance 1. For Marty, Loes's utterance 4 is exactly what should follow his utterance 3, and as is apparent from his "Yeah" in utterance 5, it restores progressivity in interpreting action and reference in the sequence they are creating (although not for YNIs as Arundale 2020: 329–30).

Note then that this three-position organization of a speaker's given first position utterance, a recipient's next adjacent second position utterance, and the same (or another) speaker's further next adjacent third position utterance provides *both the speaker and the recipient of the given utterance* with working evidence of how the given first position utterance has been interpreted in that particular interaction. The evidence of a speaker's interpreting of a given first position utterance that its recipient gains in interpreting a third position utterance is just as important to the recipient of the given utterance in advancing the interaction as is the evidence that the speaker gains in interpreting the next adjacent second position utterance. Examining Marty and Loes's conversation is misleading in one respect. It suggests that the utterance in third position is important only when it qualifies progressivity because it is inconsistent with normative sequential expectations for what should come next after the second position utterance. That is explicitly not the case. Three positions would be just as essential for Loes to create a recipient operative interpreting of Marty's first position, "Loes, do you have a calendar," if Marty's third position talk and conduct were entirely consistent in sustaining progressivity, as in his reaching out to take the proffered desk calendar and perhaps saying "Thanks."

What then is the *participant's procedure* for creating interpretings in everyday interaction? Returning to Sacks, Schegloff, and Jefferson (1974), the participant's display, in subsequent utterances, of their interpretings of the talk and conduct appearing in prior utterances, is the key resource participants employ in interpreting prior utterances. It is the key resource because a recipient's display of his or her provisional interpreting enables a speaker to assess his or her provisional interpreting of his or her prior utterance. In that assessing, the speaker confirms or modifies his or her provisional interpreting of that prior utterance so that it becomes useable or operative as a basis for designing and delivering further utterances fitted to and grounded in the particular interpretings emerging in the current, situated interaction. If one grants not only that participants assess utterances in sequence in view of the default presumption that the next adjacent utterance is linked in some way to the immediately prior utterance, but also that a participant's initially provisional interpreting of an utterance becomes an operative interpreting as he or she assesses nextness, then: (1) *from the perspective of the speaker* of a given first position utterance, the participant's procedure involves assessing the nextness of another participant's next adjacent utterance so as to directly establish the speaker's operative interpreting of that first position utterance; and (2) *from the perspective of the recipient* of another's first position utterance, the participant's procedure involves not only assessing the nextness of the speaker's or another participant's third position utterance so as to directly establish an operative interpreting of the recipient's own second position utterance, but also using that operative interpreting as the grounds for indirectly (i.e., inferentially) establishing an operative interpreting of the speaker's first position utterance. Because speakers and recipients alternate in interaction, both must engage the participant's procedure from both perspectives. As two or more participants engage the procedure across overlapping sets of three contiguous utterances they create the temporal order of their particular interaction.

Again, the participant's procedure for interpreting utterances *in tempore* in everyday interaction is distinct from the analyst's *post hoc* procedure for doing so, even though both participants and analysts utilize the same interaction-internal evidence. The participant's procedure for establishing interactionally grounded, speaker and recipient operative interpretings of a given first position utterance is a direct reflection of the three-position temporal organization of next adjacency noted above. Elsewhere I identify this three-position temporal organization as the "conjoint co-constituting" of participant interpretings in everyday interacting (Arundale 2010, 2020: Ch. 3). The three-position temporal organization of conjointly co-constituting both a speaker's and a recipient's operative interpretings of a given first position utterance embeds the two-position organization of interactionally achieving a speaker's operative interpreting of a given first position utterance. I argue that this more encompassing, triadic account of the temporal organization of interaction is fully consistent with Garfinkel's ([1948] 2006: 184) early insight on understanding in interaction as a procedural matter (Arundale 2020: 90–1). Although it might appear that establishing the recipient's operative interpreting of a given first position utterance is simply the overlapping of two, two-position interactional achievements of speaker operative interpretings, with speaker and recipient roles reversed, the conjoint co-constituting account makes apparent that that is not the case. Specifically, in the process of conjointly creating interpretings across any three-position sequence of next adjacent utterances, the speaker's and the recipient's operative interpretings of the first position utterance become systemically interdependent. That interdependence defines the speaker and the recipient as a nonadditive social system, rather than as an additive collectivity, and cannot either practically or formally be accounted for in terms of interactionally achieving two successive speaker operative interpretings across two overlapping two-position sequences (Arundale 2020: 79–86, 385–90).

2.4 The Three-Position Organization of Next Adjacency and Action Ascription

Again, as Section 2.2, the three-position temporal organization of adjacency, nextness, and progressivity in interaction is generic and always in play as participants assess the nextness of each next adjacent utterance, but participants cannot assess nextness except in terms of one or more normative organizations of elements, e.g., turns in a sequence of turns, actions in a sequence of actions, and repair initiations in a sequence of utterances. Participant's assessments of nextness draw as well upon normative nonsequential moral orders in interaction, as in matters of cost–benefit (Clayman & Heritage 2014), epistemics (Heritage 2012a, 2012b), and deontics and emotional expression (Stevanovic & Peräkylä 2014). Quite commonly two or more normative organizations are coincident in assessing the nextness of a given next adjacent utterance, although whether a given utterance should or should not come next may well differ across those organizations. With regard

TURN	TRIAD	ADJ. PAIR	REPAIR
	1		
1 M: loes, do you have a calendar,	| 2	**1a**	**P1** ←
2 L: yeah ((reaches for her desk calendar))	| | 3	**1b**	**P2** ↑
3 M: do you have one that hangs on the wall?	| | |	**2a**	**P3** ↑
4 L: oh, you <u>want</u> one.	| |	**2b**	**P4** →
5 M: yeah	|		

Key: 1st Adjacency Pair: 1a: Request
1b: Grant
2nd Adjacency Pair: 2a: First pair part reworking post-expansion
2b: Reworked grant

Figure 2.1 Four coincident sequential organizations

to the sequential organization of turn-taking, the five utterances of Marty and Loes's conversation shown in Figure 2.1 comprise five TCUs in five contiguous positions in a turn-taking sequence. With regard to the temporal organization of next adjacency, those five utterances are coincident with three overlapping, three-position triads of next adjacent utterances: utterances 1–3, utterances 2–4, and utterances 3–5. With regard to the sequence organization of action, the five utterances are also coincident with two successive two-position adjacency pairs: a request and a subsequent granting across utterances 1 and 2, followed by one type of "first pair part reworking post-expansion" (Schegloff 1992: 1322 n14, 2007: 162–8) in utterance 3 that reworks the initial request and enables a reworked granting in utterance 4. With regard to the sequential organization of repair, utterances 1–4 comprise a fourth position repair initiation sequence (1992: 1326–7).[2]

As participants engage their procedure for interpreting utterances they draw on all relevant sequential and nonsequential normative organizations, although I focus here only on the coincidence of the three-position temporal organization and the two-position sequence organization of action (Schegloff 2007). In designing and delivering a given first position utterance, a speaker uses his or her knowledge of adjacency pair organization in anticipating the interpreting of action that his or her recipient will ascribe to that utterance. That anticipating is the speaker's provisional interpreting of the first position utterance.

[2] Sequences of next adjacent utterances must be both initiated and terminated (Arundale 2020: 86–7). Openings establish participant's expectations for next adjacent utterances where interaction does not yet exist (e.g., Pillet-Shore 2018), and apart from the abrupt dropping of a communication link, closings terminate sequences once interaction has been established by obviating the participant's expectations for next adjacent utterances (e.g., Schegloff & Sacks 1973).

The speaker draws on that same knowledge in assessing the nextness of the recipient's next adjacent, second position utterance as he or she identifies the interpreting of action that the recipient has ascribed to the first position utterance in this particular situation, and in so doing creates his or her operative interpreting of its action. Where the action of next adjacent second position utterance is what should come next, the action that the speaker anticipated would be ascribed to his or her utterance is confirmed and progressivity in the action sequence is sustained. Where the action of the next adjacent utterance should not come next the anticipated action is not confirmed and progressivity in the action sequence is qualified, leading the speaker to reconfigure his or her initial provisional interpreting of the first position utterance in creating his or her speaker operative interpreting of its action.

As it has been widely understood in terms of adjacency pair organization, then, action ascription is a matter of recipients indicating in a next adjacent utterance what action they have ascribed to a speaker's prior utterance. Returning briefly to Excerpt 2.1, Loes's reaching for her desk calendar is a next adjacent, second position utterance recognizable and interpretable as her action of granting that type of calendar, and thus of her ascribing to Marty the action of having requested some type of calendar in first position. From his perspective as speaker, Marty engages his knowledge of adjacency pair organization in assessing the nextness of Loes's second position utterance and creates his speaker operative interpreting of his first position action: an interpreting that enables him to continue designing and interpreting utterances because he now has evidence for how Loes has interpreted his action in their particular interaction. But Drew (2011: 1) makes a very important observation about what is occurring as recipients an ascribe action to a speaker's utterance: "when a recipient treats the prior speaker as having done something, *they* are doing something (i.e., ascribing an action is itself an action)." Loes's reaching for her desk calendar is a second position utterance that functions in ascribing an action to Marty's first position utterance. But Loes's second position utterance is, in and of itself, a recognizable and interpretable action of granting one type of calendar that likewise requires that a recipient of that second position utterance indicate in a next adjacent, third position utterance what action he or she has ascribed to it. From her perspective as speaker of the second position utterance, then, Loes engages her knowledge of adjacency pairs in assessing the nextness of Marty's third position utterance and creates her speaker operative interpreting of her second position action. That interpreting is interactionally grounded, enabling her to continue designing and delivering utterances fitted to their particular conversation.

It follows from Drew's (2011: 1) observation that *understood in terms of two-position adjacency pair organization, action ascription is a matter both of the recipient of a first position utterance indicating in a next adjacent, second position utterance what action they have ascribed to the first position utterance, and of a recipient of the second position utterance indicating in a next adjacent, third position utterance what action they have ascribed to the second position utterance.* Returning to the participant's procedure makes apparent, however, that even taking into account Drew's elaboration of the process, framing action ascription in terms of adjacency pair organization entails accounting for it solely from the perspective of the speakers of the first and of the second position utterances, and hence providing an account only of how each of them create a speaker operative interpreting of the action of their own utterance. What is missing in view of the participant's procedure is an account from the perspective of the recipient(s) of the first position utterance, and hence an account that incorporates how a recipient of a first position utterance creates his or her recipient operative interpreting of its action. It follows that *understood in terms of two-position adjacency pair organization, as well as in terms of the coincident three-position temporal organization of next adjacency, action ascription is a matter not only of the recipient of first position utterance indicating in a next adjacent, second position utterance what action they have ascribed to the first position utterance, and of a recipient of the second position utterance indicating in a next adjacent, third position utterance what action they have ascribed to the second position utterance, but also of the recipient of the first position utterance using the action ascribed to the second position utterance as the basis for establishing the action ascribed to the first position utterance.*

In forwarding the position that action ascription entails a three-position organization of conjointly co-constituting operative interpretings, coincident with a two-position organization of interactionally achieving them, I am not adding something previously unseen. Rather I am adopting a procedural perspective in identifying and examining characteristics of the three-position, generic temporal organization of next adjacency that are entailed as participants create sequences of operative interpretings, and tracing their implications for understanding and examining both the procedural bases of human interaction in general, and of how participants ascribe actions to utterances in particular. These implications have not been apparent in conceptualizing interaction principally as a two-position organization of interactionally achieving interpretings (Arundale 2020: 89–95), and in the absence of examining the continual sequential movement in interaction from provisional to operative interpretings (2020: 58–66).

2.5 Assessing Nextness and Progressivity in Ascribing Action

The process of assessing nextness warrants more detailed consideration because it is central to progressivity in ascribing action. Returning to

Schegloff's characterization, the default relationship defining the "nextness" of elements in sequence is that "each should come next after the prior" (2007: 14), to which he adds that "[m]oving from some element to a hearably-next-one with nothing intervening is the embodiment of, and the measure of progressivity," and that "[s]hould something intervene between some element and what is hearable as a/the next one due . . . it will be heard as qualifying the progressivity of talk, and will be examined for its import" (2007: 15). In other words, if the next adjacent utterance does not intervene there is maximal progressivity in the sequence of elements, that progressivity being qualified if the next adjacent utterance intervenes in some way. But if participant's assessments of nextness in forming operative interpretings entail assessing both progressivity and its import, then assessments of nextness cannot be simply assessments of *whether* a next adjacent utterance does or does not intervene, or should or should not come next. Assessments of nextness must also entail the participant's assessing of *how or in what way* a next adjacent utterance affects not only his or her interpreting of a prior utterance, but also his or her designing of subsequent utterances in the sequence-in-progress. In other words, assessing nextness must entail assessing the procedural consequentiality of each next adjacent utterance (Schegloff 1991: 53), and in so doing, how or in what way progressivity in the current sequence is sustained or qualified.

In Excerpt 2.1, as Marty assesses the nextness of Loes's second position utterance he finds that her action of granting him her desk calendar is what should come next in that it displays her ascribing to him the action of requesting "a calendar," even though the type of calendar she indexes is not what he expected. Her action is procedurally consequential both in his creating his operative interpreting of action for his first position utterance, and in his designing his third position utterance. For Marty, progressivity in their sequence has been sustained with regard to action, but qualified with regard to reference. As Loes in turn assesses the nextness of Marty's third position utterance, she finds that his reissuing of his initial request is not an action normatively expected to come next after her action of granting, leaving her with the tasks of assessing how or in what way his reissuing is procedurally consequential not only for creating operative interpretings of the actions of her second position and of his first position utterances, but also for the action she will ascribe to him in her fourth position utterance. For Loes, progressivity in ascribing action has been significantly qualified, and her next adjacent fourth position utterance could well be instrumental in restoring it. Framed in terms of the participant's procedure, Marty as speaker of the first position utterance creates his speaker operative interpreting of progressivity in ascribing action to his utterance as he assesses the nextness of Loes's next adjacent second position utterance, and Loes as recipient of the first position utterance creates not only her speaker operative interpreting of progressivity in ascribing action to her utterance, but also her recipient operative interpreting of progressivity in ascribing action to his utterance, as she assesses the nextness of Marty's next adjacent third position utterance.

Excerpt 2.1 is a single, specific example of everyday interaction, but it reflects a generic characteristic of the temporal organization of next adjacency: the successive utterances of different persons in a sequence of utterances are *always* next adjacent to one another. That implies that in assessing the nextness of each next adjacent utterance, participants like Marty and Loes are also *always* assessing progressivity in the sequence they are creating. And because the process of assessing nextness *always* creates operative interpretings, *in assessing nextness participants are always creating operative interpretings of progressivity*: operative interpretings not simply of whether progressivity is or is not present, but of how or in what way progressivity in the sequence is sustained or qualified at the point each next adjacent utterance appears. That said, it is also the case that Marty and Loes cannot assess nextness in the temporal organization of next adjacency, and more specifically, cannot assess progressivity in ascribing action, except as they draw on their respective knowledges of the sequence organization of action. The two organizations have distinct characteristics, one specific characteristic of the sequence organization of action being particularly relevant in assessing nextness and progressivity in ascribing action: whereas in the temporal organization successive utterances in a sequence of utterances are always next adjacent, in the sequence organization of action understood as adjacency pairs, successive actions in a sequence of action need not be next adjacent. Consider the examples in Excerpts 2.2 and 2.3 of departures between successive utterances and successive actions in interaction, and the implications for examining progressivity in ascribing actions to utterances in sequence. Because the term "position" is defined differently in these two organizations, I use "*adjacent* position" to refer to a position in the temporal organization of next adjacency, and "*sequential* position" to refer to a position in the sequence organization of action, or in another sequential organization like repair (Arundale 2020: 102).

As in Excerpt 2.1, the four utterances in Excerpt 2.2 comprise two adjacency pairs, but in this case one of these pairs (utterances 2 and 3) is an insertion expansion embedded within the other adjacency pair (utterances 1 and 4) (Schegloff 2007: 97–168), so that the sequential positions in adjacency pair 1 and 4 do not map onto adjacent positions. Where Merritt (1976: 333) identifies the customer in this service encounter as A and the provider as B, I substitute Amy and Bob to make the discussion less abstract.

Excerpt 2.2

```
01 AMY:    may i have a bottle of mich?
02 BOB:    are you twenty-one?
03 AMY:    no
04 BOB:    no
```

As Amy assesses the nextness of Bob's utterance 2, she finds that his YNI request for information is not an action normatively expected to come next following her YNI request for a bottle of a particular brand of beer. For Amy, Bob's utterance 2 is procedurally consequential in two ways. First, because his YNI does not ascribe an action to her utterance, she cannot use his utterance 2 in creating an operative interpreting of the action of her utterance 1, so that her interpreting of its action remains provisional. Second, she must now design her utterance 3 to address the new action sequence Bob has initiated in utterance 2. As Amy assesses nextness she creates a speaker operative interpreting that progressivity in ascribing action to her utterance 1 has been deferred pending completion of the new action sequence Bob has initiated in utterance 2. As Bob in turn assesses the nextness of Amy's utterance 3, he finds not only that it conforms to normative expectations for uptake, but also that it is consequential in creating both his speaker operative interpreting of his YNI in utterance 2 as having been addressed, and his recipient operative interpreting of Amy's utterance 1 as a request for a beverage to which she is not entitled because she is not of legal age. As he assesses nextness Bob creates both a speaker operative interpreting that progressivity in the action sequence he initiated in utterance 2 has been sustained, and a recipient operative interpreting that progressivity in the action sequence Amy initiated in utterance 1 has been restored.

As Amy assesses the nextness of Bob's "No" in utterance 4, she finds both that it is tied back to and addresses her YNI request in utterance 1 (Sacks 1992: 557–60), and that (likely despite her desires) it is an action normatively expected to come next following her request. Bob's utterance is in fourth adjacent position, but in second sequential position as the second pair part of the request and grant/deny adjacency pair Amy initiated in utterance 1. For Amy, Bob's "No" is procedurally consequential in creating her speaker operative interpreting of her utterance 1 as a request that has been denied, which has clear implications for her subsequent activities in their situation. In assessing procedural consequentiality Amy creates a speaker operative interpreting that the progressivity in ascribing action to her utterance 1 that had been previously deferred has now been restored. Merritt's (1976) transcript of her tape recording provides no utterance 5 by Amy, as for example in verbally acknowledging or visibly turning away, but her activity in fifth adjacent position would provide Bob with the basis for creating his recipient operative interpreting of her utterance 1.[3]

In his argument for the omnirelevance of action in interaction, Schegloff (1995: 193) examines the much more extended deferral in Excerpt 2.3 from a telephone call. His penetrating analysis rewards a careful reading.

Excerpt 2.3 (DON = Donny, MAR = Marcia)

```
09 DON:    ˙hh my ca:r is sta::lled.
10         (0.2)
11 DON:    ('n) i' m up here in the glen?
12 MAR:    oh::.
13         {(0.4)}
14 DON:    {˙hhh }
15 DON:    a:nd.hh
16         (0.2)
17 DON:    i don' t know if it' s po:ssible, but {˙hhh} /0.2} see
18         i haveta open up the ba:nk.hh
19         (0.3)
20 DON:    a:t uh: (˙) in brentwood? hh=
21 MAR:    =yeah:- en I know you want- (˙) en i whoa- (˙) en i
22         would, but- except i' ve gotta leave in aybout five
23         min(h)utes.[(hheh)
24 DON:                [okay then i gotta call somebody
25         else.right away.
26         (.)
27 DON:    okay?=
28 MAR:    =okay [don    ]
29 DON:          [thanks] a lot.=bye-.
30 MAR:    bye:.
```

Among the features of this excerpt that Schegloff considers are Marcia's "silent receipts" at lines 10, 13, 16, and 19, each of which he argues is "as fully fledged an event in the conversation as any utterance and as consequential for the ensuing talk" (1995: 198). Schegloff argues that each of these silent receipts is an occasioned absence of action in that it is a point "at which intervention from Marcia with an offer of help might be relevant" (1995: 199),

[3] Note two points. First, Amy's speaker operative interpreting and Bob's recipient operative interpreting of her utterance 1 are systemically interdependent, even though they are not conjointly co-constituted because they are not created across three next adjacent utterances (Arundale 2020: 79–86, 105). Second, had Bob initiated a repair sequence in utterance 2 with "A bottle of what?" one would likely find a similar pattern in how or in what way the ascribing of action to Amy's utterance 1 had been deferred.

but at which no offer is forthcoming, even though Marcia's utterance at lines 21–3 makes evident that she interprets Donny's line 9 "My car is stalled" as an action of announcing that implements a complaint and a request for help.

Take Donny's line 9 as the given first adjacent position in the temporal organization of next adjacency, and as the first sequential position and a first pair part in the sequence organization of action. Drawing on Schegloff's (1995: 198) analysis, Marcia's line 10 is *recognizable* as a silent receipt by a different participant given the conditional relevancy of an offer of help. As an occasioned absence the silent receipt qualifies as an utterance (Section 2.2), and hence as the second adjacent position in the organization of next adjacency. However, because her silent receipt is not *interpretable* as an action that might be expected to come next, it does not qualify either as a second sequential position or as a second pair part. In providing a silent receipt at line 10, Marcia passes an opportunity for a turn at talk, and in assessing the nextness of that silent receipt Donny finds that she has not ascribed an action to his line 9. Because he cannot use her line 10 utterance in creating an speaker operative interpreting, Donny's interpreting of the action of his line 9 utterance remains a provisional interpreting. That interpreting is nevertheless procedurally consequential, as is evident in his electing to continue in line 11 by designing and delivering an increment that elaborates his first sequential position, first pair part "My car is stalled." In the process of assessing the nextness of Marcia's silent receipt and finding that Loes has not ascribed an action, Donny creates a speaker operative interpreting that progressivity in interpreting his first pair part action of announcing-complaining-eliciting help has been deferred, pending subsequent uptake from Marcia that is interpretable as a second pair part action. As it turns out, Donny's line 11 increment after Marcia's line 10 silent receipt is the first of his four elaborative increments following silent receipts, which together comprise "a multiply renewed effort . . . to elicit help from Marcia, without ever requesting it . . . explicitly" (1995: 199).

Donny's line 11 "('n) I'm up here in the Glen?" is the third adjacent position utterance in the organization of next adjacency, and in assessing nextness Marcia finds that his informing her of his location is something that could come next following her silent receipt. But because her second adjacent position silent receipt provides no interpretable uptake and hence no display of an action she ascribes to his first adjacent position utterance, Marcia cannot use Donny's third adjacent position in creating either a speaker operative interpreting of action for her second adjacent position utterance, or in turn a recipient operative interpreting of action for his first adjacent position utterance, so that both interpretings remain provisional. That those provisional interpretings are procedurally consequential is evident in her delivering "Oh::." in line 12 as an acknowledgment or a "receipt of the informing, once again with no response to the complaint" (Schegloff 1995: 199–200). In assessing the nextness of Donny's line 11 increment, Marcia creates a speaker operative interpreting of her second adjacent position silent receipt as having deferred progressivity in interpreting action for Donny's first utterance. She evidently uses his utterance to elaborate her recipient provisional interpreting of his first adjacent position utterance, but that interpreting is not at this point interactionally grounded. Donny and Marcia repeat the sequence of her silent receipt followed by his increment across lines 13–15, lines 16–18, and lines 19–20, which are respectively the fifth and sixth, seventh and eighth, and ninth and tenth adjacent positions. As they assess the nextness of each successive utterance across these ten adjacent positions in the temporal organization their respective interpretings of the action of Donny's line 9 first pair part remain provisional because Marcia has yet to provide an utterance interpretable as its second pair part in the sequence organization of action. In assessing the procedural consequentiality of each next adjacent utterance as they do so, they continually create operative interpretings that progressivity in interpreting the action of line 9 has been deferred.

Unlike her silent receipts, Marcia's lines 21–3 are interpretable as an action that might come next after Donny's line 9. Her utterance, albeit in eleventh adjacent position, qualifies as the second sequential position and the second pair part in the adjacency pair initiated in first adjacent position. The first TCU in Marcia's line 21 ties her utterance back to Donny's utterance in line 9 (Sacks 1992: 557–60), and in assessing the nextness of her utterance Donny finds that she has ascribed to him the action of eliciting help, but that for the reason she offers she cannot provide the help he was requesting. Her utterance is procedurally consequential in his creating a speaker operative interpreting of the action he initiated first sequential position, as well as for designing his next utterance, and he creates a speaker operative interpreting that progressivity in interpreting his action of announcing-complaining-eliciting help has been restored. In twelfth adjacent position in lines 24–5, Donny acknowledges Marcia's inability to help and formulates its implication for him. As Marcia assesses the nextness of his acknowledgment, she finds that he has ascribed to her the actions of acknowledging but declining. His utterance is procedurally consequential in her creating a speaker operative interpreting of the action of her eleventh adjacent position utterance, and by inference her recipient operative interpreting of Donny's line 9 first sequential position utterance as an announcing-complaining-eliciting of help that has now been addressed, as well as in providing her with the bases for participating in the closing sequence that follows immediately. In assessing consequentiality Marcia creates a recipient operative interpreting that progressivity in action in the adjacency pair he initiated in first adjacent position has now been restored.

Excerpts 2.2 and 2.3 make evident that as participants assess the nextness of each successive utterance in the temporal organization of next adjacency, they create operative interpretings of progressivity in ascribing action as sustained, qualified, restored, or in some cases terminated. Yet because successive actions in the sequence organization of action as adjacency pairs need not be in next adjacent positions, participants are not necessarily creating operative interpretings of action as each successive utterance appears. The sequence organization of action is distinct from the temporal organization of next adjacency, and where successive actions depart from successive utterances, interpretings of action remain provisional until the participants encounter an utterance interpretable as a second pair part to an earlier first pair part. First and second pair parts become separated in a number of ways: Sacks (1992: 528–9) pointed to what he termed "delay sequences," and Schegloff (2007: Ch. 6) identifies a number of variants of insertion sequences that include other-initiated repair sequences. To these one need add both pre-expansions before a first pair part (2007: Ch. 4) and post-expansions following a second pair part (2007: Ch. 7). Insertion and expansion sequences increase the complexity of the process of ascribing actions to utterances, but participants demonstrably orient to and track progressivity in that process as they create operative interpretings of action in interaction.[4]

2.6 Conclusion: Third Position Utterances in Ascribing Action

There is a long-standing presumption that the speaker of a given first position utterance is doing one of two things as he or she designs and delivers a third position utterance: either progressing the current sequence of talk and conduct in some normatively expected manner and thereby tacitly (versus explicitly) confirming "the displayed understandings in the sequence so far" (Heritage 1984: 258; cf. Levinson 2013: 104), or initiating repair on some problematic aspect of the recipient's interpreting of the first position utterance that the recipient has displayed in his or her second position utterance. In other words, third position utterances have been understood principally as locations in which the speaker of a first position utterance engages in activity either to confirm or to repair the recipient's interpreting of the first position utterance. In that confirming or repairing the

[4] In view of Sacks's (1987) observations regarding preferences for agreement and contiguity, Stivers and Robinson's (2006) findings regarding a preference for progressivity in certain question-answer sequences, and the argument here that participants are always creating operative interpretings of progressivity as they ascribe actions to utterances, let me offer for future research the conjecture that there is a systematic privileging of sustaining of progressivity in creating operative interpretings of action, vis-à-vis qualifying that progressivity in some manner.

speaker of the first position utterance displays his or her understanding of the "state of the talk" (Heritage 1984: 259; cf. Rawls 2006: 30).[5]

The participant's procedure reveals this presumption to be too narrow. Third position utterances are indeed locations in which the speaker of a first position utterance (or another participant) designs and delivers a next adjacent utterance that displays some aspects of his or her provisional interpreting of the second position utterance, including at times an indication that repair is warranted. But that is not all. A recipient of the first position utterance also inspects that third position utterance in assessing nextness with regard to the second position utterance, in view of the expectations currently invoked in the sequence organization of action. The outcomes of that assessing are the recipient's operative interpretings of the action both of the second position utterance, and in turn of the speaker's first position utterance. It is only as the third position utterance is complete that the speaker's and the recipient's operative interpretings of the first position utterance become interdependent, that *both the speaker and the recipient* of the first position utterance have established the state of the talk between them, and that both have created bases for designing and interpreting utterances beyond third position that are interactionally grounded in the contingencies of their situated interaction (Arundale 2020: 92–3). As the speaker's and the recipient's operative interpretings become interdependent at the point of the third position utterance, they become a dyadic social system (Section 2.3).[6]

Considered in view of the triadic organization of interaction, third position utterances are just as essential as second position utterances in confirming, delimiting, or reconfiguring interpretings of first position utterances, and hence in creating operative interpretings in the sequence organization of action. The action ascribed to a second position utterance by a third position utterance has implications that extend backward to the action ascribed to a first position utterance because the second position utterance was designed as uptake to that first position utterance. That is the case *whether or not* the first, second, and third sequential position utterances appear in next adjacent positions (Arundale

[5] This understanding of the function of third position utterances has had the effect of constraining research both on ways of modifying prior interpretings other than repairing them, and on what comprises the "normal" development of a sequence in the absence of third position repair (Arundale 2020: 93–4).

[6] Note another long-standing presumption that at the point third position utterances appear, the participants are establishing or sustaining a "context of publicly displayed and continuously updated intersubjective understandings" (Heritage 1984: 259; cf. 2016: 209), "intersubjectivity" being often understood in this context as some form of "common understanding" between the participants. I argue that the establishing and sustaining of interdependent operative interpretings of a given first position utterance specifically does not entail "intersubjectivity" conceptualized as common understanding. Addressing these complex issues is well beyond the scope of this chapter, but see Arundale (2020, 95–102).

2020: 105). The procedural account developed here recognizes the centrality of third position utterances in creating operative interpretings of first position utterances, as did Garfinkel ([1948] 2006: 184). The procedural account both makes more apparent the complexities involved in ascribing actions to utterances in everyday interaction, and provides resources for examining those complexities from the participant's perspective.

My observation is that the more narrow understanding of the function of third position utterances has prevailed, so that until recently they have remained understudied, despite earlier work by Jefferson and Schenkein (1978) and Maynard (1989), for example. Current studies of third position utterances as confirming, delimiting, and reconfiguring interpretings of first position utterances include, but are by no means limited to Gardner (2013) and Kevoe-Feldman and Robinson (2012) on three-position sequential patterns, Heritage (2016) on change-of-state tokens in third position, Hayashi and Yoon (2009), Kim (2013), Schegloff (2007: 118–37) and Seuren (2018) on third position utterances that in closing a sequence delimit and reconfigure interpretings of first or second positions in adjacency pairs, and Haugh (2017) and Haugh and Pillet-Shore (2018) on third position utterances designed to distinguish among potential interpretings of first position utterances. These and other studies make evident not only that participants orient to third position utterances as procedurally consequential in confirming, delimiting, and reconfiguring interpretings of first position utterances (Arundale 2020: 102–9), but also that third position utterances are one key means by which "participants, themselves, make distinctions within gross categories of action" (Pomerantz and Heritage 2013: 223).

The argument that third position utterances are central in ascribing action rests on examining the triadic temporal organization of adjacency, nextness, and progressivity, specifically from the perspective of the participant as he or she forms an interactionally grounded interpreting of a given utterance in assessing the nextness of the utterance that another participant places adjacent to it. Examining the participant's procedure in doing so reveals a fundamental asymmetry in interpreting in everyday interacting (Arundale 2020: 75–7). With regard to the temporal organization of next adjacency in general, the speaker of a given first position utterance needs only a second adjacent position utterance by another participant to interactionally ground his or her interpreting of the given utterance, whereas the recipient of the given utterance needs a further third adjacent position utterance to interactionally ground his or her interpreting of the given utterance. With regard to the sequence organization of action in particular, the utterances comprising an adjacency pair need not be next adjacent, but the asymmetry remains. The speaker of a given first position utterance needs only another participant's ascription of action in a second sequential position utterance to form an interactionally grounded interpreting of the action of his or her utterance. But the recipient of the given utterance needs another participant's (often the initial speaker's) ascription of action in a further third sequential position utterance to form an interactionally grounded interpreting of action for the given utterance. In short, the triadic temporal organization of everyday interacting points to third position utterances as essential for the recipient in ascribing action to any given first position utterance, and as a consequence, essential for the speaker and for the recipient in together establishing the state of the talk and conduct between them.

REFERENCES

Arundale, R. B. (2010). Constituting face in conversation: Face, facework, and interactional achievement. *Journal of Pragmatics*, 42, 2078–105.

(2020). *Communicating and Relating: Constituting Face in Everyday Interaction.* Oxford: Oxford University Press.

Arundale, R. B. & Good, D. A. (2002). Boundaries and sequences in studying conversation. In A. Fetzer & C. Meierkord, eds., *Rethinking Sequentiality: Linguistics Meets Conversational Interaction.* Amsterdam: John Benjamins, pp. 120–50.

Clayman, S. & Heritage, J. (2014). Benefactors and beneficiaries: Benefactive status and stance in the management of offers and requests. In P. Drew & E. Couper-Kuhlen, eds., *Requesting in Social Interaction.* Amsterdam: John Benjamins, pp. 55–86.

Drew, P. (2011). Reflections on the micro-politics of social action in interaction. Paper presented the 12th International Pragmatics Association Conference, University of Manchester.

(2013). Turn design. In J. Sidnell & T. Stivers, eds., *Handbook of Conversation Analysis.* Chichester: Wiley-Blackwell, pp. 131–49.

Gardner, R. (2013). Conversation analysis in the classroom. In J. Sidnell & T. Stivers, eds., *Handbook of Conversation Analysis.* Chichester: Wiley-Blackwell, pp. 593–611.

Garfinkel, H. (1961). Aspects of the problem of common-sense knowledge of social structures. In K. H. Wolff, ed., *Transactions of the Fourth World Conference of Sociology (1959).* Louvain: International Sociological Association, pp. 51–65.

([1948] 2006). *Seeing Sociologically: The Routine Grounds of Social Action.* Boulder, CO: Paradigm Publishers.

Haugh, M. (2017). Prompting offers of assistance in interaction. *Pragmatics and Society*, 8(2), 183–207.

Haugh, M. & Pillet-Shore, D. M. (2018). Getting to know you: Teasing as an invitation to intimacy in initial interactions. *Discourse Studies*, 20(2), 246–69.

Hayashi, M. & Yoon, K. (2009). Negotiating boundaries in talk. In J. Sidnell, ed., *Conversation Analysis: Comparative Perspectives.* Cambridge: Cambridge University Press, pp. 250–78.

Heritage, J. (1984). *Garfinkel and Ethnomethodology.* Cambridge: Polity.

(2012a). Epistemics in action: Action formation and territories of knowledge. *Research on Language and Social Interaction*, 45(1), 1–29.

(2012b). The epistemic engine: Sequence organization and territories of knowledge. *Research on Language and Social Interaction*, 45(1), 30–52.

(2016). On the diversity of "changes of state" and their indices. *Journal of Pragmatics*, 104, 207–10.

Jefferson, G. & Schenkein, J. (1978). Some sequential negotiations in conversation: Unexpanded and expanded versions of projected action sequences. In J. Schenkein, ed., *Studies in the Organization of Conversational Interaction*. New York, NY: Academic Press, pp. 155–72.

Kevoe-Feldman, H. & Robinson, J. D. (2012). Exploring essentially three-turn courses of action: An institutional case study with implications for ordinary talk. *Discourse Studies*, 14(2), 217–41.

Kim, H. R. S. (2013). Retroactive indexing of relevance: The use of "well" in third position. *Research on Language and Social Interaction*, 46(2), 125–43.

Lerner, G. H. (2019). When someone other than the addressed recipient speaks next: Three kinds of intervening action after the selection of next speaker. *Research on Language and Social Interaction*, 52(4), 388–405.

Levinson, S. C. (2013). Action formation and ascription. In J. Sidnell & T. Stivers, eds., *Handbook of Conversation Analysis*. Chichester: Wiley-Blackwell, pp. 103–30.

Maynard, D. W. (1989). Perspective-display sequences in conversation. *Western Journal of Speech Communication*, 53(2), 91–113.

Mazeland, H. (2013). Grammar in conversation. In J. Sidnell & T. Stivers, eds., *Handbook of Conversation Analysis*. Chichester: Wiley-Blackwell, pp. 475–91.

Merritt, M. (1976). On questions following questions in service encounters. *Language in Society*, 5(3), 315–57.

Pillet-Shore, D. (2018). How to begin. *Research on Language and Social Interaction*, 51(3), 213–31.

Pomerantz, A. & Heritage, J. (2013). Preference. In J. Sidnell & T. Stivers, eds., *Handbook of Conversation Analysis*. Chichester: Wiley-Blackwell, pp. 210–28.

Rawls, A. W. (2005). Garfinkel's conception of time. *Time and Society*, 14, 163–90.

(2006). Respecifying the study of social order: Garfinkel's transition from theoretical conceptualization to practices in details. In A. W. Rawls, ed., *Seeing Sociologically: The Routine Grounds of Social Action by Harold Garfinkel*. Boulder, CO: Paradigm Publishers, pp. 1–97.

Raymond, G. (2003). Grammar and social organization: Yes/no interrogatives and the structure of responding. *American Sociological Review*, 68(6), 939–67.

Robinson, J. D. (2013). Overall structural organization. In J. Sidnell & T. Stivers, eds., *Handbook of Conversation Analysis*. Chichester: Wiley-Blackwell, pp. 257–80.

(2016). Accountability in social interaction. In J. D. Robinson, ed., *Accountability in Social Interaction*. Oxford: Oxford University Press, pp. 1–44.

Sacks, H. (1987). On the preferences for agreement and contiguity in sequences in conversation. In G. Button & J. Lee, eds., *Talk and Social Organisation*. Clevedon: Multilingual Matters, pp. 54–69.

(1992). *Lectures on Conversation, Volume 2*. Oxford: Blackwell.

Sacks, H., Schegloff, E. A. & Jefferson, G. (1974). A simplest systematics for the organization of turn-taking for conversation. *Language*, 50(4), 696–735.

Schegloff, E. A. (1981). Discourse as interactional achievement: Some uses of "uh huh" and other things that come between sentences. In D. Tannen, ed., *Analyzing*

Discourse: Text and Talk. Washington, DC: Georgetown University Press, pp. 71–93.

(1988). Discourse as interactional achievement II: An exercise in conversation analysis. In D. Tannen, ed., *Linguistics in Context*. Norwood, NJ: Ablex Publishing, pp. 135–58.

(1991). Reflections on talk and social structure. In D. Boden & D. H. Zimmerman, eds., *Talk and Social Structure*. Cambridge: Polity, pp. 44–70.

(1992). Repair after next turn: The last structurally provided defense of intersubjectivity in conversation. *American Journal of Sociology*, 97(5), 1295–345.

(1995). Discourse as interactional achievement III: The omnirelevance of action. *Research on Language and Social Interaction*, 28(3), 185–211.

(2007). *Sequence Organization in Interaction: A Primer in Conversation Analysis*. Cambridge: Cambridge University Press.

Schegloff, E. A. & Sacks, H. (1973). Opening up closings. *Semiotica*, 8(4), 289–327.

Seuren, L. M. (2018). Assessing answers: Action ascription in third position. *Research on Language and Social Interaction*, 51(1), 33–51.

Sidnell, J. & Stivers, T., eds. (2013). *Handbook of Conversation Analysis*. Chichester: Wiley-Blackwell.

Stevanovic, M. & Peräkylä, A. (2014). Three orders in the organization of human action: On the interface between knowledge, power, and emotion in interaction and social relations. *Language in Society*, 43(2), 185–207.

Stivers, T. & Robinson, J. D. (2006). A preference for progressivity in interaction. *Language in Society*, 35(3), 367–92.

3 The Micro-Politics of Social Actions

Paul Drew

3.1 Introduction

This is an enquiry into how participants can manoeuvre for position in managing certain social actions in interaction, and equally how they can manage to avoid implementing certain actions. This will involve considering participants' attributions of social actions to one another's talk, including their 'selective' attributions and contested attributions.

As the editors remind us in their introduction to this volume, a recipient's next turn has been taken by conversation analysts to be the key to, and to give us (as analysts) access to, action ascription. Given the possibilities for alternative understandings, or alternative action attributions, a recipient's response to a prior turn displays their analysis of the action they take as being implemented in that prior turn (Atkinson and Drew 1979: 50–1). Thus, we find in recipients' responses their understandings of prior turns, including their understandings of the actions they take those prior turns to be implementing. This is what in Conversation Analysis is known as a 'proof procedure', which according to Sacks et al. is a by-product of the turn-taking system for conversation. They say that

> When A addresses a first pair-part such as a 'question' or a 'complaint' to B, . . . A selects for B that he next perform a second pair-part for the 'adjacency pair' A has started, i.e. an 'answer' or an 'apology' . . . respectively. B, in doing so, not only performs that utterance type, but thereby displays (in the first place to his co-participants) his understanding of the prior turn's talk as [having been] a first part, as a 'question' or 'complaint'.

They continue,

> Herein lies a central methodological resource for the investigation of conversation . . . It is a systematic consequence of the turn-taking organization of conversation that it obliges its participants to display to each other, in a turn's talk, their understanding of other's turn's talk. (Sacks et al. 1974, §6.3: 728)

The editors give a fuller account of this corollary of the turn-taking system in their Introduction. But in brief, a recipient's response displays their understanding of what the prior speaker was doing in their prior turn; the recipient ascribes to the other, to the prior speaker's turn, an action – this is *action ascription in action*.

It is perhaps unfortunate that Sacks et al. chose to refer to this consequence of the turn-taking system as a *proof* procedure – unfortunate because it suggests, and has been taken to mean, that whatever particular action a recipient ascribes to the prior turn, as displayed in their response, *proves* that that is indeed *the* action that the speaker enacted or performed, or conducted or however one chooses to describe *doing*. This is misleading; a response in a next turn's talk displays *an* analysis of the action implemented by the prior speaker's turn.

The recipient's response displays the way she takes or chooses to understand that prior turn. The recipient is in effect *selecting*, from among some possible understandings of the prior turn, the action implication that they judge best suits their interactional purposes. In this respect – and this is my central argument here – *action ascription is itself a social action*; recipients are 'doing' something when they treat a prior turn as having implemented a given action.

3.2 The 'Value' and 'Dis-value' of Actions

My starting point is somewhere out of left field – it is that certain actions are 'valued' over others, in what are not restricted to pairs of possible actions (therefore not restricted to adjacency pairs). An informal example: in many situations it is considered 'better' (for one's self-image? for one's future career?) to resign, rather than to be fired. For instance, there seems to be a value attached to having the opportunity to *resign* (to 'fall on one's sword') rather than be *dismissed* – a value that is particularly apparent when that opportunity is denied, or, as sometimes happens, when someone is given the opportunity to resign or retire, in circumstances in which it is felt by some that they should have been fired. Such cases are reported frequently in the media; for instance, it was recently said about the one-time advisor to President Trump, Roger Stone, that 'Stone initially had a role with the Trump campaign, but in August 2015 he and the candidate had a falling-out, and Stone left. (Trump said he was fired; Stone said he quit)' (Toobin 2019: 30). Another similar example concerned the 'removal' of Stanley O'Neal as the chairman and chief executive of Merrill Lynch in 2008, in response to his role in the subprime exposure of the bank and thereby in the financial crisis of that year and beyond. 'As the hearing drew to a close, the committee's chairman, Henry Waxman, reprimanded John Finnegan, who represented Merrill Lynch's board at the hearing, for allowing O'Neal to retire, with his stock and options intact, rather than firing him.' (This quote appears in an editorial comment that O'Neal, the former CEO of Merrill Lynch, was 'forced to resign' [Cassidy 2008: 78].)

I said above that "certain actions are 'valued' over others": it may be noticed in this example that any such value may be attached by one of the participants, but not by the other(s). Although resigning/retiring may have been valued by O'Neal (literally – he received what was described as a payoff of $162 million, on retirement), that was plainly not the action that was valued by the committee chairman. Likewise, with apologies: the offended party may seek and therefore value an apology, whilst the putative offender may resist giving one. In the same account of the congressional hearing cited above, it was reported that "O'Neal made no apology for Merrill's role in marketing securities tied to subprime mortgages" (Cassidy 2008: 78). Again, demands and failures to give apologies are frequently reported in the media (for an account of the avoidance of giving apologies, see Drew and Hepburn 2015).

Considering the manoeuvring between participants as to who does what, a speaker can avoid explicitly inviting the recipient to some event by instead managing the talk in such a way that the other asks (requests) to come – by the speaker 'reporting' some circumstances (about an event), to which the other can respond by asking if they can come (Drew 1984). A particularly notable example – one that was perhaps seminal in conversation analysis – of such manoeuvring was Sacks's observation that in the opening of a call to a suicide prevention centre (SPC) line, in response to the counsellor's opening self-identification ('This is Mr Smith of the emergency psychiatric centre can I help you?') the caller avoided reciprocating with his name by initiating repair ('I can't hear you') (Sacks 1992a: 3–11). The sequential slot in which the caller would relevantly have identified himself by name is thereby elided, and the call continues without the caller having given his name.

An outstanding example of such manoeuvring is Irvine's account of the jockeying for position by the Wolof when they greet one another. One aspect of the relationship that becomes visible in Wolof greetings is that the one who initiates the greeting exchange "has control of all options until the very end" of the conversation (Irvine 1974: 173). However, the Initiator and Respondent roles may entail "a tacit agreement on their relative positions", such that the one who initiates adopts a self-lowering position and the Respondent self-elevates. But, Irvine cautions, it should not be assumed that each interactant will necessarily aim to take the higher-status position of respondent, because a higher-rank person (i.e., respondent) runs the risk that the other, the lower-status Initiator, may ask them, then or later, for a loan – high-status persons have financial obligations towards lower-status persons. "One may, therefore, wish to be lower than another and dependent on him; and the greeting can be used to help define such a relationship. By taking the lower-status role in the greeting, person A hints that he or she expects sometime to call on the higher-status person B for financial assistance" (Irvine 1974: 175). Irvine describes the ways in which people encountering one another may manipulate the slots in the greeting exchange so as to lay claim to the lower-status role by initiating the exchange ("If both parties are trying to be the Initiator, it may require some effort for a person to assure himself of the role: he must move quickly toward the other, and speak loudly and rapidly, the instant he has caught the other's eye or even before the other has noticed him" (Irvine 1974: 176).

This is a quite formalised example of sequential manoeuvring or manipulation (in Irvine's terms), to secure the position (slot) of opening the greetings exchange, if one sees the chance and has the aim to borrow money from the other (hence the situated value of initiating the greetings exchange). Others, such as the manoeuvring that Sacks reports enabling callers to the SPC to avoid giving their name in the appropriate sequential slot in call openings, and the management of the talk in such a way that the other asks if they can come to/join the event (self-invite), are less formalised, less conventionalised. There are other cases reported in the literature where *normative* seems more appropriate than 'formalised'; an outstanding example is Pomerantz's finding that 'my side' tellings can elicit from the other an account of where they were, what they were doing, to whom were they speaking, and so on.

Excerpt 3.1 Rahman II:1 (JEN = Jenny, IDA = Ida)

```
Jen:  Hello there I rang yeh'rlier b'tchu w'r ou:t,
      (•)
Ida:  Oh: ah musta been et Dez's mu:m's.
```

In telling Ida that she had tried to speak to her earlier in the day, Jenny reports that Ida 'was out', which is an inference she made from not having received an answer. Jenny's is a 'my side' telling about an event which Ida, of course, knew about first-hand; Ida knew she was not at home and knew where she was. In Pomerantz's terms, Jenny's 'my side' telling is about a matter which for her is a type 2 knowable, but which for Ida is a type 1 knowable, by virtue of her first-hand experience. Pomerantz refers to a speaker asserting a type 2 knowable to a recipient for whom what is asserted in a type 1 knowable, as a 'fishing' device (Pomerantz 1980). Pomerantz's account of this 'fishing' device suggests that there is a normative organisation that inhibits directly or explicitly asking someone where they were; the fishing device is a resource for finding out, by affording the recipient the opportunity to volunteer that information.

Such examples illustrate, rather informally, the sense of the 'value' that might be attached to an action, reflected in the manoeuvrings to implement that action and to avoid another. In some respects, this might seem to converge with the notion of preference in CA (Pomerantz & Heritage 2014). However, there are differences, one being the situated character of 'value' explicated above. In CA, preference attaches to action types in whatever sequential or other circumstances an action type occurs. By contrast, in these informal examples the 'value' associated with or attributed to certain actions is not intrinsic to the action; rather, it is situated, insofar as value may be differentially associated with particular interactional circumstances, and the interactional roles and interests of the parties involved (e.g., the one who has 'resigned' and the other who is critical; the offended party and the putative transgressor; the one who is holding the event and the one they might wish to come). In these and other ways, 'value' is a situated property of an action, 'belonging' to one or the other participant but not generally or usually equally to both. By the way, I have placed 'value' in scare marks to alert the reader to the somewhat ill-defined character of what I am referring to as 'value': it is perhaps easier to see that rejections or dismissals are not valued by the recipients of those actions, but 'value' in the case of Pomerantz's 'fishing' device is a less secure matter – its 'value' evident perhaps only in the manoeuvring in which participants engage, to elicit information by 'fishing' rather than by asking directly. That is to say, the situated value an action may have is evident in the sequential manoeuvring or managing the interaction so as to promote or inhibit such actions. The situated and contingent nature of 'preferred/dispreferred' turns might help to account for the complex and sometimes unexpected findings reported by Kendrick and Torreira (2015) concerning the relative timings of preferred and dispreferred responses in adjacency pairs.

The examples considered above involve participants manoeuvring in such a way as to avoid certain actions or possible action attributions – for instance, to avoid seeming to have been fired from a position; to avoid taking the initiative in inviting someone but instead to have them invite themselves; to avoid identifying oneself by name; by initiating greetings, thereby to avoid being in the position of being asked for a loan, for instance; and to avoid officially or accountably asking the recipient where they were, whom were they talking to and so on. It might be possible, across the operations through which speakers manage the talk so as to avoid some 'unwanted' action, in each of these examples, to discern some common interactional operations, or operations that are common to some of these 'avoidings'. However, there may be particular dimensions of social interaction that underlie the situated 'value' of one or the other possible actions, one such dimension being voluntarism. For instance, Pomerantz's 'fishing' device allows participants to volunteer where they were, rather than having to provide that information in answer to a direct question. 'Resigning' one's position entails choice in the matter; the one who resigns takes the initiative in volunteering to go, in contrast to their being forced out (fired) (hence the oxymoronic character of the phrase, again not uncommon in the media, that, as was quoted above regarding O'Neal's departure from Merrill Lynch, someone was 'forced to resign'). I will not develop the possibility that a dimension of voluntarism underlies (some of) the action manoeuvrings discussed here, except to note the probable connection with Parsons's voluntaristic theory of action (Alexander 1978; Parsons 1937). Moreover, it is likely that other social dimensions will also underlie the 'value' that some actions might have, in situ. For instance, 'value' may lie at the intersection between voluntarism, social solidarity, and the matter of 'who benefits' (Clayman & Heritage 2014), as well as with other social dimensions concerning epistemic and deontic rights (which might almost be regarded a privileges) and epistemic and deontic authority (Heritage 2012a, 2012b; Stevanovic & Perakyla 2012) underlying certain social action, and the 'recognition of what others are doing' (Stevanovic & Perakyla 2014). Other possible dimensions might include the problematic normative associations or implications of some action (e.g., that 'enquiring' might be regarded as 'prying', or the negative associations that might attach to the 'presumption' of inviting someone who is 'higher' on some measure of social position or 'desirability'). But for the time being, this informal consideration of voluntarism will have to suffice.

I refer to the micro-politics of action because politics involves the allocation of scarce and therefore valued resources – 'action' certainly fits that bill.[1] But it is likely that this sense of the (political) value of action is congruent with Levinson's "exploration of the economy of question asking". Noting that "one of the most prominent differences between questions and assertions is the obligation to respond", Levinson engages in an enquiry that

> begin(s) by laying out a model of a conversational economy of information, and later come(s) back to explaining its motivation. We need two kinds of currency. The one measures the value of the information exchanged ... The other kind of currency is a social measure, a measure of social IOUs or social 'feel good' factors or 'brownie points'. (Levinson 2012: 21)

Noting further the possible social costs of asking questions, he predicts that "If speakers can ask a question without being on record as doing so, they will do so ... (and that) across languages speakers will exploit question-equivocal forms, like the Labov and Fanshel queclarative, the question in declarative form" (Levinson 2012: 13). In an exploration across ten languages, Levinson finds that there is indeed mostly, though not invariably, evidence to support his predictions, including "statistical tendencies for polar questions to outnumber Wh-questions two-to-one across languages", and an "(apparent preference) in all languages to disguise their polar questions as declaratives". Added to which, in Yeli Dnye "self-repairs always seem to replace the socially expensive Wh-question with the cheaper polar one, not the other way around"

[1] My title is derived from Emerson and Messinger's *The Micro-Politics of Trouble* (1977).

(Levinson 2012: 31). Levinson's prediction that languages will exploit question-equivocal forms, to 'ask without asking' by using declarative forms to find out information, is of course exactly reflected in Pomerantz's account of how speakers can exploit the 'fishing' device of a declarative report of a 'my side' type 2 'my side'.

All that being said, however, the micro-politics of social action is evident in the manoeuvres in which participants engage, in such a way as to *implement* or to *avoid* certain actions, always remembering that the relative value of an action is a situated attribute. In what follows, I will consider some, but only some, of the systematic ways in which participants 'position' themselves with respect to certain action environments. From among the many and varied ways participants manoeuvre and position themselves regarding implementing and avoiding action, three stand out:

- Avoiding taking an action, in such a way that the other responds as though to the (absent action) implication (other's attribution to self of an action self might have been avoiding).
- Disguising an action, through (mis)attributing to one's own speech an action which may differ from the action that is thereby implemented (self-attribution).
- Treating a prior turn/action as having been what it was not officially designed to be/do (denying, disclaiming and 'misattributing' actions) (other-attribution).

3.3 Action Avoidance

The brief outline given above of the practice identified by Pomerantz – in which a speaker asserts something from her perspective (type 2 knowables, or K–; Heritage 2012a, 2012b), about which the other has first-hand knowledge (type 1 knowables) – suggests that this 'fishing' practice serves to avoid asking or enquiring directly about where the recipient was or to whom they were speaking. That information is left to be given, voluntarily, by the other, in response to the declarative. Here is an example closely resembling Excerpt 3.1 above.

Excerpt 3.2 NB:II:2:1 (NAN = Nancy, EMM = Emma)

```
Nan:  Oh: 'I:::'ow a:re you Emmah:
Emm:  FI:NE yer LINE'S BEEN BUSY.
Nan:  Yea:h (.) my u.-fuhh h-.hhhh my fa:ther's wife ca:lled me,h
      .hhh So when she ca:lls me::,h .hh I always talk fer a lo:ng
      ti:me cz she c'n afford it'n I ca:n't.hhh hhh °huh°
```

Pomerantz (1980)

Emma's report that Nancy's (telephone) line has been 'busy' elicits from Nancy information about whom she was talking to and why it's been 'busy' for so long. Eliciting that information has been managed without Emma asking directly, or officially. Here is an example in which a declarative, an announcement, similarly elicits from the recipient an 'initiating' response that saves the speaker asking.

Excerpt 3.3 Rahman:B:1:IDJ(12) (JEN = Jenny, IDA = Ida)

```
Jen:  Hello?,
      (0.5)
Ida:  Jenny?
      (0.3)
Ida:  It's me:,
Jen:  Oh hello I:da.
Ida:  Ye:h..h uh:m(0.2)I've jis rung tih teh-eh tell you(0.3)
      uh the things ev arrived from Barker'n Stone'ou[:se,
Jen:                                                  [oh:::::.
      (.)
Jen:  O[h c'nah c'm rou:nd,h[h
Ida:   [An'                 [ye[s please[that's w]'t=
Jen:                           [ha ha   [.a : h]
Ida:  =I wantche tih come rou:nd.
```

Ida reports/announces that *the things have arrived from Barker and Stonehouse* (a furniture store). In response, Jenny's request to 'come over' to see the new furniture that Jenny evidently knew was to be delivered, saves Ida having to ask her over – or rather, stands in place of asking Jenny over. It is clear from Ida's response to Jenny's request (lines 12–14) that her announcement was made in the service of 'asking' Jenny over, which she has achieved without having officially or explicitly to ask. In essence, Ida has managed the interaction in such a way that Jenny invited herself; Ida only 'admits' to having given her the news about the arrival of her new furniture, because she 'wants' Jenny to come round to see them (line 14); for more on how speakers' reportings, such as Ida's here, prompt self-invitations, see Drew 1984. This is as clear a case of positioning as occurs in Irvine's Wolof greetings, or in the 'positioning' whereby a caller avoids giving their name in the openings of calls to a suicide prevention centre.

In the next example, the caller, Charlie, has bad news (Schegloff 1988) to tell Ilene; he is not after all going to drive up to Syracuse this weekend – the consequence of which, for Ilene, is that he will not be able to give her a lift (ride) in his car. But that is not quite the news he actually delivers.

Excerpt 3.4 Trip to Syracuse (CHA = Charlie, ILE = Ilene)

```
Cha:  hhhe:h heh .hhhh I wuz uh:m:(·).hh I wen'ah:-
      (0.3) I spoke teh the gi:r- I spoke tih Karen.
      (.hhhh)/(0.4)And u:m::(·) ih wz rea:lly ba:d
      because she decided ofa:ll weekends fuh this one
      tih go awa:y
      (0.6)
Ile:  Wha:t?
      (0.4)
Cha:  She decidih tih go awaythis weekend.
Ile:  Yea:h,
Cha:  .hhhh=
Ile:  =.kh[h
Cha:      [So tha:[:t
Ile:              [k-khhh
Cha:  Yihknow I really don't have a place tuh sta:y.
Ile:  .hh Oh:::::.hh
      (0.2)
Ile:  .hhh so yih not g'nna go up this weeken'?
      (0.2)
Cha:  Nu::h I don't think so.
```

Charlie's 'bad news' (line 3) is that the friend with whom he was going to stay (Karen) is not now going away for the weekend. Leaving aside some of the intricacies of this example (including Ilene's 'open class' repair initiation in line 7, foreshadowing trouble; Drew 1997), and the hiatus that follows (lines 10–14), Charlie summarises the news as being that he 'doesn't have a place to stay' (line 15). It is Ilene who finds and articulates the implication of his not having somewhere to stay, the upshot being that he is not going up his weekend (line 18). Hence his 'news' is delivered in a stepwise fashion (Jefferson 1984), in such a way that it is left to *Ilene* to make explicit the 'real' news that he is not after all going up to Syracuse. In this way, the putative recipient of the bad news is the one to 'tell' that news. That much is well known (e.g., Schegloff 1988); however, what I am drawing particular attention to here is the 'teller's' (Charlie's) use of stepwise formulations through which he edges towards but does not quite articulate the news, thereby manoeuvring the talk in such a way as to avoid telling Ilene that he is not going, positioning himself to avoid the (un-)valued action, whilst leaving it to her, Ilene, to articulate the news.

The positionings or manoeuvrings illustrated in Excerpts 3.2–3.4, are managed through speakers telling recipients something, some news (e.g., Ida's 'I've just rung to tell you', line 7 in example 3) that have a 'my side' character (Pomerantz 1980), told from the speaker's perspective. These 'tellings' elicit responses that articulate the implications or upshots of the circumstances which the speaker has reported. (Speakers') reportings (Drew 1984) is a practice for eliciting from recipients an action that absolves the speaker from a relevant but 'unwanted' action; it is a practice which thereby repositions teller and recipient.

The ubiquity of this practice can be grasped by considering its use in what might broadly be termed service encounters, when customers, clients, and the like may simply report some circumstances, again from their perspective, leaving it to sales staff or other professionals to figure out the action implication of what is reported. Here are two brief illustrations, which will have to do duty for the overwhelmingly common use of this practice in our everyday lives. These examples are not perhaps from the everyday – one is from the opening of a medical (primary care) consultation, the other from an emergency call to the police.

Excerpt 3.5 Frozen shoulder (DOC = Doctor, PAT = Patient)

```
Doc:  So what can I do for you today.
Pat:  W' ll-(.) I have (.) som:e shoulder pa:in
      a:nd (0.2) a:nd (.) (from) the top of my a:rm. A:nd (0.2)
      thuh reason I,m here is because > a couple years
      ago < I had frozen shoulder in thee other a:rm, an,
      I had to have surgery . And ( ) this is starting to
      get stuck, and I want to stop it before it gets stuck.
      (0.4)
Doc:  Adhe:sive capsulitis
```

Heritage & Robinson (2006: 53)

In response to the doctor's opening enquiry in Excerpt 3.5, the patient reports the problem she has been experiencing with pain and stiffness in her shoulder (lines 2 and 7); as Heritage and Robinson observe, her account includes a self-diagnosis ('frozen shoulder'), to which the doctor responds with the more medical term, 'adhesive capsulitis' (Heritage & Robinson 2006: 53). The patient does not answer the doctor's opening enquiry, 'So what can I do for you today?', line 1); she does not respond with a request or any similar solicitation of assistance in resolving the problem – she simply reports the problem she is experiencing (her side), without articulating the implication for what the doctor might do to resolve the problem. It is noticeable that in none of the examples Heritage and Robinson show does the patient make a request, or do anything other than report the problem (the clue being in the title of their chapter, 'giving reasons' for seeking medical care).

In this excerpt from an emergency (999) call to the police, the caller likewise reports only the problem she is experiencing; she does not ask for – request – police assistance.

Excerpt 3.6 999 call, UK (CAL = Caller, COM = police call-taker)
(An emergency call to the police.)

```
Com:   Hello police
Ca:    Yeah hello (becca)uh I live at (address)
       (.)
Com:   Y[eah
Ca:    [Right and I'm (not home)my daughter was there(who is
       thirteen) and she's home and somebody has broken the house
       (.)
Com:   (oh=one=seven)(.)what's the address you want police to go
       to
```

This example has been included because the police communicator's response makes visible the request that he attributed to the caller's report, when he asks to what address the caller *wants* the police to go (line 8). In all such cases, a speaker reports some circumstances, leaving it to the other, the recipient, to determine the action implications of the report. They thereby save themselves from making a request for assistance.

3.4 Disguising an Action

It has been implicit in Section 3.1 that some actions can have associated costs, for one or the other (the giver or the receiver). For example, whilst offers might in some circumstances be a 'preferred' action, according to CA orthodoxy (but see Kendrick & Drew 2014), offering something might carry the implication that the other 'needs' what is being offered (Curl 2006), which implies 'want'; furthermore, an offer can be taken to impose (reciprocal) obligations on the other. It may be that such interactional costs lie behind the high incidence of rejections of offers, at least in the first instance. More immediately, they may also account for offers being disguised as other actions, as happens here when Gladys calls a near neighbour, Emma, to 'offer' her the use of her daily paper.

Excerpt 3.7 NB:IV:5:1 (EMM = Emma, GLA = Glady)

```
Emm:  ...oney=OH:I'                    [M f:i::ne?hhh
Gla:                                   [(I-)
Gla:  Well goo:d, ah:'ll tell you I:: .hh have a proposition:
      uhm.t.hhu-Bill:u-o:f course goes off on that uh (0.2)
      ↑tou↓:r: (.) Mondee< (.) i-his reguluh ↑go:lf ga:me.
Emm:  Ye:ah:?=
Gla:  =An'now I've got(.)tuh wash my hair en get the↑goop
      out'v it'n evrything? .hh 'n ah have the↑paper here I
      thought chu might li:ke tih↓have it. ↓.hhhh[h
Emm:                                            [Th[a:nk you.
Gla:                                               [en then
      you: could return it ub(.) ↑Oh along about noo:n,
```

The account Gladys gives (lines 7–8), that she is about to wash her hair and all that entails, has the implication that she cannot use and therefore does not need her newspaper during the morning. Her 'offer' to Emma to borrow the newspaper is constructed in an almost indirect manner ('you might like to have it', lines 8–9). Emma responds to what she takes to have been an offer by Gladys, 'thank you' (line 10). However, Gladys prefaced her account by 'naming' her action as being 'a proposition' (line 3). In this respect, therefore, she has disguised what is to be an offer to Emma (to lend Emma her newspaper for the morning) as a proposition, a *proposal* to 'let her have' the newspaper for the morning. I used scare quotes, 'let (Emma) have', to indicate that, whilst one might say *offer to lend*, it does not seem apt to say *proposal to lend*, because offers and proposals have quite different associations and affordances, especially regarding 'who benefits' and possible reciprocal obligations are concerned. At any rate, whilst offering something to someone implies a need (or want) on the part of the recipient, in other words *out of consideration* for and to assist the other, proposals, by contrast, do not convey another's need, nor assistance, and are made *for the other to consider*.

Here is an example in which the speaker names his action as 'offering'; this is from a conversation between the doctor and parents of a baby born very prematurely and whose survival is unlikely.

Excerpt 3.8 Neonatal (DOC = Doctor)

```
Dr:   And I don't think there's any chance of him having any,
      (.) meaningful(0.3)survival.
      (1.2)
Dr:   <And>>I think< our feeling as a tea:m,is that- (0.4)
      we should,(1.2)offer,(.)to:(0.2)palliate
      him an' to,(0.4)discontinue intensive care.
      (.)
Dr:   I think that would be in his best interest.=(and
      ultimately) he would die.
```

Whilst in line 4 the doctor refers to 'our feeling as a team' that they should 'offer' palliative treatment instead of the intensive care being given at present, it is plain to see that the doctor is recommending a course of action. In Excerpt 3.7 Gladys disguised her offer as a 'proposal'; here in Excerpt 3.8 by contrast, the doctor attributes the action of 'offer' to what is a proposal or recommendation.[2] It is perhaps unnecessary to consider more closely what is at stake in this example, as regards benefit and the desirability of the course of action 'offered' for the recipients. But it is evident that the affordances of an 'offer' differ markedly from those associated with 'recommendation', the former allowing the recipient(s), here the baby's parents, greater choice in whether to accept or decline the offer, than do the affordances associated with a recommendation (coming as that does with the authority of a medical team).[3] At any rate, it is enough for our purposes to see that differentially labelling actions as either 'proposals' or 'offers' manages, through these action attributions, the differing 'values' each action has for the different participants.

I should add a caveat here. In these cases, action attribution is managed and manifest through naming – through attaching an action label to what a speaker is 'doing', that is labelling her action as an offer, a proposal and so on. It should be noted that participants' action ascriptions may be done through and manifest in other much less explicit and visible ways, which we will consider below. My point here is only that when a speaker names what she is doing as making a proposition, she takes first rights to say what that action is (i.e., before a recipient has treated that turn as having been a certain action), and thereby takes the opportunity to label what she is doing (e.g., proposal) in a way that disguises or elides the obligations or other social dimensions associated with the 'unnamed' action (e.g., offer).

The affordances associated with 'offering', particularly those concerning the benefit to the recipient of an offer, are likewise deployed in this next example, also from a medical context, in which a nurse is trying to recruit a patient to join a randomised control trial for various treatments for the condition from which he is suffering.

2 Shaw et al. (2020) report that in a half of their sample of cases in which doctors initiated decision points concerning the future treatment of very premature babies in intensive care, doctors use this 'single-option choice format', in which a 'choice' is offered but without listing the options that might be available.

3 On the affordances associated with treatment recommendations, see Stivers et al. (2018).

Excerpt 3.9 Randomised control trial – recruitment (NUR = Nurse, WIF = patient's wife, PAT = patient)

```
Nur:   So>what I< have to ask you no:::w, HHH [.HHH
Wife:                                          [Mmmhmm
Nur:   U::m:(0.4)if you've got no other ques:tions,
       [.h h  is-  u ::]m: (0.6)>would you like
Pat:   [No can't think of any]
Nur:   to< be- °randomised today°.
```

Donovan et al. (2001)[4]

Recruiting patients to randomised control trials is managed through nurses asking patients whether they would agree to be 'randomised' – which is to say, through 'requesting' patients to join the trial. It is quite apparent in this example that the nurse has some difficulty in asking the patient whether he would join the trial. (In randomised control trials, the principle is that a patient who has agreed to be 'randomised' is randomly assigned to one of the available treatments for a medical condition; one of those 'treatments' may include, if medically and ethically appropriate, 'no treatment'.) Without going into great detail, her difficulty is evident in her prefatory *what I have to ask you now* in line 1, the use of the constraining *have to* in that preface (line 1), in her stretching certain sounds (lines 1 and 4), her audible intake of breath (lines 1 and 4), the softness with which she articulates *randomised today* (line 4), and above all in the construction through which she asks the patient *would you like* to be randomised today – which is one of the constructions through which offers are conventionally made (Curl 2006). In short, the nurse is hesitant to ask the patient to be randomised, and hence transforms her request into offering the patient something from which he will not benefit (the benefit is of course for medical knowledge and research, and so to patients in the future.)

Gladys's and the doctor's 'disguise' of their actions in Excerpts 3.7 and 3.8 were managed through action ascriptions, by naming their actions in line with the different in situ values that those actions might have, in relation to the actions for which they stand as surrogates. The disguise in Excerpt 3.9 was rather more subtle; the nurse does not name her action, but uses a form associated with a different action (offer) than that which she is in reality implementing (a request). Likewise in this next example, an extract from a call by a high school truancy officer (Off) to the mother (Mom) of a student who has been 'reported absent' from classes for almost three days and who is therefore suspected of being truant. Having established that the school records show the student as having been absent, and that she (the daughter) has not been at home with some medical condition, the truancy officer summarises what should be done.

[4] I am grateful to Jenny Donovan and Merran Toerien for permission to show this excerpt.

Excerpt 3.10 Medeiros 2 (Call from a US high school truancy office) (OFF = officer, MOM = mother)

Off: Yea:h. Well, u::h the- obviously she's not going to
her cla:sse:s an' we need tuh find out where she is:
going would you: talk t'her about it tonight'n .hhh
send her into the attendance office tomorrow morning so
that we c'n straighten these out.
Mom: Mmmkay[:: I'll see what she says about it.
Off: [Uh:: we have a new-
Off: .hhh Okay:. We have a new uh:: detention system now
(.)
Off: that if they don' clear the:se they'll become truants.
(.)
Off: .hh A:nd she will need to come in en clear them up.
(.)
Mom: Nnk[ay
Off: [Okay?
Mom: Do:I have tuh get back t'you 'r (.) jus' sending her is that enough.

The truancy officer advises Mom about what she should do ('would you talk to her . . .' etc., lines 3–5). Mom acknowledges this advice, 'Mmmkay::' (line 6), towards the end of which they collide when Mom continues, 'I'll see what she says about it' (line 6), just as the officer simultaneously begins giving her what will turn out to be information about 'a new detention system'. The overlap between them results in the officer dropping out of her turn (line 7), which she resumes after the completion of Mom's now-completed prior turn. The officer's resumption in line 8 is notable for both a change from, then a similarity to, her aborted turn in line 7. She now adds the preface *Okay*, thereby marking both a break from but at the same time a continuity with her previous turn, displaying a transition to something further (Beach 1993). However, that 'something further' begins exactly as did her previous attempt, when she repeats 'We have a new', before continuing and completing her turn. She might otherwise have resumed her turn after 'new', by going straight to 'detention system now'; instead, she restarts the turn (again, restarting with the inserted preface *Okay*) in which she goes on to deliver information about the 'new system'. Restarting in this way, by repeating what was first done in overlap, is an indication of something like the importance or significance of what is being said, of the importance for the speaker of not 'losing' what she is saying in the overlap. By referring to the detention system as 'new', the officer constructs the information as newsworthy; she is giving Mom information about a system that she will not have encountered before. At any rate, the officer is *informing* Mom about their system; delivering this as an informing about something new, and incorporating 'if they don' clear the:se up they'll become truants', serves to mitigate or detoxify the warning ('if you don't do X then Y will happen'). Indeed, whilst a warning is conveyed here (albeit that conditionally constructed warnings avoid directly accusing someone of a transgression; the officer does not accuse the daughter/student of being truant), the turn is designed overall as an informing, as news, of which a warning is only a part or an implication.

Having considered ways in which speakers can disguise the actions they are implementing, and thereby in a sense avoid certain other possible (or likely) action ascriptions, we turn now to consider manoeuvres on the part of recipients, involving their ascriptions to a speaker's prior turn/action.

3.5 'Mis'-attributions: Deniability, Defeasibility, and Disclaimers

In Section 3.1 I outlined briefly – as the editors do more fully in their Introduction to this volume – our reliance in Conversation Analysis on what has been termed the 'proof procedure' afforded by responses to prior turns, in which (that is to say, in the responses) next speakers display their analysis not only of who has been selected to speak (turn-taking allocation), but also what they take the speaker in that prior turn to have 'done', what action has been implemented in that prior turn. I further outlined why we might now find that unsatisfactory, or at least simplistic, that reason being that a next speaker selects one or some from among alternative possible understandings of the actions to be (accountably) found in that prior turn. They respond to one (or possibly some) of the potential understandings/actions they identify in prior turns. In selecting, participants are acting, so that *action ascription is itself a social action.*

The selection from among alternative possible understandings or action implications is relatively transparent in this example, in which Emma has phoned Margy to thank her for a luncheon party she gave. This excerpt begins at the point at which Emma is apologising for and explaining the delay in calling to thank Margy.

Excerpt 3.11 NB:VII:2 (EMM = Emma, MAR = Margy)

```
Emm:  =I shoulda ca:lled you sooner b't I don't know where the
      week we::n[t,
Mar:            [u-We:ll::=
Mar:  =Oh-yEmma you don'haftuh call me up=
Emm:  =[I wa::nt [ to:.  ]
Mar:  =[I wz jus [tickled] thetche-
      (.)
Mar:  nYihkno:w w'n you came u:p en uh-.hhh=
Mar:  =W'l haftuh do tha[t more]o[:ft en.]
Emm:                    [.hhhhh] [Wul w]hy don't we:uh-m:
      Why don't I take you'n Mo:m up there tuh: Coco's.
      someday fer lu:nch. We'll go, buzz up there tu[h,
Mar:                                                [k Goo:d.
Emm:  Ha:h?
Mar:  That's a good deal..hh-.hh=
Emm:  =Eh I'll take you bo:th [up
Mar:                           [No:::: we'll all go Dutch.=
Mar:  =B't[le t's do that. ]
Emm:      [No: we wo:n'    ]t.
```

Emma responds to Margy's good natured suggestion, 'We'll have to do that more often' (line 9), with a reciprocal action, which was first formed as a suggestion or proposal, 'Why don't we (go up to Coco's someday)', but which is transformed by the self-correction, 'Why don't we uhm why don't I' (lines 10 and 11), into an invitation (for a closer analysis of this excerpt, see Drew 2005: 89–90). The ambivalence in the action construction evident in Emma's turn in lines 10–12, poised as it is between being a proposal and an invitation, affords Margy the opportunity to select which of those actions she responds to. It is to be supposed that a recipient would select/respond to the 'nearest' action, to the one placed in second position, on the basis of the principle of contiguity (Sacks 1987). In this case, that 'second' action is an invitation. However, Margy chooses to respond instead to the 'first' action, the action that would have been implemented had Emma completed 'Why don't we [go up there to Coco's someday for lunch]' – a proposal. In doing so, she avoids or ignores the invitation that is recognisable in Emma's corrected version, to 'take you and Mom' up to Coco's someday for lunch. (By the way, this ambivalence in the construction of Emma's turn is evident not only through the self-correction, but also in the 'someday' nature of the invitation, as well as the negative construction *why don't we why don't I* in lines 10–11, negatively constructed proposals being associated with environments in which trouble has occurred or is anticipated: Drew 2013). The selection that Margy makes between, on the one hand, the possible but uncompleted proposal, and on the other hand the (more proximate) invitation, is manifest in her response in line 13, 'Goo:d'. *Good* is an appropriate response to a proposal or suggestion, but not to an invitation (in a corpus of invitations there are none that go *A: Would you like to come over for dinner at the weekend? B: Good*). The discriminative character (power) of adjacency pairs provides Margy with a resource to indicate that she is treating Emma's prior turn as having been a suggestion (to go and have lunch together at Coco's sometime), rather than an invitation (i.e., Emma's treat).

There follows a struggle between them regarding whether Emma is inviting Margy and her mother to lunch – her treat ('I'll take you both up', line 16); or whether they'll have lunch together but 'go Dutch' (i.e., pay separately) (line17), which Emma steadfastly rebuts (line 19) in pursuit of her invitation (again, for an extended analysis of this struggle, see Drew 2005: 89–90). This struggle represents precisely the micro-politics of social action; was Emma's turn in lines 10–12 an invitation, as she supposes and advocates, or was it a suggestion or proposal, as Margy chooses to regard it? The next turn, Margy's response, is not a 'proof' procedure, but rather the means by which she contests her co-participant's action attribution, and advocates her own quite different attribution. Each has a different understanding than the other about what action was being implemented by Emma in her turn in lines 10–12; neither Margy's response nor the struggle that follows 'proves' what action Emma produced in that turn.

A similar struggle between different 'understandings' of the same turn occurs in this next extract, in which Emma is talking to her sister, Lottie.

The call is winding down, when Emma begins to draw it to a close with her reference to *seeing her* one of these days (lines 4–5).

Excerpt 3.12 NB:1:6:4 (LOT = Lottie, EMM = Emma)

```
Lot:  °Oh I love tuh gee I ride mine all [th' ti:me.°
Emm:                                     [°Ye:ah.°
Lot:  I love it.
Emm:  .hhh WELL honey? ()Ah:ll (.) pob'ly SEE yih
      one a'these da:y[s,
Lot:                  [Oh: Go:d yeah [(ah wish)]=
Emm:                                 [ehh huh  ]=
Lot:  =But I c- I jis [couldn' git do:w[n (   )
Emm:                  [Oh-u             [OhI know=
Emm:  =I'm not as[kin yih tih]c'm dow-]
Lot:             [Jee:ziz    ]I m e an] I jis
          (0.2)
Lot:  I didn' have five minutes yesterday.
Emm:  Ah don' know how yih do i:t.
          (0.3)
Lot:  Ah don' kno:w. nh huh
Emm:  You wuh:work all day tih da:y.
```

The construction of this turn, *Well honey I'll probably see you one of these days* (lines 4–5), is susceptible to at least two alternative understandings; that is, the construction might be described as ambivalent (as in ambi-valent). First, it is a properly constructed reference to a future 'getting together', fitted to its pre-closing sequential environment (Schegloff & Sacks 1973). Though this reference is generalised, by not specifying a time and a place, for instance, it can be taken to be one of those pretty standard routines to open up the call closing (e.g., *I'll see you around, Talk to you later, I'll call sometime*). However, the form of this pre-closing is also consistent with a second understanding, that it is a complainable – implying a complaint that she has not seen much of the other (here, Lottie), and perhaps also an indication (request?) that she like to see her 'one of these days'. It is this latter understanding that Lottie attributes to Emma's turn in line 4, as is evident in lines 6, 8, 11, and 13 in which Lottie variously excuses not having been able to 'get down' to see Emma. In her turn in line 10, *I'm not asking you to come down*, Emma contests Lottie's understanding that she (Emma) was complaining about not having seen Lottie. She thereby treats Lottie as having misattributed that action to her turn. Her denial that she was asking her to come down underscores the defeasibility of action attributions to speakers' turns at talk (Hart 1960). In such circumstances (i.e., in which 'first speaker' initiates repair on or directly contests the action attribution revealed in a response), that response, and the first 'speaker's' response to the other's response, are evidence that a response is not a proof procedure – it is not a proof, but it is a procedure for attributing action, though a defeasible action attribution.

When in Excerpt 3.11 above Margy responded *Good* (line 13), she treated Emma as having made a suggestion or proposal – she treated Emma *as if* she had suggested having lunch together, rather than having offered to treat her (and her mother) to lunch. Thus, although a response/next turn does not 'prove' what the prior action was, nevertheless it does attribute an action to the prior turn, whether or not the speaker 'intended' that action, i.e., constructed their (prior) turn to perform that action. A response can thereby be a resource or a device to attribute to a prior turn an action that the recipient values, but which was not evident in that prior turn. Which is to say that recipients may treat the prior turn action as having implemented an action that it was putatively *not* designed to be/do.

Take responses that treat the prior speaker as having apologised. The standard response to an apology is a common form of absolution, *That's alright*, as illustrated in this next example.

Excerpt 3.13 Field:C85:3:1 (MYR = Myra, LES = Leslie)

```
Myr:  =I'm dreadf'ly sorry,[ it's hhh] hones]tly ah-ah-this=
Les:                       [That's^al]ri:ght]
```

In response to Myra's explicit and fulsome apology for being unable to make a meeting that evening, Leslie right away accepts her apology (line 2) (Drew & Hepburn 2015). That simple form of absolution is deployed in this next extract, Excerpt 3.14, as a means, a device, to treat the prior turn *as if* the prior speaker had apologised, although an apology is not visible in that prior turn.

Excerpt 3.14 Rahman:1:2:1 (DES = reception desk, KEN = Jenny)

```
Desk: Hello Goodzwin,
Jen:  Ehm good morning. eh it's Missiz Rah:man here,I ca:lled
      in on Thursday: tih see: if uh I c'd make en appointment
      t'see Mistuh (Thornley,)
      (1.2)
Jen:  An', I haven't heard anything'n I wz wondring if: uh:m
      (Ic'd possibly see im) one day next week.
      (0.8)
Desk: Uh:m I'll j's check iz diary c'n you hold a minute(eh
      [please).
Jen:  [yes,
Desk  (    ),
      (7.0)
Desk: Hello:,
Jen:  Hello?
Desk: Uh what name was it again[please
Jen:                           [Missiz Rah:man. R-a-hm-a-n.
Desk: R-a-hm-a-n. .h Right. Ken you just hold on one moment.
Jen:  eYes.
Desk: Thank you,
      (15.0)
Tho:  Hello:::,
Jen:  Hello?
Tho:  I tried tuh ring you  on: Thursday evening. b't
      I couldn'get'ny reply::.
Jen:  Oh dea:r. ehh hnh[h
Tho:                   ['T's alright Now?, when uh::dihyou
      wan'tuh come in
      Monda:y?,
```

Jenny has called her opticians and reports to the reception desk something complainable, 'I haven't heard anything' (line 6) (on complainable matters, see Sacks 1992b, e.g., pp. 46, 47, 438, and 441), which is to say that her optician has not phoned her back to arrange an appointment. Desk passes the message on to the optician (Mister Thornley), who comes to the phone and straightaway informs Jenny that he did try to phone her but 'I couldn't get any reply'. So whilst Jenny had represented herself as the 'offended' party, it now appears from Thornley's turn (lines 24/25) that she is the 'offender' (not being at home on Thursday evening). Her response to the news that Thornley had indeed tried to call her is to treat her not being home as having been a misfortune, 'Oh dear', (line 26). She does not apologise for being out, nor in any respect treat herself as having been at fault. His response to her response, ''T's alright', absolves her of blame for a transgression which she has not acknowledged or to which she has not admitted; through his absolution he accepts an apology that was not given – he treats her turn in line 26 *as if* she had apologised.

The absolution offered by the recipient in Excerpt 3.15 is rather more elaborate than in Excerpt 3.14.

Excerpt 3.15 Field:U88:1:4:3 (DAN = Dana, GOR = Gordon)

```
Dana: And I was so a[ngry
Gor:                  [kuhhhh.hh-[h
Dana:                             [a:n'(0.3)(   )
      ( [   ) an' oh::: Ghhhod.[C'z-
Gor:    [.hhhhhhhhhh           [But was: was the ↓film good.↓
      (0.3)
Dana: Yes it wa[s b't
Gor:           [Did you en↓joy it.↓
      (0.6)
Dana: Yes but it's: (.) oo I can't hardly remember the film
      Becuz I got so (bucked) up 'n ↓mm:-mm:.
Gor:  ehhhhh [Oh-:-:-oo,hh]
Dana: It's not you:r fault, but it's just becuz (0.3)
      Christie's ((w)) °so damn thick.°
```

It is unnecessary to go into the detail of what Gordon has done to have made Dana *so bucked up* (line 11) (by which she meant here something like distracted by the anxiety at Gordon having phoned late the previous evening, drunk). Through expressing sympathy in response, *Oh::* (line 12), he treats her state of distraction likewise as a misfortune, not a blameable matter, and therefore not something for which he should apologise. Dana's response to his sympathy is the more elaborate form of absolution, *It's not your fault* (line 13). As happened in Excerpt 3.14, Dana treats Gordon's prior turn as if it had been an apology, where none was given.

In these cases, then, recipients treat the prior turn/action as having been what it was putatively *not* designed to be or do. By treating the prior speaker as if they had admitted doing something wrong and apologising, recipients are mobilising the resources of 'next turn' to attribute to the other an action – an apology – which the other did not make, but should have made. These and examples like them are suffused with struggles between participants about fault, blame, and appropriate recompense.

3.6 Conclusion

I have argued that some actions, in interaction, are 'valued' whilst others are not; those that are valued may be sought, whilst those that are not may be avoided. I have further argued that the value or otherwise that may be attached to an action is not intrinsic to that action, but is rather a situated property, associated with such matters as from whose perspective, who benefits, voluntarism vs. compulsion,[5] interactional circumstances and sequential environments, and so on. I have further argued that the situated value an action may have is evident in the sequential manoeuvring or positioning through which the interaction is managed in such a way as to promote or inhibit those actions. We have seen evidence for these situated values in examples of three types of manoeuvring – in speakers avoiding actions through positioning their turns in certain ways; through disguising a (putative) action as another; and through the attributions of actions by recipients/next speakers of actions to prior speakers' prior turns. Insofar as those attributions display recipient understandings

[5] COVID-19 alert: One aspect of the reactions by the public, citizens, and by, e.g., particular occupational groups to the circumstances and strictures associated with the coronavirus pandemic, has been whether what might loosely be regarded as 'assistance' is given voluntarily or under some form of pressure or even coercion ('compliance vs. compulsion', as it is being summarised in the UK's media). For instance, there are stories of workers in different sectors either volunteering to take cuts in salary, whilst others are being obliged (required) to 'agree' to salary cuts during the period of lockdowns and temporary cessation of certain commercial activities. This dimension of voluntarism vs. the pressure of obligation is evident in accounts of how football clubs in the English Football League, and groups of club players, have responded to the opportunities to assist in the present crisis, one possibility being that super-rich clubs might donate money to the NHS to support the manufacture of necessary protective equipment. Some individual players began making donations, but clubs were slow to respond: "That said it was obvious football might get a kicking weeks ago and the players, the Professional Footballers' Association and the Premier League should have anticipated it. In mid-March, donating a large sum to the NHS would have been a massive PR win. Now it looks like they are being shamed into it, while also appearing out of touch with fans" (*The Guardian*, 6th April 2020). Insofar as being 'shamed' into offering financial assistance might be regarded as less worthy, in PR terms at least, acting sooner, voluntarily, is represented here as the more valued conduct.

of the actions they treat the prior turns as having implemented, attributions involve *selecting* an action from among the possible actions to be found in that prior turn. And to reiterate, this requires us to recognise that action ascription is itself a form of social action, the significance of which is evident in the sequential unfolding and the contingent dynamics of sequences of interaction.

REFERENCES

Alexander, J. (1978). Formal and substantive voluntarism in the work of Talcott Parsons: A theoretical and ideological reinterpretation. *American Sociological Review*, 43, 177–98.

Atkinson, J. M. & Drew, P. (1979). *Order in Court: The Organisation of Verbal Interaction in Judicial Settings*. London: Macmillan.

Beach, W. (1993). Transitional regularities for 'casual' *Okay* usages. *Journal of Pragmatics*, 19, 325–52.

Cassidy, J. (2008). Subprime suspect. *The New Yorker*, March 31.

Clayman, S. & Heritage, J. (2014). Benefactors and beneficiaries: Benefactive status and stance in the management of offers and requests. In P. Drew & E. Couper-Kuhlen, eds., *Requesting in Social Interaction*. Amsterdam: John Benjamins, pp. 55–86.

Curl, T. (2006). Offers of assistance: Constraints on syntactic design. *Journal of Pragmatics*, 38, 1257–80.

Donovan, J. L., Mills, N., Smith, M. et al. (2002). Improving design and conduct of randomised trials by embedding them in qualitative research: ProtecT (prostate testing for cancer and treatment) study. *British Medical Journal*, 325, 766–70.

Drew, P. (1984). Speakers' reportings in invitation sequences. In J. M. Atkinson & J. Heritage, eds., *Structures of Social Action: Studies in Conversation Analysis*. Cambridge: Cambridge University Press, pp. 129–51.

(1997). 'Open' class of repair initiators as responses to sequential sources of troubles in conversation. *Journal of Pragmatics*, 28, 69–101.

(2005). Conversation analysis. In K. Fitch & R. Sanders, eds., *Handbook of Language and Social Interaction*. Mahwah, NJ: Lawrence Erlbaum, pp. 71–102.

(2013). Conversation analysis and social action. *Journal of Foreign Languages*, 37, 2–20.

Drew, P. & Hepburn, A. (2015). Absent apologies. *Discourse Processes*, 1–18.

Emerson, R. M. & Messinger, S. L. (1977). The micro-politics of trouble. *Social Problems*, 25, 121–34.

Goffman, E. (1967). On face work. In *Interaction Ritual: Essays on Face-to-Face Behaviour*. Harmondsworth: Penguin, pp. 5–46.

Hart, H. L. A. (1960). *The Concept of Law*. Oxford: Oxford University Press.

Heritage, J. (2012a). Epistemics in action: Action formation and territories of knowledge. *Research on Language and Social Interaction*, 45(1), 1–29.

(2012b). The epistemic engine: Sequence organization and territories of knowledge. *Research on Language and Social Interaction*, 45(1), 30–52.

Heritage, J., Raymond, C. & Drew, P. (2019). Constructing apologies: Reflexive relationships between apologies and offences. *Journal of Pragmatics*, 141, 185–200.

Heritage, J. & Robinson, J. (2006). Accounting for the visit: Giving reasons for seeking medical care. In J. Heritage & D. Maynard, eds., *Communication in Medical Care: Interaction between Primary Care Physicians and Patients*. Cambridge: Cambridge University Press, pp. 48–85.

Irvine, J. (1974). Strategies of status manipulation in the Wolof greeting. In R. Bauman & J. Sherzer, eds., *Explorations in the Ethnography of Speaking*. Cambridge: Cambridge University Press, pp. 167–91.

Jefferson, G. (1984). On stepwise transition from talk about a trouble to inappropriately next-positioned matters. In J. M. Atkinson & J. Heritage, eds., *Structures of Social Action: Studies in Conversation Analysis*. Cambridge: Cambridge University Press, pp. 191–222.

Kendrick, K. & Drew, P. (2014). The putative preference for offers over requests. In P. Drew & E. Couper-Kuhlen, eds., *Requesting in Social Interaction*. Amsterdam: John Benjamins, pp. 87–114.

Kendrick, K. & Torreira, F. (2015). The timing and construction of preference: a quantitative study. *Discourse Processes*, 52, 255–89.

Lerner, G. (1996). Finding "face" in the preference structure of talk-in-interaction. *Social Psychology Quarterly*, 59, 303–21.

Levinson, S. (2012). Interrogative intimations: On a possible social economics of interrogatives. In J. P. de Ruiter, ed., *Questions: Formal, Functional and Interactional Perspectives*. Cambridge: Cambridge University Press, pp. 11–32.

Parsons, T. (1968/1937). *The Structure of Social Action*. New York, NY: The Free Press.

Pomerantz, A. (1980). Telling my side. "Limited access" as a "fishing" device. *Sociological Inquiry*, 50, 186–99.

(1984). Agreeing and disagreeing with assessments: Some features of preferred/dispreferred turn shapes. In J. M. Atkinson & J. Heritage, eds., *Structures of Social Action: Studies in Conversation Analysis*. Cambridge: Cambridge University Press, pp. 57–101.

Pomerantz, A. & Heritage, J. (2014). Preference. In J. Sidnell & T. Stivers, eds., *Handbook of Conversation Analysis*. Chichester: Blackwell, pp. 210–28.

Sacks, H. (1987). On the preferences for agreement and contiguity in sequences in conversation. In G. Button & J. Lee, eds., *Talk and Social Organisation*. Clevedon: Multilingual Matters, pp. 54–69.

(1992a). *Lectures on Conversation, Volume 1*. Oxford: Blackwell.

(1992b). *Lectures on Conversation, Volume 2*. Oxford: Blackwell.

Sacks, H., Schegloff, E. A. & Jefferson, G. (1974). A simplest systematics for the organization of turn-taking for conversation. *Language*, 50(4), 696–735.

Schegloff, E. A. (1988). On an actual virtual servo-mechanism for guessing bad news: A single case conjecture. *Social Problems*, 35, 442–57.

Schegloff, E. A. & Sacks, H. (1973). Opening up closings. *Semiotica*, 8(4), 289–327.

Shaw, C., Connabeer, K., Drew, P. et al. (2020). Initiating end-of-life decisions with parents of infants receiving neonatal intensive care. *Patient Education and Counseling*, 103(7), 1351–7.

Stevanovic, M. & Peräkylä, A. (2012). Deontic authority in interaction: The right to announce, propose and decide. *Research on Language and Social Interaction*, 45 (4), 297–321.

(2014). Three orders in the organization of human action: On the interface between knowledge, power, and emotion in interaction and social relations. *Language in Society*, 43(2), 185–207.

Stivers, T., Heritage, J., Barnes, R. K. et al. (2018). Treatment recommendations as actions. *Health Communication* 33(11), 1335–44.

Toobin, J. (2019). Time in the barrel. *The New Yorker*, February 18 & 25.

4 Action Ascription, Accountability and Inference

Michael Haugh

4.1 Introduction: Action Ascription as Social Action

Actions are behaviours that bring about changes in the world. A *social* action arises when those changes are brought about by one party initiating and another party responding (therefore presupposing that we are talking of *inter*-action). Work in ethnomethodological conversation analysis has demonstrated that social actions are formed through assemblages of practices that are "account-able" – that is, intelligible and reportable – as initiating and responding by virtue of those practices themselves (Garfinkel 1967: 1; Garfinkel & Sacks 1970: 342). A central question that this raises is what exactly are participants initiating? For participants of inter-action this question is pervasively approached through the lens of "why that now?" (Schegloff & Sacks 1973: 299). This question lies at the heart of the practical reasoning underpinning account-able inter-action. In short, participants need to engage in inferencing about what other parties are doing through these assemblages of practices. In accomplishing social action through responding in inter-action, however, a key question that also arises for participants is 'what next?' More specifically, what is an appropriate or legitimate response given any response not only construes the other party as account-ably initiating an action, but that response is itself also an account-able action? Practical reasoning thus not only concerns account-able inferences made available through current actions (i.e., 'why that now?'), but inferences made available through responses to those actions (i.e., 'why that next?').

Consider the following extract from a first conversation between Lily and Naomi who have been talking for some time about the advantages of living on one's own, and not with other housemates. Lily has been describing the granny flat she is currently renting.

Excerpt 4.1 CAAT: AusAus02 18:29 (LIL = Lily, NAO = Naomi)

```
01 LIL:   it's all i need (0.5) it's nice.
02        (0.1)
03 LIL:   [i like it]
```

```
04 NAO:       [goodness]
05            (0.1)
06 NAO:       if you ever move out let me[know or]
   nao:                                *points to self*
```

Figure 4.1 NAO pointing to self

```
07 LIL: ->                               [tsk well:]
08 NAO:      [↑HEH ha ha ha ha ha ha ha ha ha ha ha he]
09 LIL: -> [i' ve got (.) that' s what i was gonna say]
   lil: -> *points to NAO*
```

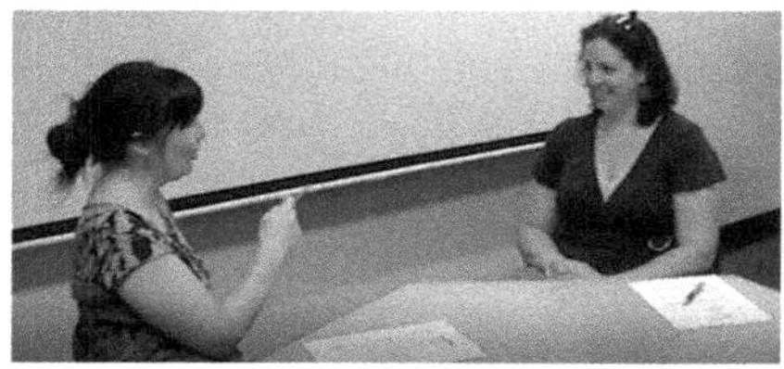

Figure 4.2 LIL pointing to NAO

```
10      -> i- if i do move out in february i ↑will
11      -> [let you know, because yeah]
12 NAO:    [yea:h?  hh ha ha ha  ha ha ]
13 LIL:    they' re .hh and the (0.2) the
14 LIL:    um: (0.1) the owners are lovely.
15 NAO:    mm.
```

Following positive assessments by Lily about the place she lives, Naomi responds with what appears, on the surface at least, to be a 'request' that is implemented through a conditional imperative format tagged with a turn-final 'or' (line 6), accompanied by Naomi lifting her hand to point to herself (Figure 4.1). Naomi subsequently adds post-completion stance-marking laughter (line 8). This post-completion laughter frames it as a non-serious 'request', and can also be heard as inviting laughter from Lily. Naomi's turn is also hearable, however, as an 'appreciative' or 'complimentary' assessment, that is, an expression of appreciation for the other's good fortune or expression of envy, through which Naomi implements upgraded agreement with Lily's own positive assessment of that granny flat (lines 1, 3).[1]

If we return, however, to the action Naomi initiates in line 6, the question facing Lily is how to respond in that moment. In order to figure out 'what next?', that is, what would count as an "appropriate response" here (Enfield & Sidnell 2017a: 524), she makes inferences about what Naomi is doing through that prior turn. After all, what counts as an 'appropriate response' critically depends on what one is responding to. Thompson, Fox and Couper-Kuhlen (2015) thus argue that "in order to respond, a participant must have ascribed some action to a prior turn, even if that ascription is only a best guess" (p. 3). In short, Lily needs to engage in action ascription in order to respond.

Action ascription is defined by Levinson (2013a) as "the assignment of an action to a turn as revealed by the response of a next speaker" (p. 104). In this case, Lily does not simply laugh in response, thereby responding to Naomi's prior turn as implementing an 'appreciative' or 'complimentary' assessment. Instead, she responds with a conditionally formatted promissory 'offer' confirming that she will let Naomi know if she moves out (lines 10–11). In so doing, Lily appears to be treating Naomi's prior turn (line 6) as (unofficially) 'fishing' for an 'offer'. However, as Heritage (2018) points out, action ascription is not just a matter of participants "recognising" what action(s) might be at play here, but also a practical matter of how one "frames" one's response to it (p. 39, see also Figure 4.2). In other words, a response to prior turns "displays *an* analysis of the action implemented by the prior speaker's turn" (Drew, Chapter 3 in this volume), an analysis which is "presented indirectly and must be inferred" (Heritage 1984a: 260) by the speaker of the prior turn.

The relative granularity (Schegloff 2000) of Lily's 'offer' (across lines 7, 9–11, see also Figure 4.2) makes available a number of inferences about how that 'offer' is being positioned with respect to Naomi's prior turn. Specifically, Lily frames her 'offer' as not simply responsive to Naomi's 'request' or 'appreciative' assessment, but one that is properly 'pre-emptive' of any genuine 'request' in claiming that she had already 'intended' to make such an 'offer' ("that's what I was going to say"). In other words, Lily is evidently concerned with her 'offer' being heard as 'volunteered' as opposed to being touched off by Naomi's 'request' or 'appreciative' assessment. It follows that Lily is not just simply treating the action implemented by Naomi in line 6 as either a 'request'

[1] This latter hearing of Naomi's action in line 6 is arguably underscored through Naomi's self-pointing, which is used here to upgrade this assessment (Turk 2007). I would like to thank Paul Drew for drawing this to my attention.

or an 'appreciative' assessment that is 'fishing' for an 'offer' (Levinson 2013a; Sidnell 2017a), but construing that 'fishing' as potentially precipitate.[2] A complication arising here, however, is that at the same time Lily is framing her offer as 'volunteered', Naomi is framing construing her 'request' as one that is equivocally (non-)serious, thereby modulating the degree to which she can be held accountable for having implemented a serious (i.e., genuine) 'request'. What is notable here is Lily persists with this ascription even though Naomi is at the same time appending post-completion laughter that modulates the valence of that 'request', thereby conferring a greater degree of equivocation on it (Drew 2018a). And despite Naomi's response to Lily's 'offer' also being equivocal with respect to whether or not she is accepting it (line 12), Lily persists in treating it as a matter for serious consideration (lines 13–14).

All in all, then, there appear to be some significant 'micro-politics' (Drew, Chapter 3 in this volume) at play here in the course of Lily ascribing an action to Naomi's prior turn, as both parties appear to be working to avoid being held accountable for accomplishing a straightforward 'request-granting' sequence. They are accomplishing a "sequential version" of something (Sacks 1992: 331). The question then is what is that 'something'? Or to put it another way, in evidently orienting to not only 'why that now?' but also 'why that next?', as well as the inferences they make available through the design of their respective turns, what is the 'that' in question?

While the growing body of research on requests, offers and recruitments (e.g., Couper-Kuhlen & Drew 2014; Curl 2006; Floyd, Rossi & Enfield 2020; Kendrick & Drew 2016; Thompson, Fox & Couper-Kuhlen 2015) can no doubt shed some light on unravelling aspects of this particular example, it is nevertheless also evident here that action types are not always so straightforwardly ascribed to prior turns as some accounts of action ascription might seem to presume. Yet it is also not simply a matter of Lily inferring what she believes to be Naomi's 'intention' or 'goal' here, and then responding 'appropriately'. For a start it is not clear what would count as an 'appropriate response' here. It is also notable that Lily's response frames her 'offer' as one that should properly have been made before ("that's what I was going to say"). The question, then, is not so much what would count as an 'appropriate response' or what Naomi's 'intention' or 'goal' here might have been here, but rather why does Lily calibrate her response here so finely? The answer here is, I would submit, that Lily is not treating her response as simply a matter of

[2] As Goodwin and Goodwin (1987) note, "rather than presenting a naked analysis of the prior talk, next utterances characteristically transform that talk in some fashion – deal with it not in its own terms but rather in the way in which it is relevant to the projects of the subsequent speaker" (p. 4). In this case, the terms of that prior talk are, of course, not self-evident. However, the point is well made that responses to prior actions do not always straightforwardly display the recipient's understanding of that prior action.

recognising what Naomi is doing in her prior turn, but orienting to the fact that she herself will be accountable for that response. In short, action ascription is, as Drew (2011, Chapter 3 in this volume) has astutely observed, itself an account-able social action, the 'something' or 'that' which is the raison d'être of conversation analysis.

Recognising that action ascription is a form of social action in its own right has significant implications, a number of which are explored in other chapters in this volume (see Arundale, Chapter 2 in this volume; Drew, Chapter 3 in this volume). The aim of this chapter is to explore the implications that follow from just two of these in further detail. The first is that action ascription not only involves the accomplishment of intersubjectivity, but also concerns matters of accountability. In treating action ascription as a social action we have formal grounds for the claim that analyses of action ascription must necessarily include inspection of third positioned actions (see also Arundale, Chapter 2 in this volume), as ascribing action is an account-able action in its own right. The second is that the accomplishment of action ascription as a social action provides grounds for the surfacing, as well as suppressing, avoiding or undercutting of practical reasoning by participants (Garfinkel & Sacks 1970), and thus procedural grounds for examining the inferences made available through action ascription. In order to provide an empirical anchor for these two rather broad claims, I will draw on a collection of instances of 'offers' that are occasioned or 'touched off' (Sacks 1992) by some prior action and are variously designed to be heard as such (Haugh 2017a). I do not mean these instances to be taken as proving these claims, as providing such proof lies well beyond the confines of a single chapter. Instead, they are meant to illustrate the pressing need to analyse action ascription as itself a form of accountable social action.

4.2 Accountability and the Three-Position Procedural Infrastructure of Action Ascription

It is well established that third position is a site for confirming or repairing participants' understandings of the import of the first-positioned initiating action. Heritage's (1984a: 254–60, 270–90) ground-breaking claim that participants' understandings of first actions formally requires (at least) three turns has been borne out in subsequent research on the interactional accomplishment of intersubjectivity (Arundale 1999, 2010, 2020, Chapter 2 in this volume; Deppermann 2015; Schegloff 1992; Sidnell 2014; Tsui 1989). However, it also has important implications for action ascription. Heritage (2018), for instance, has recently reiterated his position that "the intersubjective recognition of actions and understandings of their import ... are the objects of temporally extended courses of action, comprising three basic positions" (p. 30). In other words, action ascription occurs over three positions not two.

This claim might seem counter-intuitive on the grounds that the next-turn proof procedure only refers to next turns. Macbeth and Wong, for instance, argue

> there is no evidence that natural conversation could actually ever go on this way, in a regime of third-turn confirmations. But perhaps, alternatively, this is not a procedure for securing the understandings of the parties; those understandings are routinely in hand through the on-going work of next turns. (Macbeth & Wong 2016: 587)

In short, the argument seems to be that participants indicate through next turns how they have understood the prior turn, and unless something goes 'wrong', this will in normal circumstances be treated as sufficient by those participants. At first glance such an argument seems compelling. After all, the basic structure of social action is initiation–response (with adjacency pairs being a more specific instantiation of that underlying structure). In one party initiating an 'offer', and the other party responding to it as an 'offer' (through granting, refusing and so on), for instance, the parties in question have thereby jointly accomplished an 'offer'. On that view, action ascription is properly analysed through examining responsive, second-positioned actions, and we only need to formally check third position if something has gone awry. In other words, just because we can confirm or repair understandings of the import of the first-positioned action in third position, this does not mean this is what participants regularly do (Heritage & Atkinson 1984: 10).

If we carefully inspect how inferences about the understandings of participants are made available through temporally ordered next turns (Garfinkel [1948]2006; Rawls 2005), however, it becomes clear that both parties do not have the same formal grounds for inspecting the inferences made available through a responsive action at second position (Arundale 1999, 2010, 2020, Chapter 2 in this volume; Deppermann 2015). In second position, the party initiating the action can infer the understanding of other party of that action from the latter's response. However, the party responding to that action does not yet have grounds for inferring how the initiating party might be understanding that initiating action in light of their response. It is only when the initiating party responds in third position that the latter has grounds for making that inference. In other words, "the *intersubjective* recognition of actions and understandings of their import" (Heritage 2018: 30, emphasis added) formally requires three positions.

However, displaying an analysis of the action import of a prior turn through responding in next position, thereby ascribing an action to it, is not just a matter of intersubjectivity (that is, coordination between participants on the action[s] ascribed to a first position utterance). It is also a matter of accountability. Action ascription involves not only issues of intelligibility, but also responsibility (Garfinkel 1963, 1967; Garfinkel & Sacks 1970; Heritage 1984a; see also Heritage 1998; Robinson 2016; Sidnell 2017a). Accountability as intelligibility refers to participants' account-ability not only for what action (s) their conduct recognisably implements, but for also ensuring the action import of their conduct is recognisably implemented (Garfinkel 1963). Accountability as responsibility is sometimes taken to refer to overt explanations or accounts for conduct (Heritage 1988). However, it refers more broadly to practical reasoning by participants about the material and moral contingencies that are oriented to and invoked through those actions (Garfinkel 1967). For that reason, Garfinkel and Sacks (1970) emphasise that "accountable phenomena" are "observable and reportable phenomena" (p. 342) that arise through "methods for producing observable-reportable understanding" (p. 343). The next actions by which participants ascribe actions are the most basic method by which participants in interaction hold others account-able for (just) prior actions. However, since in framing that response they are also construing the prior action in a particular way, this response is itself an account-able action.

Consider the following excerpt in which Lesley 'offers' to lend her mother warm clothes during her visit.

Excerpt 4.2 Holt:X (C):1:2:7 (LES = Lesley, MUM = mother)

```
LES:     ↑don' t bring↑ too much
         (0.2)
MUM:     ↑oh that' s w' i wz g' n t' tell ↓you i' m:- (.) i' m ↑not
         bringing an (.) I' m not bring any big j:ump- (.) big
         ca:rdigans
         (0.2)
LES:     no: y[ou c' n
MUM:          [or a dressing gow:n i- .a (0.2) i[c' n ba-
LES:                                             [no-
         (.)
LES: ->  you c' n[↑borrow mi↓:ne
MUM:             [(      )-
MUM: ->  yeh i thought w' l i' d brin:g the small case ('n
         [just)
LES: ->  [eeyes do.
```

Mum responds to Lesley's 'trouble-responsive offer' (Curl 2006) that she can lend her warmer clothes during her visit (line 11) by producing an account as to why she won't be bringing those clothes herself (line 13), namely, the smaller case she will be bringing – which is easier for her to travel with – won't easily fit larger, bulky clothes. Lesley responds, in turn, with an imperatively formatted confirmation (line 15).[3] The mother's response, in line 13, holds Lesley accountable for making good on her offer (and thus accountable for the material and moral consequences of not making good on it), but does not straightforwardly accept it. Lesley's response, in line 15, orients to this non-straightforward acceptance of the offer by urging her mother to do just that (line 11). In so doing, Lesley is holding her mother account-able for committing to borrowing clothes during her visit (if that turns out to be necessary). Her initial 'offer' is sequentially modulated from being a contingent possibility to a likely eventuality through "displaying willingness to do an action on behalf of the recipient" (Hofstetter & Stokoe 2015: 741). The offer is no longer simply 'proposed' as a possibility; rather it has been 'announced' as a future course of action to which they are contingently committed. We have evidence here, then, that action ascription is "a temporally extended work-in-progress that is managed through the serial interlocking of actions in a process of successive confirmation and specification" (Clayman & Heritage 2014: 57).

However, in responding to Lesley's initial offer, her mother is not simply recognising it as an offer; she is herself accountable for having treated it as an offer, an accountability Lesley addresses through her subsequent response to her mother's response to the offer. Action ascription is thus a specific kind of reflexive action. That is, action ascription involves an action *acting upon* prior action. It is not simply displaying an analysis of the action import of the prior turn. This has three important upshots.

First, we have additional grounds for positing that the procedural infrastructure of action ascription necessarily involves three basic positions, not two. Not on the grounds that third position is a site for confirming or repairing what was 'meant' by the first-positioned initiating action – although it is just such a site to be sure (Arundale, Chapter 2 in this volume; Deppermann 2015; Heritage 1984a, 2018; Schegloff 1992; Sidnell 2014) as previously discussed – but rather because action ascription is itself an action. In constituting an action in its own right, it is account-able as a response and thereby accomplished as a social action accordingly. Action ascription minimally involves one party initiating and one party responding in adjacent turns, which in the case of adjacency pairs are recursively extendable through pre-, insert- and post-expansions (Levinson 2013b; Schegloff 2007). The focus in analysing action

[3] The 'offer' in line 11 follows an earlier attempt by Lesley to make such an offer in line 7. However, this is abandoned when Lesley's mother goes on to describe other 'heavy' clothes she won't be bringing (line 8). Notably, Lesley restarts this offer in line 9, but this is also cut off when her mother goes on to start what appears to be a possible 'proposal' ("I can borrow . . ."), which is also abandoned at the same time, before Lesley finally goes on to make the offer in question. There therefore appears to be some 'competition' here between the two of them about whether Lesley's mother is going to be first in making a 'proposal' to borrow clothes or Lesley will beat her to it in making an offer first (Drew, personal communication).

ascription has therefore tended to be on turn design (i.e., turn design as analytical resource) and response design (i.e., response as analytical resource). Analysing action ascription as an account-able social action, however, entails recognising that it involves not only responding to a prior action, but responding to that response.[4] Action ascription is itself an interactional achievement. It follows, then, that the interactional achievement of action ascription involves not only actions in second position acting upon the prior action in first position, but also the responsive action in third position acting upon both the responsive action in second position, and the initiating action in first position. In other words, action ascription arises through second *and* third position responses.

Second, we have procedural grounds for participants to engage in what Drew (Chapter 3 in this volume) terms the 'micro-politics' of social action. It is widely acknowledged that next turns are sites in which recipients display '*an* analysis' of the prior turn (Drew, Chapter 3 in this volume; see also Coulter 1983: 370; Heritage 2018: 28; Lynch 2011: 555), thereby allowing room for recipients to exercise agency in the way in which they frame their response (Goodwin & Goodwin 1987: 4; Heritage 1984a: 260; Heritage & Atkinson 1984: 11). While second position is procedurally an opportunity for the recipient to display *an analysis* of the prior action, thereby framing it in ways relevant to the recipient, third position is procedurally a site in which *an analysis of that analysis* can be offered. In other words, the ascription of action can be shaped, contested, and so on in the course of the participants accomplishing a particular "sequential version" (Sacks 1992: 331) of that social action.

If, for instance, we return to consider her mother's response to Lesley's offer in Excerpt 4.2 above, it appears that just such 'micro-politics' are indeed at play here. Rather than straightforwardly accepting Lesley's offer, her mother implies acceptance through registering the offering ("yeh"), and then producing a *well*-prefaced account that is embedded within reported talk quotative ("I thought w'l I'd brin:g the small case").

Excerpt 4.3 from Excerpt 4.2 above (LES = Lesley, MUM = mother)

```
LES:     you c' n[↑borrow mi↓:ne
MUM:             [(       )-
MUM: ->  yeh i thought w' l i' d brin:g the small case ('n
         [just)
LES:     [eeyes do.
```

4 While the way in which responses beget responses means closing sequences of actions is indeed a practical problem for participants, as Schegloff and Sacks (1973) argued, there are a range of methods by which participants close (or extend) sequences in third position, which thereby overcome the potential recursivity of action ascription as social action. This raises the question, in turn, of what count as adequate responses to second-positioned responses more broadly, but this is an empirical question that lies outside of the scope of the present chapter.

In responding in just this way, Lesley's mother is not only backgrounding what Lesley has offered to do for her (i.e., lend her some warm clothes during her visit if she needs them), and foregrounding the justification for such an offer being forthcoming (i.e., it will enable her to bring a small case); she also asserts her own agency and independent grounds for accepting the offer (i.e., she had already planned to do so prior to Lesley's offer).

Reported thought is sometimes associated with presenting a "silent criticism" (Haakana 2007: 176). In this case, this assertion of agency in her response to Lesley's offer follows her previously responding to Lesley 'advising' her mother not to bring too much luggage (line 1), by announcing through a 'touched-off' recalling that she plans to travel light (lines 3–5).

Excerpt 4.4 Holt:X(C):1:2:7 (LES = Lesley, MUM = mother)

```
01 LES:       ↑don't bring↑ too much
02            (0.2)
03 MUM: ->    ↑Oh that's w' i wz g'n t' tell ↓you i'm:- (.) i'm ↑not
04      ->    bringing an (.) i'm not bring any big j:ump- (.) big
05      ->    ca:rdigans
06            (0.2)
07 LES:       no: y[ou c'n
08 MUM:             [or a dressing gow:n i- .a (0.2) [c'n ba-
09 LES:                                              [no-
10            (.)
11 LES:       you c'n[↑borrow mi↓:ne
```

On that analysis, then, the offer by Lesley that eventuates in line 11 appears designed to be heard as prompted by the mother's declaration of her plans (in lines 3–5). The mother's response to that offer (lines 13–14), in turn, appears designed to resist just such a construal (Haugh 2017a), as well as reasserting her own agency in making those plans, thereby addressing the 'unsaid' criticism that Lesley's initial advice can be heard as implicating (Shaw & Hepburn 2013). In short, Lesley's mother brings off her acceptance of Lesley's offer not as merely responsive to Lesley's initial advice that she avoid bringing too much luggage, but that avoiding this was something about which she was already cognisant. Lesley's response in line 15 to her mother's response to the offer can be therefore heard as confirming that her mother will likely be taking up that offer, but on grounds somewhat independent of the grounds on which it was initially proffered by Lesley (Keevallik 2017). It is notable, then, that the way in which Lesley's mother responds to Lesley's offer, and Lesley responds in turn, is itself responsive to the advice-giving sequence Lesley initiated and the mother's subsequent responses appear designed to resist.

This points towards a third upshot of a treatment of action ascription as a reflexive social action involving action *acting upon* prior actions – namely, that the contingencies of sequences accomplished prior to the current sequence can be invoked in ascribing action to the just-prior turn (see also Mondada, Chapter 5 in this volume). In other words, in ascribing actions, participants not only consider that prior action, but prior sequences leading up to the just-prior action. As Goodwin (2013) argues,

> actions exist as rich, temporally unfolding process. Individual actions emerge from, and use, a consequential past shaped through chains of prior action, providing current participants with a dense, present environment, a rich now, containing many different kinds of resources that can be selectively decomposed, reused and transformed to build a next action, a proposal for how the future will be organized. (Goodwin 2013: 21)

To further illustrate this point, let us return to the example initially discussed at the beginning of this chapter. As noted in that rather brief analysis, Lily formulates her 'offer' (lines 7, 9–11) as one that is more properly delivered prior to Naomi's (equivocal) 'request' (line 6), while Naomi frames her 'request' as half-joking or equivocally non-serious (Holt 2016). Both parties therefore appear to be engaging in 'micro-politics' of a sort with respect to what Naomi is doing through her 'request' in line 6.

Excerpt 4.5 CAAT: AusAus02 18:31 (NAO = Naomi, LIL = Lily)

```
04 NAO:     [goodness]
05          (0.1)
06 NAO:     if you ever move out let me[know or  ]
   nao:                               *points to self*
07 LIL: ->                                  [tsk well:]
08 NAO:     [↑HEH ha ha ha ha ha ha ha ha ha ha ha he]
09 LIL: ->  [i'`ve got (.) that's what i was gonna say]
   lil:     *points to N*
10          i- if i do move out in February i ↑will
11          [let you know, because yeah]
12 NAO:     [yea:h? hh ha ha ha  ha ha]
```

The question for both parties, then, is not simply 'why that now?' with respect to Naomi's 'request', but 'why that next?' with respect to Lily's 'offer' being designed to be heard as 'first'. Lily is clearly not responding to just anything; rather she is exposing something in the inferential substrate she presumes to be available to both her and Naomi.

Further inspection of their conversation prior to this sequence suggests that it may be that Lily is orienting to Naomi's prior assertions that she would like to live in a granny flat herself rather than a shared house. Indeed, Naomi claims on two occasions that she has been looking for one for herself. In Excerpt 4.6, which occurs nearly five minutes earlier in their conversation, Naomi responds to Lily's self-disclosure that she lives in a granny flat that she's "jealous" (line 3), because she has been "looking for" one (line 5).

Excerpt 4.6 CAAT: AusAus02 14:35 (NAO = Naomi, LIL = Lily)

```
01 LIL:     hh yeah mm i- i' m living by myself at the moment?
02          um just in like a little granny ↑flat
03 NAO:     .HHH [i' m very jealous [that' s] =
04 LIL:                            [it' s very cu:te  [yeah   ]
05 NAO: ->  =what i' ve been £looking for£.
06 LIL:     yeah?=↑we:ll i think u:m (0.1) oh .tch >i dunno know<
07          i' ve i- i' ve lived there? (.) i moved there in february,
08 NAO:     mm.
```

This expression of jealousy from Naomi overlaps with Lily's positive assessment of her flat (line 4), and so also implements, in this sequential context, an 'upgraded' appreciative assessment.

Following an extended complaint about her current housemate, whose behaviour is one of the reasons for wanting to live by herself she has previously offered (data not shown), Naomi reiterates this desire again two minutes later (line 4).

Excerpt 4.7 CAAT: AusAus02 16:44 (NAO = Naomi, LIL = Lily)

```
01 NAO:     but a granny flat.
02          (0.1)
03 LIL:     [ye:ah]
04 NAO: ->  [.tsk ] i mean i' ve been looking for one and .hhhhh
05 LIL:     mm.
06 NAO:     there' s a great article in um (0.3) oh some (0.3)
07          hairdressing magazine that i was flipping through one
08          da(hh)y ha um about (0.4)an- y- demographically th- the
09          idea of solitaires? and people who .hh (0.2) are
10          perfectly social they' re not sort of hermits
((24 lines of omitted text))
35 NAO:     i was thinking ye:sf why don' t people (0.4) bui:ld
36          more of those [you know] (like)=
37 LIL:                   [yeah yep]
38 NAO:     =because .hhh
39 LIL:     [it' s true]
40 NAO: ->  [<i mean   ] that sort of thing would be perfect>
41      ->  all I need is somewhere:
42          (0.4)
```

```
LIL:    mm. (0.2) yep=
NAO:    =bed (0.5) some kind of socialising area.
        (0.2)
LIL:    [yeah
NAO:    [preferably not (0.2) all in the one space
```

This then leads into a telling about an article she read about the seeming lack of suitable places to rent for people who prefer to live on their own but don't want to be squeezed into a one room apartment (lines 6 onwards). She concludes by reiterating again that she would like to rent just such a place (lines 35–47). Notably, in both cases, the assertion of this desire is prefaced with "I mean", indicating an orientation to this being heard as a 'complaint', and not something else (Maynard 2013), such as a 'masked' or 'disguised' request (Drew, Chapter 3 in this volume). Thus, despite reporting this 'desire' a number of times these reports do not appear to be designed as prompts for an offer of assistance from Lily (Haugh 2017a); at any rate Lily treats them as only informings through response tokens that acknowledge that desire (Gardner 2001). However, just like any report of troubles, difficulties or needs, they could nevertheless be heard as prompting or recruiting an offer of assistance (Kendrick & Drew 2014), a possible hearing that perhaps accounts for Lily's 'offer' rather than simply laughing in response (see Excerpt 4.5). The latter would have amounted to a treatment of Naomi's 'request' as implementing yet another 'appreciative' assessment (see line 3, Excerpt 4.6). However, Lily does not laugh, but rather responds non-straightforwardly with an 'offer' that suppress inferences that might otherwise arise (e.g., that making such an offer had not previously occurred to Lily prior to Naomi raising that possibility through the 'request').

In sum, while the procedural infrastructure of action ascription minimally consists of three positions, it is evident that participants can orient to the contingencies of sequences accomplished prior to those three positions in question. There is evidence, then, that interaction generates an inferential substrate (Haugh 2017b; see also Deppermann 2012, 2018; Drew 2018a) that participants can selectively draw upon in ascribing action. The following section considers this inferential substrate and its role in action ascription in more detail.

4.3 Action Ascription and Practical Reasoning

There is a long tradition of (social) action being associated with controlled, purposive or intentional behaviour. However, while there is no doubt human beings always have their own goals, even if they not always consciously experienced, a key insight that can be derived from ethnomethodolgy and CA is that such intentions or goals are first and foremost *products* or *outcomes* of inter-action (Arundale 2008; Drew 1995; Garfinkel [1948]2006; Haugh 2013; see also Deppermann & Kaiser, Chapter 6 in this volume).[5] To define actions in terms of putative, *a priori* intentions, then, is not consonant with the way in which social actions are demonstrably interactional accomplishments. In short, while participants may indeed make inferences about the putative intentions or goals of speakers, these do not determine social actions, but rather are attributed to speakers in the course of the interactional accomplishment of social actions. To define social actions in terms of individual speaker goals or intentions, then, is to put the cart before the horse, as it were. Claims that action ascription primarily involves inferences about speaker goals (e.g., Enfield & Sidnell 2017a, 2017b), or plans (e.g., Levinson 2013a, 2017), thus arguably conflate action ascription with action formation. As Levinson (1995) has previously noted, while reasoning from goals or plans to conduct is relatively straightforward, reasoning from conduct back to goals or plans is not. For that reason, while it may be entirely reasonable to define a 'request' as (intentionally) recruiting assistance of some or another for self (or on behalf of others), one cannot simply reverse this line of reasoning in examining action ascription.

A range of different types of inferential processes are implicated in action ascription (Deppermann 2012, 2018; Drew 2018b; Elder & Haugh 2018; Haugh 2009; Levinson 2013a, 2017). Not all of these are, however, directly observable through the analysis of talk-in-interaction, although their probable shape and nature can, of course, be inferred to some extent. There is, in addition, a vast inferential substrate that participants draw upon, as Garfinkel (1967) first demonstrated, although this is also not directly observable unless participants work to expose those inferences in the course of interaction (Haugh 2017b). What is clearly tractable for analysis, though, is the methods of practical reasoning (Garfinkel & Sacks 1970; Pomerantz 2017; Sacks 1992) that participants themselves draw upon in ascribing action.[6] These methods of

[5] This echoes an earlier line of argumentation from ordinary language philosophers in which the analysis of action was decoupled from intentions, and linked to uptake by recipients (e.g., Austin 1962; Melden 1961; Mills 1940), a move that was subsequently undone in the work of Searle (1969), who reinstated intention as central to the analysis of speech acts.

[6] In engaging in this sort of practical reasoning, participants are almost invariably orienting to both moral and material (including spatio-temporal) contingencies. The nature of those contingencies with respect to action ascription has been the subject of significant attention in recent years (Deppermann & Haugh, Chapter 1 in this volume; see also Deppermann 2021), but as Heritage (2012a, 2012b, 2013, 2018) notes, there is still much to be done to properly elucidate these different principles and orders of interaction. Systematic consideration of these thus lies beyond the scope of the present chapter.

practical reasoning make available inferences that progressively shape the ascription of action through the temporal and sequential placement of responses to prior actions.

One sequential environment in which practical reasoning recurrently surfaces is in cases where *want*-formatted offers that explicitly reference the recipient's presumed or potential 'desires' (Curl 2006; Deppermann 2018) occasion non-straightforward *well*-prefaced responses (Haugh 2017a). It has been observed that *want*-formatted offers are canonically used when troubles or needs of the recipient are educed (from prior talk), as opposed to having been overtly stated (Curl 2006), and so occur in particular sequential environments (Drew, Walker & Ogden 2013). Clayman and Heritage (2014) also observe that formulating offers in this way foregrounds the recipient's needs or desires. These observations create cross-cutting preferences with respect to accepting such offers. On the one hand, it has been claimed that offers (canonically) prefer acceptances (Schegloff 2007: 60), and so a rejection of an offer should typically be implemented with a dispreferred format (although cf. Kendrick & Drew 2014). On the other hand, accepting a *want*-formatted offer tacitly endorses the presumption that the party making the offer has educed what the recipient 'desires' (Curl 2006: 1274). One way of dealing with these cross-cutting preferences is to respond non-straightforwardly to the offer.

In the following example, for instance, the initial *well*-prefaced response (line 3) to Alice's offer is treated by Alice as projecting rejection. In this case, then, a dispreferred action (i.e., rejection) is projected through a *well*-prefaced dispreferred format, a rejection that Alice forestalls (Jefferson 1986) through a subsequent version of the offer (Davidson 1984).

Excerpt 4.8 SBL2.1.6.R (ALI = Alice, BET = Betsy)

```
ALI:      d' you wan' any pots
          f' r coffee er a[ (nything? )]
BET:                      [W E :LL? i  ] : have[-v]
ALI:                                           [ h] yihknow
          i have that great big glass: °coffee m:° hhh maker
          it makes ni:ne cu:p[s.
BET: ->                      [w' l sa:y now that' s' n idea
          YE:s i would like tih use[tha:t.]
ALI:                               [n  o :w] i: c' n i:' ll
          bring the: insi:de to it y' see
```

However, the subsequent *well*-prefaced response to Alice pressing Betsy to accept her offer, in contrast to the first instance, indexes a non-straightforward acceptance of that offer (i.e., a preferred response implemented with a dispreferred format). Notably, Betsy's acceptance of Alice's offer to lend her coffee pots is framed as one that has just occurred to her in that very moment ("that's an idea"), as opposed to being something she had been 'wanting' Alice to offer her. Betsy thus undermines the inference made available through a *want*-formatted offer that this what she had been 'wanting' all along. In responding in that way, then, the offer itself is construed by Betsy as not responsive to prior 'prompting' by her, but rather one that Alice had 'volunteered' of her own accord.

We can observe similar occurrences of non-straightforward acceptances of offers in the following set of examples.

Excerpt 4.9 DS00007 (MIK = Mike, MAR = Mary)

```
01 MIK:      do you want one?
02 MAR: -> u::m yea- (.) well it' s le- less messier actually.
03 MIK:      okay.
```

Excerpt 4.10 NB:IV:10:R (EMM = Emma, LOT = Lottie)

```
01 EMM:     if[you wa] nt ↑ME TO go to the beauty parlor i wi:ll,
02 LOT:       [°oh:.°]
03          (.)
04 LOT: ->  ↑well i just thought maybe we could go over to richard' s for
05          lunch then after i get my hair ↓fixed.
06 EMM:     alri :ght.
```

Excerpt 4.11 TC1(a):14:2-5 (BEN = Ben, ALB = Albie)

```
01 BEN:     >want me to bring anything?<
02          (0.6)
03 ALB: ->  u-we:ll w(h)hy yer own bodies?' n: sumpn tuh dri:nk,hh
04          (0.2)
05 BEN:     oka:y?
```

In each case, the *well*-prefaced response implements a non-straightforward acceptance of the offer in question.

In Excerpt 4.9, Mary accepts Mike's offer to get her a plate on the grounds that it addresses a potential 'trouble'. In Excerpt 4.10, Lottie accepts Emma's offer (or proposal), which follows a series of inquiries from Lottie as to whether Emma would like to go the beauty parlour (Clayman & Heritage 2014: 81–2), on the grounds that it would enable them to have lunch together. Finally, in Excerpt 4.11, Albie non-straightforwardly accepts Ben's offer to bring something to the party through a joke-first response (Schegloff 1987). In all three cases, the non-straightforward acceptance appears designed to defeat the inference that is made available through accepting a *want*-formatted offer that this is indeed what they had been 'wanting'. In so doing, the offer is construed as 'volunteered', as opposed to being 'responsive' to prior 'fishing' on their parts to prompt just such an offer through reporting some kind of trouble, need, absence and the like (Haugh 2017a; Kendrick & Drew 2014, 2016; Sidnell 2017a), or what Curl (2006: 1269) terms an "educed problem offer". In short, through their non-straightforward acceptances recipients are not just accepting any offer, but a specific kind of offer (Drew 2013: 154), namely, a 'volunteered' offer that foregrounds the agency of the party accepting that offer (Keevallik 2017; see also Drew, Chapter 3 in this volume).

In each case, there are particular moral, material and interactional contingencies with respect to action ascription that these non-straightforward acceptances appear designed to address. In the case of Mike's offer to Mary, for instance, we can see in the more extended excerpt below that Mike's offer is itself occasioned by a prior offer from Mary.

Excerpt 4.12 DS30007 (MAR = Mary, MIK = Mike)

```
MAR:     ↑o:h. ((while eating))
         (0.8)
MIK:     [°m:m°
MAR:     [i haven't gotten y' a bread 'n butter plate
         but (0.4) there's one in the cupboard if you want one.
MIK:     mm? o::h ↑sho:uld be okay? i'll j[u-
MAR:                                      [yo[:u  alright?]
MIK:                                         [d' yu    d' yu]
         do you want one?
MAR: ->  u::m yea- (.) well it's le- less messier actually.
MIK:     okay.
MIK:     ((gets up and goes to the kitchen))
```

The sequence in question actually begins with a *want*-formatted offer from Mary to Mike that he can get himself a plate if he "wants one" (line 5). Mary's offer is launched with a 'noticing' that registers, through "oh" (Heritage 1984b) (line 1), an absence that serves as an account (line 4) for her subsequent offer. Mike initially responds with a rejection of Mary's offer (line 6). However, pursuit of the matter by Mary (line 7) appears to prompt an interpolated (Goodwin 2017) *want*-formatted offer to get a plate for Mary (lines 8–9). The granular design of Mary's response in line 10 to that offer is instructive.

Mary initially launches a type-conforming (Raymond 2003) acceptance of the offer. However, this is sequentially deleted through a self-initiated self-repair that launches a non-straightforward acceptance of the offer consisting of three components: *well*-prefacing, an account, and turn-final "actually". The *well*-prefacing indicates that her response to Mike's query is non-straightforward (Heritage 2015; Schegloff & Lerner 2009), the account foregrounds the potential 'trouble' engendered by eating without a plate thereby implementing a dispreferred format (Pomerantz & Heritage 2013), and the turn-final "actually" marks Mary's response as counter to Mike's expectations (Clift 2001). In this case, Mary does not position herself not as the beneficiary of an offer that addresses her 'desire' to have a plate; rather she positions both her and Mike as beneficiaries of an offer that addresses a possible 'trouble' that might otherwise arise.

However, her response to Mike's offer does more than simply that. It was noted in Section 4.2 that responsive actions can also act on first-positioned actions, not only second-positioned actions. In this case, Mary's non-straightforward acceptance of Mike's *want*-formatted offer also defeats the inference that Mike offering to get plates for them both was what she 'wanted' all along. This is not only relevant to the offer made by Mike (lines 8–9), but also to Mary's initial offer (lines 4–5). Through her non-straightforward response Mary undercuts the inference made available by Mike's *want*-formatted offer that her initial offer was designed to 'recruit' (Kendrick & Drew 2016) or 'prompt' (Haugh 2017b) just such an offer from Mike.

In sum, through non-straightforward responses to offers, participants display an orientation to the ascription of a specific kind of that action (Drew 2013: 154; Pomerantz & Heritage 2013: 223), specifically a 'volunteered' offer that foregrounds the agency of the party accepting – and benefiting from – that offer. In this respect, then, action ascription is clearly a participants' concern. The granular design of these responses (Schegloff 2000) indicates an orientation on the part of those participants to both moral (Heritage 2013; Stevanovic & Peräkylä 2014) and interactional (Drew 2018a) contingencies in the ascription of action. Attention to these contingencies is not just important for the ascription of gross categories of action, however, but is needed to tease out the ways in which participants orient to *particular kinds* of that action. It is this orientation to specific kinds or 'tokens' of action that thereby provides warrant for the assignment of action types by analysts. While it is evident that participants are not, for the most part, much concerned with specifying or naming action types (Enfield & Sidnell 2017a, 2017b, Chapter 12 in this volume; Sidnell 2017a, 2017b), they are evidently concerned with specifying the moral and material import of those actions. As we have seen here, our understanding of how participants ascribe particular kinds of actions can be furthered through paying close attention to the practical reasoning that surfaces in interaction, for instance, through non-straightforward acceptances of offers.

4.4 Conclusion

Action ascription in CA has sometimes been treated as essentially synonymous with action recognition. It has thus sometimes been assumed that analysing next turns offers analysts sufficient proof of the actions that have been ascribed by participants to the prior turn. In this chapter, it has been argued that such a view arises from conflating action ascription with action formation, and that conflating these leads to an impoverished account of the former. An alternative view that has emerged more recently is that action ascription is not simply an inferential operation underpinning the recognition of action types, but is a form of social action in its own right (Drew 2011, Chapter 3 in this volume). In this chapter, I have explored two implications the follow from this understanding of action ascription as a form of social action.

The first is that action ascription is not just a matter of intersubjectivity, but is also a matter of accountability. Participants are account-able for responding to a prior action in just that way, and the ascription of action is thus interactionally achieved through responses to responses. The underlying accountability of action ascription is what engenders, in turn, what Drew (Chapter 3 in this volume) refers to as the 'micro-politics' of social action, the potential framing and reframing of the specific kind of action that is held to be accomplished by those participants. The procedural infrastructure of action ascription is thus premised on three basic positions, not two.

The second is that inferences are made procedurally available, as well as suppressed, avoided or undercut in the course of ascribing action through participants' methods of practical reasoning. This claim was illustrated through examining non-straightforward acceptances of *want*-formatted offers, that is, cases in which the preferred action (i.e., acceptance of the offer) is implemented through a dispreferred format. It was argued that these non-straightforward responses are designed to undercut the inference that is otherwise made available by accepting *want*-formatted offers that this was indeed what the recipient had 'wanted' all along. This reflects, in turn, an orientation on part of those participants to the moral and material contingencies of ascribing particular kinds of offers.

The far-reaching implications of Drew's (2011, Chapter 3 in this volume) explicit call to treat action ascription as a social action have still to be fully worked through. This chapter is intended as a modest contribution to that endeavour. The hope here is that it will encourage further research in CA that builds on Sacks' ([1964/1965]1989) original interest in elucidating the inferential machinery of practical reasoning and inferencing that both affords and constrains the interactional accomplishment of accountable social action.

Acknowledgements

I would like to thank Bob Arundale and Paul Drew for their very insightful comments on an earlier version of this chapter. Any mistakes remain, of course, my own.

REFERENCES

Arundale, R. B. (1999). An alternative model and ideology of communication for an alternative to politeness theory. *Pragmatics*, 9(1), 119–54.

(2008). Against (Gricean) intentions at the heart of human interaction. *Intercultural Pragmatics*, 5(2), 229–58.

(2010). Constituting face in conversation: Face, facework and interactional achievement. *Journal of Pragmatics*, 42, 2078–105.

(2020). *Communicating and Relating: Constituting Face in Everyday Interacting*. Oxford: Oxford University Press.

Austin, J. L. (1962). *How to Do Things with Words*, Cambridge, MA: Harvard University Press.

Clayman, S. & Heritage, J. (2014). Benefactors and beneficiaries: Benefactive status and stance in the management of offers and requests. In P. Drew & E. Couper-Kuhlen, eds., *Requesting in Social Interaction.* Amsterdam: John Benjamins, pp. 55–86.

Clift, R. (2001). Meaning in interaction: The case of "actually." *Language*, 77(2), 245–91.

Coulter, J. (1983). Contingent and *a priori* structures in sequential analysis. *Human Studies*, 6, 361–76.

Couper-Kuhlen, E. & Drew, P., eds. (2014). *Requesting in Social Interaction.* Amsterdam: John Benjamins.

Curl, T. (2006). Offers of assistance: Constraints on syntactic design. *Journal of Pragmatics*, 38, 1257–80.

Davidson, J. (1984). Subsequent versions of invitations, offers, requests and proposals dealing with potential or actual rejection. In J. M. Atkinson & J. Heritage, eds., *Structures of Social Action. Studies in Conversation Analysis*. Cambridge: Cambridge University Press, pp. 102–28.

Deppermann, A. (2012). How does "cognition" matter to the analysis of talk-in-interaction? *Language Sciences*, 34(6), 746–67.

(2015). Retrospection and understanding in interaction. In A. Deppermann & S. Günthner, eds., *Temporality in Interaction.* Amsterdam: John Benjamins, pp. 57–94.

(2018). Inferential practices in social interaction: A conversation-analytic account. *Open Linguistics*, 4(1), 35–55.

(2021). Social actions. In M. Haugh, D. Kádár & M. Terkourafi, eds., *Cambridge Handbook of Sociopragmatics.* Cambridge: Cambridge University Press, pp. 69–94.

Drew, P. (1984). Speakers' reportings in invitation sequences. In J. M. Atkinson & J. Heritage, eds., *Structures of Social Action: Studies in Conversation Analysis.* Cambridge: Cambridge University Press, pp. 129–51.

(1995). Interaction sequences and anticipatory interactive planning. In E. Goody, ed., *Social Intelligence and Interaction*. Cambridge: Cambridge University Press, pp. 111–38.
(2011). Reflections on the micro-politics of social action, in interaction. Paper presented at the 12th International Pragmatics Association Conference, University of Manchester.
(2013). Turn design. In J. Sidnell & T. Stivers, eds., *Handbook of Conversation Analysis*. Chichester: Wiley-Blackwell, pp. 103–30.
(2018a). Equivocal invitations (in English). *Journal of Pragmatics*, 125, 62–75.
(2018b). Inferences and indirectness in interaction. *Open Linguistics*, 4(1), 241–59.
Drew, P., Walker, T. & Ogden, R. (2013). Self-repair and action construction. In M. Hayashi, G. Raymond & J. Sidnell, eds., *Conversational Repair and Human Understanding*. Cambridge: Cambridge University Press, pp. 71–94.
Elder, C.-H. & Haugh, M. (2018). The interactional achievement of speaker meaning: Toward a formal account of conversational inference. *Intercultural Pragmatics*, 15, 593–625.
Enfield, N. J. & Sidnell, J. (2017a). *The Concept of Action*. Cambridge: Cambridge University Press.
(2017b). On the concept of action in the study of interaction. *Discourse Studies*, 19, 515–35.
Floyd, S., Rossi, G. & Enfield, N. J., eds. (2020). *Getting Others to Do Things: A Pragmatic Typology of Recruitments*. Berlin: Language Science Press.
Gardner, R. (2001). *When Listeners Talk: Response Tokens and Listener Stance*. Amsterdam: John Benjamins.
Garfinkel, H. (1963). A conception of, and experiments with, "trust" as a condition of stable concerted actions. In O. J. Harvey, ed., *Motivation and Social Interaction: Cognitive Determinants*. New York, NY: Ronald Press, pp. 187–238.
(1967). *Studies in Ethnomethodology*. Englewood Cliffs, NJ: Prentice-Hall.
([1948]2006). *Seeing Sociologically: The Routine Grounds of Social Action*, Boulder, CO: Paradigm Publishers.
Garfinkel, H. & Sacks, H. (1970). On formal structures of practical action. In J. C. McKinney & E. A. Tiraykian, eds., *Theoretical Sociology. Perspectives and Developments*. New York, NY: Appleton-Century-Crofts, pp. 338–66.
Goodwin, C. (2013). The co-operative, transformative organisation of human action and knowledge. *Journal of Pragmatics*, 46(1), 8–23.
(2017). *Co-operative Action*. Cambridge: Cambridge University Press.
Goodwin, C. & Goodwin, M. H. (1987). Concurrent operations on talk: Notes on the interactive organization of assessments. *IPrA Papers in Pragmatics*, 1, 1–54.
Haakana, M. (2007). Reported thought in complaint stories. In E. Holt & R. Clift, eds., *Reporting Talk. Reported Speech in Interaction*. Cambridge: Cambridge University Press, pp. 150–78.
Haugh, M. (2009). Intention(ality) and the conceptualisation of communication in pragmatics. *Australian Journal of Linguistics*, 29, 91–113.
(2013). Speaker meaning and accountability in interaction. *Journal of Pragmatics*, 48 (1), 41–56.

(2017a). Implicature and the inferential substrate. In P. Cap & M. Dynel, eds., *Implicitness: From Lexis to Discourse*. Amsterdam: John Benjamins, pp. 281–304.

(2017b). Prompting offers of assistance in interaction. *Pragmatics and Society*, 8(2), 183–207.

Heritage, J. (1984a). Garfinkel and Ethnomethodology. Cambridge: Polity Press.

(1984b). A change of state token and aspects of its sequential placement. In J. M. Atkinson & J. Heritage, eds., *Structures of Social Action. Studies in Conversation Analysis*. Cambridge: Cambridge University Press, pp. 299–345.

(1988). Explanations as accounts: A conversation analytic perspective. In C. Antaki, ed., *Analysing Everyday Explanation: A Casebook of Methods*. London: Sage, pp. 127–44.

(2012a). Epistemics in action: Action formation and territories of knowledge. *Research on Language and Social Interaction*, 45(1), 1–29.

(2012b). The epistemic engine: Sequence organization and territories of knowledge. *Research on Language and Social Interaction*, 45(1), 30–52.

(2013). Action formation and its epistemic (and other) backgrounds. *Discourse Studies*, 15, 551–78.

(2015). *Well*-prefaced turns in English conversation: A conversation analytic perspective. *Journal of Pragmatics*, 88, 88–104.

(2018). The ubiquity of epistemics: A rebuttal to the 'epistemics of epistemics' group. *Discourse Studies*, 20, 14–56.

Heritage, J. & Atkinson, J. M. (1984). Introduction. In J. M. Atkinson & J. Heritage, eds., *Structures of Social Action: Studies in Conversation Analysis*. Cambridge: Cambridge University Press, pp. 1–15.

Hofstetter, E. & Stokoe, E. (2015). Offers of assistance in politician–constituent interaction. *Discourse Studies*, 17, 724–51.

Holt, E. (2016). Laughter at last: Playfulness and laughter in interaction. *Journal of Pragmatics*, 100, 89–102.

Jefferson, G. (1986). Notes on "latency" in overlap onset. *Human Studies*, 9, 153–83.

Keevallik, L. (2017). Negotiating deontic rights in second position: Young adult daughters' imperatively formatted responses to mothers' offers in Estonian. In M.-L. Sorjonen, L. Raevaara & E. Couper-Kuhlen, eds., *Imperative Turns at Talk: The Design of Directives in Action*. Amsterdam: John Benjamins, pp. 271–95.

Kendrick, K. & Drew, P. (2014). The putative preference for offers over requests. In P. Drew & E. Couper-Kuhlen, eds., *Requesting in Social Interaction*. Amsterdam: John Benjamins, pp. 87–114.

(2016). Recruitments: Offers, requests, and the organization of assistance in interaction. *Research on Language and Social Interaction*, 49(1), 1–19.

Levinson, S. C. (1995). Interactional biases in human thinking. In E. Goody, ed., *Social Intelligence and Interaction*. Cambridge: Cambridge University Press, pp. 221–60.

(2013a). Action formation and ascription. In J. Sidnell & T. Stivers, eds., *Handbook of Conversation Analysis*. Chichester: Wiley-Blackwell, pp. 103–30.

(2013b). Recursion in pragmatics. *Language*, 89, 149–62.

(2017). Speech acts. In Y. Huang, ed., *Oxford Handbook of Pragmatics*. Oxford: Oxford University Press, pp. 199–216.

Lynch, M. (2011). On understanding understanding. *Journal of Pragmatics*, 43, 553–55.

Macbeth, D. & Wong, J. (2016). The story of "oh," Part 2: Animating transcript. *Discourse Studies*, 18, 574–96.

Maynard, D. (2013). Defensive mechanisms: *I-mean*-prefaced utterances in complaint and other conversational sequences. In M. Hayashi, G. Raymond & J. Sidnell, eds., *Conversational Repair and Human Understanding*. Cambridge: Cambridge University Press, pp. 198–233.

Melden, A. I. (1961). *Free Action*, London: Routledge & Kegan Paul.

Mills, C. W. (1940). Situated actions and vocabularies of motive. *American Sociological Review*, 5(6), 904–13.

Pomerantz, A. (2017). Inferring the purpose of a prior query and responding accordingly. In G. Raymond, G. Lerner & J. Heritage, eds., *Enabling Human Conduct: Studies of Talk-in-Interaction in Honour of Emanuel A. Schegloff.* Amsterdam: John Benjamins, pp. 61–76.

Pomerantz, A. & Heritage, J. (2013). Preference. In J. Sidnell & T. Stivers, eds., *Handbook of Conversation Analysis*. Chichester: Wiley-Blackwell, pp. 210–28.

Rawls, A. W. (2005). Garfinkel's conception of time. *Time & Society*, 14, 163–90.

Raymond, G. (2003). Grammar and social organization: Yes/no interrogatives and the structure of responding. *American Sociological Review*, 68(6), 939–67.

Robinson, J. D. (2016). Accountability in social interaction. In J. D. Robinson, ed., *Accountability in Social Interaction*. New York, NY: Oxford University Press, pp. 1–44.

Sacks, H. ([1964/1965]1989). The inference making machine. *Human Studies*, 12, 379–93.

(1992). *Lectures on Conversation*. Oxford: Blackwell.

Sacks, H., Schegloff, E. A. & Jefferson, G. (1974). A simplest systematics for the organisation of turn-taking for conversation. *Language*, 50(4), 696–735.

Schegloff, E. A. (1987). Some sources of misunderstanding in talk-in-interaction. *Linguistics*, 25, 201–18.

(1992). Repair after next turn: The last structurally provided defense of intersubjectivity in conversation. *American Journal of Sociology*, 97(5), 1295–345.

(2000). On granularity. *Annual Review of Sociology*, 26, 715–20.

(2007). *Sequence Organization in Interaction: A Primer in Conversation Analysis*. Cambridge: Cambridge University Press.

Schegloff, E. A. & Lerner, G. H. (2009). Beginning to respond: *Well*-prefaced responses to *wh*-questions. *Research on Language and Social Interaction*, 42, 91–115.

Schegloff, E. A. & Sacks, H. (1973). Opening up closings. *Semiotica*, 8(4), 289–327.

Searle, J. (1969). *Speech Acts: An Essay in the Philosophy of Language*. Cambridge: Cambridge University Press.

Shaw, C. & Hepburn, A. (2013). Managing the moral implications of advice in informal settings. *Research on Language and Social Interaction*, 46(4), 344–62.

Sidnell, J. (2014). The architecture of intersubjectivity revisited. In N. J. Enfield, P. Kockelman & J. Sidnell, eds., *Cambridge Handbook of Linguistic Anthropology*. Cambridge: Cambridge University Press, pp. 364–99.

(2017a). Distributed agency and action under the radar of accountability. In N. J. Enfield & P. Kockelman, eds., *Distributed Agency*. Oxford: Oxford University Press, pp. 87–96.

(2017b). Action in interaction is conduct under a description. *Language in Society*, 46(3), 313–37.

Stevanovic, M. & Peräkylä, A. (2014). Three orders in the organization of human action: On the interface between knowledge, power, and emotion in interaction and social relations. *Language in Society*, 43(2), 185–207.

Thompson, S., Fox, B. & Couper-Kuhlen, E. (2015). *Grammar in Everyday Talk: Building Responsive Actions*. Cambridge: Cambridge University Press.

Tsui, A. (1989). Beyond the adjacency pair. *Language in Society*, 18, 545–64.

Turk, M. (2007) Self-referential gestures in conversation. *Discourse Studies*, 9, 558–66.

5 Attributing the Decision to Buy

Action Ascription, Local Ecology, and Multimodality in Shop Encounters

Lorenza Mondada

5.1 Introduction

5.1.1 Action Formation and Action Ascription

Action formation and action recognition or ascription are central issues in Conversation Analysis, lying at the foundations of sequential organization, its emergent and projective temporality, and the way they are locally treated by the participants to social interaction. In this framework, actions are considered from a double perspective: for how they are built by their doers, prospectively projecting and constraining next actions, and for how they are responded to by their recipients, who retrospectively attribute them a meaning. In order to describe the intelligibility, recognizability, and accountability of actions, Conversation Analysis has insisted on these two dimensions (Levinson 2013; Schegloff 2007), combining the analysis of projections and the analysis of responses – considered as a "next turn proof procedure" (Sacks, Schegloff & Jefferson 1974) – in order to provide for a rigorous study of the turn by turn, or more generally step by step, sequential organization of actions in social interaction.

Recent debates on action formation have pointed at puzzles not yet fully solved: What defines the meaning of an action, given that it cannot be reduced to the resources to build it in the first place? How to treat the fact that an action can be multi-barreled and in service of other actions (Schegloff 2007)? How to account for its inevitable indexicality (Garfinkel & Sacks 1970) and yet participants unproblematically recognize it? Conversation Analysis has developed its original approach of the accountability of action based on sequential organization – on the location and environment of actions, positioned as prior vs. next, as first vs. second, etc. However, other aspects have been pointed out too. How to conceive different levels of sequential organization, more local vs. more global, as they define the meaning of an action? How to relate an action both to the adjacent one and to larger projects or activities and activity types (Levinson 2013)? How to finely integrate sequential and categorical aspects (Sacks 1972), the latter also generating normative expectations and inferences? How to understand intentions and attributions of intentions within interaction (Duranti 2015)? How to articulate turn formats, epistemic statuses/stances, and action ascription (Heritage 2012)? How to precisely and finely treat the temporality of embodied practices and resources and ascertain what consequences this has for the conception of sequentiality (Mondada 2018a)? How to reconcile different types of granularity – that is, as put by Levinson, "to what extent are actions finely coded in linguistic detail, or to what extent is recognition or ascription dependent on tracking complex sequential context?" (2013: 116–17). This chapter addresses these questions by discussing a specific kind of attribution – attribution of a decision to the other party.

5.1.2 The Phenomenon

This chapter contributes to these issues by studying how participants interpret and recognize an action as manifesting decision-taking and the extent to which they are confident enough with that ascription to progress in the activity and proceed to the next actions, having inferred that decision. In order to explore how variations in the systematic unfolding of actions might respond to some of the questions asked above, the chapter focuses on a particular setting in which a recurrent set of actions are observable in a specific sequential environment: deciding to buy a product after having tasted it in gourmet shops. In these shops, customers are routinely offered samples to taste. The outcome of tasting is often a positive assessment. The starting point of this chapter is the observation that such a positive assessment is often treated as a decision to buy the tasted product. The chapter explores how such an ascription of meaning to an action – and indeed of intentions to a participant – is made possible. How is decision-taking imputed and attributed to the customer, without any explicit reference to it?

The focus on this very particular activity and sequential environment, highlights how in some configurations participants can ascribe actions to one another in a very implicit and yet very consistent way. The inquiry into how this is systematically possible and into possible variations of this pattern contributes to a better understanding of sequentiality. Fundamentally, it shows the importance of larger projects and their embodied trajectories, and the way previous actions can have durable sequential consequences: an action is not only interpreted by the co-participants by addressing the immediate previous actions, but in relation to more remote sequential implications. A turn can address diverse previous actions and implement several actions – and its multimodal organization is crucial for enabling these possibilities.

5.1.3 Data

In order to investigate the systematic, methodic, and yet situated and indexical, aspects of action ascription and their sequential variations, I focus on a particular context, encounters in food shops specializing in cheese products, gathered across Europe in twelve languages and fifteen cities (a mean of 4 hours of recordings was collected in each city). This diversity is not exploited here within a comparative perspective searching for differences across countries and languages, but rather to reveal a systematic organization of the environment studied – post-tasting assessments leading to the decision to buy a product. Ordinary encounters between shopkeepers and customers selling and buying cheese were video-recorded, with the collaboration of the shop owners and the informed consent of all of the participants. Video-recordings were collected during extensive fieldwork, using two cameras documenting the ecology of the shop, and additional microphones on the seller and the counter. Data were then transcribed using Jefferson's (2004) conventions for talk and Mondada's (2018a) conventions for multimodality.

5.1.4 Ascribing Decision-Taking to the Customer

The starting point of the study is the following extract, recorded in a cheese shop in Germany.

Excerpt 5.1 FRO_D_FREI_CLI24_01.38.45 (CUS = customer, SEL = seller)

```
1  CUS:  gut`n ta:g=
         good morning
2  SEL:  =gut`n ta:g?
         good morning
3        (0.5)
4  CUS:  tsk (1.4) ich würd mir gern `nen schönen brie empfehlen lassen,
         tsk (1.4) I would like to have recommended a nice Brie
((13 lines omitted, about customer's preferences and some options))
18       (0.3) * (0.6)
   sel         *grasps Coulommier--->
19 SEL:  °le coulommier°. (0.2) wollen sie mal ein bissel probieren?
         °the Coulommier° (0.2) do you want to taste a bit?
20       (0.4)
21 CUS:  °(ja xx[xxx)°
         °(yes xx[xxx)°
22 SEL:         [(fein,)* es isch schon e aromisch brie:, (0.5)
                [(fine) it is yet an aromatic Brie (0.5)
                     =>*cuts a bit--->
23       so schön (0.2) und kräftig,
         so nice (0.2) and strong
```

```
24          (0.5)*
   Sel        ->*hands over sample to taste->
25          ±# (2.7) +± (0.3) ±#
   cus      ±puts in mouth and chews->
   cus  ->          +points fwd->
   cus  ->          ±head toss±
   fig      #fig.5.1             # fig.5.2
```

Figure 5.1 Tasting the cheese

Figure 5.2 Outcome of the tasting

```
26  CUS: ->  °sehr+  le •+ * cker°*
             very tasty
                ->+ ,,,,+
    sel                 •looks down at cheese ->
    sel  ->               *.....*positions knife, ready to cut ->
27           (1.1)#
    fig             #fig.5.3/5.4
```

Figure 5.3 Establishing the quantity to be bought

Figure 5.4 Establishing the quantity to be bought (detail)

```
28 CUS:     .msk +ja. +
            .msk yes
                 +nods+
29          (0.2) * (0.5) * (2.4)
   sel         ->*cuts-*
```

In this excerpt, the customer asks for a recommendation concerning a Brie (line 4). In response, the seller inquires about his preferences and offers some options (5–17), finally proposing a Coulommiers (19), which she offers for tasting (19). As she cuts a sample, she describes its main characteristics (22–3), and hands over the sample (24).

The tasting is accomplished in silence (25, Figure 5.1) (see Mondada 2018b) and its outcome is displayed in different ways: first, by the hand pointing and the head tossing (25, Figure 5.2); second, by a positive assessment (26), constituted only by an intensified adjective (*sehr lecker*/ 'very tasty', 26).

This global multimodal Gestalt is interpreted by the seller as warranting her next action, the establishment of the quantity to the bought – which presupposes the decision to buy. This action is performed manually and in silence: the seller looks down at the cheese, positions her knife in such a way to suggest a possible cut (27, Figures 5.3–5.4). The customer merely agrees with the particle *ja*/'yes' (28) and a nod, and the seller operates the irreversible action of cutting a slice of Coulommiers corresponding to that measure and defining now that phase of the customer's purchase.

In this example, the positive assessment at line 26 (formatted in a complex multimodal Gestalt) is immediately understood as displaying a decision to buy. This decision can be ascribed to the customer not just by virtue of the immediate previous action, but by virtue of the initial actions opening the encounter: a request for a recommendation which is syntactically formatted in a peculiar way, as a request for a specific type of cheese to be advised about. The tasting is an action that enables the customer's evaluation of the recommendation. If the recommendation is accepted, the product proposed is considered as matching what the customer wanted.

This excerpt shows the importance of previous actions for the interpretation of subsequent ones. It also casts light on a specific institutional organization of action. For instance, it highlights the paradoxes of tasting, as a gift given for free but strongly embedded within the current economic transaction. The possibility that the seller can understand a positive assessment of a tasted sample as a decision to buy that product shows that tasting is not a gratuitous act done for the pleasure of discovering new flavors. Rather, its outcome is sequentially positioned within a series of possible responses that impinge on the possible continuation of the transaction. Since tasting is often offered after the customer has already committed to buy a more or less precise product, but is hesitating between various options (Mondada in press), the outcome of tasting is interpreted in the light of these previous commitments, as a way to solve problems of choice and to allow for the encounter to progress; the positive assessment is interpreted as implying the final decision to buy.

5.1.5 Outline

Decision-taking is a key moment in shop encounters. It is the moment in which the process of buying is achieved, which transforms the potential customer into a buying customer and a future possessor of the product. Decision-taking is thus pivotal in terms of rights and obligations, commercial engagements, and change of a *buyable* into a *bought* product.

Contrary to *request sequences*, in which the purchase is achieved by a customer's requesting a product and the seller granting the request by fetching it (Fox & Heinemann 2015; Mondada & Sorjonen 2016), other types of sequences recurrent in shops – such as when customer utters a *generic request for a type of product, a request for recommendation, or a question*, responded to by an *offer or an invitation to taste* by the seller – are sequentially more elaborated, and often completed by an explicit decision-taking of the customer, announced as such, in a turn devoted to it.

In this chapter, I discuss the latter environments, and I focus on cases in which the seller has proposed some candidate products and has offered a taste. The typical environment in which the seller invites the customer to taste a sample emerges after some options have been mentioned and a choice has not yet been made (see Mondada in press). The analysis concentrates here on sequences that emerge *after* tasting (see Mondada 2018b for a systematic analysis of the organization of tasting, which will not be considered here in all detail).

This chapter analyses the way in which the decision to buy is attributed to the customer by the seller in the post-tasting sequential environment. In some cases, the customer explicitly expresses his/her decision to buy; but in other cases, this is much more elusive (as shown in Excerpt 5.1). The chapter discusses various actions encountered in this environment – for example requests for confirmations – that show that more than just assessing is at stake. The analysis is organized along a cline going from the most explicit decisions to buy to the more elusive ones, and presents the evidence of different ways in which the seller attributes to the customer a decision to buy and checks it.

5.2 Customer's Explicit Decision-Taking

In the most explicit sequences following tasting, the customer declares their decision to buy the product just tasted. In this section, I discuss two recurrent environments in which decision-taking is explicitly announced: in the first, tasting is completed with a positive assessment proffered by the customer, followed by their decision to buy; in the second, tasting is directly followed by the decision to buy, without any assessment.

5.2.1 Tasting Occasions a Positive Assessment and a Decision to Buy

In the most explicit cases, the outcome of tasting is displayed in an assessment, followed by an explicit decision to buy, uttered by the customer, as in this fragment, recorded in Madrid:

Excerpt 5.2 FRO_E_MDR_cli14_1.52.49 (CUS = customer, SEL = seller)

```
1          (0.7)
   cus     >>tasting, chewing->
2  CUS: -> está (bueno)
           it's (good)
3          (1) ±+(0.7)±(0.4)+ %⊥
   cus  ->    ±nods-±
   cus          +points----+
   cus                        ->%
   cus                          ->⊥gazes at SAL->>
4  CUS: -> tsk. dame medio
           tsk. give me a half
5          (0.6)
6  SEL:    muy *bien
           very good
               *grasps a piece and cuts it->>
```

The customer tastes and chews in silence for a short moment. He then produces a positive assessment (2), followed by a nod and a pointing gesture towards the cheese. He also shifts his gaze towards the seller, and requests the quantity of cheese he decides to buy (4). This is responded to by the seller (6), by cutting the requested piece in two. Cutting represents the next step: the cut is specifically tailored for the customer, is an irreversible action, and presupposes that a decision to buy has been taken.

A similar pattern is observable in the following encounter between a seller and two French customers, recorded in London:

Excerpt 5.3 FRO_UK_LDN_0304_1.36.40 cheddar FR-CLI71.1/2 (CU1 = customer 1, CU2 = customer 2, SEL = seller)

```
1              (1.6) +(0.4)+ (0.5)
   cus2        >>tasting->
   cus2  ->          +lateral head shake+
         ->          +and eyebrows raise+
2  CUS2: -> très +bon. +
           very good
         ->      +eyebrows+
```

```
3              (1.0)
4   SEL:       c'est pas mal hein?
               it's not bad, huh?
5              +(0.3)
    cus2       +nods->
6   CUS1:      mh [hm
7   CUS2:         [ouais+
                  [yeah
    cus2             ->+
8              (0.7) + (0.4) +
    cus2             +circular index gest+
9   CUS2: ->   +j'vais pren+dre un morceau d'celui-là=
               I will take a bit of this one
               +points in fr of her+
```

The tasting is completed and its outcome is displayed by facial expressions (1) and a positive assessment (2) co-occurring with an eyebrow raise. This multimodal assessment is followed by a request for confirmation by the seller (4), in the form of a positive assessment built on a litotes, and a particle seeking agreement. The customer (CU2) confirms, with a nod (5) and a positive token (7), and her husband (CU1) with an aligning *mh hm* (6). The request for confirmation generates the agreement of both customers (whereas the assessment was made by only one of them). After this confirmation of the positive assessment, the customer announces her decision (9), co-occurring with some gesticulation and pointing.

So, in this case, the tasting is followed by (a) a positive assessment, (b) occasioning a sequence requesting for confirmation initiated by the seller and confirmed by the customers, (c) followed by an explicit decision to buy.

5.2.2 Tasting Directly Engenders the Decision to Buy

Tasting can be followed directly by a decision to buy, as in the following case, from Madrid. It is worth noting that a request for a particular cheese is issued before tasting (3–4), including a preliminary announcement of the willingness to buy (4). Tasting is occasioned here by an inquiry about the knowledge the customer has of that cheese (5–6): the seller orients to the customer as not knowing, on the basis of his formatting of the request with a multimodal indexical expression and an account referring to visual aspects (3–4). This is interpreted as a negative epistemic stance, which often generates an offer to taste (Mondada, in press).

Excerpt 5.4 FRO_E_MDR_0104_cam2_1.25.15 (CUS = customer, SEL = seller)

```
1   SEL:    algo más queríais?
            do you want something more?
2           (0.7)
3   CUS:    sí eh+:: este de aquí que:+ tiene buen aspecto
            yes eh:: this of here that is good looking
                 +points————————————+
4           pues me llevo un trozo
            PRT I take a piece
5   SEL:    el a- el azul este lo conocéis? es un azul
            the b- the blue this one do you know it? it's a blue
6           que elaboramos nosotros
            that we produce ourselves
7   CUS:    no lo conozco
            I don't know it
8   SEL:    en valladolid en nuestra quesería
            in Valladolid in our creamery
9           mira probalo a ver qué os parece
            look try it and see what do you think
10          (8.2)
11  SEL:    esto es* leche leche de vaca cruda, °y bueno° un
            this one is milk milk of cow raw °and well° a
                   *hands over a sample-->
12          queso muy: *+muy interesante +muy rico
            cheese very very interesting very tasty
                      ->*
    cus                  +takes——————————+puts into mouth->
13          (0.8)
((5 lines omitted: SEL offers a taste to CUS's wife, who refuses))
19          (0.2) ± (0.5)+
    cus                 ->+
    cus           ±'cutting' gesture, w vertical palm->
20  CUS: -> me ±llevo un trozo de ese
            I take a piece of this one
             ->±
```

The seller offers a sample to taste (9), which he describes while handing it over (12). The customer's tasting is completed by a gesture made with his palm moving vertically, in a 'cutting' gesture and the decision to buy (20). We can notice that the decision to buy (20) uses the same format and words as the initial request (4): in this way, the customer displays that the decision following tasting reiterates his initial decision – fortified by the tasting and its positive outcome. This fragment shows in a particularly clear manner that the decision does not only depend on tasting, but closes a larger project that was initiated by a much earlier request. In this sense, what follows the tasting both refers retrospectively to the immediate previous action (as an outcome of the tasting, and made possible by it) and to a more distant previous action (the initial request).

In some cases, this larger retrospective orientation is further manifested by a turn-initial particle preceding the decision to buy. The next excerpt, from Helsinki, is an instance of this particular turn-format, in which the particle ties the post-tasting turn back to the more global project.

The customer utters a rather vague request ('something to put on top of the bread' (3); in response the seller offers an Alpzirler (18–21), inviting the customer to taste it (23):

Excerpt 5.5 FRO_FIN_1704_16–15 (Austria small talk CUS2) (CUS = customer, SEL = seller)

```
1   SEL:     päivää.
             good morning
2            (0.8)
3   CUS: •   hei, (.) tota, (0.3) jotai leivämpäälle,
             hi (.) uhm (0.3) something (to put) on bread
4            (0.5)
((12 lines omitted))
17           (1.4)
18  SEL:     (no) mä voisin kaupata sulle >mä oon< tänään
             (well) I could sell for you I am today
19           niin innostunut tässä on tä*mmönen ↑Alpzirler, (0.2)
             so excited     here is a kind of Alpzirler (0.2)
                                       *fetches Alpzirler-->
20           itäva*ltalainen tilsi*tteri; (0.8) suhteellisen.
             an Austrian tilsiter (0.8) relatively
                  *shows————————*unpacks->
21           tuoksuva.
             fragrant
22  CUS:     joo.=
             yes
23  SEL:     haluatsä maistaa tä.<
             do you want to taste this
23  CUS:     ↑joo; (.) joo.
             yes  (.)  yes
((20 lines omitted - tasting and small talk))
44           (0.2) + (0.8)
    cus              +chews 2d bit—>>
45  CUS: ->  ↑joo, (.) (otetaas)  yks pala
             yes  (.) let's take one piece
46           (1.2)
```

The tasting is completed by the customer with a turn prefaced by the particle *joo* (45), then followed by the explicit announcement of the decision to buy that cheese (45). The particle *joo* in that position is not merely responsive to the immediate prior action – the tasting – but also to an action located much earlier: the offer by the seller of the Alpzirler (18–19). In her extensive study of the particles *joo* and *nii* in Finnish, Sorjonen (2001) shows that *joo* responds to the factual character of a prior utterance and registers it as understood. *Joo* is also closure relevant, addressing larger background talk. In this particular case, *joo* might not only orient to the still open and active relevance of the offer made by the seller at the beginning of the larger episode, but also to the fact that this main action has been delayed and in a certain way held up by some small talk: in this sense, *joo* also orients to the resumption of the main commercial business activity.

The presence of a turn-initial particle after tasting – which often happens during an extended period of silence – and before decision-taking is therefore an interesting detail that reveals an orientation towards broader sequential tying practices. The particle prefacing the decision to buy operates retrospectively by linking that turn to a previous action – occurring before the tasting: the initial request. The presence of the particle shows more globally that the turn achieving decision-taking refers back to the entire project and not only to the immediate prior action.

5.3 Seller Attributes Decision to Buy and Asks for Confirmation

The previous instances show how, upon completion of tasting, the customer might explicitly display their decision to buy the product. However, often the customer does not produce such an explicit turn. In this section, I explore an alternative format, in which it is the seller who formulates, in a try-marked way, the final outcome and decision, and requests confirmation. In this case, it is the seller who attributes to the customer the decision to buy. This section explores a recurrent sequential environment characterizing these turns at talk.

A first occurrence of this pattern is observable in the following extract, recorded in Madrid. The customer initially requests half of a piece of Pasiego (1). As in Excerpt 5.4 above, the seller inquires whether the customer knows the cheese he is requesting (4), and upon a negative answer (6), he offers a taste (7).

Excerpt 5.6 FRO_E_MDR_3012_cam2_2.30.41-CLI18 (CUS = customer, SEL = seller)

```
1   CUS: • mira, eh: me pones: medio +de: pa+siego de este?
           look eh you give me a half of this Pasiego?
                                           +points+
2   SEL:   claro
           sure
3          (1) * (0.6) * (2.5)
               *takes one piece and puts it on counter*
4   SEL:   lo conoces ya?
           you know it already?
```

```
5             (0.6)
6   CUS:      >no<
              no
7   SEL:      no lo conoces? querías probar un poquito?
              you don't know it? do you want to taste a bit?
8   CUS:      pues sí tío
              PRT yes friend
((8 lines omitted: SEL cuts and gives sample))
17            +(5.0) + (0.7) ± (0.6) ±
    cus       +tastes->
    cus                +nods->
    cus                       ±gesture±
18  CUS:      bueno.+
              good
                  ->+
19            (0.2)
20  SEL:      sí?
              yes?
21            +*(0.2)+
    cus       +nods--+
    sel  ->    *looks down at cheese and prepares to cut w knife->>
22  SEL: ->   mitad entonces?
              half (of this) then?
23            (0.4)
24  CUS:      sí
              yes
```

The tasting (17) is completed by the customer nodding and doing a gesture towards the cheese, before uttering a positive assessment (18). This assessment is followed by a request for confirmation by the seller (*sí?*/'yes?', 20), responded to positively by the customer with a nod (21). The confirming sequence is immediately followed by the seller turning to the cheese (21) and producing a yes/no question concerning the amount of cheese desired, thus attributing a decision to buy to the customer. The use of *entonces*/'then' (22) refers back to the initial request (1) and treats the tasting as having confirmed the desire to buy. In this sense, the request for confirmation is used to verify information already established in prior talk (Seuren & Huiskes 2017).

This sequential environment is characterized not only by the fact that the seller imputes the decision to the customer. The use of the yes/no interrogative strongly projects and shapes a positive response (Raymond 2003), implying that there are good reasons to do so – that is, good reasons to infer from the assessment a decision to buy. The request for confirmation after the assessment displays that more than just assessing is at stake.

In a similar way, in the next case, recorded in London, tasting is followed by an assessment, a confirmation sequence and an attribution of the decision to buy by the seller to the customer. The customer is searching for a cheese that he had bought in the past; the seller proposes something to taste, which the customer is tasting at line 1.

Excerpt 5.7 FRO_UK_LDN_0104_50–00_several_tastings-1.15 (CUS = customer, SEL = seller)

```
1            +(1.6)
   cus       +tastes->
2  CUS:      m:,
3            (0.5)
4  SEL:      (then) co:w, (0.4) triple cream, (1.7) and just (      )
5            (1.6)
6  CUS:      mm::,
7            (1.8)
8  CUS:      nice flavor
9            (0.4)
10 CUS:      it's delicious
             (0.6)+
   cus         ->+
11 SEL:      yea*h?*
                *smiles*
12           (1.8)
13 CUS:      yeah.
14 SEL: ->   let's go for that?
15           (0.6)
16 CUS:      definitely (      )
```

The outcome of the tasting is a double positive assessment by the customer (8, 10), followed by a request for confirmation of the seller (*yeah?*, 11), aligned to by the customer (*yeah*, 13). On this basis, the seller's yes/no question projects a positive response, attributing the decision to buy to the customer, which is confirmed by him (14).

In a nutshell, in all these cases, tasting is followed by a positive assessment, which is checked by the seller (e.g., with the particle *yeah?* with interrogative prosody) and confirmed by the customer (with the same particle or a nod). This check constitutes the basis for attributing to the customer the decision to buy the positively assessed product – and indeed the customer aligns with this attribution.

5.4 After Customer's Positive Assessment, Seller Requests a Simple Confirmation and Proceeds to Cut

The cases examined in Section 5.3 have shown the crucial importance of a request for confirmation formatted in a minimal way, which is likewise responded to minimally (*yeah?*/'yeah'). This paves the way for an attribution of decision-taking to the customer in a Y/N question. In some cases, addressed in this section, this confirming sequence enables the seller to directly proceed to cutting the cheese – an action that presupposes that the customer has taken the decision to buy. This represents a more concise version of the sequential environment highlighted in the previous section.

The next fragment, from a shop in Madrid, presents such an instance. Like the Excerpts 5.4 and 5.6, the seller checks whether the customer knows the cheese he is proposing (1). The negative response prompts the seller to offer a tasting, while he continues to explain the particularities of the cheese.

Excerpt 5.8 FRO_E_MDR_301215cam2_1–57-49_casin.mov_3627 (CUS = customer, SEL = seller)

```
1  SEL:   ca*sín, lo cono*•ces?
           Casín   do you know it?
             *points at cheese*
                             •looks at CUS->
2          +(0.9)
   cus     +leans over casín and looks at it——>
3  CUS:    no.•
           no
   sel      ->•
((5 lines omitted: SEL gives to taste))
9          +(0.6)
   cus     +approaches sample to mouth->
10 SEL:    es, +tsk. se*gún eh:: los ra+bilados >que tenga va cogiendo
           it's tsk. depending on eh the rolls it goes through it gets
                      ->*
   cus       ->+smells——————————————+chews——————————————>1.18
11         como intensidad.< es un queso *mu:y •inten*so ±eh?±
           kind of an intensity. it's a cheese very intense eh?
                                        *opens both H*
                                             •looks at CUS->
   cus                                                  ±nods±
12         ±(0.4)
   cus     ±nods continuously->
13 SEL:    >sabes?< >es como que necesita< un vino±
           >y'know?<  >it like  needs<     a red
   cus                                       ->±
14         tin:%to [±sa%±bes?± de esos pi•can:%±tes.±%#
           wine     [y'know      of these spicy ones
15 cus:             [±sl%±
                    [yes
                     ±nods±nods±               ±nods±
                 %points %                     %points%
   fig                                                   #fig.5.5
16         (0.6) %  (0.6)  %  (0.3) • (0.2)# % (0.3)  *%
   Cus           %........%points————————————%,,,—————%
   Sel                               ->•looks at cheese ——>>
   Sel                                                *....moves hand fwd->
   fig                                      #fig.5.6
```

```
17 SEL:     si?#
            yes?
   fig         #fig.5.7
18 cus:     si.+*
            yes
             ->+swallows
19          (0.3) * (0.4) Ø 0.2) *  (0.8)  +  (13.0)
  Sel    ->      ->*grasps piece-*
  Sel    ->                Øwalks to register——————————>>
  Cus                               ->+walks along counter->>
```

Figure 5.5 Seller's gaze is still on customer

Figure 5.6 Seller's gaze follows customer's pointing

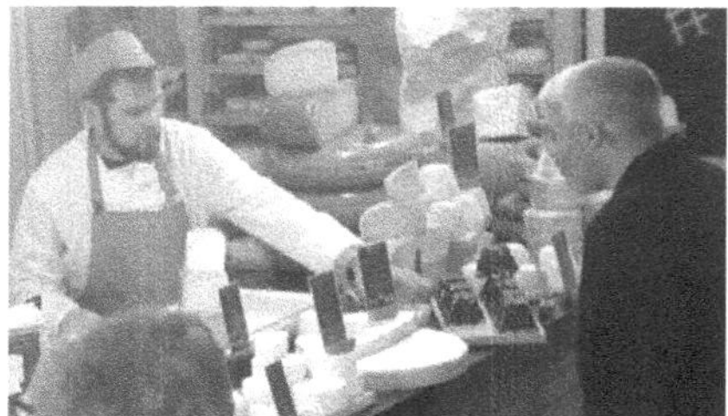

Figure 5.7 Seller moves hand to cheese

The seller's explanation (10–14) is formatted in a way that actively pursues a response from the recipient (*eh?* 11, > *sabes?* < 13, *sabes?* 14), and that is indeed actively responded to by the customer (nodding repeatedly, 11–13, as well as nodding while responding *sí*, 15, and pointing, 15–16). In particular, the last response of the customer is a pointing gesture, which prompts a change in the posture of the seller: the seller shifts his gaze from the customer (Figure 5.5) to the cheese (Figure 5.6), and while he extends his hand towards the cheese, he initiates the confirmation sequence (*sí?*, 17), which is promptly aligned to by the customer (*sí*, 18) (Figure 5.7). The confirmation is immediately followed by the seller grasping the piece of cheese, and carrying it to the register. The customer follows the seller, aligning with his trajectory. So in this case, the attribution of the decision to buy the cheese is achieved in an embodied way: it emerges directly after the tasting, in the seller's reorientation towards the product, and it is achieved after a sequence of minimal confirmations.

In this case, the piece of cheese was sold by unit; in other cases, it is the gesture of cutting and its preparation – bringing the knife to the cheese, positioning it in a way that indicates and projects a possible portion – that presupposes that the customer has taken the decision to buy and that the seller can therefore move to the next step, the determination of the quantity desired.

This is the case of the next fragment, from Germany, in which a customer accompanied by his wife requests a medium strong Camembert (1), which is offered for tasting (6):

Excerpt 5.9 FRO_D_FREI_CLI3_15.44 mittelkr camemb (CU1 = customer 1, CU2 = customer 2, SEL = seller)

```
1  CUS1: •  [ein mittelkräftigen camembert
            [a not so strong Camembert
2  CUS2:    [ein bis-
            [a bit-
3           (0.5)
4  SEL:     ja,
            yes
5           (3.7)
6  SEL:     (>jetzt<) probieren sie mal. von dem ein *bisschen,
            (now) have a taste of this one a little bit
                                                   ->* cuts slice->
7           (1.1)
8  CUS1:    gerne.
            with pleasure
9           (0.5)
10 CUS2:    ((clears throat)) *(albert) d`s+ schmeckt (dir)+*imma (0.3)
                               (albert) you always like that (0.3)
   sel                      ->* hands over the slice ————*
   cus1                                   +..............+takes->
11          ((lau[ghing))   +
12 SEL:          [°und wenn:+ xxx ein bisschen dann >ka mä auch<
                 [and when xxx a little bit then we can also
   cu1                   ->+chews slice—>>
13          n± bisschen (0.2) was kräftigeres°.
            a little bit (0.2) of something stronger
14 CUS1:    s:%ehr gut.%
            very good
              %index pts up and down%
15          •(0.2)
   sel      •looks down at cheese->
16 SEL:  => ja?*
            yes?
        ->     *...*positions knife to cut->
17          (0.3)
18 CUS1: => °perfekt°
           perfect
```

```
19 SEL:  -> (so ein stück?)
            (a piece like this?)
20 CUS1:    ja.
            yes
            (1.0) * (2.2)
   sel          ->*cuts—>>
```

The tasting ends with a positive assessment (16), which co-occurs with an index finger moving up and down. The seller responds to this turn in two ways: first, she looks down at the cheese (see Excerpt 5.8, line 16), projecting a next action that implies its manipulation (idem), further projected as she positions the knife on the cheese. Second, she initiates the confirmation sequence *ja?*/'yes?' (18), responded to by the customer with a confirming °*perfekt*°/'perfect', (20). Next, a precise quantity is proposed (21) and accepted (22). In this case, the positioning of the knife ready to cut is achieved even *earlier* in its sequence than in the previous fragment: the projection is initiated after the first pair part of the confirmation sequence, that is, when the customer has not yet responded. This further shows that a positive response is strongly projected at that point.

So, the attribution of the decision emerges within this post-tasting moment, along the assessment and with the change of gaze and posture, shifting from the customer to the product. The request for confirmation prolongs the closing assessment and highlights its relevance for the next step. It projects and secures the transition to the next sequence, the establishment of the quantity wanted, which is projected not only by the gaze on the product but its manipulation, foreshadowing cutting. Cutting, as an irreversible transformation of the product tailored for the customer, presupposes that the customer has decided to buy that cheese.

5.5 Customer's Simple "Yes" After Tasting

By contrast with the excerpts analyzed in the previous section – in which the customer's assessment was expanded by a confirmation sequence initiated by the seller before proceeding to cut – in other cases, the post-tasting sequences can be more minimal. A simple "yes" from the customer is enough for the seller to proceed to the cut.

We join the next excerpt in Madrid, as the customer requests a Manchego (1) and the seller proposes an Iniesta Manzanaro (11), which he offers to the customer to taste (8):

Excerpt 5.10 FRO_E_MDR_301215_cam2_2–27-20_si_CLI17 (CUS = customer, SEL = seller)

```
1  CUS: • manchego qué tenéis?
          Manchego what do you have?
((5 lines omitted, SEL proposes a cheese))
7         (1.5) * (0.3)
                *hands out bit to taste->
```

```
8  SEL:     prueba a ver qué te parece. (.) leche*+ cruda de oveja
            try to see what it seems to you (.) raw milk of sheep
                                               ->*
   cus                                            +takes, puts in mouth->
9           (0.4) + (0.4)
   cus         ->+chews——>>
10 SEL:     se llama iniesta manzanaro.
            it is called Iniesta Manzanaro
11          (1.1)
12 CUS:     ±°sí. °±+•
            yes
   cus      ± nods±
   cus            +looks at Manzanaro->
   sel             •gz at cheese->>
13 SEL:     *sí?
            yes?
        ->  *...grasps 2 other pieces->
14          (0.8)
15 SEL: ->  qué tal alguna de *estas cuñas?±
            what about one of these corners?
        ->                  ->* shows 3 pieces->
16          (0.6)
17 SEL:     estás es más grande: más •pequeña•
            this one is bigger smaller
                                   ->•looks at CUS•
18 CUS:     la más grande sí
            the bigger one yes
```

Here the client tastes (from line 8 on), and at line 12 utters a simple °*sí*°/ '°yes°', while nodding. Just after the particle, he looks at the cheese, as does the seller. The seller produces a simple *sí?*/'yes?' with an interrogative prosody (13). Without waiting for any response, he grasps a few pieces of cheese, offering them for the customer's selection – which presupposes that he has attributed to the customer a decision to buy one of them. In this case, the customer does not produce any assessment, but only the positive particle, which is reminiscent of the particle *joo* that was prefacing the decision to buy in the Finnish example (Excerpt 5.5 supra).

The post-tasting sequence can be even more reduced, as in the following case in which all the customer does is nodding and saying *sí* /'yes', treated as sufficient by the seller to propose a choice between a half or an entire piece:

Excerpt 5.11 FRO_E_MDR_301215_cam2_2–26-11 si_after req for advice (CUS = customer, SEL = seller)

```
1  SEL:     alguna cositas más?
            something else?
2           (0.2)
```

```
3   CUS:     sí sí
             yes yes
4            (4.2)
5   CUS: •   ( ) a llevar. alguno cremosito, ( ) (fuerte).
             ( ) to take. something quite creamy ( ) (strong)
((9 lines omitted: SEL offers some Puigpedros))
15           *(0.6)
    sel      *gives bit to taste->
16  SEL:     y es un queso como muy cremoso e inten*+so.
             and it's a cheese kind of very creamy and intense
                                                    ->*
    cus                                                +takes->
17           yo creo que es justo la descrip+ción que has dicho
             I think that it corresponds to the description you made
    cus                                    ->+puts whole bit in mouth->
18           (0.5)
19  SEL:     quizás está un poquito frío eh que a- tiene que ponerse un
             perhaps it's a bit cold eh that a- it needs to be a
20           poquito má:s: a una temperatura un poquito mayor
             bit more at a slightly higher temperature
21           ±(0.4)± (2.4) ±(0.3)
    cus      ±nods-±       ±nods->
22  CUS:     >sí.<±=
             yes
                 ->±
23  SEL: ->  =ese es *mitad o *ente*ros
             this one is either by half or as a whole
                      *points-*,,,,*
24           (1.0) +  (0.3)  +
    cus            +vertic gest+
25  CUS:     mita*d
             a half
    sel          *grasps->>
```

The customer utters a general request for something creamy and strong (5) and the seller proposes a Puigpedros. The customer engages in tasting, while the seller utters a caveat about the fact that the cheese is not expressing its fullest flavor due to its temperature (19–20). The tasting ends with some nods (21–2) and a simple *sí*/'yes' (22). This is enough for the seller to announce the standard quantities in which the cheese can be bought (23). The customer chooses the first option, expressed both verbally (*mitad*/'half' 25) and with a vertical gesture, as if cutting the cheese in two.

5.6 Positive Assessments Understood as Decision-Taking

In the previous sections, I showed how the post-tasting positive assessment was often followed by either the customer announcing the decision to buy that cheese (Section 5.2), or the seller asking for a confirmation about that decision

(Section 5.3), with a frequent insert sequence merely constituted by a pair of positive tokens like *yes* (Sections 5.4–5.5).

These environments showed the importance of the assessment, considered not only as an evaluation of the sample tasted but as an action paving the way for the next steps and crucial for the progressivity of the economic transaction. Indeed, in some transactions, as seen in Excerpt 5.1, the assessment itself is treated as equivalent to a decision-taking. In these cases, the assessment is followed by the seller indicating on the cheese the portion to cut, which presupposes the decision to take a piece from that cheese.

In the next excerpt, recorded in London, the assessment is responded to by a request for confirmation, establishing the grounds for further actions. The transaction features a customer accompanied by her partner searching for a cheese she has bought in the same shop in the past but does not remember the name of. After some inquiries, the seller finds out what it was. Although this is immediately acknowledged by the customer, the seller offers her a taste:

Excerpt 5.12 FRO_UK_LDN_0304_CLI64_00–34-45 finAss (CU1 = customer 1, CU2 = customer 2, SEL = seller)

```
1            (5.0)
   cus1      >>tastes->
   cus2      >>tastes->
2  SEL:      really creamy:: really milky
3            (0.8)
4  SEL:      what do you think?
5            (0.7)
6  CUS1:     really good=#
   fig                   #fig.5.8
7  SEL:      =really [goo*d?#
8  CUS2:             [yes
   sel                   *turns to cheese->
   fig                      #fig.5.9
```

Figure 5.8 Seller shifts posture

Figure 5.9 Seller turns from customer to cheese

```
9            (0.8)
10 SEL:      perfe:*ct.#
          ->     ->*carries cheese to the counter->
   fig                 #fig.5.10
```

```
11          (3.7) * (0.2) +±#
   sel   ->    ->*puts cheese on balance->
   cus1                ->+
   cus2                 ->±
   fig                     #fig.5.11
```

Figure 5.10 Seller carries cheese to counter

Figure 5.11 Seller weighs cheese

Figure 5.12 Seller positions knife on cheese

```
12 SEL:   -> s:*o:::this is one ki*lo (.) how much *do you like?#
          -> *weights—————————*puts on the board *knife on cheese->
   fig                                                    #fig.5.12
13          (0.2)
14 SEL:     (e::r) (.) this is one hundred gram (.) just to give you an idea
15          (2.0)
16 CUS1:    hm::: (0.3) two hundred
```

While the two customers are tasting (1), the seller produces an evaluative description (2), and asks for their opinion (4). The answer is a highly positive assessment (6). The seller repeats it with an interrogative prosody, asking for confirmation (7), which is given by the other member of the couple (2) (see above, Excerpt 5.3, where the request for confirmation asked to a couple generates the agreement of both members of the couple). As soon as this confirmation sequence is completed, the seller shifts his posture (Figures 5.8–5.9) from the customer to the cheese (8) and while uttering a closing implicative *perfe:ct* (10) he grabs the cheese, carries it to the counter on the other side of the shop (Figure 5.10), where there is a balance and the register. He weighs the piece (Figure 5.11) and uses the total weight as basis for a calculation of what the customers might want, explicitly solicited (12). The assessment and its confirmation, then, are treated as a sufficient basis for attributing to the customer(s) the decision to buy and for moving to the next step, the verbal negotiation of the quantity requested, also embodied by putting the knife in the position of the possible cut (Figure 5.12).

This sequential environment might be sensitive to the fact that the customer had requested the cheese she had already bought and she liked, and that, after finding out which cheese that was, she has enthusiastically displayed her willingness to buy it. The tasting in this case intervenes as an extra check warranting the decision.

Whereas in the previous fragment the assessment was further confirmed by the seller, in other cases the post-tasting positive assessment is enough for the seller to interpret it as a decision to buy. This is the case of Excerpt 5.1, from Germany, partially reproduced here, in which the customer asks the seller to recommend a Brie (4):

Excerpt 5.13 FRO_D_FREI_CLI24_01.38.45 (see excerpt 1) (CUS = customer, SEL = seller)

```
4   CUS: •  tsk (1.4) ich würd mir gern `nen schönen brie empfehlen lassen
            tsk (1.4) I would like to have recommended a nice Brie
((20 lines omitted))
25          ±(2.7) + (0.3)
    cus     ±puts sample in mouth and chews->
    cus            +points fwd->
26 CUS:     °sehr+ le•+*cker°*
            very tasty
            ->+,,,,+
    sel              •looks down at cheese->
    sel  ->            *......*positions knife, ready to cut->
27          (1.1)
28 CUS:     .msk +ja.±+
            .msk yes
                  ->±
                 +nods+
29          (0.2)*(0.5) *(2.4)
    sel        ->* cuts--- *
```

In response to the request for recommendation, the seller selects a Brie that is given to the customer to taste (25). The customer puts it into his mouth, chews it, and concludes the tasting with a pointing gesture in front of him (towards the cheese/the seller), before producing a positive assessment (*sehr lecker*, 26). Even before the adjective is completed, the seller looks at the cheese and moves her knife, positioning it in a way that indicates the quantity and that is ready to cut. This is done without a word, but the seller's movement is understood by the customer as a proposal of quantity, to which he responds with a simple *.msk ja*/'.msk yes' (28). This sequence is particularly minimal, in the sense that the tasting is merely closed by a positive assessment, immediately followed by the silent embodied indication of the quantity to be bought. In this case too, the initial request paves the way for an interpretation of the tasting outcome as displaying his willingness to buy. So, again, the attribution of decision-taking is built not only on the local understanding of the assessment, but also by tying the positive outcome of tasting to the previous request for a recommendation.

In other cases, the seller not only attributes the willingness to buy to the customer, but even suggests the positive assessment as an outcome of the tasting activity. In the next fragment, recorded in France, the customer points at a cheese claiming not to know it. Her turn is *and*-prefaced, displaying that it is part of a list of purchases she is building (she has already selected a first product); it is further formatted with only the mention of the name of the cheese with interrogative prosody, followed by *j'connais pas*/'I don't know' (1). This is not yet a request, but rather a query about an unknown product. As a result, the seller gives her a sample to taste (8–10).

Excerpt 5.14 FRO_F_THO_1804_CLI41_2.22 termignon (CUS = customer, SEL = seller)

```
1  CUS: • et l'bleu d'termignon? (.) j'con+nais pas.
          and the blue of Termignon? (.) I don't know (it)
          >>looks at cheese-----------------------+
((6 lines omitted)
8  SEL:   c'est un bleu ru:sti*que,•
          it's a rustic blue
                               ->*holds it out to CUS->
                                     •looks at CUS->
9         (2.1)
10 CUS:   merci*±
          thanks
   sel       ->*
   cus         ±takes and puts in mouth->
11        (0.2) • (0.2) ± (2.1) • (0.3) ‡     (2.5)   ‡
   cus                  ->±chews->
                                        ‡various nods‡
   sel       ->•looks away----•looks at cus--->
12 SEL:   c'est pas mal *hein?
          it's not bad, right?
       ->               *moves knife, ready to cut->
13 CUS:   mmh.
14        (1.4)
15 CUS: ->la moitié de ce morceau?
          the half of this piece?
16 SEL:   mais bien sûr.
          but sure
```

The customer completes her tasting with some nods (11), but does not (yet) produce any verbal assessment. It is the seller, looking at her, who proposes an assessment (*c'est pas mal*/'it's not bad', 12), followed by the particle *hein?*/'right?' soliciting a response (cf. Excerpt 5.3 supra, from London). While uttering this request for confirmation, and without waiting for the (minimal) response of the customer (13), the seller also moves her knife on the cheese. The timing of this movement shows that even *before* the alignment of the customer, the seller has attributed to her the decision to buy, and is progressing towards the negotiation of the quantity. The latter is explicitly addressed in the form of a turn with high-rise intonation (15), having also been anticipated and projected by the positioning of the knife on the cheese (12).

5.7 Conclusion

This study describes a range of sequential variations characterizing the way in which participants in shop interactions organize and interpret the customer's decision to buy a product. In order to highlight the systematicity of these practices, I have focused on a precise sequential and praxeological environment – assessments and decision-taking following tasting moments, which are routinely offered when the customer does not know the product, hesitates between some options, or is given a recommendation by the seller. This environment is observable across countries and languages in Europe, presenting a quite remarkable stability and generality. It also presents some systematic variations, which are interesting for the contrast they present between maximally explicit series of sequences of actions (tasting → closing positive assessment → announcement of the decision to buy the product; Section 5.2) and quite minimal, reduced, and yet clearly recognizable ones (tasting → assessment or 'yes' → ascription of the decision to buy by the seller; Section 5.6). Interestingly, in the corpus there are no instances of repairs, corrections, complaints, or contestations of these ascriptions. The confidence with which sellers attribute the decision to buy to customers, and the systematic unproblematic alignment of customers to that ascription, confirms that this is an exemplary environment in which to study action ascription and more particularly that the way assessments are produced, within a multimodal Gestalt including facial expression, head movements and other gestures, achieves more that just assessing, and is understood so. Intermediary cases, in which requests for confirmations feature in systematic ways, show how sellers can check and build grounds for the ascription of the decision (Sections 5.3–5.5). These cases show how participants indeed address the issue of how the recognizability of action is interactively achieved.

The data also show how participants orient to actions in their local sequential environments – such as assessments responding to tasting and constituting the public outcome of tasting – but also within larger sequential environments – such as initial requests, leading to tasting and to selection and decision. The analyses show the relevance of larger projects, in which an action is tied back to previous talk (Levinson 2013): for instance, a positive assessment might be formatted in a way that not only responds to the invitation to taste and the tasted item but also to a prior action, such as a question about the product, or, most often, an initial request.

The fact that an assessment can be responsive both to the immediate previous action and to an action that has initiated a larger project raises questions about possible elements in its formatting that hint at that retrospective tying. The analysis has shown the importance of turn-initial particles in this respect. But other aspects – related to how assessments are implemented as multimodal Gestalts – might contribute to that too. For example, it seems that some forms of pointing gestures co-occurring with assessments tend to be interpreted by the seller as doing more than assessing, and as tilting the action towards a decision to buy. Nods – especially big nods – are another type of embodied display that might be interpreted in that way, although they also have a strong local responsiveness (as positive assessments responding to tasting).

Other embodied resources contribute to the multimodal organization of the ascription of action and its emergent conditions. For instance, a convergent change of posture of both participants, seller and customer, shifting from mutual attention to gazing at the product after the assessment sequence, is enough to index a common alignment towards considering that product as a buyable. The seller's embodied orientation towards the product is further expanded by putting the knife on the cheese, in a position that projects cutting. This movement displays the ascription of the decision to buy to the customer; it projects an action that presupposes the decision to buy and that constitutes the next step in the activity. In some cases, this movement is anticipated quite early on, for instance before the sequence requesting for confirmation is closed. This is a case in which various sequential trajectories and projections are initiated, launched, and maintained in parallel.

In this context, requests for confirmation constitute interesting sequences. Sellers requesting a confirmation for a just-uttered positive assessment display that they orient to it as doing more than just assessing. The initiation of minimal confirmation sequences ("yes?" – "yes.") before an attribution of decision-taking also shows an orientation to the relevance of further actions relevant for doing action ascription. The very fact that these sequences mobilize minimal tokens (such as "yes?") reveals the use of highly indexical resources for doing both a local sequential job and for referring back to previous actions and engagements. The exact reference of what is checked and accepted with "yes?"–"yes." remains undetermined, and it is precisely this indetermination that achieves the local as well as global interactional job of these sequences.

These issues emerge from the specificity of the corpus and the systematic analyses that it enables. They point at features that might contribute more generally to our understanding of what an action is, how it is progressively made intelligible by the participants in a reflexive and interactive way, and how that action is located within different levels of sequential organization by the participants themselves.

Note on Transcription Conventions

Talk has been transcribed following the conventions of Gail Jefferson (2004). Embodied conducts were transcribed following the conventions of Lorenza Mondada (see 2018 for a conceptual discussion, and www.lorenzamondada.net/ multimodal-transcription for a tutorial).

REFERENCES

Duranti, A. (2015). *The Anthropology of Intentions: Language in a World of Others.* Cambridge: Cambridge University Press.

Fox, B. & Heinemann, T. (2015). The alignment of manual and verbal displays in requests for the repair of an object. *Research on Language and Social Interaction*, 48(3), 342–62.

Garfinkel, H. & Sacks, H. (1970). On formal structures of practical actions. In J. D. McKinney & E. A. Tiryakian, eds., *Theoretical Sociology.* New York, NY: Appleton-Century Crofts, pp. 337–66.

Heritage, J. (2012). Epistemics in action: Action formation and territories of knowledge. *Research on Language and Social Interaction*, 45(1), 1–29.

Jefferson, G. (2004). Glossary of transcript symbols with an introduction. In G. H. Lerner, ed., *Conversation Analysis: Studies from the First Generation.* Amsterdam: John Benjamins, pp. 13–31.

Levinson, S. (2013). Action formation and ascription. In T. Stivers & J. Sidnell, eds., *Handbook of Conversation Analysis*. Chichester: Wiley-Blackwell, pp. 103–30.

Mondada, L. (2018a). Multiple temporalities of language and body in interaction: Challenges for transcribing multimodality. *Research on Language and Social Interaction*, 51(1), 85–106.

(2018b). The multimodal interactional organization of tasting: Practices of tasting cheese in gourmet shops. *Discourse Studies*, 20(6), 743–69.

(in press). Offers to taste in gourmet food shops: Small gifts in an economy of sale. In B. Fox, L. Mondada & M.-L. Sorjonen, eds., *Encounters at the Counter.* Cambridge: Cambridge University Press.

Mondada, L. & Sorjonen, M.-L. (2016). First and subsequent requests in French and Finnish kiosks. *Language in Society*, 45, 733–65.

Mosegaard Hansen, M.-B. (1998). *The Function of Discourse Particles*. Amsterdam: John Benjamins.

Raymond, G. (2003). Grammar and social organization: Yes/no interrogatives and the structure of responding. *American Sociological Review*, 68(6), 939–67.

Sacks, H. (1972). An initial investigation of the usability of conversational data for doing sociology. In D. Sudnow, ed., *Studies in Social Interaction.* New York, NY: The Free Press, pp. 31–74.

Sacks, H., Schegloff, E. A. & Jefferson, G. (1974). A simplest systematics for the organization of turn-taking for conversation. *Language*, 50(4), 696–735.

Schegloff, E. A. (2007). *Sequence Organization in Interaction: A Primer in Conversation Analysis*. Cambridge: Cambridge University Press.

Seuren, L. M. & Huiskes, M. (2017). Confirmation or elaboration: What do Yes/No declaratives want? *Research on Language and Social Interaction*, 50(2), 188–205.

Sorjonen, M.-L. (2001). *Responding in Conversation: A Study of Response Particles in Finnish*. Amsterdam: John Benjamins.

Part II

Practices of Action Ascription

6 Intention Ascriptions as a Means to Coordinate Own Actions with Others' Actions

Arnulf Deppermann and Julia Kaiser

6.1 Introduction

When speakers in social interaction produce turns-at-talk, their co-participants are sometimes unable to figure out which action the prior turn is implementing. Among other means, next speaker can try to resolve this problem by explicitly ascribing an intention to prior speaker and in doing so, explicate the meaning of their behavior. Yet, as our article will show, explicit ascriptions of intentions to the partner in response to their adjacent prior turn can also have uses other than seeking to clarify meaning. They can be used to index some problem with the prior turn, e.g., that the prior turn projects a course of future actions which is considered to be inadequate, or it can be used to expose the concealed, "real" meaning of the prior turn.

This article deals with the use of intention ascription as a member's interpretive and pragmatic resource to arrive at a public understanding of others' actions. It focuses on explicit intention ascription through the use of the German intentional modal verb in second person *du willst/Sie wollen* ('you want').

The theoretical debate over how intentions figure in social actions has focused on methodological and ontological questions about the role of intentions in the constitution of action. After a short review of the competing views on this issue in Section 6.2, we zoom in on our research question, namely, the role of intentions in the interpretation of actions. Thus, our study is not concerned with the essentialist question whether and how intentions are involved in bringing about an action per se. Instead we will ask: When, why and how does the ascription of (certain aspects of) intention matter for action ascription in interaction by participants? While it is clear that action ascription mostly does without any overt ascription of intention, we are interested in cases in which the appeal to intention is used to make sense of an action.

In Section 6.3, we discuss prior studies of other practices by which the meaning of a prior turn is formulated. In Section 6.4, we describe our research object, intention ascription in response to a partner's prior turn using *du willst/ Sie wollen*, in more detail. Section 6.5 introduces the data. The main body of the article (Section 6.6) consists of an analysis of different uses of intention ascription in response to another's prior turn. Intention ascriptions differ with respect to the aspect of the prior action they address, the action they perform themselves, and the next action they make relevant from the prior speaker. In Section 6.7, we conclude that beyond these differences, intention ascriptions are used to deal with three concerns:

(a) clarifying and intersubjectively grounding the meaning of a prior action which otherwise would remain underspecified, ambiguous, unmotivated, or indeterminate in its projective properties and with regard to larger joint and individual projects;
(b) stating and/or obtaining information about the partner's (henceforth: S01) action orientations, which is necessary for the ascriber (henceforth: S2) in order to be able to coordinate successfully their own future actions with those of their partner;
(c) sometimes, but not always, the intention ascription can index a problem with the prior turn, inviting the partner to refrain from future actions, which they can be held to have projected by the prior turn.

6.2 The Debate over Intentions in Actions

From early on, the role of intentions in the constitution of actions has been disputed in the philosophy of action and in the various approaches to pragmatics derived from it. In a nutshell, there are two opposing perspectives on the issue. Intentionalistic approaches to action assign intentions a constitutive role both for the constitution and for the meaning of some stretch of behavior as action. Although they differ on the details at a number of points, both approaches from phenomenology and from analytic philosophy share two basic tenets: (i) intentions are crucial as motivations for actions, and (ii) action meaning is at least to some extent defined by the intention of its producer. Phenomenological approaches,[1] such as those of Merleau-Ponty (1945) and Schütz and Luckmann (1979), the anthropological account by Duranti (2015) building on Husserl (1950, 1976), as well as the analytic theories of action by Grice (namely his theory of implicatures; Grice 1989) and Searle (1983) and more recent accounts such as Gibbs' psycholinguistic (Gibbs 1999) and Sidnell and Enfield's anthropological approach (Enfield & Sidnell 2017; Sidnell & Enfield 2014), subscribe to this view. The competing perspective

[1] Lat. *intentio* was introduced as a philosophical notion already in medieval philosophy in order to distinguish between a direct epistemic relation between a cognizer or a sign and an object (*intentio prima*) and an indirect one (*intentio secunda*). Its rise as a core term in modern philosophy began with the phenomenologist Brentano (1874), who took intentionality, the property of being directed at something, to be the basic property of consciousness.

argues that intentions do not play a necessary or (in a stronger version) an essential role for the meaning of behavior as action. One account appeals to rules and conventions as the grounds for action meaning (Ryle 1949; Wittgenstein 1950; Searle 1969); these operate independently of people's intentions. Duranti's earlier studies on the cultural dependency of intention ascription and action interpretation are consistent with this line of theorizing (Duranti 1993), although they speak against the universalist assumptions underlying much work in analytic philosophy. A different approach is taken by scholars who claim that action meaning depends on social meta-pragmatic processes. According to this approach, interactive negotiation and social accountability of behavior are seen as key constituents of meaning. This position is taken in some studies from Conversation Analysis (Heritage 1984a), in Discursive Psychology (Potter & Edwards 2013) and in pragmatic theories such as those by Arundale (2008) and Haugh (2008, 2013).

In contrast to these general methodological and ontological questions, our study focuses on the role of intention ascriptions for action ascription in cases in which they are used as an explicit interpretational resource by discourse participants.

6.3 Intention Ascription as a Type of Formulations

Intention ascriptions are one type of formulations, i.e., they formulate the meaning of some prior stretch of talk explicitly (see Heritage & Watson 1979). Formulations of prior speakers' talk are overwhelmingly organized according to the same sequential pattern: S01: action which will be formulated subsequently – S2: formulation of the prior action (with differing degrees of certainty) – S01: confirmation/disconfirmation of the action ascription. Prior research has shown that formulations of prior talk are a means to transform its meaning according to institutional goals (e.g., Antaki 2008, 2012; Antaki, Barnes & Leudar 2005; Barnes 2007; Deppermann 2011; Drew 2003; Heritage & Watson 1979; Weiste & Peräkylä 2013) and that different grammatical constructions embody varying degrees of certainty concerning the assumed intersubjective validity of the formulation (Deppermann & Helmer 2013; Helmer & Zinken 2019). In making the (putative) meaning of a prior turn explicit, intention ascriptions can check the understanding of a prior turn (Antaki 2012; Pomerantz 1988) or rather make a claim about it. As we will see, intention ascriptions can not only be used to clarify meanings, but also to problematize the prior turn, indexing that it is in need of revision.

Studies on the formulation of others' talk and on repair-initiation have not dealt with intention ascriptions yet (but see Helmer, Chapter 7 in this volume on the ascription of strategic action, which always involves the presumption of intentionality). Intention ascriptions have been studied in police interrogations, where police officers try to assess the degree to which some incriminated behavior was produced intentionally (Edwards 2008). In contrast to our study, Edwards did not deal with the ascription of intentionality to prior verbal actions, but to bodily actions, and the actions in questions were not witnessed by the inquirer, but occurred remotely in place and time. Childs (2012a, 2012b) studied self-ascriptions of intention concerning practical actions; Deppermann (2014) has dealt with self-ascriptions which are used to reinterpret a speaker's own prior talk. In contrast to these studies, the current study focuses on other-ascriptions of adjacent prior talk.

6.4 The Object of the Study: Intention Ascription with German *du willst/Sie wollen*

Our study deals with intention ascription through the use of the German volitional modal verb *wollen* in second person singular as an immediate response to a prior speaker's turn. Our study includes instances of the declarative (*du willst/Sie wollen*) and the interrogative variant (*willst du? Wollen sie?*) as well as zero-argument cases without subject pronoun (*willst*). We chose this construction because such instances of *wollen* in second person are particularly clear cases of intention ascription. Excerpt 6.1a is an example.[2] It is from an informal conversation among students, talking about coming back from a semester abroad and then having to rent a new room:

Excerpt 6.1a FOLK_E_00055_SE_01_T_06_c76 (S01 = student 1, S02 = student 2) (Informal conversation among students)

```
01 S01:     also falls es wirklich so SEIN sollte dass du
            so in case it would really be like this that you
04          dann (.) noch nichts NEUes hast,=
            then still won't have anything new
05          =oder auch nich[ts neues ] SUchen willst dann;
            or that you don't want to search anything new either
            then
08          wär ja MIR geholfen,
            this would help me
21 S02: ->  du willst   mir          das      ZIMmer anbieten.
            you want.2SG me.PRO.DAT DEF.ART room   offer.INF
            you want to offer me the room
22 S01:     ((sighs)) °h=geNAU;
                       Exactly
```

[2] This is a shortened excerpt from a longer extract which is represented as Excerpt 6.1b in Section 6.6.1. Therefore, line numbering is not always consecutive.

The modal verb *wollen* in second person singular is used to ascribe (or ask for) a prototypical intention with the following properties:[3]

- the intention motivates S01's prior action;
- it defines an aspect of the meaning of the action as ascribed by S02;
- it accounts for the goal-directedness of this ascribed action;
- S01 is conscious of the intention;
- and responsible for their action;
- the ascribed action is under conscious control of the agent; and
- the action is chosen by free will (not enforced upon the agent).

The intention ascription is retrospective and responsive to the preceding turn which it interprets, but it is never projected by the prior turn as a second pair part of an adjacency pair; instead, it often introduces an insertion sequence or is realized as a post-expansion (Schegloff 2007). Certain kinds of intention ascriptions with *du willst/Sie wollen* are excluded from analysis when they do not concern an immediately preceding turn or when their object is a bodily action of S01 which is not a communicative action.[4]

6.5 Data and Distributions

Our study builds on the FOLK corpus of the IDS in Mannheim (accessible via http://dgd.ids-mannheim.de). We used the 2018 release, which includes 230 hours (2.2 million words) of audio- and video-recordings of talk-in-interaction from various private, institutional and public interaction types (e.g., dinner table, university viva, public mediation). We identified and analyzed sixty-three instances of our phenomenon, including the informal *du willst* (forty-four tokens) and the formal *Sie wollen* (nineteen tokens).

[3] These properties are commonly taken as conceptually implied by a strong notion of 'intentionality' (e.g., Gibbs 1999); they are also strongly associated with the notion of an 'agent' (see Dowty 1991 on the "proto-agent").

[4] Those cases are in particular:

- ascriptions of general preferences or intentions of S01 which are not tied to individual actions;
- intention ascription to refocus prior/suspended topics or activities;
- repetitions of intentions which were already declared by S01;
- ascriptions in narratives concerning past actions of interlocutors before the present encounter;
- contexts of indirect speech, quotes etc.;
- ascriptions of intention concerning bodily action or object transfer which can be inferred from others' behavior, physical condition, etc.;
- intention ascription to objects and animals;
- *if you want X then Y*-conditionals used for argumentation, rule formulation or offers (see Curl 2006);
- intention ascriptions with a generic *you*; and
- modality repairs of prior turns.

No plural forms were attested. Forty-nine instances are in present tense, fourteen in past tense. The tenses are used systematically: while intention ascriptions to self in first person are mostly realized in past tense, indexing self-repair and continuity of intention at the same time (Deppermann 2014), intention ascriptions to others are mostly realized with present tense and focus more on the interactive "here and now". The study includes thirty-nine declarative, verb-second instances (*du willst/Sie wollen*), twelve cases with interrogative, verb-first syntax (*willst du/wollen Sie*), six verb-final uses in a subordinate clause, and six cases with subject omission (ø *willst* ø).[5] All these variants can be used for understanding-checks (Heritage 1984b: 318–20) concerning the correctness of the intention ascription. Yet, the declarative variant conveys a higher degree of certainty and commitment of the speaker concerning the validity of the ascription (Heritage 2012: 6). The most important lexemes prefacing the intention ascription were *ach(so)* (n = 7, which corresponds to the change-of-state token 'oh') and *also* (n = 6, inferential 'so').

6.6 Four Practices of Intention Ascription

A proper response to a prior action does not necessarily require an intention ascription and, *a fortiori*, not an overt intention ascription. Still, in talk-in-interaction participants sometimes produce intention ascriptions in response to a prior turn for various reasons: for resolving ambiguity, clarifying indirectness, dealing with unexpectedness, identifying the relevance of the action with respect to larger strategies, etc.

A main aim of our study is thus to determine which aspects of action meaning become an object of intention ascription. This will help us to understand better both participants' conceptualization of 'action' and their understanding of how intentions figure in interaction.

In our data, we found that when an intention is ascribed using second person *wollen*, different aspects of action meaning may be addressed:[6]

- the basic action type (n = 29/63; Section 6.6.1);
- the response expected from S02 (n = 5/63; Section 6.6.2);
- the projection of S01's future actions (n = 18/63; Section 6.6.3);
- S01's individual project, strategy or motive (n = 23/63; Section 6.6.4).

[5] Subject omission can either be analyzed as pro-drop within a V1-interrogative frame or as topic drop within a declarative sentence frame. Six instances were found in subordinate clauses with the verb in final position.

[6] Some instances had to be assigned to several categories. The sum of the numbers for the four types therefore exceeds the total number of instances.

These four aspects indicate that and how different facets of intentions may be addressed by participants. Our study shows that these four kinds of intention ascriptions are used for clarifying (explicating, disambiguating) the meaning of a prior action to (re-)establish intersubjectivity, and for successfully co-coordinating the participants' action orientations in ongoing joint activities. An additional use of these intention ascriptions, which, however, is not present in all cases, is to index that the prior turn is considered as being problematic in some way and thus in need of revision.

For each of the four types of intention ascription, we analyze the following properties:

- the larger sequence in which the intention ascription occurs;
- the linguistic form of the intention ascription;
- the action that is performed by the intention ascription itself;
- its relevance for the participants' future action coordination;
- the interpretive sources S02 draws on to construct the ascription.

6.6.1 Clarification of the Basic Action Type

An intention ascription can be used in order to check which type of action the prior turn was to implement. In our data, there are two kinds of prior turns which give rise to this kind of confirmation check. Prior turns may be hard to understand because they are marked by multiple self-repairs, cut-off, hedges, or allusive or indirect wording. The prior action is thus in need of clarification (Excerpt 6.1). Alternatively, the prior turn lends itself either to a literal, direct, conventional interpretation or to an indirect understanding which is also conventionalized, even though to a lesser degree. The task of the intention ascription then is to resolve this ambiguity (Excerpt 6.2).

Excerpt 6.1b, which is an extended version of Excerpt 6.1a, is from an informal everyday conversation among students. They are talking about going abroad and then coming back to their home university, where they have to rent a new room.

Excerpt 6.1b FOLK_E_00055_SE_01_T_06_c76 (S01 = student 1, S02 = student 2) (Informal conversation among students)

```
01 S01:    also falls es wirk[lich so] SEIN sollte dass du ähm;
           so in case it would really be like this that you uhm
02 S02:                      [JA,     ]
                             yes
03         (0.51)
04 S01:    dass du dann (.) noch nichts NEUes hast,=
           that then you still won't have anything new
05         =oder auch nich[ts neues ] SUchen willst dann;
           or that you don't want to search anything new either then
```

```
06 S02:                    [hm_HM,  ]
                           uhum
07          (0.22)
08 S01:     wär ja MIR geholfen,
            this would help me
09          weil ich dich KENN,
            because I know you
10          und dir dann au[ch verT]RAU,
            and because then I trust you too
11 S02:                    [JA;    ]
                           yes
12 S01:     und wei[ß lieber DI]CH als [jemand AN]ders?=°hh
            and (because I) know rather you than someone else
13 S02:            [KLAR weil; ]
                    sure because
14                                     [JA,      ]
                                        yes
15 S01:     aSO- ((laugh particle))
            well
16          gott [des klingt jetz AUCH wieder] beschEUert;=
            oh my god now this sounds silly again too
17 S02:          [JA,=na JA,                 ]
                  yes well
18 S01:     = [gell,      ]
               right
19 S02:     [NEIN,=aber ich] verS[TEH was du meinst]
            no but I understand what you mean
20 S03:[7]                       [ulrike           ]
                                 ulrike
21 S03:     ja das_s  [cool     ]
            yeah that's  cool
22 S02: ->  ((laughs))[du   willst]  mir          das       ZIMmer anbieten.
                      you want.2SG me.PRO.DAT DEF.ART room  offer.INF
                      you want to offer me the room
23 S01:     ((sighs)) °h=geNAU; (.)
                         exactly
24          [geNAU;]
            exactly
25 S02:     [ja    ]
            yes
26 S03:     [S     ]Ü[ß; ]
            sweet
27 S01:               [und]
                       and
28 S02:     al[so ich FI]ND_S äh-
            well I find it
29 S01:       [also     ]
               so
```

[7] S3 is a third participant who comments on S01's and S02's conversation but who is not involved in the focal exchange.

```
30 S02:   JA,=dOch ich w
          yeah of course I w
31        (0.43)
32 S01:   da [aso dass mer_s zu]mindest mal BEIde ins Auge [fasse]n,
          so that at least we both consider it
33 S02:      [auf jeden FALL,  ]
              definitely
34                                                         [JA,   ]
                                                            yes
35 S01:    °h und ich wollt_s [dir JETZ schon sagen;       ]
               and I wanted to tell it to you already now
36 S02:                       [DAS würd ich gern (nEhmen;) ]
                               I would like to (take) it
37 S01:   damit [du A]UCH dann;
          so that then you also
38 S02:         [JA, ]
                 yes
```

In lines 1–12, S01 produces a complex, lengthy turn, with conditional and causal subordinate clauses; she lists pre- and side-conditions and consequences of looking for a new room and having a new roommate; finally she produces a self-directed devaluating comment concerning her own formulation (line 16). S02 reacts to S01's formulation-problems by an understanding-claim 'I understand what you mean' (line 19), already indicating that her following intention ascription is to give a valid formulation of the action S01 intended to produce, that is, an offer: 'You want to offer me the room' (line 22). The intention ascription is realized with declarative syntax and falling intonation; still the utterance is used (and confirmed) as a candidate understanding (Pomerantz 1988; Antaki 2012) to check the correctness of the ascription. The intention ascription draws on the discourse topic and the statements made in the prior turn: from the stated conditions, causes and consequences, S02 can draw the inference that an offer is intended. Given that S01 was about to make the offer but did not exactly produce it yet, the inchoative meaning aspect of the verb *wollen* (see Fritz 2000) becomes apparent.

S01 confirms the ascription ('exactly', 23–4), whereupon S02 accepts the offer (28, 30, 33, 36). Yet S01 downgrades the commitment which the offer and its acceptance establish for both parties (32). The design of S01's action and her later downgrading index the potentially sensitive, dispreferred character of the offer. The potential dispreferredness seems to be transferred from the second to the first pair part, probably because offers can force the respondent to commit themselves to either acceptance or refusal, thus constraining their freedom of future action and creating the potential for face-threats for both parties (see Kendrick & Drew 2014: 92–6).

In Excerpt 6.2, three friends are having dinner together. S01 and S03 are drinking red wine, S02 a white ice tea. S01 asks S02 how 'the white one' (line 4) tastes, thus jocularly referring to the ice tea as if it was wine.

Excerpt 6.2 FOLK_E_00293_SE_01_T_04_c890 (S01 = friend 1, S02 = friend 2, S03 = friend 3) (Informal table talk among friends)

```
01 S03:     bin (dann) gut SATT nachher;
            so I have had quite enough afterwards
02          (0.21)
03 S01:     ICH auch;
            me too
04          [*wie SCHMECKT_n eigentlich] der weiße,*
             how does actually the white one taste
   s01       *head nod towards glass-------------------*
05 S02:     [((chuckles))                     ]
06          +%(0.89)      +
   s02      +gaze at glass+
   s01       %gaze towards glass->
07 S02:     +ja GUT,=
             yes good
   s02      +gaze towards S01-------->
08 S02: ->  =willst  proBIERN jetz;+
             want.2SG try.INF  now
             want to try now
   s02      ----------------------------->+
09 S01: ->  %NEE grad NICH;%
            no not at the moment
   s01      %gaze towards plate, slight head shake%
10 S01: ->  DANke;=h°
            thanks
11          (10.0)
```

In line 7, S02 first responds to the literal meaning of S01's turn in line 4. S02 treats it as a question asking for an assessment and responds accordingly ('yes good'). S02 expands her turn by a pro-drop-formatted intention ascription ('want to try now', line 8), which might index more certainty than a V1-interrogative. S02's turn literally implements a question; yet, it is also a conventional way of offering. S01 declines the offer ('no not at the moment', line 9).

S01's question concerning the taste of the beverage in line 4 is an instance of a turn-type which is systematically ambiguous not only in the particular context, but more generally by virtue of its turn-design. It has both a direct, literal interpretation as a question and an indirect, non-literal interpretation as a pre-request (to be allowed to try the beverage). S02 initially responds to the first, literal interpretation (question) in line 7 and then to the possible second, non-literal interpretation (pre-request) in line 8. The second response, the offer, builds on the first, the positive assessment, as it anticipates and at the same time preempts S01's possible request to have a sip (Haugh 2017). S01's refusal in line 9 displays that he did not intend his turn in line 4 to be heard as a request, but only as an elicitation of information. The inferential intention ascription is thus declined in favor of the literal action meaning of the critical turn.[8]

6.6.2 *Clarification of Expected Response*

If an intention ascription makes the type of action that the prior turn is to implement explicit, then this often implies that a certain responsive action by S02 will be due (or not). Yet, an overt intention ascription can also directly address the kind of response which S01's prior turn expects from S02, without explicitly assigning a particular type of action to the prior turn itself.

In Excerpt 6.3 from a university viva, the examiner (S01) asks the student (S02) a question about methods for teaching literature (line 4). Instead of answering directly, S02 ascribes to S01 a more specific expectation, namely that the student should describe the representation of drama as a method (lines 8/12), and presents it for confirmation.

Excerpt 6.3 FOLK_E_00034_SE_01_T_01_c493 (S01 = student 1, S02 = student 2) (University viva)

01 **S01:** **hm_HM,=°h**
uhum
02 **dann äh gehen wir vielleicht (.) lieber (.) wieder zu den meTHOden,**
then er maybe let's better return to the methods
03 **wir hatten ja jetzt schon die handlungs und produktionsorientierte methode beLEUchtet bezÜglich (1.19) ((lip-smack)) des DRAmas;**
so far we had already dealt with the action and the production oriented method concerning drama
04 **°h welche WEIteren methoden des literaturunterrichts KENnen sie denn,**
so which other methods of literature instruction do you know
05 **(1.57)**
06 **S02:** **ÄHM;**
uhm
07 **(1.42)**
08 **S02: -> also sie wollen jetz (.) drauf hiNAUS,=öhm;**
so you want.2SG now thereon.PrepObjPro onto.DIR uhm
so now you are getting at uhm
09 **(0.95)**

[8] One might argue here that the offer is simply a next action instead of an interpretation of the prior. Yet, offers often build on an inference about others' wants and needs. And although the intention ascription does not get a confirmation by S01, there is still an inferential link between the two possible action-meanings relying on their conditional relationship: if someone is interested in the taste of something, they might want to taste it.

```
10 S02:  äh
         er
11       (0.42)
12 S02:  drama DARstellen als metho[de;=Oder-]
         to represent drama as a method or
13 S01:                             [nEIn-=
                                     no
14       =ich] bin jetz allgemein bei meTHOden des literaTURunter[richts;]
         I'm talking about methods of literature instruction in general
15 S02:                                                          [hm_HM? ]
                                                                  uhum
```

In response to the examiner's question (line 4), the student – after a delay and a filled pause – produces an intention ascription concerning the more precise topic of the expected answer (lines 8/12). The student's turn has declarative syntax with the verb in second position. It starts with *also*, which indexes that S02 takes his reformulation to be an explication of something which S01 has meant, but not said (Deppermann & Helmer 2013). The final *oder* with level intonation displays that there might be (unarticulated) alternatives to the student's hypothesis about the examiner's intention which the examiner prefers (see Drake 2016). The student uses the idiomatic expression *auf etwas hinauswollen* ('to be driving/getting at something').[9] In contrast to Excerpts 6.1 and 6.2, the intention ascription in this idiomatic format does not concern the basic action type of the prior turn (a question), but the precise topic of her response that is expected. Interestingly, the explicit reference on a response expectation makes it explicit that the basic action type of S01's turn is already obvious and unequivocal. The intention ascription serves as a pre-second, inserted candidate understanding, because the adequacy of S02's answer depends on the recognition of what the examiner precisely expects S02 to deal with. The intention ascription draws on common ground concerning the subject matter of the exam. It reflects the student's orientation to standards for a good performance in the exam, thus indexing the specific participation roles in this setting. This kind of intention ascription points to the strategic nature of examinations, in which question design often is not maximally cooperative, so as to test if the student is able to produce correct answers without being given a hint in advance about what is relevant. With the intention ascription, S02 displays her orientation to this strategical aspect of the examination question as a knowledge testing and thereby tries to unveil and intersubjectively ground S01's more precise expectation. The examiner,

[9] In our data, this construction is used only in university vivas, although its use is certainly not restricted to this setting.

however, disconfirms the ascription (line 13) and insists on her original topic formulation (line 14, cf. line 4). In terms of the potentially strategic, ambiguous intentional aspects which the ascription addresses, this example shows some similarities with the cases we will examine in the following sections.

6.6.3 Clarification of Projected Action of S01

Intention ascriptions not only concern the type of prior action by S01 (Section 6.6.1) or S01's expectations regarding S02's response (Section 6.6.2). They can also be used in order to anticipate the future course of S01's actions in the context of the current overall activity. In this case, S01's prior turn is treated as projecting specific next actions by S01. If these actions affect the future interaction between S01 and S02, S01's projected actions are also immediately consequential for the feasibility, adequacy, relevance, success, etc. of S02's own possible next actions (Excerpt 6.4). In other cases, S01's projected actions do not affect S02 (Excerpt 6.5).

Excerpt 6.4 is from an informal telephone conversation among friends, which has been going on already for 62 minutes. As S01 yawns and asks for the time (lines 1–2), S02 interprets this as an index that S01 wants to close the call next.

Excerpt 6.4 FOLK_E_00084_SE_01_T_03_c694 (S01 = friend 1, S02 = friend 2) (Informal telephone conversation among friends)

```
01 S01:     <<yawning>oh °h GOTT;>
                          oh my god
02          wie viel UHR is es;=h°
            what time is it
03          (0.74)
04 S02:     ACHTzehn uhr fün_ndrEIßig;
            six thirty-five p.m.
05          kannst auch wir könn_auch gleich (.) SCHLUSS machen;
            you also can we can hang up just now
06          (0.22)
07 S02:     °h
08          (0.2)
09 S02: ->  ((laughs)) du  willst  schon  AUFlegen;
                       you want.2SG already hang up.Inf
                       you already want to hang up
10          hast kein BOCK mehr mit mir zu rEden;
            you're not in the mood anymore for talking to me
11 S01:     ((sniffs))
12 S01:     NEE,=Aber;
            no but
13          ich muss mich noch bei LEYla melden und ich muss noch SCHLAfen;
            I still have to call leyla and I still have to sleep
```

As in Excerpt 6.2, in line 4 of Excerpt 4 S02 first answers to the literal meaning of S01's question (here: about time, line 2). She then offers to close the call, thus anticipatorily complying with what could be guessed as the motive for S01's question about time (line 5). S01's intention ascription in line 9 ('you already want to hang up') responds to a series of S01's prior actions: yawning (line 1), asking for the time (line 2), not responding to S02's offer to close the call (lines 6–8). The intention ascription is produced with declarative syntax and falling intonation. Although this turn-design embodies a high degree of certainty about her inference, a confirmation of S02's formulation is still relevant, because it concerns S01's epistemic domain. S02 adds a relationship-threatening motive for the ascribed intention ('you're not in the mood anymore for talking to me', line 10), which makes clear that this intention is being treated as problematic and thus upgrades the relevance of a response by S01. S01 disconfirms this motive and gives an alternative account, which does not refer to her attitude towards S02, but attributes the need to close the call to social obligations and physical necessity ('I still have to call Leyla, I still have to sleep', lines 12–13). In fact, this account implicitly confirms S02's first intention ascription that S01 wants to hang up, yet trying to remove its relationship-threatening implications.

The intention ascription in Excerpt 6.4 is immediately consequential for the joint project of the phone call. It is implicative for both S01's own next actions and for the cooperative response expected by S02: both should stop topical talk and initiate the closing of the encounter. The example shows how intention ascriptions rely on cumulative evidence in the prior sequential context. While each of S01's actions by themselves may be ambiguous (yawning, asking for the time, not responding to or not rejecting the offer to close the call), they give joint evidence for a clear-cut intention, namely, projecting the closure of the call.

Excerpt 6.5 also shows an instance of an intention ascription which implies an inference about what future action has been projected by S01's prior turn. In contrast to Excerpt 6.4, however, the intention ascription does not have an implication for S02's own future actions. In Excerpt 6.5, a daughter (S01) is preparing a cake while she talks with her mother (S02).

Excerpt 6.5 FOLK_E_00331_SE_01_T_01_c109 (S01 = daughter 1, S02 = mother) (Informal baking interaction)

```
01 S01:   #SO;
           alright
   s01    #closes oven door->
02        (1.22)
```

```
03 S01:     ich brauche HUN#dertachtzig grad;
            I need 180 degrees
   s01      ————————————>#
04 S02: -> <<h> willst   du  JETZ  schon   vorheizen?>
                want.2SG you now   already preheat.INF
           do you want  to  preheat already
05          (1.33)
06 S01:     <<creaky> JA-> (.)
                      yes
07          [NEIN,            ]
             no
08 S02:     [ja da  sind die  ] +KNÖPfe da;
             yeah there are buttons there
   s02      ..................+points to oven—>
09          [SIEHST+ du doch;]
             you see PTCL
   s02      ———————+,,,,,,,,,,
10 S01:     [NEIN,         =d]u hast RECHT;
             no             you are right
11          ich brauch EH lange glaub ich;=oder? °hh
            I need a lot of time anyway I guess right
12 S02:     wie lang\
            how long
13          (0.82)
14 S01:     äh h°
            erm
15 S02:     zum VORheizen brauch der backofen (0.42) hm-
            for preheating the oven needs            erm
16          (1.06)
17 S02:     vielLEICHT;
            perhaps
18          (0.53)
19 S02:     fünf miNUten oder so; (.)
            five minutes or so
20          wenn überHAUPT,
            if at all
21          (4.25)
```

When S01 announces that she needs 180 degrees (line 3), she closes the door of the oven. S02's intention ascription by way of a polar interrogative in line 4 interprets S01's announcement as indexing that S01 wants to preheat the oven immediately. The ascription is produced as a request for confirmation. However, also due to the stressed temporal adverb ('JETZ') and to the adverb 'schon', which can index that the planned action is premature, it can be heard as a challenge that prompts S01 to reflect on the adequacy of the inferred action plan and to take a public stance on it. In addition, asking for confirmation of an intention that is unproblematically inferable from the prior turn can be seen to call for an account for the intention (Raymond & Stivers 2016). Indeed, after a rather delayed initial confirmation of the intention ascription (line 6), S02 publicly abandons the intention to preheat the oven immediately afterwards (line 7) and accounts for this by referring to the time she needs for the preparation of the ingredients of the cake (line 11). Interestingly, S01 explicitly treats S02's intention ascription as challenging her inferred action plan by avowing that S02 is right (line 10).

If the ascription makes an intention explicit which may be heard as a violation of normative expectations that hold in the current context, the intention ascription can be used and understood (as Excerpts 6.4 and 6.5 show) as a conventional format to convey criticism and disagreement in order to resist a course of future action which can be seen to be projected by S01's prior turn.[10]

6.6.4 Revealing Individual Projects, Strategies and Motives

While the intention ascriptions in Section 6.6.3 concern inferences for planned, immediate next actions by S01, it is also possible that a larger individual project, a more general strategy of acting or (hidden) motives are attributed to S01 by virtue of their prior turn. Projects and strategies are characterized by "in-order-to motives" (Schütz 1974 [1932]). They exhibit an orientation towards a goal. The prior turn which gives rise to the intention ascription is treated as standing in a part-whole relationship to a larger project or strategy, being one step of its implementation. In contrast to projects or strategies, "because-motives" (Schütz 1974 [1932]) are causes or reasons for actions, which often cannot be paraphrased as goals. Motives are sometimes events or states of affairs which can be identified already in the past, independently from the action which gives rise to their ascription.

Excerpt 6.6 is an instance of the ascription of an individual project or an overarching strategy. Seven peers, who have known each other for a long time, are playing the game 'football manager'. We join the action when S01 and S02 are bidding for a specific football player in order to compose teams who will play against each other afterwards.[11]

[10] In addition to normative inadequacy of the intention, features of the design of the ascriptive turn, such as interrogative syntax, marked prosody, temporal adverbs, and grading particles, can index that it is meant to problematize the partner's intention and (projected) action.

[11] The interaction between S03 and S04 is a side sequence.

Excerpt 6.6 FOLK_E_00021_SE_01_T_02_c1107 (S01 = friend 1, S02 = friend 2, S03 = friend 3, S04 = friend 4 (Informal gaming interaction)

```
01 S02:     SECHzehn,
            sixteen
02          (0.37)
03 S01:     SIEBzehn,
            seventeen
04          (1.26)
05 S03:     hast du noch so_n (.) getränk_a,
            do you have another one of drink_a
06          (1.57)
07 S04:     JA_a,
            yeah
08          (0.9)
09 S04:     PAAR müssten noch da sein;
            there should be some left
10          (0.47)
11 S02: ->  du willst_n                      HAben;=oder?
            you want.2SG=him.Pro.3SG.M.Acchave.Inf or
            you want to have him don't you
12          (0.77)
13 S01:     UNbedingt;
            absolutely
14          (0.41)
```

As S01 produces an enhanced bid (line 3), which outdoes S02's prior, S02 interprets S01's bid as indexing a larger individual project to buy the football player by the ascription 'you want to have him, don't you' (line 11). The ascription is produced with declarative syntax and a tag which asks for confirmation, still expressing a rather high degree of certainty. S02's ascription does not simply highlight the intentionality of the act of bidding itself. S02 seems to ascribe to S01 a determination to buy the player regardless how much he will cost, which is explicitly confirmed by S01 ('absolutely', line 13). S02 produces no further bid and leaves the football player to S01, presumably because the detection of S01's intention makes him aware that he would have to pay much more for the player than he is willing to.

Since the whole bidding sequence is competitive and, moreover, performed in a playful key, the validity of S01's confirmation in line 13 cannot be assessed. Like most competitive games, this game requires strategical acting and the players have to adapt their behavior according to the others' factual and expectable actions. In this context, both the intention ascription and its (dis-)confirmation can be produced strategically – the ascription as a kind of a challenge in order to tease out the real objectives of other participants, the (dis-)confirmation in order to mislead or puzzle the competitors. In any case, the validity of these actions is often dubious and intransparent, at least at the moment when they are produced. Sources for the intention ascription here are the common ground of default actions and putative goals in the interaction type, the game, together with the prior sequence of bids.

The revelation of an individual project or strategy can involve the identification of a hidden agenda of S01, which S01 may want to conceal. With an intention ascription, S02 can purport to expose and criticize S01's "real", unavowed motives, which are potentially contradicting the motives that S01 has publicly asserted. Excerpt 6.7 is an instance of the ascription of a "because-motive" for action. As in all cases of serious motive ascriptions in our data,[12] the ascription is to reveal a hidden motive of S01, which accounts for the real intention that S01 has tried to conceal from S02's view. Excerpt 6.7 is from a conversation between a couple. S02 (the woman) has told S01 about her sister, whose boyfriend preferred to go out with his friends when she was ill, instead of staying at home with her. S02 now insistently asks her boyfriend S01 how he would act in a similar situation. We join the conversation after S01 refuses to take a stance on the issue.

Excerpt 6.7 FOLK_E_00047_SE_01_T_02_c431 (S01 = woman, S02 = man (Informal conversation between a couple)

01 **S02:** **WArum kannst du des so pa[uschal nich sAgen,]**
why can't you say it sweepy
02 **S01:** **[°h des w]äre situaTIONS (.) bedingt.**
this would be situation-dependent
03 **(1.1)**
04 **S02:** **warum kanns_u des nich SAgen;**
why can't you say this
05 **S01:** **weil (.) man dazu keine AUSsage machen kann.**
because one cannot make a statement about *this*
06 **(0.7)**
07 **S02:** **((laughs)) °h**
08 **-> du will[st jetz nur kein ÄRger kr]iegen;=Oder,**
you want.2SG now only no trouble get.Inf or.Tag
you're only trying to avoid trouble now don't you
09 **S01:** **[((laugh particle))]**
10 **((laughs softly))**
11 **S01:** **°h ich will dazu nix SAgen weil ich_s nich SAgen kann;**

12 There are also instances of teasing motive ascriptions which can be clearly critical or done just to create amusement by ascribing an absurd motive. The next case presented below is a "serious" one despite the laughing and seemingly de-escalating effect: This becomes clear in the further sequential deployment after the ascription.

```
           I don't want to say anything about this because I can't say it
12       (1.14)
13 S02:  ha was IS_n daran bitte sui f f-
         ha so what in this is sui
14       was is denn situaTIONSbedingt;
         so what is situation-dependent then
15       was IS denn,
         so what is
16       was müsste denn da EINtreffen;
         so what would have to happen then
17       (1.28)
18 S01:  wie da muss GAR nix eindreffen;
         what there doesn't have to happen anything
19 S02:  ja aber ich MEIN-
         yes but I mean
20       [WArum kannst_e des] denn nich sagen jetz;
         so why can't you say this now
21 S01:  [((laughs))        ]
22 S02:  <<laughing> un (willst/kannst) es denn nich jetz nich entSCHEIden;>
                    and so why (can't you/don't you want to) decide it now
23 S01:  °h damit mal später °h keine VORhaltungen kommen;
           just in order to avoid reproaches later
```

Faced with S01's evasive answers (lines 2/5), S02 accounts for them by ascribing to S01 the intention of trying to avoid trouble with her (line 8). This intention ascription clearly is not a formulation of the prior action(s), but a challenging account for its/their motive. It is produced to explain why S01 gives a response which is commonly known to be dispreferred (at least from S02's point of view). The ascription is formulated with declarative syntax and the tag *oder*, with rising intonation, pursuing S01's confirmation and indexing a moderate degree of certainty (König 2020: 174–7). The ascription purports to reveal the "hidden", "real" motive of S01's uncooperative actions. It is also relevant for the interlocutors' future action coordination, because it indexes that S02 is not fooled by S01's avoidance and will urge S01 to reveal his "real" attitude. The source for S02's motive ascription here is the series of evasive, uncooperative answers by S01, which may be seen as rational moves in order to avoid the dilemma of either lying (i.e., making a promise he does not intend to keep) or violating expectations concerning loyalty in the interlocutors' romantic partnership.

At first, S01 does not confirm the intention ascription and provides a competing account instead (line 11). Yet, a little later he confirms the motive ascription and justifies his refusal saying that he did not want to commit himself ('to avoid later reproaches', line 23). Interestingly, the latter formulation can be understood as a paraphrase of S02's motive ascription in terms of a strategy (or goal) formulation, this being an instance of the interchangeability of "in-order-to-" and "because-motives".

6.7 Summary and Conclusion

Our study has shown that intention ascription in response to a partner's prior turn can address different aspects of action meaning of this prior turn. They can concern the basic type of action implemented by S01's turn (Section 6.6.1), the response S01 expects from S02 (Section 6.6.2), the projection of S01's own future actions (Section 6.6.3), and S01's larger individual project or strategy and S01's motives for the prior turn (Section 6.6.4). These different meaning aspects offer insights into a putative ontology of the possible intentional foundations of action from a member's point of view. They show which facets of an action are considered to be controlled by intentions, thereby providing for the local meaning of the action from the ascriber's point of view. This does not mean that participants always interpret actions according to these four dimensions of intention; it shows that participants use intentions as one resource to account for an action's meaning and motivation.

Various properties of the prior action can give rise to an intention ascription: ambiguity, indirectness (Section 6.6.1), unexpectedness, the assessment of the prior turn as being inapposite in the given context (Section 6.6.3), its unclear situated relevance (Section 6.6.1 and 6.6.3), or a lack of transparency as to what S01 expects from S02 as a response (Section 6.6.2). While the prior turn itself may be sufficiently understood, there may be a need to anticipate S01's next future actions (Sections 6.6.3 and 6.6.4), their larger individual projects and strategies or their motives in order to understand what the projection is for a future course of joint action (Section 6.6.4).

However, intention ascriptions in interaction are not just inferences and interpretations. They perform discursive actions which do specific interactional work in their sequential context (Drew, Chapter 3 in this volume). They are not solicited, but self-initiated by S02. They stall the sequential progression of the interaction, especially if they are produced when a conditionally relevant action from S02 is due next (like an answer or a complying action). Intention ascriptions in response to partner's prior turn are a kind of understanding-check or repair-initiation. We have seen that they can be used to index a problem with the prior turn, ranging from adumbrating disagreement to straightforward challenge. The kind of problem indexed is not stated, but is to be inferred from a mismatch relationship between norms, states of affairs and expectations which can be considered to hold in the local situation and the intention which is ascribed.

Looking into the details of the situated uses of intention ascriptions, our study has shown that they are not a uniform practice. Although we have focused on the use of only one specific linguistic resource (the volitional modal verb *wollen,* 'want' in second person singular referring to the immediately prior turn of an interlocutor), we have seen that both the prior context and the actions performed by intention ascriptions are quite diverse. More specifically, it seems that there are systematic links between the intentional aspect addressed by the ascription and the action which the ascription itself performs. While the ascription of the basic action type and of response expectations serves to clarify action meaning as a basis for proper response generation (Section 6.6.1), the ascription of S01's next future actions can sometimes instead be designed as critical of these actions (Sections 6.6.3 and 6.6.4), working as a repair-initiation inviting S01 to revise their plans. The revelation of larger strategies and individual projects can be used for clarifying the terms of future cooperation (Section 6.6.2), but in more strategic and competitive contexts can perform a challenge or a cue in order to elicit more information about the interlocutor's strategy (Sections 6.6.3 and 6.6.4). Finally, because-motives (Schütz 1974[1932]) in our data are ascribed/addressed to expose "real", concealed motives which are normatively problematic, run counter to joint commitments, or contradict S01's public claims (Section 6.6.4). Motive ascriptions are thus always critical; they show that S02 is not led astray by the partner's action. In some cases, the exposure of motives implies that S01 has tried to deceive S02 by feigning misleading motives. The systematics of the different action uses of intention ascription will certainly be a rewarding area for more in-depth future research.

The same applies to responses to intention ascriptions. Since they are typically built as confirmation checks, it is most likely that the interlocutor to whom the intention is ascribed will take a stance towards it in next turn. However, in only twenty-one out of sixty-three instances did we find a straightforward confirmation of the intention ascription. In nineteen instances, the ascription is rejected. In fifteen instances, S01 responds with another action (such as laughter, topic change, or giving an account). Since only some of our data extracts were from video-recordings, nonverbal responses to the intention ascription could not always be taken into account. It will be rewarding to explore in more detail why and when intention ascriptions are not confirmed, which, as our data suggest, is probably related to the fact that intention ascriptions often problematize the prior turn in some way.

In sum, intention ascriptions are generally produced as confirmation checks which embody more or less certainty (indexed by clause type and the use of tags and depending on prior interaction) apart from the very few cases in which S02 claims to know S01's intentions without a doubt (sometimes better than S01 themselves, thereby rejecting their claims). They are produced in the service of three concerns, which build on each other:

(a) Intention ascription serves to clarify and ground intersubjectively the meaning of an action in first position which otherwise would remain underspecified, ambiguous, unmotivated or indeterminate in its projective properties and with regard to participants' larger joint and individual projects.

(b) By establishing the intelligibility of S01's prior action, intention ascriptions support the coordination of S02's future actions with S01. This is because the intention ascription clarifies aspects of S01's action which are relevant for S02's action planning, e.g., in terms of responses expected from S02, the appropriateness, success and feasibility of S02's future actions depending on S01's future actions.

(c) Intention ascriptions are sometimes used to index a problem with the partner's prior action, inviting them to revise the prior action, to refrain from a projected course of future action or to give up on trying to mislead interlocutors concerning the meaning of the partner's actions.

Beyond the more fine-grained level of the intentional facets of intention ascription and the actions they perform themselves in particular contexts, a general, superordinate motivation for intention ascription is thus to foster intersubjective coordination of future actions in interaction, by accomplishing intersubjective action meanings, by obtaining information about a partner's action orientations and by deflecting unwanted future actions of the partner.

Acknowledgments

We thank Elizabeth Couper-Kuhlen, Alexandra Gubina and Michael Haugh for valuable comments on prior versions of this text.

REFERENCES

Antaki, C. (2008). Formulations in psychotherapy. In A. Peräkylä, C. Antaki, S. Vehviläinen & I. Leudar, eds., *Conversation Analysis and Psychotherapy.* Cambridge: Cambridge University Press, pp. 26–42.

(2012). Affiliative and disaffiliative candidate understandings. *Discourse Studies*, 14 (5), 531–47.

Antaki, C., Barnes, R. & Leudar, I. (2005). Diagnostic formulations in psychotherapy. *Discourse Studies*, 7(6), 627–47.

Arundale, R. B. (2008). Against (Gricean) intentions at the heart of human interaction. *Intercultural Pragmatics*, 5(2), 229–58.

Barnes, R. (2007). Formulations and the facilitation of common agreement in meetings talk. *Text & Talk,* 27(3), 273–96.

Brentano, F. (1874). *Psychologie vom empirischen Standpunkt.* Leipzig: Duncker & Humblot.

Childs, C. (2012a). Directing and requesting: Two interactive uses of the mental state terms "want" and "need." *Text & Talk*, 32(6), 727–49.

(2012b). "I'm not X, I just want Y": Formulating "wants" in interaction. *Discourse Studies*, 14(2), 181–96.

Curl, T. (2006). Offers of assistance: Constraints on syntactic design. *Journal of Pragmatics*, 38, 1257–80.

Deppermann, A. (2011). The study of formulations as a key to an Interactional Semantics. *Human Studies*, 34(2), 115–28.

(2014). Handlungsverstehen und Intentionszuschreibung in der Interaktion I: Intentionsbekundungen mit *wollen*. In P. Bergmann, K. Birkner, P. Gilles, H. Spiekermann & T. Streck, eds., *Sprache im Gebrauch. Räumlich, zeitlich, interaktional. Festschrift für Peter Auer*. Heidelberg: Winter, pp. 309–26.

Deppermann, A. & Helmer, H. (2013). Zur Grammatik des Verstehens im Gespräch: Inferenzen anzeigen und Handlungskonsequenzen ziehen mit *also* und *dann*. *Zeitschrift für Sprachwissenschaft*, 32(1), 1–40.

Dowty, D. (1991). Thematic proto-roles and argument selection. *Language*, 67(3), 547–619.

Drake, V. (2016). German questions and turn-final *oder*. *Gesprächsforschung – Online-Zeitschrift zur verbalen Interaktion*, 17, 168–95.

Drew, P. (2003). Comparative analysis of talk-in-interaction in different institutional settings: A sketch. In P. Glenn, C. Lebaron & J. Mandelbaum, eds., *Studies in Language and Social Interaction: In Honor of Robert Hopper*. Mahwah, NJ: Lawrence Erlbaum, pp. 293–308.

(2018). Inferences and indirectness in interaction. *Open Linguistics*, 4(1), pp. 241–59.

Duranti, A. (1993). Truth and intentionality: Towards an ethnographic critique. *Cultural Anthropology*, 8(2), 214–45.

(2015). *The Anthropology of Intentions: Language in a World of Others*. Cambridge: Cambridge University Press.

Edwards, D. (2008). Intentionality and mens rea in police interrogations: The production of actions as crimes. *Intercultural Pragmatics*, 5(2), 177–99.

Enfield, N. J. & Sidnell, J. (2017). On the concept of action in the study of interaction. *Discourse Studies*, 19, 515–35.

Fritz, G. (2000). Zur semantischen Entwicklungsgeschichte von “wollen.” Futurisches, Epistemisches und Verwandtes. In G. Richter, J. Riecke & B.-M. Schuster, eds., *Raum, Zeit, Medium – Sprache und ihre Determinanten. Festschrift für Hans Ramge zum 60. Geburtstag*. Darmstadt: Hessische Historische Kommission, pp. 263–81.

Gibbs, R. W. (1999). *Intentions in the Experience of Meaning*. Cambridge: Cambridge University Press.

Grice, H. P. (1975). Logic and conversation. In P. Cole & J. L. Morgan, eds., *Syntax and Semantics 3, Speech Acts*. New York, NY: Academic Press, pp. 41–58.

(1989). *Studies in the Way of Words*, London: Harvard University Press.

Haugh, M. (2008). The place of intention in the interactional achievement of implicature. In I. Kecskes & J. Mey, eds., *Intention, Common Ground and the Egocentric Speaker-Hearer*. Berlin: de Gruyter, pp. 45–85.

(2013). Speaker meaning and accountability in interaction. *Journal of Pragmatics*, 48 (1), 41–56.

(2017). Implicature and the inferential substrate. In P. Cap & M. Dynel, eds., *Implicitness: From Lexis to Discourse*. Amsterdam: John Benjamins, pp. 281–304.

Haugh, M., ed. (2008b). Intention in pragmatics. *Special issue of Intercultural Pragmatics*, 5(2), 99–260.

Helmer, H. & Zinken, J. (2019). *Das heißt* ("that means") for formulations and *du meinst* ("you mean") for repair? Interpretations of prior speakers' turns in German. *Research on Language and Social Interaction*, 52(2), 159–76.

Heritage, J. & Watson, D. R. (1979). Formulations as conversational objects. In G. Psathas, ed., *Everyday Language: Studies in Ethnomethodology*. London: Irvington, pp. 123–62.

Heritage, J. (1984a). *Garfinkel and Ethnomethodology*. Cambridge: Polity.

(1984b). A change-of-state token and aspects of its sequential placement. In M. J. Atkinson & J. Heritage, eds., *Structures of Social action: Studies in Conversation Analysis*. Cambridge: Cambridge University Press, pp. 299–345.

(2012). Epistemics in action: Action formation and territories of knowledge. *Research on Language and Social Interaction*, 45(1), 1–29.

Husserl, E. (1950). *Husserliana 3: Ideen zu einer reinen Phänomenologie und phänomenologischen Philosophie. Erstes Buch: Allgemeine Einführung in die reine Phänomenologie*, ed. by W. Biemel. The Hague: Martinus Nijhoff.

(1976). *Husserliana 6: Die Krisis der europäischen Wissenschaften und die transzendentale Phänomenologie. Eine Einleitung in die phänomenologische Philosophie*, ed. by W. Biemel. The Hague: Martinus Nijhoff.

Kendrick, K. & Drew, P. (2014). The putative preference for offers over requests. In P. Drew & E. Couper-Kuhlen, eds., *Requesting in Social Interaction*. Amsterdam: John Benjamins, pp. 87–114.

König, K. (2020). Prosodie und *epistemic stance*: Konstruktionen mit finalem *oder*. In W. Imo & J. Lanwer, eds., *Prosodie und Konstruktionsgrammatik*. Berlin: de Gruyter, pp. 167–99.

Merleau-Ponty, M. (1945). *Phénoménologie de la perception*. Paris: Gallimard.

Pomerantz, A. (1988). Offering a candidate answer: An information seeking strategy. *Communication Monographs*, 55(4), 360–73.

Potter, J. & Edwards, D. (2013). Conversation analysis and psychology. In J. Sidnell & T. Stivers, eds., *Handbook of Conversation Analysis*. Chichester: Wiley-Blackwell, pp. 701–25.

Raymond, C. W. & Stivers, T. (2016). The omnirelevance of accountability: Off-record account solicitations. In J. D. Robinson, ed., *Accountability in Social Interaction*. Oxford: Oxford University Press, pp. 321–53.

Ryle, G. (1949). *The Concept of Mind*. New York, NY: Hutchinson's University Library.

Schegloff, E. A. (2007). *Sequence Organization in Interaction: A Primer in Conversation Analysis*. Cambridge: Cambridge University Press.

Schütz, A. (1974 [1932]). *Der sinnhafte Aufbau der sozialen Welt*. Frankfurt am Main: Suhrkamp.

Schütz, A. & Luckmann, T. (1979). *Strukturen der Lebenswelt, Vol. 1*. Frankfurt am Main: Suhrkamp.

Searle, J. (1969). *Speech Acts: An Essay in the Philosophy of Language*. Cambridge: Cambridge University Press.

(1983). *Intentionality: An Essay in the Philosophy of Mind*. Cambridge: Cambridge University Press.

Sidnell, J. & Enfield, N. J. (2014). The ontology of action, in interaction. In N. J. Enfield, P. Kockelman & J. Sidnell, eds., *The Cambridge Handbook of Linguistic Anthropology*. Cambridge: Cambridge University Press, pp. 423–46.

Weiste, E. & Peräkylä, A. (2013). A comparative conversation analytic study of formulations in Psychoanalysis and Cognitive Psychotherapy. *Research on Language and Social Interaction*, 46(4), 299–321.

Wittgenstein, L. (1950). Philosophische Untersuchungen. In L. Wittgenstein, ed., *Werkausgabe, Vol. I*. Frankfurt am Main: Suhrkamp, pp. 225–580.

7 Strategy Ascriptions in Public Mediation Talks

Henrike Helmer

7.1 Introduction

Action formation has long been the focus of research on actions in interaction (cf. Schegloff 2007) and can be analyzed in terms of turn design and bodily resources. The ascription of an action instead can typically only be inferred by the *next-turn proof procedure* (Sacks, Schegloff & Jefferson 1974), i.e., by observing next speakers' subsequent reactions to an action. It is influenced by several factors such as turn design, sequential position, and the overarching activity and social roles of the participants (Levinson 2013). Producing a turn in third position (a confirmation or disconfirmation) is crucial for establishing intersubjectivity: "An intersubjectively shared and socially valid action ascription thus is neither warranted by the agent's intention nor by the recipient's response but is the outcome of an interactional process of mutual displays and possibly negotiation" (Deppermann & Haugh, Chapter 1 in this volume, p. 000). However, establishing intersubjectivity about ongoing actions in a three-step process is sometimes not feasible for or not a primary goal for participants. Not feasible, because in some (especially institutional and public) settings, specific rules may partly determine or completely formalize the turn-taking system and do not allow immediate reactions to prior speakers. And not the main goal, because in specific situations, e.g., in conflict talk, other motives like self-positioning or winning an argument are more relevant to participants. In this case, the specific type of interaction (see Levinson 2013) and its intrinsic characteristics (such as a conflict between different parties and different relevant ideologies, see Deppermann 2015) can systematically enter into ascribing actions to prior talk in second position. Being on one side of opposing parties may influence both, which "kind of action [is presupposed] as a condition" (Deppermann & Haugh, Chapter 1 in this volume, p. 18) for a response, and which kind of action the response itself constitutes.

In public debates, speakers regularly ascribe strategies to participants of another party as a practice of overt action ascription. When speakers employ what I call 'strategy ascriptions', they overtly ascribe an action and spell out what kind of interactional plan they think opponents pursue, typically by exposing their means (rhetorical devices, asking challenging questions, the structure of logical conclusions, etc.) and their ends (in the sense of underlying intentions such as confusing others, concealing uncomfortable truths, etc.). Consequently, ascribing strategies goes hand in hand with overtly claiming ('You do X in order to do Y') or at least tacitly indicating that speakers use those strategies intentionally. Ascribing strategies does not only reveal how participants construe prior talk, but by accusing opponents of covert intentions and questionable means of achieving them, is itself a vehicle for an action.

In this chapter, I examine the ascription of strategies in a public mediation setting that resembles a (mediated) public debate. In Section 7.1.1, I sketch the discursive framework of public debates and the particular properties and conditions for strategy ascription it establishes. Section 7.1.2 deals with strategies as a discursive practice and Section 7.1.3 specifically with strategy ascriptions in public debates. In Section 7.2, I introduce the complex participation framework and turn-taking system of the mediation talk under examination. Section 7.3 is devoted to analyses of sequences in which speakers in a public mediation session ascribe a strategy to an opponent. The chapter ends with a conclusion of the practices of strategy ascriptions in public mediation sessions and of the relevance of this chapter as a contribution to studies on (mediated) public debates and action ascription (Section 7.4).

7.1.1 Public Debate and Its Confrontational Characteristics

In specific situations and types of interactions, participants of opposing sides exchange arguments. This applies to informal conflict talk, but even more to some types of institutional and public interaction, such as courtroom interaction (Komter 2013), mediation talks (Nothdurft 1997), TV debate shows (Hutchby 1997), news interviews (Clayman 2013), and political debates (Burkhardt 2003). In many of these settings, such as courtroom interactions and mediations, coming to some kind of agreement is imposed upon participants as one main goal of the (mediated) conflict. The roles of participants such as judges and mediators are grounded in the institutional characteristics of the interaction type, and even adversative moves and actions (like accusations and defenses in courtroom interaction, cf. Komter 2013) serve this overarching main goal. This is different in some confrontational formats like specific TV talk shows, panel debate shows, and public political debates, in which participants are part of a "spectacle of confrontation" (see Hutchby 2006: 65). Participants of opposing sides orient to the public as an overhearing audience that they seek to influence and persuade (cf. Atkinson 1984; Clark & Schaefer 1992; Hutchby 2006). This may result in what has been termed "pseudo-dialogue" (cf. Burkhardt 2003: 278), in which the argumentation has the underlying main goal to strengthen the position of the speakers' party and discredit the position of the opponents, not only on a factual but also on a moral level. In those debates, speakers use several practices in order to accuse the opponents of specific shortcomings and publicly discredit them and their credibility (cf. Deppermann, [1997] 2005: 188). One of these practices is strategy ascription with which participants indicate a violation of normative rules and moral expectations.

7.1.2 Ascription of Strategies and Intentions as a Discursive Practice

The notion of (pragmatic) 'strategies' implies a certain goal-orientation, i.e., that speakers employ strategies in order to achieve some effect or serve a plan of action (see Leech 1983: 15; Brown & Levinson 1987). This however, "may still be (but need not be) unconscious" (Brown & Levinson 1987: 85), i.e., rather than consciously intended it is routinized in being part of "shared sociocultural knowledge" (Culpeper 2016: 442). In line with that, researchers in the field of Conversation Analysis have pointed out that analyzing strategies cannot mean analyzing 'pre-strategies' (Hopper 2005; Heritage 1990/1991) that are grounded in presumptions of interlocutors' *a priori* intentions (Haugh 2008). The recourse to *a priori* intentions for ascribing strategies may not only be superfluous, but even problematic due to the fact that evidence is rare and "usually cannot be located precisely in time" (cf. Hopper 2005: 149).

The notion of 'intentions' always plays at least tacitly a role when considering strategies, yet only as a part of a discursive practice of ascription – as with all cognitive phenomena, it is not methodologically feasible to make assumptions about cognitive states of interlocutors (see Heritage 1990/1991; Hopper 2005) and get down to speakers' "real" intentions. When cognitive issues are considered as an object for CA studies (e.g., understanding, knowledge ascriptions, epistemic stance; see for example Heritage & Raymond 2005; Deppermann 2014; Reineke 2016), they are examined in relation to practices and interactional outcomes.

Similarly, researchers in the field of Discursive Psychology, as main advocates for an approach that considers ascriptions of cognitive phenomena as a discursive practice, emphasize that "'intention' here is not treated by the analyst as the driver of behavior, but is taken as a members' resource for accountability within particular everyday and institutional settings" (Potter & Edwards 2013: 718). Furthermore, ascribed intentions are defeasible even if they become an explicit topic in an ongoing interaction (see Edwards 2008).

Consequently, scholars in CA consider 'strategies' as an emergent process (Hopper 2005: 140), in which participants mutually display how they ascribe (which) sense to each other (Deppermann 2014). Still, interlocutors regularly display that they (also) base their understanding of each others' actions upon cognitive issues such as knowledge (e.g., Heritage & Raymond 2005) or intentions, strategies, and plans (Levinson 2013). This is directly observable in statements about own intentions (Deppermann 2014) and overt ascriptions of others' intentions (Deppermann & Kaiser, Chapter 6 in this volume). Ascribing intentions as a discursive practice typically occurs for the sake of clarification and intersubjective grounding, through which speakers not only ascribe meaning to each other's actions, but also coordinate future actions (see Deppermann & Kaiser, Chapter 6 in this volume). Analysts cannot identify real intentions behind strategies, but "if an action is predicated, ascriptions of intention (and still other cognitive states, such as epistemic stances) are implied as part of its (social) semantics" (Deppermann 2012: 763). Strategy ascriptions (and thus overtly or tacitly intentions) are a form of overt action ascriptions. As a discursive practice, they are systematically used with specific interactional outcomes, especially in some interactional settings such as political debates.

7.1.3 Strategies and Strategy Ascriptions in Political Debates

Speakers' orientation to (presumed) strategies and intentions is an especially interesting topic in conflictual interaction such as political debates. Especially when strategies and the underlying intentions are overtly ascribed, the ascription is not just a response in the sense of a display of understanding of a prior speaker's action, but the overt strategy ascription is itself an action in its own right (as noted by Walker, Drew & Local [2011] on indirect responses). Prior research has shown that participants in adversational contexts, such as political debates, expose strategies and hidden motives in order to criticize the inadequacy of their interlocutors' actions (e.g., Luginbühl 1999). In public debates, speakers use strategies in order to prevail over their adversaries in an exchange of argument as well as with regard to their conversational status in the overarching discussion: strategies may have an effect on the own and the opponents' credibility, expertise, and distribution of speaking rights.

Conversely, exposing an opponent's use of conversational strategies has a comparable effect itself. Speakers treat strategies they expose as intentional, morally contaminated (i.e., as unfair), and concealed (i.e., in contrast to what the speaker overtly claims to do). When speakers spell this out, they accuse opponents of using strategies that violate the normative rules of a conversation. Especially when participants display that they hold their opponents morally responsible for their actions (Robinson 2016) and impose commitment to a specific (discredited) standpoint onto their opponents (cf. Kampf 2013: 5), this may have effects on the course of interaction and the conversational status of the speakers.

The larger interaction type enters fundamentally into strategy ascriptions. Some public political debates comprise not only (at least) two opposing sides with category-bound expectations (Sacks 1972, 1992) about members of the opposing party, but also an absent or present overhearing audience that is ought to be convinced (see Section 7.1.1). Purporting to uncover opponents' strategies is thus a vehicle for accusations that ought to strengthen the own party, weaken the other, and persuade the audience.

Prior research has shown that exposing opponent's strategies is used in order to deal with face-threatening prior turns such as leading questions, loaded statements or overt accusations (cf. Deppermann 2015: 30). Participants claim a shortcoming in their opponents' conduct and indicate that political interests of their party are an underlying scheme of any of their actions (Deppermann 2015: 33). A prototypical example is the accusation of untruthfulness of other participants, when speakers point out that their opponents are concealing information that would be relevant for evaluating the subject (Luginbühl 1999: 206). When interlocutors treat knowledge as a moral domain (Stivers, Mondada & Steensig 2011), speakers hint at their opponents' moral shortcomings. Other accusations operate on a moral domain too, e.g., when speakers claim that opponents employ distractions to avoid a direct answer to a question (Luginbühl 1999: 210), or act strategically with a view to future elections (Luginbühl 1999: 214). Exposing those strategies has always a twofold function: speakers judge their opponents by high moral standards that they claim for themselves (Luginbühl 1999: 207) for the sake of strengthening their own positions and weakening the others'. This is typical of public political debates and the public mediation that I discuss in this chapter.

7.2 Data

All data samples in this chapter stem from three sessions (ca. 16 hours in total) of a public mediation that took place in 2010 in Stuttgart, Germany. The reason and background for the mediation go back to the 1990s. In 1994, Deutsche Bahn (DB, 'German Railways') presented a railway and urban development project called "Stuttgart 21" ("S21" for short), which included a plan for restructuring Stuttgart main station from a terminus station to an underground through station. The project was controversial, and the public and politicians discussed it over a number of years, especially in terms of cost risks and environmental protection. In 2010, these discussions led to massive protests and a serious conflict between supporters and opponents of the project, in the course of which more than a hundred people were injured during demonstrations. To solve the conflict, the federal state of Baden-Württemberg appointed a mediator and set up mediation talks spanning nine sessions from October 22 to November 30, 2010, at Stuttgart town hall. Due to the public interest, the mediation was broadcast live on German TV. During the mediation sessions, the problems were discussed by around seventy participants from the opposing sides and/or persons with technical expertise. More concretely, the participation framework can be summed up as follows (cf. Reineke 2016: 70):

- The mediator, Heiner Geißler,[1] served as the chair of the sessions. He was responsible for assuring compliance with the structure and schedule of each session, for distributing the right to speak (i.e., for turn allocation), and for formulating a binding arbitral verdict at the end of the mediation process.
- On the side of the supporters of project S21 there were several politicians (especially members of the regional government at that time) and German Railways representatives.
- On the side of the opponents of S21 there were representatives and politicians of other German parties.
- Each side had recruited experts who contributed to the discussion, for example by providing (and debating) expert reports regarding technical questions (tunnel construction, environmental protection, etc.).
- Some neutral accountants were in charge of evaluating the financial plans of the project.

Apart from these actively contributing and debating participants there were several passive attendants, that is, people who were not given the right to contribute to the discussion: journalists, a transcript writer, and several assistants.

The mediation sessions could be observed by spectators on a screen outside the mediation hall. In addition, two German TV stations broadcast the sessions.[2] Since the presentations and discussions were designed for an audience, the interaction type ranged between a mediation and a public political debate. Due to these circumstances, publicity is a central aspect and even a central purpose of the mediation. The purpose is not only to find and formulate a binding arbitral verdict, but also to lay out the details of the project and its problems for the public and to provide the audience with information about the complex facts (see Reineke 2016: 66).

Not only are the setting and participation framework complex, but the mediation sessions themselves follow a complex course of action (cf. Reineke 2016: 68). In each session, there are several thematic slots with predetermined presentations about specific topics. Each slot is restricted in time and comprises presentations in favor and against the project with regard to the determined topic. Each slot is followed by a mediated discussion. For the

[1] Throughout this chapter, I will be using real names, not pseudonyms, because the interactions are public data.

[2] The fact that the mediation sessions were broadcast implies a problem regarding a potential multimodal analysis of the data: usually only the current speaker is visible; there are only few long shots in which it is clearly retraceable to which specific participants current speakers are addressing their talk. On account of this problem, multimodal analyses of the extracts are not provided (systematically) in this chapter, but only where it is possible and adequate.

mediated discussion, speakers indicate their intention to contribute; the mediator compiles a list of prospective speakers, and then works through the list more or less in the order in which persons expressed their intent to speak. Due to this strict handling of turn allocation, reactions of recipients of certain presentations may be more or less adjacent (after a turn allocation of the chair/mediator), but more often they occur with some (and sometimes quite long) latency relative to the related prior turn. The public mediations talks therefore are similar to what Greatbatch (1992) analyzes as *panel interviews*: each party's turns are elicited by intervening questions and turn allocation devices by a moderator who mediates the contrasting statements and positions.

Only the mediator Heiner Geißler himself is authorized to interrupt speakers during a contribution in order to clarify something or to rebuke a certain type of behavior. Geißler pursues neutrality in his assertions (cf. Clayman 1992) and strives for moderately formulated ascriptions, evaluations, etc. by other speakers. This leads to the exigency of employing potentially challenging actions without personal attacks, because Geißler rebukes overt and personal accusations as well as 'unauthorized' direct quarrels between participants.

When a participant switches to the status of current speaker, their microphone is turned on; otherwise it is turned off. Heckles by non-current speakers do still occur, but are not always audible (at least not for the public) and are not always dealt with by current speakers.

This distinctive turn-taking system has consequences for speakers' turn designs: once they have been allocated the right to speak, they can produce long turns in which they can develop complex arguments without having to fear interruptions by opponents.

In the 16 hours of video recordings, I found sixty-seven cases of strategy ascriptions, in which participants ascribe actions to opponents when responding to their prior talk. I excluded all cases of strategy ascriptions that did not refer to prior talk, but to overarching strategic conduct of the parties (such as refusing to distribute specific documents) or to quotations of absent agents of parties (cited in newspaper articles, etc.). I identified three main types of strategy ascription, the most frequent being the exposure of untruthfulness, followed by the exposure of using a rhetorical strategy and the exposure of using false premises as a basis for an argument (basically equally distributed, see Table 7.1). As the first type is typically designed in a less overt way, I start with the more clear-cut cases for my analysis.

7.3 Strategy Ascriptions in the "Stuttgart 21" Mediation

As shown in Table 7.1, speakers in the mediation talks ascribe different strategies to other participants, typically spelling out both the devices their opponents use as well as exposing or at least hinting at the "hidden motives" (cf. Deppermann & Kaiser, Chapter 6 in this volume, p. 150) as a

Table 7.1 *Main types of strategy ascriptions in the public mediation sessions*

Type of strategy ascription	Number (%)
Exposing untruthfulness/lies/telling half-truths (consciously revealing knowledge)	28 (41.8)
Using a rhetorical strategy	14 (20.9)
Using false premises for argumentation	12 (17.9)
Other	13 (19.4)
Total	67

presupposition of the turns to which they are responding. I will illustrate the exposure of three strategies that speakers ascribe to prior speakers, and I will trace how speakers use strategy ascription as accusations for the sake of strengthening their own position.

7.3.1 Exposing a Rhetorical Strategy

In one of the mediation sessions, the plenum discusses the construction risks and the consequences of the construction for mineral springs and ground water. Walter Wittke, a professor for geotechnics and an expert in favor of the supporters of the S21 project, had presented information about problems and solutions regarding the construction of tunnels for the project. One of the main problems is that constructing new tunnels could cause an influx of water. When water gets into contact with the nearby mineral anhydrite, it swells and can destroy the walls of the tunnels, leading to additional repair costs.

In the discussion, Boris Palmer (an opponent of S21) addresses Walter Wittke after his presentation:[3]

Excerpt 7.1 FOLK_00069_SE_01_T_03_c161ff.

(BPA = Boris Palmer [mayor of Tübingen, member of the Green Party Die Grünen, against S21],
WWI = Walter Wittke [professor of geotechnics, expert on the side of the S21 supporters],
HGE = Heiner Geißler [mediator, chair])

```
01 BPA:  und jetzt möcht ich herrn wittke n paar FRAgen stellen.
         and now I'd like to ask Mister Wittke some questions
02       °hh sIE haben wenn ich sie richtig verstanden hab (.) geSAGT,
         if I understood you correctly, you said
03       es ist nicht (.) Überall möglich wasserzutritte vollständig
         AUSzuschließen.
         it is not possible everywhere to entirely avoid influxes of water
```

[3] All extracts follow GAT2-conventions (Selting et al. 2009).

04 **(0.2)**
05 BPA: **°hh kann ich (.) daraus FOLgern,**
can I deduce from that
06 **dass auch SIE nicht sAgen;**
that you, too, are not saying
07 **es ist hundert prozent SIcher;**
it is a hundred percent certain
08 **(0.2)**
09 BPA: **dass bei den tunneln die hier gebaut werden (.) NIRgendwo (.) das quellproblem AUFttritt.**
that with the tunnels that are being built here the problem with swelling will not arise anywhere
10 **oder können sie des hUndertprozentig AUSschließen.**
or can you exclude that hundred percent
11 **das is meine ERSTte frage.=**
that's my first question
12 **=[meine zwei-]**
my secon-
13 WWI: **[ei_moment] darf ich die frage der REIhe nach beant[worten.**
]
just a moment may I answer the question in order
14 BPA: **[wenn sie sie**
[mit ja order NEINbeantworten,]
if you answer them with yes or no
15 HGE **[ja-BITte schön- beANTwo] rten sie-**
yes please answer
16 **kommen dann gleich weider DRAN herr [palmer.]**
((it'll)) be your turn again right after master palmer
17 BPA: **[gut,]**
fine
18 WWI: **[ich würde] gurne die fragen (.) der REIhe nach beantworten.**
I'd like to answer the.questions.in.order
19 HGE: **[ja-]**
yes
20 WWI: => **[weil es] ein übliches verfahren is zehn [FRAgen zu stellen und] (.) redner zu verwIRren,**
Because it is a common procedure to ask ten questions and confuse speakers
21 HGE: **[ja vöilling RICHtig;]**
Yes absolutely correct
22 WWI: => **ansichließend frag (sind/ist) die erste frage verGESsen.**
Afterwards ques- the first question (has/have) been forgotten
23 **hhh das möcht ich ni most ich nich (.) äh möch.ich.nich äh [dem AUSgesetzt]sein;**
that I don't want I don't want (.) eh.i don't want (.) to be exposed to
That

```
24 HGE:       [wie würden SIE den;]
               how would you
25 HGE:   ja-
          yes
26 WWI:   °h
27 HGE:   gut oKAY.
          fine okay
```

Palmer begins with what could be interpreted as a request for clarification (lines 2–10) due to the epistemic hedge (line 2) and the interrogative format (see lines 5/10). However, Palmer's inference turns out to be a challenge. If Wittke really said that he cannot exclude the influx of water in the range of the tunnel constructions (line 3), this would imply that he cannot exclude anhydrite coming into contact with that water and causing the problem with 'swelling' ("quellproblem", line 9). Admitting this would not only imply a high risk of problems with the tunnel constructions and unplanned additional costs, but would also be threatening for Wittke's positive face (see Brown & Levinson, pp. 61), as he had previously denied such risks.

Palmer is about to ask a second question (line 12), but is interrupted by Wittke (line 13), who indicates that he wants to answer each part of the questions in turn. After a short verbal exchange and the approval of the chair, Heiner Geißler (lines 15, 16), Wittke moves to meta-pragmatic talk (see Haugh 2008: 25). In an impersonal claim, he states that it is a 'common procedure' ("übliches verfahren", line 20), i.e., a rhetorical strategy, to ask a lot of questions in order to confuse speakers and make them forget the first question. Wittke indicates that the prior action ('to ask ten question') is a means to an end ('confuse speakers'). Wittke uses an impersonal construction ("es [...] is", 'it is', line 20), avoiding a personal attack on the opponent. Yet his "weil" ('because'), with which he connects his explication back to his prior request, works on a discourse level rather than on a propositional level (see Gohl & Günthner 1999). Thus, Wittke turns the ascription of the rhetorical strategy into a justification on a discourse level, exposing it as a potential risk that his opponent Palmer must at least be potentially aware of. Even if the strategy is not openly ascribed to Palmer (so that Wittke himself could not be held accountable for accusing his opponent of acting strategically), Wittke's statement lets the other participants infer that Palmer is using this rhetorical strategy and is morally accountable for using it. Wittke uses the meta-pragmatic strategy ascription as a vehicle for an accusation and designs it to challenge his opponent's motives for asking questions in the way he does (i.e., not [only] in order to retrieve information). When justifying his wish to proceed directly, Wittke states that he does not want to be 'exposed' ("AUSgesetzt sein;", line 23) to this strategy, a word choice that suggests his status as a potential victim.[4]

In Excerpt 7.1, exposing the use of a rhetorical strategy has positive interactive consequences for Wittke: he is allowed to answer the question after Geißler's turn allocation. Interestingly, Geißler had moved to grant his wish twice (line 15, line 19), before Wittke explicitly refers to the rhetorical strategy. This suggests that the exposure of the strategy serves not only to get the floor, but also to discredit Palmer in front of the other participants and the audience for at least potentially using unfair means to weaken the case of the S21 supporters. Thus Palmer is under suspicion of trying to violate the normative rules of a successful communication and discussion. The fact that Geißler strongly agrees (line 21), neither denying nor rebuking Wittke's ascription, may support Wittke's depiction of Palmer.

7.3.2 Exposing the Use of False Premises

In one of the mediation sessions, the plenum discusses the financial plan of the project, which reaches back to the 1990s. After the currency changeover from the Deutsche Mark to the euro in 2002, the costs for S21 were calculated for an in-house document of the German Railways (called BAST: *Betriebliche Aufgabenstellung für die Umsetzung der Konzeption Netz 21*, 'Operational task for the realization of the concept Net 21') to amount to 4.2 billion euro. However, the German Railways officially communicated a total sum of 2.5 billion euro in the same year and corrected it only in 2010 to a total of 4.1 billion euro. The opponents of the project believe that German Railways had already known of the higher sum in 2002, and they take the BAST document as support for this accusation. German Railways, on the other hand argues that the persons responsible for the document made a simple currency error: they accidentally calculated using D-Marks instead of euros (4.2 billion D-Mark = ca. 2.5 billion euro), even though all other prices were given in euro.

Subsequently to this discussion, Michael Holzhey (an economist on the side of the opponents of S21) shows a slide that reveals unrealistic planning costs. He presents a value (5.22 billion euro), which according to him would be more realistic and insinuates that the planners are either deceiving the public consciously or engaging in poor planning. However, he had calculated his own value based on the presumably correct value (4.2 billion euro instead of 2.5 billion euro). Volker Kefer, a supporter of S21, who had explained that the

[4] In fact, given the complex participation framework, there is a high risk that recipients of questions or accusations may not get an opportunity to react. Participants frequently orient to this risk and also treat the lack of anticipated answers as a proof of lack of knowledge.

value in the BAST document was based on a typo (D-Marks vs. euros), reacts to this in Excerpt 7.2:

Excerpt 7.2 FOLK_E_00070_SE_01_T_04_DF_01_c726ff.

(VKE = Volker Kefer [board member of German Railways, S21 supporter],
MHO = Michael Holzhey [economist, consultant and expert of the S21 opponents],
HGE = Heiner Geißler [chair, mediator])

```
01 VKE:   herr HOLZhey;
           Mr. Holzhey
02        zweitausendZWEI der wert;
          two thousand and two that value
03        (.) die vier ZWANzig;
              the four twenty
04        wo kommen die HER;
          where do they come from
05        (1.05)
06 MHO:   bast;
          BAST
07        (0.55)
08 VKE:   das is der wert den ich vorhin RICHtiggestellt ha[be. ]
          that is the value that I corrected earlier
09 MHO:                                                     [ja; ]
                                                             yes
10        (0.32)
11 MHO:   ich SAG j[a;]
          well, like I say
12 VKE:            *[a ]HA.
                     I see
  vke              *smiles ->
  fig              #fig.7.1
13 MH=:       [(der aktuelle)]
               (the current)
14 VKE: => °h    [des heißt als    ]o mit falschen zAhlen wern* falsche arguMENte
          auf[gebaut.     ]
              so that means with false numbers false arguments are being
          constructed
  vke     -----------------------------------*
15 MHO:       [<<t,f>nein,]
                      no
16        ich habe-
          I said
17        (.) ich habe offen gesagt ich habe hier den BAST wert eingetragen;-
              I said openly ((that)) I inserted the BAST-value here
18        =ich hab sogar gesagt dass ich NICHT station und service drin habe;
           I even said that I did not have station and service included
19 VKE:   ich hatte grade ausgeführt dass des DE mark warn un nicht EUro.
          I had just laid out that that was D-Mark and not Euro
20 MHO:   ich hatte ausgeführt dass ich ihnen nicht GLAUbe.
          I had laid out that I do not believe you
```

```
21       °h und ich da steht jetzt erst mal aussage gegen AU[Ssage,  ]
         and I now for the moment it's one person's word against another's
22 HGE:                                                  [na GUT ab]er-
                                                           fair enough but
23       aber des GEHT nicht;
         but that's not okay
24       (.) nich wahr;=des ham wer ja nun erÖRtert-
         right we have already discussed that
```

As in Excerpt 7.1, Volker Kefer begins with a challenging question, asking about the origin of the value of 4.2 billion euro. After Holzhey admits that he took the figure from the BAST document (lines 6), Kefer claims that he had rectified the value (line 8). Holzhey confirms this (line 9) and starts to give an account (line 11) that is abandoned due to Kefer's interruption. Kefer uses the change-of-state token "aHA" ('I see', line 12), which typically indexes a receipt of new information (cf. Imo 2009). In this case, Kefer's smile (Figure 7.1) indicates that he had already expected the answer and has discovered Holzhey's strategy.

Still smiling and again in overlap with Holzhey (line 13), Kefer exposes the strategy that he believes Holzhey is applying: "des heißt also mit falschen zAhlen wern falsche arguMENte aufgebaut" ('so that means with false numbers false arguments are being constructed', line 14). As in Excerpt 7.1, Kefer indicates that (parts of) the prior action ('using [false] numbers') is used as a means to an end ('constructing [false] arguments'). Kefer's ascription is formulated in the passive voice, avoiding a personal attack on the opponent. Yet, the connectors *das heißt* and *also* indicate a logical conclusion (cf. Deppermann & Helmer 2013; Helmer & Zinken 2019) that Kefer is drawing on the basis of his opponent's claims and premises (false values) and on the presupposition that his own estimates are correct. It works similar to an *if-then*-construction: Kefer's accusation about the incorrectness of Holzhey's arguments operates as an *apodosis* to the *protasis* (that the BAST-value is wrong and the value Kefer has declared is correct), implying that using the corrected value would have been adequate and expected (cf. Günthner 2000: 109).

The implication of course is not only that Holzhey's argument and calculated total sum are obsolete and that Kefer is right on a factual level. In

Figure 7.1 Kefer's smile at the beginning of "aHA" (line 12)

addition, the strategy ascription is a vehicle for an accusation: Kefer is discrediting his opponent as morally questionable (see Andone 2013), since he is suspected of using the wrong value intentionally for his own argument and against his better knowledge (see Stivers, Mondada & Steensig 2011).

Holzhey orients to this moral level when he defends himself and stresses his consequent transparency about his calculations (lines 17–18). When Kefer repeats that he had already laid out that the BAST-value is based on a typo (line 19), this brings Holzhey to openly state that he doesn't believe Kefer, implying that Kefer is lying, which is a strong accusation in service of discrediting an opponent (see Deppermann [1997] 2005: 128–41; Luginbühl 1999: 205–17). There is evidence for this interpretation in Heiner Geißler's conduct: Heiner Geißler intervenes and cuts off the discussion (lines 22–4). In the later course of interaction (not shown), the mediator further accuses Holzhey and the other opponents of acting within the range of speculation and downgrades the relevance of the whole discussion.

Considering this sanction, Kefer's move to expose Holzhey's (alleged) strategy works for him as a way to prevent Holzhey from continuing his argument about the unrealistic total sum the S21 supporters had communicated, which had been challenging and thereby face-threatening for the S21 supporters.

7.3.3 *Exposing the Telling of a Half-Truth*

The mediator treats accusations of using a rhetorical strategy or spelling out incorrect conclusions (see Excerpts 7.1 and 7.2) less as a personal attack than accusations of lies or concealment of facts (see end of Excerpt 7.2). Nevertheless, most frequently (see Table 7.1) speakers suggest that opponents intentionally tell only half-truths and thereby conceal uncomfortable facts that could weaken an argument. In order to deal with potential interventions of the mediator, these cases are designed implicitly rather than overtly, and the boundaries between propositional content and meta-pragmatic talk are much fuzzier compared to instances when speakers expose rhetorical strategies or wrong conclusions. This is illustrated by the following exchange of arguments in another mediation session. Excerpt 7.3 shows a quite implicit strategy ascription, Excerpt 7.4 a more overt one.

During one session, the feasibility of shorter passenger transfer times (one goal of the S21 project) is discussed. The S21 supporters had presented a movie clip showing a platform of the station in Bad Cannstatt (an outer district of Stuttgart), where only a few passengers are present, so that a train leaves without delay. Later, the opponents of S21 had presented a short movie clip showing another platform in the same station during rush hour, so that it is overcrowded with passengers, who need more than five minutes to get off or on the waiting train. The S21 opponent Boris Palmer had suggested that the first movie clip presented by German Railways had been shown to prove that trains in a through

station can leave quicker than in the current terminus station (due to technical and staff reasons). He believes that German Railways wants to use this to build an argument for reconstructing Stuttgart main station as a through station for the sake of shorter transfer times. Palmer had claimed that for a correct estimation of the transfer time, it would be necessary to consider commuter traffic with a high occupancy of trains. Tanja Gönner, the then-minister for environment of the federal state of Baden-Württemberg, and a supporter of S21, reacts to Palmer's assumption and his claim. In her reaction, she implicitly indicates that Palmer is hiding the fact that the supporters actually recorded the video during a time span that qualifies as rush hour.

Excerpt 7.3 FOLK_E_00068_SE_01_T_02_c237
(TGO = Tanja Gönner
[minister for environment, Baden-Württemberg, member of the Christian Democratic Union party, supporter of S21])

```
01 TGO:    °h lieber herr PALmer;
           dear Mr. Palmer
02 TGO:    (.) SIEBzehn uhr dreißig bad CANNstatt war des was wir
           vorgeführt haben-
             five thirty pm Bad Canstatt was what we presented
03 TGO: => °h ich finde es erstaunlich dass bei ihnen siebzehn uhr dreißig
           seit neustem (.) !KEIN! °h äh (.) rushhour mehr isch;=
           I find it astonishing that for you five thirty pm is as of most
           recently no longer rush hour
04 TGO:    =weil im übrigen genau zu diesen zeiten °h auch die frage
           des äh (.) beRUFSverkehrs isch;=
           because by the way these are the exact times for which the
           question about commuter traffic comes up
```

After clarifying that the movie clip of the S21 supporters had been recorded at 5:30pm (line 2), Gönner insinuates that Palmer has just recently decided that the time is not classifiable as rush hour. Using irony, she implies her belief that Palmer must know that 5:30 pm qualifies as 'rush hour'. She insinuates that Palmer is intentionally keeping the time of day secret when he accuses the supporters of using an unsuitable movie clip. Claiming "ich finde es erstaunlich" ('I find it astonishing', line 3), she ironically marks this as counter to her own expectations and hints at Palmer's incredulity. With "seit neustem" ('as of most recently', line 3) she alludes to the fact that Palmer's argument is contradictory to common sense and prior opinions – the S21 supporters had already considered rush hour as an important factor. Clearly, her goal in this extract is not (only) to clarify the time of the video-recording on a factual level, but to show that and why Palmer's claim is (morally) questionable and not a valid argument for the discussion. However, by avoiding an explicit and personal accusation, she leaves the audience to decide whether Palmer's

position exhibits incompetence (not considering 5:30 pm as rush hour) or reveals a strategy of serving unavowed goals (e.g., concealing inconvenient truths). In other comparable extracts, too, speakers use expressions like ‘all of a sudden’ or ‘recently’ to suggest that a change or inconsistency in an opponent’s conduct points to hidden dishonest motives. Sometimes they explicitly contrast two incompatible utterances and indicate moral double standards (‘when you talk about your side, you say X, but when you talk about the other side, you say Y’).

After a short discussion with the mediator, Palmer is allowed to respond to Gönner’s accusation. He in turn exposes Gönner’s strategy of telling a half-truth and concealing the whole:

Excerpt 7.4 FOLK_E_00068_SE_01_T_02_c342ff.
(BPA - Boris Palmer
[mayor of Tübingen, member of Die Grünen, opponent of S21])

01 **BPA: sie haben züge (.) gewählt die schwach AUSgelastet sind;**
you have chosen trains that are sparsely frequented
02 **wir nehmen einen vOll ausgelasteten beRUFSverkehr?**
we take commuter traffic operating at full capacity
03 **=> °h statt zuzugeben dass es so IS sagt frau gönner,**
instead of admitting that it is so Ms. Gönner says
04 **(0.22)**
05 **wir haben AUCH einen zug im berufsverkehr genommen.**
we took a train in commuter traffic too
06 **(0.28)**
07 **siebzehn uhr DREIßig;=**
five thirty pm
08 **=stimmt.**
that is true
09 **=> °hh aber ich finde sie sollten dann so EHRlich sein zu sagen,=**
but I think then you should be so honest to say
10 **=dass sie einen zug richtung stuttgart HAUPTbahnhof genommen haben,=**
that you took a train towards Stuttgart main station
11 **=und dass des die SCHWACHlast richtung ist;**
and that that is the less frequented direction
12 **°h es fahren eben abends um sechs relativ wenig leute nach stuttgart REIN?**
there are just relatively few people going to Stuttgart in the evening
13 **die meisten fahren RAUS.**
most of them leave (the city)
14 **so isch des.**
that’s the way it is
15 **(0.27)**
16 **in STUTTgart.**
in Stuttgart

17 => °h un wenn sie so (.) nEtt wären uns nicht mit solchen NEbelkerzen aufzuhalten,=
and if you would be so kind not to distract us with such red herrings

18 => =sondern zuzugeben dass sie_n zug genommen ham wo wenig LEUte ein und aussteigen,=
but admit that you took a train on which few people get on and off

19 =kommen wir bei diesen schlichtungsgesprächen besser voRAN.
we ('d) make better progress in these mediation sessions

Palmer repeats the prior claim he wanted to make with his movie clip (lines 1–2). The argument that is spelled out here, is the following. The time of the opponents' recording (5:30 pm) may indeed qualify as rush hour (lines 5–8). Yet the train recorded by the supporters was not leaving Stuttgart, but going into the city, so that the track showed only a few commuters (because the typical commuters, who work in the city and live outside it, are on another track; lines 9–14).

During his argument, Palmer indicates that Gönner is using a strategy ('deliberately not telling the whole truth') as a means to an ends ('distracting the mediation process and potentially deceiving the public'). Exposing this strategy again is used as a vehicle for accusations in order to discredit Gönner and question her credibility. Palmer alludes to this four times (lines 3, 9, 17, 18). He accuses her of not admitting that the supporters – in contrast to the opponents of the project – deliberately recorded a sparsely frequented train (lines 1–3 and line 18). With "statt zuzugeben" ('instead of admitting', line 3) and "sondern zuzugeben" ('but admit', line 18) he overtly exposes the strategic (and thus intentional) concealment of significant details that might be compromising for German Railways and the supporters of S21. By exposing that Gönner is acting strategically, Palmer discredits her motives (cf. Deppermann [1997] 2005: 128) and points to her moral responsibility (Robinson 2016).

After confirming the correct time (5:30 pm) he uses a deontic suggestion to allude to Gönner's strategic untruthfulness: "aber ich finde sie sollten dann so EHRlich sein zu sagen," ('but I think then you should be so honest to say', line 9). His turn operates on a logical level, since *dann* ('then') pretends to be an *apodosis* of a conditional, drawing a conclusion from prior utterances. The *protasis* would be the fact that Gönner claims to have shown a train during commuter traffic (basically, 'if you claim to show a train during rush hour, you should at least admit that it's the wrong direction'; see also Deppermann & Helmer 2013: 23). The deontic suggestion includes the modal verb *sollten* ('should'; see Couper-Kuhlen 2014) in *irrealis* (and not with past perfect: *hätten tun/sein sollen*, 'should have done/been'). *Sollten* is ambiguous as a deontic expression – on the one hand it is used to refer to a past action, but on the other hand it can also recommend a future action (here, to tell the whole truth subsequently). Palmer, however, reveals the truth himself (lines 10–14) so that Gönner has no option but to account for her action in the first place.

Continuing his talk, Palmer formulates another deontic suggestion that alludes to Gönner's strategy (as a means) and her intention (as an end): "wenn sie so (.) nEtt wären uns nicht mit solchen NEbelkerzen aufzuhalten" ('if you would be so kind not to detain us with such red herrings', line 17); "kommen wir bei diesen schlichtungsgesprächen besser voRAN" ('we['d] make better progress in these mediation sessions', line 19). He accuses her of at least potentially inhibiting the progress of the mediation itself. The accusation of using distractions is another variety of accusing opponents of being untruthful (see Luginbühl 1999: 210). Palmer questions Gönner's willingness to cooperate or to come to an agreement at all, which would undermine the fundamental basis of the mediation (the 'willingness to reach agreement', cf. Nothdurft & Spranz-Fogasy 2005). He strives to prove that Gönner's handling and presentation of reality is fundamentally biased and that she is acting strategically in order to strengthen her position instead of acting cooperatively for the sake of the mediation.

The exposure of Gönner's strategy has a positive effect for Palmer which can be seen in the subsequent interaction:

Excerpt 7.5 FOLK_E_00068_SE_01_T_02_c350
(HGE = Heiner Geißler
[chair, mediator])

01 **HGE: °h herr PALmer-**
Mr. Palmer
02 **°h äh die nebelkerzen lass_ich ZU?**
uh I tolerate the red herrings
03 **°h ähm aber (.) wenn sie sagen- sie SOLLten so ehrlich sein,**
but when you say you should be so honest
04 **°h des FINde ich,**
I find that
05 **äh des is halt so ne sache die °h äh an die grenze DESsen geht-**
that is just a thing that pushes the envelope of
06 **=> (.) °h äh (.) obwohl er in der SAche, (.)**
however factually
07 **=> hat er da RECHT frau gö (.) frau gönner;=nicht?**
he is right Ms. Gönner isn't he
08 **=> °h sie ham also (.) die falsche ZUGrichtung (.) öh gema-**
so you (chose) the wrong direction of the train

The mediator Geißler sanctions Palmer for committing a personal attack on Gönner's credibility by accusing her of being dishonest (lines 3–5). This intervention demonstrates again that exposing untruthfulness and personal attacks are riskier than other strategy ascriptions and impersonal formulations or use of the passive voice (cf. Excerpts 7.1 and 7.2). Yet, the mediator concedes ("obwohl", 'however/although', line 6) that at least factually Palmer has a point and that the S21 supporters used a train going in the wrong direction. About a minute later when he tries to close the topic (not shown here), he explicitly refers to the potential strategy of telling only half-truths, recommending that all participants deliver complete information.

In sum, ascribing the strategy of untruthfulness to someone is a strong personal attack (see Luginbühl 1999: 205), because it serves to imply that the speaker is violating basic rules of communication. This in turn may have consequences for the speaker to whom it is ascribed (cf. Deppermann [1997] 2005: 122). Locally, it may lead to a decrease in the opponent's speaking rights (through a cutting-off of the ongoing argument); globally, it may change how strictly the mediator treats similar violations, and it may even result in a decrease in the credibility of the opponent's future arguments. As a second function, Palmer implicitly claims the high moral value of honesty for himself (Luginbühl 1999: 207). Revealing Gönner's strategy is thus itself an accusation that serves to strengthen his own position.

7.4 Conclusion

This chapter has analyzed when and how speakers in a public mediation session employ strategy ascriptions as an overt form of action ascriptions and what short- and long-term interactive consequences strategy ascriptions have. Furthermore, I have shown that strategy ascription constitutes an action itself – in public debate, mainly an accusation.

Speakers who employ a strategy ascription do not only or primarily orient to the prior turn's primary action (such as a question, a request, an offer, etc.). They also orient to an "off-record action" (Levinson 2013: 107) such as a challenge, avoidance of an answer, etc. that is constituted by the prior turn. Exposing these off-record actions in second position, speakers make publicly available "why [opponents do] that now" (Schegloff & Sacks 1973: 299). Spelling out how opponents employ an action as a means to an underlying end serves their position and status and damages that of the others.

During debates, speakers typically employ overt strategy ascriptions in response to prior turns that threaten the face of currently arguing participants or challenge their party's position. Exposing strategies of their opponents, such as the use of rhetorical strategies, false premises, or untruthfulness, is used as a vehicle for accusations.

Speakers frequently accuse their opponents of asking too many questions at once so that they do not get a fair chance to answer them (see Excerpt 7.1). Sometimes speakers accuse opponents of still owing them a (straight) answer and concealing this with rhetorical strategies. Speakers expose the strategic use of false premises in order to accuse their opponents of using incorrect conclusions (see Excerpt 7.2). The premises are directly or indirectly (e.g., by requesting proof) challenged or marked as incorrect. The accused opponents typically are not able to react properly to the accusation, e.g., due to lack of time or because proof would require actions beyond the ongoing debate. Exposing opponents as telling only half-truths (as shown in Excerpts 7.3 and 7.4) is one of the stronger and riskier strategy ascriptions. Speakers using rhetorical strategies might also be evaluated as skilled and eloquent orators (see, e.g., Atkinson 1984), and the use of false premises may be explained due to non-intentional aspects like ignorance or wrong calculations so that judging stays on the level of propositional (in)correctness. In contrast, exposing the strategy of telling only half-truths often goes hand in hand with knowledge ascriptions that are strong vehicles for accusations (see Reineke 2016: 141–59), claiming that concealing knowledge violates social norms and is a morally accountable choice (Stivers, Mondada & Steensig 2011: 17, 19). All overt strategy ascriptions serve to strengthen the speaker's own position and weaken that of others.

Turn design across all types of strategy ascriptions mostly exhibits the passive voice and other impersonal formulations, for instance using metonymies ('German Railways' for the specific person[s] in charge). When more direct attacks that can be attributed to one specific person are employed, the mediator typically intervenes with a rebuke. Yet, when strategy ascriptions are designed within the normative rules of a critical discussion, they are quite effective. The chair locally concedes a point to the speaker (see Excerpts 7.1, 7.2, and 7.5), globally rebukes the specific usage of the strategy, or at least the accusation of using a strategy is articulated and may have an effect on the audience, especially if the opponents do not have the opportunity to react to it properly. Strategy ascriptions to local actions are consequently controlled globally for the sake of discrediting opponents and strengthening the speaker's own position.

Acknowledgments

I would like to thank Sven Bloching for his valuable assistance with screening, systematizing, and preparing the data, and the two reviewers for their helpful comments on this chapter.

REFERENCES

Andone, C. (2013). *Argumentation in Political Interviews: Analyzing and Evaluating Responses to Accusations of Inconsistency*. Amsterdam: John Benjamins.

Atkinson, J. M. (1984). *Our Masters' Voices: The Language and Body Language of Politics*. London: Methuen.

Brown, P. & Levinson, S. C. (1987). *Politeness: Some Universals in Language Usage*. Cambridge: Cambridge University Press.

Burkhardt, A. (2003). *Das Parlament und seine Sprache: Studien zu Theorie und Geschichte parlamentarischer Kommunikation*. Tübingen: Niemeyer.

Clayman, S. E. (1992). Footing in the achievement of neutrality: The case of news-interview discourse. In P. Drew & J. Heritage, eds., *Talk at Work: Interaction in Institutional Settings*. Cambridge: Cambridge University Press, pp. 163–98.

(2013). Conversation analysis in the news interview. In J. Sidnell & T. Stivers, eds., *Handbook of Conversation Analysis*. Chichester: Wiley-Blackwell, pp. 630–56.

Clark, H. & Schaefer, E. (1992). Dealing with overhearers. In H. Clark, ed., *Arenas of Language Use*. Chicago, IL: University of Chicago Press, pp. 248–73.

Couper-Kuhlen, E. (2014). What does grammar tell us about action? *Pragmatics*, 24(3), 623–47.

Culpeper, J. (2016). Impoliteness strategies. In A. Capone & J. L. Mey, eds., *Interdisciplinary Studies in Pragmatics, Culture and Society*. Cham: Springer, pp. 421–45.

Deppermann, A. [1997] (2005). *Glaubwürdigkeit im Konflikt*. Radolfzell: Verlag für Gesprächsforschung.

(2012). How does "cognition" matter to the analysis of talk-in-interaction? *Language Sciences*, 34(6), 746–67.

(2014). Handlungsverstehen und Intentionszuschreibung in der Interaktion I: Intentionsbekundungen mit *wollen*. In P. Bergmann, K. Birkner, P. Gilles, H. Spiekermann & T. Streck, eds., *Sprache im Gebrauch: Räumlich, zeitlich, interaktional. Festschrift für Peter Auer*. Heidelberg: Winter, pp. 309–26.

(2015). Gleiche Wörter – inkommensurable Bedeutungen: Zur interaktiven Entstehung von Undurchschaubarkeit in politischen Diskussionen am Beispiel von "Ökologie" in den Schlichtungsgesprächen zum Bahnprojekt "Stuttgart 21." In U. Tuomarla, J. Härmä, L. Tiittula et al., eds., *Miscommunication and Verbal Violence: Du malentendu à la violence verbale: Misskommunikation und verbale Gewalt*. Helsinki: Société Néophilologique, pp. 25–41.

Deppermann, A. & Helmer, H. (2013). Zur Grammatik des Verstehens im Gespräch: Inferenzen anzeigen und Handlungskonsequenzen ziehen mit *also* und *dann*. *Zeitschrift für Sprachwissenschaft*, 32(1), 1–40.

Edwards, D. (2008). Intentionality and mens rea in police interrogations: The production of actions as crimes. *Intercultural Pragmatics*, 5(2), 177–99.

Gohl, C. & Günther, S. (1999). Grammatikalisierung von *weil* als Diskursmarker in der gesprochenen Sprache. *Zeitschrift für Sprachwissenschaft*, 18(1), 39–75.

Greatbatch, D. (1992). On the management of disagreement between news interviewees. In P. Drew & J. Heritage, eds., *Talk at Work: Interaction in Institutional Settings*. Cambridge: Cambridge University Press, pp. 268–301.

Günthner, S. (2000). *Vorwurfsaktivitäten in der Alltagsinteraktion*. Tübingen: Niemeyer.

Haugh, M. (2008). The place of intention in the interactional achievement of implicature. In I. Kecskes & J. Mey, eds., *Intention, Common Ground and the Egocentric Speaker-Hearer*. Berlin: de Gruyter, pp. 45–85.

Helmer, H. & Zinken, J. (2019). *Das heißt* ("that means") for formulations and *du meinst* ("you mean") for repair? Interpretations of prior speakers' turns in German. *Research on Language and Social Interaction*, 52(2), 159–76.

Heritage, J. (1990/1991). Intention, meaning and strategy: Observations on constraints on interaction analysis. *Research on Language and Social Interaction*, 24(1–4), 311–32.

Heritage, J. & Raymond, G. (2005). The terms of agreement: Indexing epistemic authority and subordination in talk-in-interaction. *Social Psychology Quarterly*, 68, 15–38.

Hopper, R. (2005). A cognitive agnostic in conversation analysis: When do strategies affect spoken interaction? In H. te Molder & Jonathan Potter, eds., *Conversation and Cognition*. Cambridge: Cambridge University Press, pp. 134–58.

Hutchby, I. (1997). Building alignments in public debate: A case study from british TV. *Text*, 17, 161–79.

(2006). *Media Talk: Conversation Analysis and the Study of Broadcasting*. Maidenhead: Open University Press.

Imo, W. (2009). Konstruktion oder Funktion? Erkenntnisprozessmarker (change-of-state-token) im Deutschen. In S. Günther & J. Bücker, eds., *Grammatik im Gespräch*. Berlin: de Gruyter, pp. 57–86.

Kampf, Z. (2013). Mediated performatives. In J.-O. Östman & J. Verschueren, eds., *Handbook of Pragmatics Online, Vol. 17*. Amsterdam: John Benjamins, pp. 1–24.

Komter, M. (2013). Conversation analysis in the courtroom. In J. Sidnell & T. Stivers, eds., *Handbook of Conversation Analysis*. Chichester: Wiley- Blackwell, pp. 612–29.

Leech, G. N. (1983). *Principles of Pragmatics*, London: Longman.

Levinson, S. (2013). Action formation and ascription. In J. Sidnell & T. Stivers, eds., *Handbook of Conversation Analysis*. Chichester: Wiley-Blackwell, pp. 103–30.

Luginbühl, M. (1999). *Gewalt im Gespräch. Verbale Gewalt in politischen Fernsehdiskussionen am Beispiel der "Arena"*. Bern: Peter Lang.

Nothdurft, W. (1997). *Konfliktstoff. Gesprächsanalyse der Konfliktbearbeitung in Schlichtungsgesprächen*. Berlin: de Gruyter.

Nothdurft, W. & Spranz-Fogasy, T. (2005). Gesprächsanalyse von Schlichtungs-Interaktion. Methodische Probleme und ihre Hintergründe. In D. Busch & H. Schröder, eds., *Perspektiven interkultureller Mediation. Bd. 2*. Frankfurt am Main: Peter Lang, pp. 341–62.

Potter, J. & Edwards, D. (2013). Conversation analysis and psychology. In J. Sidnell & T. Stivers, eds., *Handbook of Conversation Analysis*. Chichester: Wiley-Blackwell, pp. 701–25.

Reineke, S. (2016). *Wissenszuschreibungen in der Interaktion. Eine gesprächsanalytische Untersuchung impliziter und expliziter Formen der Zuschreibung von Wissen*. Heidelberg: Winter.

Robinson, J. D. (2016). Accountability in social interaction. In J. D. Robinson, ed., *Accountability in Social Interaction*. Oxford: Oxford University Press, pp. 1–44.

Sacks, H. (1972). An initial investigation of the usability of conversational data for doing sociology. In D. Sudnow, ed., *Studies in Social Interaction*. New York, NY: The Free Press, pp. 31–74.

(1992). *Lectures on Conversation*. 2 vols. Oxford: Wiley-Blackwell.

Sacks, H., Schegloff, E. A. & Jefferson, G. (1974). A simplest systematics for the organisation of turn-taking in conversation. *Language*, 50(4), 696–735.

Schegloff, E. A. (2007). *Sequence Organization in Interaction: A Primer in Conversation Analysis*. Cambridge: Cambridge University Press.

Schegloff, E.A. & Sacks, H. (1973). Opening up closings. *Semiotica*, 8(4), 289–327.

Selting, M., Auer, P., Barth-Weingarten, D. et al. (2009). Gesprächsanalytisches Transkriptionssystem 2 (GAT 2). *Gesprächsforschung*, 10, 353–402.

Stivers, T., Mondada, L. & Steensig, J. (2011). Knowledge, morality and affiliation in social interaction. In T. Stivers, L. Mondada & J. Steensig, eds., *The Morality of Knowledge in Conversation*. Cambridge: Cambridge University Press, pp. 3–24.

Walker, T., Drew, P. & Local, J. (2011). Responding indirectly. *Journal of Pragmatics*, 43(9), 2434–51.

8 Action Ascription and Deonticity in Everyday Advice-Giving Sequences

Elizabeth Couper-Kuhlen and Sandra A. Thompson

8.1 Introduction

Action ascription, according to Levinson (2013: 104), is "central to the CA enterprise," and yet "direct empirical investigations in CA are few and far between." This chapter explicitly addresses action ascription in everyday advice-giving sequences, with a focus on those sequences in which advice has not been solicited as such. It takes the perspective of a would-be next speaker, who must ascribe an action to the prior speaker in order to determine how to respond. That is, the recipient of a complaint or troubles-telling must decide whether or not it warrants advice. If advice is given, the complainer or troubles-teller must ascribe to the advice the kind of response it projects. In unsolicited advice-giving sequences, such decision-making can be relevant, for instance, for the would-be advice-giver, who, in choosing to give advice, makes a determination that an offer of 'help' is relevant, but also for the advice-recipient, who, in deciding whether to accept or resist the advice, makes a determination about the nature of the advice and the strength of the stance being taken by the advice-giver.

Advice-giving has been examined in institutional settings such as medical interaction (e.g., Heritage & Lindström 1998, 2012; Heritage & Sefi 1992; Kinnell & Maynard 1996; Pilnick 2001, 2003; Silverman 1997); student counseling and tutoring (e.g., Vehviläinen 2001; Waring 2005, 2007, 2012); help lines (e.g., Butler et al. 2010; Emmison et al. 2011; Hepburn & Potter 2011; Pudlinski 2002); and expert-layperson call-in radio programs (Hudson 1990; Hutchby 1995). In these settings, asymmetries between the interactants are institutionally given: the counselor/doctor/advisor generally has greater deontic status (Heritage 2012a, 2012b; Stevanovic & Peräkylä 2012) with respect to the future action than the layperson/patient/student.

There has been much less research on advice-giving in informal, everyday interactions, Jefferson and Lee (1981) being a notable exception. We return to their study below. Shaw and Hepburn (2013) and Shaw et al. (2015) explore advice-giving in mother–adult daughter interactions; in such interactions, though they are mundane everyday encounters, there is a generation-based asymmetry, with mothers typically treated as having the authority to advise their grown daughters, whereas in this chapter we consider everyday conversations in which there are no pre-established role asymmetries. In our data, the interactants are friends and siblings; no one interactant has *a priori* greater deontic status than the other based on social roles: who gives and who receives advice gets negotiated through deontic and epistemic stance displays that are implemented in talk (Heritage 2012a, 2012b; Stevanovic & Peräkylä 2012).

Our understanding of 'advice' in this study is narrower than that of, e.g., Heritage and Sefi (1992), who speak of advice-giving sequences where "the HV (= health visitor) describes, recommends, or otherwise forwards a preferred course of future action" (p. 368). For us, advice-giving actions are a type of 'Suggestion' (Couper-Kuhlen 2014), involving advocating, forwarding, or naming a future action for the interlocutor to carry out that will be of primary benefit to the interlocutor her- or himself (see also Clayman & Heritage 2014). In cases where advice has not been explicitly solicited, advice-giving actions are typically produced in the context of troubles talk or complaining by an interlocutor (see also Jefferson & Lee 1981). In these situations the advice is offered as a possible solution to what is treated as the interlocutor's problem. The structure of the advice-giving sequences we are looking at, in its minimal form, then, is as follows:

A: Complaint or troubles-telling turn or turns	(Position 1)
B: Advice-giving turn	(Position 2)
A: Response to advice-giving turn	(Position 3)

That is, the data lead us to treating advice-giving as a responsive rather than an initiating action.[1] This perspective allows us to distinguish advice-giving from other types of Suggestion, where putatively beneficial proposals for what the other person should do are typically volunteered as first, or initiating, actions. We speak of advice-giving being located in second 'position' rather than being a second 'pair-part' because the problem that it is presented as resolving may not be succinctly formulated in a single prior turn. Indeed, as Jefferson's (1988) work on troubles-telling has shown, in advice-giving sequences, we are dealing with a 'big package' whose component parts often extend over more than one turn at talk. The following extract from a telephone

[1] This is not to deny that complaints or troubles-telling turns, represented here as first-position actions, may themselves be responsive to prior actions by other.

conversation between two sisters, Lottie and Emma, illustrates a slightly expanded version of such a sequence:

Excerpt 8.1 "Stay down-1" (Nb 009-4) (LOT = Lottie, EMM = Emma)
(Lottie lives in Newport Beach south of Los Angeles, while her sister Emma lives in an urban conglomeration to the north. Emma owns a vacation rental at Newport Beach, to which she comes down regularly for rest and recreation. This conversation takes place when both sisters are at Newport Beach.)

```
05 LOT:    it's beautiful: day i[ bet] you've had a lotta smo::g=
06 EMM:                        [yah-]
07 LOT:    =up there haven't you.
08 EMM:     oh::: lo:ttie,hh (.) you don't kno::w,         Incipient complaint
09 LOT:    i kno[:w.
10 EMM:         [go:::d it['s been  ]                       Incipient complaint
11 LOT: ->                 [↑why don't] you stay dow::n.    Advice-giving turn
12 EMM:     .hh (0.2) oh::: ↓*I know it. i: should st*ay    Response to advice
13         ↓d*o:wn. hhhhhhh
14         (.)
15 LOT:     je:sus i: wu< ↓with a:ll that s:mo:g u[p there]  Account for advice
16 EMM:                                          [mye:a:] :h,
17 EMM:    *i ↓r*eally should ↓st*ay d*own.↓        Reiterated response to advice
18         let's see this is the end of the (0.8)
19         .t (0.4) w*e:ll maybe,h i'd say ne:xt week=
20         <i: haven't got too many clothes
```

In lines 8 and 10 Emma begins to complain about the smog she is encountering where she lives: *oh::: lo:ttie .hh (.) you don't kno::w. . .go:::d it's been*. Before she can proceed any further, Lottie offers a solution for Emma's problem: ↑*why don't you stay dow::n* (line 11), proposing that if she stays at the beach she can avoid the city smog. Note that Lottie did not have to offer advice at this point: she could easily have joined in the complaining sequence initiated by Emma by saying something like 'I know. I've been reading about it in the papers – it must be awful.' However, in the event, Lottie forgoes this option and instead makes a recommendation that she proposes would alleviate Emma's problem.

We know that Lottie's turn in line 11 is being taken as offering advice because of the way Emma responds: in a creaky voice (indicated by the asterisks), she admits to knowing that this is what she should do: *oh::: i know it. i: should stay dow:n* (line 12).[2] When Lottie provides an account for her recommendation*: je:sus i: wu< with a:ll that s:mog up there* (line 15), Emma reiterates that she herself should stay down (line 17). However, from the way

[2] Emma's creaky voice may be displaying a kind of groaning admission that this is what she should do, but that circumstances make it difficult for her to do so.

she continues this turn, we can surmise that she probably will not act on Lottie's advice, at least not over the weekend in question, because among other things, she claims not to have enough clothes with her (lines 17–19).

Our collection consists of seventy cases of such everyday advice-giving sequences from video and audio recordings of British and American face-to-face and telephone conversations among friends and family members. We will focus on action ascription at two different positions in these sequences. First, at position 2, the recipient of a troubles-telling or complaint must decide whether the prior turn makes the provision of 'help' or assistance relevant. This allows the troubles recipient to decide whether to offer advice in next turn or not.[3] Second, at position 3, the recipient of a piece of advice must decide how exactly it was meant: as a binding prescription or injunction, or as a mild suggestion for a possible way forward? This is relevant for the advice-recipient in deciding how to deal with the advice: whether to accept or reject/resist it, or to join the other in brainstorming about how to remedy the situation. Our data suggest that for action ascription at both second and third positions, the design ('composition') and the sequential location ('position')[4] of the prior turn are crucial factors. We begin by examining position 2, where the recipient of a troubles-telling or complaint must decide what to do next, that is, whether to offer advice or not.

8.2 Second Position: To Advise or Not to Advise

Not every troubles-telling or complaint action is responded to with advice. As Jefferson and Lee (1981) point out, in a troubles-telling episode, with its mutually established roles of troubles-teller and troubles recipient, moving too abruptly into suggesting a remedy for a 'problem' can transform the situation into something akin to a service encounter, where the interlocutor becomes a 'service-seeker' and the speaker a 'service-supplier' (p. 410). Troubles tellers may, initially at least, be expecting emotional reciprocity, that is, a display of empathy from the other, rather than a practical solution for how to resolve their 'problem'. In Excerpt 8.2 we see an occasion, another telephone call between Emma and Lottie one week after that in Excerpt 8.1, on which Emma again complains to Lottie, this time about the heat in the urban conglomeration where she lives. But on this occasion Lottie, rather than

[3] Although our collection consists primarily of sequences in which advice is ultimately given, for the purpose of comparison we have included several instances of troubles-telling and complaining where advice-giving is absent, e.g., Excerpt 8.2.

[4] On 'composition' and 'position' see Schegloff (1993: 121).

immediately proposing that she stay down at the beach, responds with displays of empathy:

Excerpt 8.2 "Heat" (Nb 011-5) (EMM = Emma, LOT = Lottie)

EMM: [WELL] we played go:lf? tuesday at (.) and we didn't tee o:ff
til la:te 'cause they had a t:ournament, a:nd it was so↑: smo:ggy
(0.3) and it wz ↑SO: HOT.h .hhh and i: uh: i said to the girls
i said god i can hardly stand to finish playing because
i was so red in the face and my eye:s were burning
it was ↑jus:t THICK (.) you know you c[ould taste it.] .hh] .hh
LOT: -> [°oh:::::↓ *o]h:°]
EMM: so i had to come home wash my hair and go with bud to something
and i said oh my god i got home my face was so: red i thought
i was gonna die:.
(0.3)
EMM: so[u it's terr:]ible up
LOT: -> [°O h : : : °]
(.)
EMM: ↑t's TERR:IBLE up .hhh ↑ we lie:- (0.4) we absolutely lie:
star:k naked on the be:d,
(0.2)
EMM: .hh with ↑MAYbe a sheet o:n about two o'↓clock.
(0.6)
LOT: ->it's that ho:t h[u : h ?]
EMM: [tha:t's] that ho:t.
(0.4)
EMM: be[lieve it or] no:t and] and we got the air conditioning=
LOT: -> [°o h_: : :] : : : .°]
EMM: =go:ing .hhhh ↑ we'll see HOW things come out lottie
.hh[hh

At numerous points in Emma's telling, there are opportunities for Lottie to respond (marked with arrows in the transcript). At each of these moments Lottie could offer the kind of advice she does in Excerpt 8.1 (e.g., *Why don't you stay down?)*, which – if Emma were to follow it – would allow her to escape the heat in the city. But Lottie opts instead for lengthened and prosodically marked *oh*s and a candidate understanding *it's that hot huh?* These are empathic displays that show Lottie's appreciation of Emma's situation without claiming to have experienced it herself (Heritage 2011). Each one provides Emma with a warrant for continuing her troubles-telling by adding another complainable detail. This contrasts sharply with Excerpt 8.1, where Lottie's advice-giving (line 11) puts an abrupt end to Emma's complaining.

Our point in comparing these two possible sequential trajectories is to draw attention to the decision-making that is observable at position 2, when a recipient is called upon to respond to an interlocutor's troubles-implicative turn or complaint. In Excerpt 8.2 Lottie repeatedly orients to Emma's complaints as having made empathy relevant next, thereby encouraging Emma to expand the telling, while in Excerpt 8.1 Lottie orients to Emma's incipient complaining as an opening for her to provide 'help'. By proposing a solution to what she treats as Emma's 'problem', Lottie in Excerpt 8.1 reflexively transforms Emma's prior turn into a recruitment (Kendrick & Drew 2016; Floyd et al., eds. 2020), which she can now accommodate by proposing a remedy.[5] This leads to a curtailment of the complaining, because, as we shall see below, the advice-giving raises issues of its own about how to deal with what has been proposed.[6]

Together, then, Excerpt 8.1 and 8.2 illustrate the choice that recipients have in responding in second position to a troubles-telling or complaint. While the complaint in Excerpt 8.1 is responded to with advice, the complaints in Excerpt 8.2 receive empathic displays. What happens in second position thus reveals how the prior turn was interpreted. If advice-giving takes place, this shows that the recipient of the complaint treats what the prior speaker has said as having made an offer of help relevant. We note that in our data, there is no evidence that the advice-giver presumes that the advice was sought; indeed it is sometimes not even welcome, as we shall see (e.g., Excerpts 8.5, 8.11, 8.12, and 8.14). If empathic displays are made instead, this reveals that the action ascribed to the prior speaker was seeking affiliation in a troublesome situation.[7]

8.3 Third Position: How to Deal with Advice

If, in the event, advice *is* delivered in second position, as in Excerpt 8.1 above, the advice-giving action can be implemented in different ways, which in turn influences how the advice is dealt with in the third-position next turn.

There is a complex interplay of factors that enter into what happens in third position. Normatively speaking, advisees are expected to positively evaluate the recommendation they have been given. This is what we see Karen doing in the story that her former schoolmate Clacia tells about her:

[5] Among the various methods of recruitment identified by Kendrick and Drew (2016) are "reports of needs, difficulties or troubles", which "create an opportunity for the other to volunteer assistance" (p. 6).

[6] On complaining sequences, see Couper-Kuhlen (2012), Drew (1998), Heinemann and Traverso (2009), and Selting (2012).

[7] In our discussion of Excerpt 8.2, we do not wish to imply that Lottie is wholly oblivious to the fact that there is a remedy for Emma's 'problem'. In fact, she does subsequently go on to deliver a piece of advice, *well:- (.) you ought to stay down ↓and::: get a little ...* But she breaks off her turn when Emma comes in in overlap with *yeah I didn't even bring a dre:ss.*

Excerpt 8.3 "Pack it away" (Clacia, 9:30) (CLA = Clacia)

(Clacia is telling her friend Diane a story about a former schoolmate named Karen, who has recently married and moved close by. Clacia reports that she decided to call her up one day "just for the hell of it.")

```
01 CLA:     i called her and she said, oh we got all this horrible
02          steuben glass.  so i-stop me if i told you this.
03          (0.5)
04 CLA:     she said we got all this horrible steuben glass and
05          i just can't stand it as wedding gifts.and i just
06          don't know what to do with it i just::  ˙hh and i
07       -> said why don't you pack it awa:y, and save it to give
08       -> away to other people for wedding gifts and she said
09       => hey that's a great idea.
10          (0.4)
11 CLA:     but i saw her once for lunch (and that was:,)
```

In Clacia's story, her advice to Karen, who is complaining about having received too much 'horrible' Steuben glass as wedding gifts (lines 4–6), is that Karen should stash it away and give it to others later on the occasion of their own weddings (lines 7–8). Karen's reported response is *hey that's a great idea* (line 9), implying that this is what she will do.

Indeed, having been given a piece of advice, recipients are normatively expected to indicate an intention to take it up in the future, or to provide an account for not doing so. Commitment to following the advice is, for instance, what happens at the end of the following advice-giving sequence:

Excerpt 8.4 "Leave off the meat" (Nb 014-10) (EMM = Emma, LOT = Lottie)

(Emma has been complaining to Lottie about her psoriasis and is now telling her about a report that eating turkey will cure it.)

```
01 EMM:     .hnff and this girl in the apartment came up the other day and
02          told me that (0.2) you know she read this?
03          (0.3)
04 EMM:     hh.hhhhh whe:re? a ↓doct↑or ↓cures ↑his ↓pa↑tients by eating
            turkey
05          (0.4)
06 LOT: ->  well now why don't you leave off the mea:t.=
((approx. 20 seconds later))
19 LOT: ->  i::'d uh leave o:ff the mea:t.
20 EMM: =>  °i think i ↑wi:ll.°  i haven't had a piece of mea:t since i
21          been down here.
```

In line 6 Lottie suggests that Emma should stop eating meat, by which she means 'red' meat, implying that Emma should just eat turkey. Once it has been established that Emma could also eat chicken (lines 7–18, not shown here), Lottie repeats her advice (line 19), whereupon Emma signals that this is what she intends to do: *I think I will* (line 20).

Alternatively, if recipients of advice do not wish to take up the advice, they are normatively expected to account for their lack of willingness to do so. Candidate accounts may include subjective judgments concerning the reasonableness or feasibility of the proposal and/or reports of objective states of affairs in the world that prevent them from carrying out the recommended action. Numerous instances of such accounts will be seen in the extracts discussed below.

Yet independent of personal proclivities and even of objective states of affairs, recipients have a choice as to whether to introduce these as reasons for not accepting the advice; sometimes they leave them unmentioned and declare an intention to follow up on the advice regardless. It is here that how a piece of advice is given, and specifically how strong the deontic stance taken by the advice-giver is, enters in. Stance, as we know, is conveyed, among other things, by linguistic means. We argue here that the linguistic format with which a piece of advice is given is one of the cues that advice-recipients use to ascribe a deontic stance to the advice-giving turn, which in turn is relevant for how they respond to the advice.

In the following we will first briefly review the five most frequent linguistic formats for giving advice in our everyday conversational data and then turn to an examination of how advice delivered with these formats is dealt with in next turn.

8.3.1 Linguistic Formats for Advising in English

The five most frequent formats for giving advice in our data collection are these,[8] in decreasing order of strength (see below):[9]

Do . . . !/Don't . . .!	(IMP) (*well wash them ou::t*)	[Imperative]
Why don't you . . .?	(WDY) (*why don't you stay dow::n*)	[Interrogative]
You should/ought to . . .	(S/O) (*you should make stencils*)	[Declarative]
I'd/I would/I wouldn't . . .	(I'D) (*I::'d leave o:ff the mea:t*)	[Declarative]
You can/could	(C/C) (*you can get him an album or something*)	[Declarative]

We note that these formats represent different grammatical clause types, as indicated in the square brackets. While this may seem at first glance to be

[8] The raw frequencies for these formats are as follows: IMP (25), WDY (19), S/O (7), I'D (14), C/C (5).

[9] These formats could be thought of as 'social action formats' (Fox 2007), as described in Chapter 1 of this volume.

merely a grammatical noticing, we shall see that it plays a significant role in action ascription in third position.

Each of the five formats displays a distinct deontic stance, that is, each format carries advice that advocates in one way or another an action that the speaker is claiming the interlocutor should carry out to the advisee's benefit.[10] Stevanovic and Peräkylä (2012) propose that such formats imply an 'obligation' for the recipient to do the action in question (p. 316); we suggest that these formats *recommend* the action named in the advice-implicative turn. However, as we will show, they do so with varying degrees of strength, or deontic authority.[11]

The deontically strongest advice-giving format is the use of a bald imperative (IMP). With such a format the advice-giver assumes a stance of high entitlement, i.e., unmitigated authority, to tell the other what to do, with no hint of doubt about this being the right course of action. Advice delivered with a bald imperative does not allow for there being any contingencies that might prevent its implementation: it expects full (immediate) compliance (Curl & Drew 2008; Craven & Potter 2010; Sorjonen et al. 2017). This is the form that Lottie uses in Excerpt 8.5 below to propose a solution for another of Emma's 'problems'.

Excerpt 8.5 "Wash them out" (Nb 028-5) (EMM = Emma, LOT = Lottie)
(The occasion for this call is a hefty argument that Emma has recently had with her husband Bud, which has led to his 'walking out' on her. Now Emma is discussing with Lottie her plans for hosting a Thanksgiving dinner in Newport Beach.)

```
EMM:     ... so i guess bud's coming down tomorrow ni:ght,
         (0.3)
LOT:     [oh:.]
EMM:     [.hhea] hh I: GUE:SS hi-s- but he'll be here thursday but i
         guess he has to go ba:ck friday to go to work.h
LOT:     ah hah,
         (0.3)
EMM:     [.t
LOT:     [will you stay di- oh well you[pro↓bably< ]
EMM:                                   [I'M GONNA  ] STAY .hh
         YOU KNOW I ONLY HA:VE one brassiere and pair of panties lottie,h
LOT: ->  well wash them ou:[:t.
EMM:                       [that's what i(h)'M DOING RI:GHT NOW
         i ↑just CA:ME in,
LOT:     oh:.
```

[10] As Shaw and Hepburn (2013: 348) put it, "Giving advice imposes and prescribes that an action *should* be done" (italics in the original).

[11] Similar issues are taken up by Stivers et al. (2018), who investigate some of the same formats for therapy recommendations in medical consultations, and by Shaw et al. (2015), who describe interrogatives and assessments for advice-giving in mother–daughter conversations.

```
        (0.2)
EMM:    .hh[hh
LOT:       [oh:.
```

Emma's problem is one we have encountered before. This time she wants to stay down at the beach but does not have enough fresh underwear to do so (line 11). Lottie responds immediately by offering a piece of advice: *well wash them out* (line 12). In choosing a bald imperative for her advice, Lottie takes a strong deontic stance: she implies that she knows exactly what Emma should do to resolve her problem and that there are no contingencies that might prevent Emma from implementing this solution.[12]

Somewhat less strong than a bald imperative format for giving advice is a *why don't you X?* format (WDY). This is the format we saw being used in Excerpt 8.1 above, where Lottie advises Emma on how to avoid the city smog: *why don't you stay dow::n* (line 11). With its negative interrogative + *why* form, WDY grammatically allows that there could be contingencies preventing implementation of the action being proposed, and if there are, through its grammatical format, it asks what they are. However, conventionally this format is understood to strongly recommend the action in question. In fact, it can even imply that the solution being recommended is so obvious or natural that there must be good reason *not* to embrace it (for further discussion, see also Thompson & Couper-Kuhlen, 2020).

In contrast to the imperative (IMP) and the interrogative (WDY) formats, the three other formats listed above are weaker ways of giving advice. All three are declarative clause types and thus are grammatically designed to do informing (Mori 2006; Thompson et al. 2015) or asserting (Vatanen 2018) at the same time as they forward an action proposed to be in the interlocutor's interest.

One of these formats involves the subject *you* together with the modal verb SHOULD or OUGHT (S/O). Here is an instantiation of the S/O format used to give advice in a face-to-face conversation between two sorority sisters:

Excerpt 8.6 "Your ring" [Sorority breakfast 2, p. 2] (LAU = Laurel, KEL = Kelly)

(Kelly and Laurel are having breakfast in the kitchen of their sorority house. About a minute earlier both women were rinsing their hands at the sink; Kelly is now standing at the table where Laurel is seated eating.)

```
LAU:    do you leave your ring out (.) on the sink?
KEL:    uhhuh.
        (2.4)
KEL:    ↓yeah. and i- (1.0) (did) it once before too?
```

[12] We return to the type of response that such a format for advice-giving may encounter in Section 8.3.2 below.

```
05           and i' ll be like-(0.2) mkay (0.8) like- take it off
06           wash your face and then (make sure) you' re gonna put it back
07           ↑on (and i' m like ah! oh yeah i' ll remember) (0.5) well i forgot.
08           (0.6)
09 LAU: ->  you should get (.) like (0.7) a little holder you know
10      ->  like a carrying thing?=
11 KEL:      =°yeah°. ↑usually i just- (0.3) i take it off like (0.6)
12           before i go and wash my face and stuff. but- (2.0) °°hhhh i
13           dunno°° (1.8) >i should just not take it off when i wash
14           my face.< its fine. like (   ) you know
```

In response to Kelly's story of having once taken off her ring to wash her face and forgotten to put it back on, Laurel gives Kelly a piece of unsolicited advice that would allow her to avoid the risk of forgetting her ring: she suggests, using the SHOULD/OUGHT format, that Kelly get a ring holder box that she could carry around with her (lines 9–10). As a declarative, this advice-giving S/O format makes an assertion that displays a knowing (K+) epistemic stance vis-à-vis the addressee (Heritage 2012a, 2012b). Through the subject *you* and the modal verb *should* or *ought*, it implies a recommendation for the recipient to act, but at the same time it can work as an assertion, making acknowledgment or agreement relevant in next turn. In the event, Kelly's °*yeah*° in line 11 acknowledges that she knows what Laurel is referring to; she then goes on to say that she usually takes off her ring before she goes to the sink to wash her face, implying that she has no need for a special holder.

The *I would X* or *I wouldn't X* format (I'D) for advice-giving is yet again weaker. This format, also declarative, mentions a solution that the advice-giver would adopt in a similar situation, but only indirectly recommends this solution for the advisee. Here is an example of the I'D format (see also Excerpt 8.4, "Leave off the meat" above):

Excerpt 8.7 "Go to somebody else" (Nb11–3) (EMM = Emma, LOT = Lottie)

(Emma has just been to her dentist, who announced that he wants to pull her tooth and make a gold bridge for 800 dollars.)

```
01 EMM:    .p.hhhh.h he wanted to pull it and i: said go:d no i:'m not
02         ready to have my too:th pulled toDA::Y?
03         (0.2)
04 EMM:    edith went with me and
05         (1.0)
06 EMM:    ↓we were gonna go to lu:nch 'n i wasn't ready you know go in
07         and have my tooth pu:lled my (.) .hhhhh where my bridge
08         hangs o:n so: (0.4) he says well i don't wanna even fix it.
09         becuz it's he .hh.hhh i: don't know lottie i don't (.) trust' n
10         th:en when he said (0.3) a go::ld he wants go:::ld bridge now
11         who in the hell wants a:ll (.) ↓ go::ld ↓ bridge.h=
12 LOT:    =°'n tha:t's a bunch of money-° ei:ght hundred
```

```
            do:ll[a r s?   ]
     EMM:         [↑isn' t th] at teRRIFIC?↑ h
            (0.2)
     LOT: ->°↓oh:: sh:::oot° i:'d go to somebody e[:  l  s  e.]
     EMM:                                          [i'm going] ba:ck to
            my other dentist,h
```

When Emma complains that she doesn't want an all-gold bridge (line 11) and that 800 dollars is a "terrific" sum of money (line 14), Lottie responds with an expletive and the remark that if the same thing were to happen to her, she would go to a different dentist (line 16). Nominally this is an informing about what Lottie would do in a similar situation. In an advice-implicative context, however, it implies that this is what Emma should do.

Arguably the weakest advice-giving format in our data collection is *you can X* or *you could X* (CAN/COULD). Designed once again as a declarative informing, in advice-implicative environments, this format presents a future action as a possible solution, without imposing any obligation on the recipient to embrace it. This is what happens in line 7 of Excerpt 8.8:

Excerpt 8.8 "Six shots" (Nb 014-10) (EMM = Emma, LOT = Lottie)
(Emma's skin condition, psoriasis, has led to a painful operation in which her doctor had to remove a toenail. Now Emma is explaining to Lottie that she does not want to go to that doctor again.)

```
     EMM:   ... i was going to go to my doctor up there
            i thought i'll go: and get a (.) you know let hi:m
            then i thought oh:: god he'll want to take the other toenail off
            and i don't want that to come o:ff so::,
            (0.4)
     EMM:   .t i was a:ll set to go do:wn here though,
     LOT: ->.t.hh we:ll you could go dow:n every SA-er[ THEY'RE O-uh he's=
                                                       [yah.
     LOT: ->=dow:n there sa:turda[y,  .hh] h
     EMM:                        [ye:ah.]
     LOT: -> and you only need s:ix::=
     EMM:   =ye:ah,
            (0.2)
     LOT: ->uh sho::ts an::d uh this: (.) uh i didn't talk to do:ctor nagle
            but i talked to his hea:d nu:rse she's a
            (0.2)
     EMM:   .hmhh.
```

((talk continues on topic of Dr. Nagle and where his office is located))

In this extract Lottie's advice to Emma for resolving her skin problem without having to have another toenail removed is that Emma come down Saturdays to the doctor in Newport Beach and get shots against psoriasis, of which she would need six (lines 7, 9, 11, 14). We see that Lottie formulates this advice as an assertion about a possibility, with *you could*. In doing so, she implies that this is one option, although there may be others.

From the perspective of advice-recipients, which of these formats the advice is given in is crucial for determining what their options are for responding. This is because each format makes different assumptions about deontic authority and how much 'freedom' the recipient has to exercise their own agency in deciding on future conduct. Let us look now more closely at the responses documented for these formats in our collection.

8.3.2 Responses to Advice-Giving Formats

We have shown that the deontic action of giving someone advice in everyday conversation sets up a normative expectation that the advisee will take a position on the advice in next turn and indicate whether they will commit to acting on it or not. While acceptance is often said to be the preferred response to advice on the grounds that it furthers social solidarity (Heritage 1984), in our data, where the participants for the most part have symmetrical deontic status, we find that, with strongly deontic formats, i.e., IMP and WDY, recipients display various sorts of resistance in third position. By *resistance* we mean that they either assess the proposed remedy as not a good one, or that they express unwillingness to implement what is recommended. Resisting can involve rejecting either the *content* of the recommendation or the *role of advisee* which the act of advising has put them in.

For instance, in Excerpt 8.9, we can see Shirley resisting her friend Geri's advice by providing both subjective and objective reasons for not accepting a recommendation that is offered first in a WDY format and then with imperative forms:

Excerpt 8.9 "Law school" (Geri and Shirley, p. 3) (SHI = Shirley, GER = Geri)

(Shirley has just told her friend Geri that she failed her Law School Admission Test and does not know what she will be doing in the fall.)

```
SHI:      .t.hhhh but i really don't think i'm gonna go to law school.
          (0.3)
SHI:      at least not right now.
 ( ):     .hh
GER:      are you se:rious,=
SHI:      =yeh,
          (0.2)
SHI:      very.
          (0.6)
 ( ):     .t.hh
GER: ->.hhhh shi:rley, i mean why don't you try taking it agai[:n.
SHI:                                                          [.hhh-
SHI: => .hhhhh 'cause i really don't know if i could put myself through it
```

```
14        => all over again.
15           (0.3)
16 GER: -> °.p.t° we:ll just study differently this ti:[ me.°
17 SHI: =>                                              [.t.hhh i don't
18        => kno:w it's on the saturday before final exams.
19           (0.8)
20 GER: -> just take one later than that.
21           (0.2)
22 SHI: => i ca:n't.
23 GER:    why:.
24 SHI: => because they don't let you. you have to take it by the end of
25         this year.
26         (0.4)
```

In line 11, Geri's initial advice is formatted with a WDY format, to which Shirley responds by giving a subjective reason for why she does not want to take the test again: *'cause I really don't know if I could put myself through it all over again* (lines 13–14). Geri's next piece of advice is delivered with a bald imperative, the strongest advice-giving format in our data: *well just study differently this ti:me* (line 16). Shirley's response to this begins with an alveolar click arguably functioning as part of a broadly negative stance display (Ogden 2013) and an inbreath; she now provides another subjective reason for not accepting Geri's imperatively formatted advice: *I don't kno:w it's on the Saturday before final exams*, implying that she will be busy and distracted by studying for finals (lines 17–18). Geri's final piece of advice, again delivered with an IMP format, *just take one later than that* (line 20), is again rejected, this time on objective grounds: *I can't . . . because they don't let you* (lines 22 and 24).

In Excerpt 8.10, we see other kinds of reasons being provided for resisting advice given with WDY formats:

Excerpt 8.10 "Revlon Nail" (Nb006–7) (LOT = Lottie, EMM = Emma)
(Lottie is asking Emma about her recent operation to have a toenail removed.)

```
01 LOT:    how'r you how's your foo:t.
02 EMM:    .t.hh OH IT'S HEALING BEAUTIFULLY
03 LOT:    goo:[:d.
04 EMM:        [the other one ma:y have to come o:ff on the
05         other toe i've got it in that but it's not infected
06         (0.7)
07 LOT: -> why don't you use (some) stuff [on i:t.
08 EMM: =>                                 [.t i've got peroxide i put
09         on it but eh .hhh the other one is healing very
10         we:ll. [i looked [at it the other day=
11 LOT:           [( )      [(good.)
12 EMM:    =i put a new ta:pe on it every da:y so .hhh[hhhhh
```

```
LOT: ->                                        [why don't you
     -> get that [nay- uh:: revlon nai[:l:  u  h]
EMM:             [hhhhh               [.t.hhh w]ell
     => that's not therapeutic lottie really it says on
        the (0.3) thi:ng uh- th- when yihk- ah this
        pro:vides just: uh kind of a, hh .hhh[h
LOT:                                         [what do you mean
        uh th- uh do:ctors use it,
        (0.3)
EMM:    .t.hhhh well on the little jar it says not therapeutic so::
        (0.6)
EMM:    you know what i mea:n? it doesn't kill any:: infection if
        i'm not mistaken i don't kno:w.
```

In response to Emma's complaint about her other toe being affected (lines 4–5), Lottie formulates a piece of advice with the relatively strong WDY form, *why don't you use (some) stuff on it* (line 7), presumably a reference to a medication for nail fungus which they had talked about before. But Emma resists this by saying that she has peroxide that she puts on it, implying that she does not need the 'stuff' Lottie is recommending. Nevertheless, Lottie goes on to make a more specific suggestion *why don't you get that nail- uh Revlon Nail* (lines 13–14). In lines 15–16, after an inbreath, possibly displaying that she is about to do a dispreferred action, Emma again resists this advice, now on the grounds that the Revlon Nail product is not therapeutic, an objective reason that justifies her reluctance to adopt it as a solution to her problem.

Whether there is a 'need' for what an advice-giver is recommending is often at issue when recipients respond by displaying resistance in third position. Much as Emma does with her mention of peroxide in lines 8–9 of Excerpt 8.10, recipients may claim that they do not need to do what is being recommended because they are already putting a remedy into practice. They may even present themselves as implementing the exact remedy that they are being advised to adopt. This is what we saw happening in Excerpt 8.5, "Wash them out", repeated here in shortened form and renumbered:

Excerpt 8.11 "Wash them out" (LOT = Lottie, EMM = Emma) (Nb 028-5, from Excerpt 8.5)

```
LOT:    [will you stay di- oh well you[pro↓bably< ]
EMM:                                  [I'M GONNA  ] STAY .hh
        YOU KNOW I ONLY HA:VE one brassiere and pair of panties lottie,h
LOT: -> well wash them ou:[:t.
EMM:                      [that's what I(h)'M DOING RI:GHT NOW
        i ↑just CA:ME in,
LOT:    oh:.
```

In line 13 Emma responds to Lottie's strongly deontic advice *well wash them out* by claiming that she has already thought of this solution herself and is in the process of implementing it: *that's what I'm doing right now*. That is, she aligns with the content of Lottie's advice but resists the role of advisee that it has put her in: she rejects being told what to do, all the more so since it is something she is already doing.

Why should deontically stronger forms for advice-giving (IMP and WDY) meet with resistance? We argue that these stronger forms establish a clear 'deontic gradient' (on analogy with Heritage's [2012a] 'epistemic gradient') between the interlocutors, with one party proposing – on the grounds of higher deontic authority – a *unilateral* resolution to the other's problem. With the strong deontic forms, these advice-givers position themselves as experts who know best what their interlocutor 'needs'; the interlocutor is expected to embrace the solution on the advisor's recommendation. Such formats arguably come across as face-threatening in everyday conversations where the participants' deontic statuses are symmetric. The WDY format – by raising the issue of accountability – can even be heard to imply that the solution is so simple the interlocutor should have thought of it themselves (Couper-Kuhlen & Thompson, 2021). Recipients who claim to already be doing what the advice-giver is recommending are countering such a morally tinged implication. At the same time, they are rejecting the asymmetric division of roles that strong deontic formats imply, and with it the role of advisee (Shaw & Hepburn 2013: 348).

Yet it is important to remember that third-position responses are choices. Even if recipients are already implementing remedies, they are under no obligation to say so. Rather they are free to choose how to respond to unsolicited advice. This is what Excerpt 8.4, "Leave off the meat" shows when we consider it in its entirety (renumbered here):

Excerpt 8.12 "Leave off the meat" (Nb 014-10) (expanded version of Excerpt 8.4) (EMM = Emma, LOT = Lottie)

(Emma has been complaining about her psoriasis but is now telling Lottie about a report that eating turkey will cure it.)

```
01 EMM:     .hnff and this girl in the apartment came up the other day and
02          told me that (0.2) you know she read this?
03          (0.3)
04 EMM:     hh.hhhhh whe:re? a ↓doct↑or ↓cures ↑his ↓pa↑tients by eating
            turkey
05          (0.4)
06 LOT: ->  well now why don't you leave off the mea:t.=
07 EMM: =>  =[i  A : : M.]
08 LOT: ->  =[just get tur]:key.=
09 EMM: =>  =i a:m.
10 LOT:     .hh you can bu:y turkey .hh i:: do: lo:ts of ti:mes. in the
```

```
        ja:r that lynden ha:s that tur:[key.]
EMM:                                  [ ye:] ah.
        (.)
EMM:    .hhhh well i'm gonna ha:ve chicken too and i love chicken
        (1.2)
        and i can ha:ve uh .hhhh.hhh.hhuhh (.) oh:: ↓a lot of stuff
        lottie like↓ that i mean i think i jus:(.)t[cook a]
LOT:                                               [i :'d]u-
LOT: ->i::'d uh leave o:ff the mea:t.
EMM: =>°i think i ↑wi:ll.° i haven't had a piece of mea:t since i
        been down here.
```

Using a WDY format *well now why don't you leave off the meat* (line 7) and a bald imperative *just get turkey* (line 9)[13] – both strong deontic formats – Lottie proposes a simple solution to Emma's problem. Yet Emma resists being given this advice when she declares, once in overlap and once in the clear, *I am* (lines 8 and 10). That is, leaving off 'meat' and just eating turkey are things she claims she is already doing. Moreover, Emma goes on to display autonomy by specifying that in addition to turkey she can also have chicken and a "lot of stuff" (lines 14–17). That is, in response to Lottie's deontically strong injunctions, Emma presents herself here as an agent, the master of her own fate. However, Lottie goes on to reiterate her advice in a much weaker form: *I'd uh leave off the meat* (lines 18–19), asserting what she would do if she were in Emma's situation. Tellingly, in response to this weaker format, Emma now displays a willingness to commit to what Lottie is recommending (line 20). She no longer insists that this is what she is already doing, but instead indicates that she will embrace the solution on Lottie's recommendation. This sudden 'change of heart', we would claim, is brought about by Lottie's use of a deontically weak format, one which does not take an authoritarian stance towards knowing what Emma should do, but instead merely describes what Lottie would do in similar circumstances. Such a stance does not threaten Emma's autonomy or agency in determining her own future actions in the same way as a WDY format, as in line 6.

So we see that givers of unsolicited advice in everyday conversations undergo a social risk when they advise someone to do something using deontically strong forms. The risk is that they can be heard as implying that the other is incapable of helping themselves: this deprives the other of autonomy and agency in deciding on a future course of action that concerns

[13] Alternatively *just get turkey* could be thought of as a continuation of the prior *why don't you leave off the meat; (why don't you) just get turkey.*

themselves. The following extract provides evidence that would-be advisors are sensitive to this:

Excerpt 8.13 "Christmas dress" (Nb 023-3) (EMM = Emma, LOT = Lottie)

(Emma and Lottie have just returned from a shopping trip and are now discussing issues related to Lottie's wardrobe.)

```
EMM:     you're all set now you don't have to worry about the gr:ay
         la:=:ce or (.) .t.h[hhh]
LOT:                        [aw:] : ↓no::[::.   ] i-]
EMM: ->                                  [.h  A] ND] TAKE uh: take th-
         are you gonna take that little christmas dress down to adeline
         see what sh[e si-]
LOT:                [yeah:] i think i wi↓:ll.and see:,
         (.)
EMM:     and then maybe we can ↓fix * it.↓
         (1.2)
LOT:     ye::ah:.
         (.)
LOT:     yeh i'll see what she says a↓bout it↓ you kno:w and uh:
         (.)
```

Rather than telling Lottie what to do, namely take her Christmas dress down to Adeline, Emma thinks better of it, and breaks off her imperative format *and take uh: take th-* (line 4) in favor of inquiring first whether Lottie intends to do as much: *are you gonna take that little Christmas dress down to Adeline see what she (says)* (lines 5–6). This choice turns out to be the better one, as Lottie declares *I think I will* (line 7). Emma can now frame the matter as something they can do together: *and then maybe we can fix it* (line 9), whereupon Lottie declares *yeh I'll see what she says about it you know* (line 13). Had Emma pursued the unilateral advice-giving launched in line 4, she would arguably have met with resistance from Lottie in next turn, e.g., something like 'That's exactly what I'm going to do'. As it is, the bilateral framing allows enough freedom for Lottie to formulate the solution as her own project (line 13), thereby preserving her autonomy and agency.[14]

The deontically weakest formats for unsolicited advising (I'D, CAN/COULD) meet with less resistance because, as we have noted, they do not mandate commitment. They are declarative in form, allowing the advisee the option of merely acknowledging or agreeing with the assertion in next turn.

[14] We note that Excerpt 8.13 is a boundary case (Schegloff 1997) for our generalization that advice actions typically occur as seconds to complaints or troubles-telling, in that it is not apparent what problem or complaint of Lottie's Emma's advice initiation in line 4 is responsive to. We surmise, but cannot prove, that there is a problem with Lottie's Christmas dress and that having Adeline work on it had been discussed in an earlier conversation.

In Excerpt 8.7, "Go to somebody else" we saw that Emma declares of her own accord that she intends to go back to her other dentist: this is not presented as a commitment to something Lottie has recommended but rather as an autonomous decision that she has made on her own. In Excerpt 8.8, "Six shots" Emma merely acknowledges Lottie's suggestion (*you could go down every Sat(urday))* as a possibility with *yah* (line 8) and *ye:ah* (lines 10 and 12). She does not take any position on whether she intends to do so, nor does Lottie pursue the matter. Lottie's advice thus remains simply something that the participants agree on as being a possible course of action for Emma in dealing with her problem.

In sum, the deontically weakest formats for advice-giving call on the recipient not so much to accept or reject the advice given as to acknowledge or agree that the action in question would be a possible course of action with beneficial effects. These formats then allow the advice-giver to avoid the strong deontic gradient implied in turns formatted with IMP and WDY forms. They put advice-giver and advice-recipient on more equal terms, allowing recipients to exert their agency over what they intend to do in the future. Often it is the recipients themselves who go on to find their own solutions to the problem.

The S/O format for advice-giving assumes an intermediary position between the deontically strongest and the deontically weakest forms. This is reflected in how recipients deal with such advice in third position. In Excerpt 8.6, "Your ring", for instance, Kelly responds to Laurel's *You should get (.) like (0.8) a little holder, you know like a carrying thing?* by first acknowledging that she knows what Kelly is referring to (°*yeah*°, line 11), and then explaining that she usually takes her ring off before going to the sink, implying that she has no need for a ring holder that she could carry around (lines 11–12). She then goes on to propose her own remedy: *I should just not take it off when I wash my face* (lines 13–14). This response combines features like those found in responses to deontically strong forms ('I don't need it', as in lines 8–9 of Excerpt 8.10, "Revlon nail") and those found in responses to deontically weak forms ('I'll find my own solution', as in lines 17–18 of Excerpt 8.7, "Go to somebody else"). Here is another case in point:

Excerpt 8.14 "All the kanji" (Before bed: 7) (STE = Steffi, OLI = Oli)
(Steffi and her boyfriend Oli are about to move to Japan and Steffi is worrying about how her friends will manage to address their letters to her in kanji.)

```
STE:   i found out all the kan[ji for where we live
OLI:                          [((sneeze))
STE:   cause- cause my friend warned me
       (.)
OLI:   we[(speak different types/cuts)
STE:     [we're a small-
      we're a small enough town
```

```
            but the postmaster (.) might not: (.)
            get ( . ) writing in english
            so we're gonna have to give it to everyone in english
            and in japanese and they have to write both
    OLI: -> you should make STENcils
    STE: => actually i was just g(h)onna l(h)ike hhh
            .hh se(h)nd it to them on the computer
            and then they can print it u(h)p!
```

The problem Steffi is worrying about concerns the fact that a small-town Japanese postmaster may not be able to deal with an address written in English (lines 7–9). She presents herself as having to ask their friends to write the address in Japanese as well, using kanji (lines 10–11).[15] Oli now offers a suggestion which would simplify the process: *you should make stencils* (line 12). The format he uses is deontically weaker than *why don't you make stencils?*, but deontically stronger than either *I'd make stencils* or *you could make stencils.* Steffi could respond with resistance by saying 'That's too much work!' or she could signal an intention to commit with 'I think I will'. Just as we saw Kelly doing with the advice about a holder for her ring, Steffi does neither: instead she revises her description of what she intends to do, marking this 'change of mind' with a turn-initial *actually* (Clift 2001). She now claims that she plans to send the address to her friends by computer so that they can print it out (lines 13–15). This in essence cancels the relevance of Oli's advice: it implies at once 'No need for stencils' and 'I can find a remedy myself', allowing Steffi a measure of autonomy without denying that some solution is required.

We hope to have shown that the five most frequent formats for offering advice in everyday advice-implicative contexts vary in their deontic strength, as schematized in Figure 8.1. We have argued that the choice of format has consequences for the strength of the deontic stance the advice-giver is heard to be taking, and consequently for how the recipient chooses to deal with the advice in next position. From the perspective of third position, an advice-recipient is guided by the linguistic formatting of the advice as to whether the advice is being given with strong deontic authority as a prescription or an injunction, or whether it is being offered on a flatter deontic gradient as a possible course of action or as a solution that the advice-giver might choose themselves. This affects how the advice-recipient responds. For advice given with an IMP format we found that 79 percent of all responses (excluding the 'no uptake' cases) either reject the advice or resist the advisee role. For advice given with WDY 62 percent of all responses embody rejection or resistance.

[15] Kanji are the Chinese characters used in Japanese orthography.

Figure 8.1 Continuum of deontic strength

On the other hand, the percentage for advice given with the weak format I'D comes out as the reverse: 67 percent of all responses either agree with the content or accept the advice.

We argue that the explanation for these findings is the following. An advice-recipient who responds by accepting or resisting/rejecting the advice-giver's recommendation casts the prior turn as having presented a solution to their problem in a unilateral fashion. The advice-recipient is thereby deprived of agency; if they choose to act, i.e., to embrace the advice, it will be not of their own accord but on the recommendation of the advice-giver. More often than not, these advice-recipients resist the advice on subjective or objective grounds, or they resist the subordinate role the prior action puts them in. On the other hand, an advice-recipient who responds by acknowledging or agreeing with the advice-giver that a particular course of action might be desirable or possible casts the prior turn as having invited bilateral problem-solving or brainstorming. This is particularly evident with the I'D format, which invokes a role switch with the advisor, who now takes on the hypothetical role of someone with the problem in question. With the weaker formats, advice-giver and advice-recipient are thus on more equal deontic footing. Advisees become agents, who can search freely for their own solution independent of an advisor's prescription or injunction.

8.4 Discussion: Advice-Giving and Action Ascription

The data we have been examining show how second position actions (in this case advice vs. no advice) orient to the prior turn as having made relevant either the provision of a solution to a problem or the provision of affiliation and empathy for a trouble. It is based on such ascriptions that potential advice-givers determine what to do next. If they choose to offer advice, they display that what the other has said was taken as an occasion to offer assistance.[16] If instead they co-complain or otherwise position themselves as a troubles recipient, they treat the other's actions as an occasion to offer empathy and affiliation.

[16] Once again, however, note that we are not suggesting that the complainer or troubles-teller was *seeking* assistance.

Furthermore, our data show how third-position actions either accept or resist the advice and/or the role of advisee, or acknowledge or agree on a desirable or possible course of action. In choosing how to respond to the advice, recipients thus cast the prior advice-giving turn as either imposing a solution unilaterally or inviting a bilateral search (brainstorming) for problem resolution. Both these action ascriptions treat the prior turn as proposing a suggestion with implications for recipients' future actions, but they entail different deontic positionings with respect to what this means for a recipient's agency and autonomy.

The sequential properties of environments in which advice-giving emerges are thus yet another arena within which we can see participants drawing on grammatical resources to assess a prior turn for its deontic strength in recommending a certain action. In fact, given the environment of third position in advice-giving sequences, it is as much the strength of this stance as an action that the recipient must ascribe to the prior turn. We have shown that the strength of the deontic stance imputed varies with the grammatical form of the advice: advice given with the stronger forms is treated as a unilateral command allowing no role for the recipient in determining their own future action, and may be responded to with resistance. Advice formulated with the weaker forms, in contrast, is treated as inviting the recipient to share in a joint problem-solving project. Participants' behavior in advice-implicative contexts thus involves not only lexical choices and assessing the location of the advice-giving within sequences, larger projects, and ongoing activities, but also evaluating the relative deontic strength of each recurrent grammatical format.

What our examination of action ascription in everyday unsolicited advice-giving sequences shows is that indeed more is at stake than the ascription of action categories such as "complaint" or "advice" when participants must decide on the fly what to do next and how to do it. These data show how 'action ascription' involves both 'ascribing an action' to a prior speaker's turn and choosing among more than one appropriate response types. As Sidnell and Enfield (2014) point out, recipients "can know how to respond quite reliably by working up from turn components and finding a token solution, and not by having to assign the whole turn to an action category" (p. 442). In our discussion of third position we have pointed to some of the "turn components" that contribute to "know(ing) how to respond" to a piece of unsolicited advice. More generally, we hope to have demonstrated the delicacy of a recipient's task in both second and third position of unsolicited advice-giving sequences as that recipient works to determine (a) what next actions their interlocutor's troubles-telling or complaint occasions and (b) what the deonticity of the grammatical form deployed for advice-giving implies about agency in finding a solution for the just-articulated problem or uncertainty.

Acknowledgments

Two anonymous reviewers and the series editor Paul Drew gave us valuable comments on an earlier version; we appreciate their input, and absolve them of any responsibility for the final form of this chapter.

REFERENCES

Butler, C. W., Potter, J., Danby, S., Emmison, M. & Hepburn, A. (2010). Advice-implicative interrogatives: Building "client-centered" support in a children's helpline. *Social Psychology Quarterly*, 73(3), 265–87.

Clayman, S. E. & Heritage, J. (2014). Benefactors and beneficiaries: Benefactive status and stance in the management of offers and requests. In P. Drew & E. Couper-Kuhlen, eds., *Requesting in Social Interaction*. Amsterdam: John Benjamins, pp. 55–86.

Clift, R. (2001). Meaning in interaction: The case of "actually." *Language*, 77(2), 245–91.

Craven, A. & Potter, J. (2010). Directives: Entitlement and contingency in action. *Discourse Studies*, 12(4), 419–42.

Couper-Kuhlen, E. (2012). Exploring affiliation in the reception of conversational complaint stories. In A. Peräkylä & M.-L. Sorjonen, eds., *Emotion in Interaction*. Oxford: Oxford University Press, pp. 113–46.

(2014). What does grammar tell us about action? *Pragmatics*, 24(3), 623–47.

Couper-Kuhlen, E. & Thompson, S. A. (2021). Ratschläge in der Alltagskommunikation: Zur Verwendung einer sedimentierten Form im Englischen ('Advice in everyday talk: On the use of a sedimented form in English'). In B. Weidner, W. Imo, K. König & L. Wegner, eds., *Verfestigungen in der Interaktion – Konstruktionen, sequenzielle Muster, kommunikative Gattungen*. Berlin: de Gruyter, pp. 299–322.

Curl, T. & Drew, P. (2008). Contingency and action: A comparison of two forms of requesting. *Research on Language and Social Interaction*, 41, 129–53.

Drew, P. (1998). Complaints about transgressions and misconduct. *Research on Language and Social Interaction*, 31(3–4), 295–325.

Emmison, M., Butler, C. W. & Danby, S. (2011). Script proposals: a device for empowering clients in counselling. *Discourse Studies*, 13(1), 3–26.

Floyd, S., Rossi, G., & Enfield, N.J., eds. (2020). *Getting Others to Do Things: A Pragmatic Typology of Recruitments*. Berlin: Language Sciences Press.

Fox, Barbara A. (2007). Principles shaping grammatical practices: an exploration. *Discourse Studies*, 9: 299–318.

Heinemann, T. & Traverso, V. (2009). Complaining in interaction. *Journal of Pragmatics*, 41(12), 2381–4.

Hepburn, A. & Potter, J. (2011). Designing the recipient: Some practices that manage advice resistance in institutional settings. *Social Psychology Quarterly*, 74, 216–41.

Heritage, J. (1984). *Garfinkel and Ethnomethodology*. Cambridge: Polity Press.

(2011). Territories of knowledge, territories of experience: Empathic moments in interaction. In T. Stivers, L. Mondada & J. Steensig, eds., *The Morality of Knowledge in Conversation*. Cambridge: Cambridge University Press, pp. 159–83.

(2012a). Epistemics in action: Action formation and territories of knowledge. *Research on Language and Social Interaction*, 45(1), 1–29.

(2012b). The epistemic engine: Sequence organization and territories of knowledge. *Research on Language and Social Interaction*, 45(1), 30–52.

Heritage, J. & Lindström, A. (1998). Motherhood, medicine, and morality: Scenes from a medical encounter. *Research on Language and Social Interaction*, 31(3–4), 397–438.

(2012). Advice giving – terminable and interminable: The case of British health visitors. In H. Limberg & M. A. Locher, eds., *Advice in Discourse*. Amsterdam: John Benjamins, pp. 169–94.

Heritage, J. & Sefi, S. (1992). Dilemmas of advice: Aspects of the delivery and reception of advice in interactions between health visitors and first time mothers. In P. Drew & J. Heritage, eds., *Talk at Work*. Cambridge: Cambridge University Press, pp. 359–419.

Hudson, T. (1990). The discourse of advice giving in English: "I wouldn't feed until spring no matter what you do." *Language & Communication*, 10(4), 285–97.

Hutchby, I. (1995). Aspects of recipient design in expert advice-giving on call-in radio. *Discourse Processes*, 9(2), 19–238.

Jefferson, G. (1988). On the sequential organization of troubles-talk in ordinary conversation. *Social Problems*, 35(4), 418–41.

Jefferson, G. & Lee, J. R. E. (1981). The rejection of advice: Managing the problematic convergence of a "troubles-telling" and a "service encounter." *Journal of Pragmatics*, 5, 399–421.

Kendrick, K. & Drew, P. (2016). Recruitment: Offers, requests, and the organization of assistance in interaction. *Research on Language and Social Interaction*, 49(1), 1–19.

Kinnell, A. M. K. & Maynard, D. W. (1996). The delivery and receipt of safer sex advice in pre-test counseling sessions for HIV and AIDS. *Journal of Contemporary Ethnography*, 35, 405–37.

Levinson, S. C. (2013). Action formation and ascription. In J. Sidnell & T. Stivers, eds., *Handbook of Conversation Analysis*. Boston, MA: Wiley-Blackwell, pp. 103–30.

Mori, J. (2006). The workings of the Japanese token *hee* in informing sequences: An analysis of sequential context, turn shape, and prosody. *Journal of Pragmatics*, 38, 1175–205.

Ogden, R. (2013). Clicks and percussives in English conversation. *Journal of the International Phonetic Association*, 43, 299–320.

Pilnick, A. (2001). The interactional organization of pharmacist consultations in a hospital setting: A putative structure. *Journal of Pragmatics*, 33(12), 1927–45.

(2003). "Patient counselling" by pharmacists: Four approaches to the delivery of counselling sequences and their interactional reception. *Social Science & Medicine*, 56(4), 835–49.

Pudlinski, C. (2002). Accepting and rejecting advice as competent peers: Caller dilemmas on a warm line. *Discourse Studies*, 4(4), 481–500.

Schegloff, E. A. (1993). Reflections on quantification in the study of conversation. *Research on Language and Social Interaction*, 26, 99–128.

(1997). Practices and actions: Boundary cases of other-initiated repair. *Discourse Processes*, 23(3), 499–545.

Selting, M. (2012). Complaint stories and subsequent complaint stories with affect displays. *Journal of Pragmatics*, 44, 387–415.

Shaw, C. & Hepburn, A. (2013). Managing the moral implications of advice in informal interaction. *Research on Language and Social Interaction*, 46(4), 344–62.

Shaw, C., Potter, J. & Hepburn, A. (2015). Advice-implicative actions: Using interrogatives and assessments to deliver advice in mundane conversation. *Discourse Studies*, 17(3), 317–42.

Sidnell, J. & Enfield, N. J. (2014). The ontology of action, in interaction. In N. J. Enfield, P. Kockelman & J. Sidnell, eds., *The Cambridge Handbook of Linguistic Anthropology*. Cambridge: Cambridge University Press, pp. 423–46.

Silverman, D. (1997). *Discourses of Counseling: HIV Counseling as Social Interaction*. London: Sage.

Sorjonen, M.-L., Raevaara, L. & Couper-Kuhlen, E., eds. (2017). *Imperative Turns at Talk: The Design of Directives in Action*. Amsterdam: John Benjamins.

Stevanovic, M. & Peräkylä, A. (2012). Deontic authority in interaction: The right to announce, propose, and decide. *Research on Language and Social Interaction*, 45 (3), 297–321.

Stivers, T., Heritage, J., Barnes, R. K. et al. (2018). Treatment recommendations as actions. *Health Communication*, 33(11), 1335–44.

Thompson, S. A. & Couper-Kuhlen, E. (2020). English *why don't you X* as a formulaic expression. In T. Ono & R. Laury, eds., *Fixed Expressions: Building Language Structure and Action*. Amsterdam: John Benjamins, pp. 99–132.

Thompson, S. A., Fox, B. & Couper-Kuhlen, E. (2015). *Grammar in Everyday Talk: Building Responsive Actions*. Cambridge: Cambridge University Press.

Vatanen, A. (2018). Responding in early overlap: Recognitional onsets in assertion sequence. *Research on Language and Social Interaction*, 51(2), 107–26.

Vehviläinen, S. (2001). Evaluative advice in educational counselling: The use of disagreement in the "stepwise entry" to advice. *Research on Language and Social Interaction*, 34(3), 371–98.

Waring, H. Z. (2005). Peer tutoring in a graduate writing center: Identity, expertise, and advice resisting. *Applied Linguistics*, 26(2), 141–68.

(2007). The multi-functionality of accounts in advice giving. *Journal of Sociolinguistics*, 11(3), 367–91.

(2012). The advising sequence and its preference structures in graduate peer tutoring in an American university. In H. Limberg & M. A. Locher, eds., *Advice in Discourse*. Amsterdam: John Benjamins, pp. 87–118.

9 "How about Eggs?"

Action Ascription in the Family Decision-Making Process While Grocery Shopping at a Supermarket

Takeshi Hiramoto and Makoto Hayashi

9.1 Introduction

Recent studies in conversation analysis (CA) on action formation and ascription have investigated the roles of linguistic (and other communicative) resources for constructing and recognizing social actions (see Deppermann & Haugh, Chapter 1 in this volume, for an overview). This study aims to contribute to this body of work by exploring how the deontic stances indexed through grammatical realizations of turns-at-talk in sequence-initiating position provide resources for action ascription.

In their work on the processes of making joint decisions at workplace meetings, Stevanovic and Peräkylä demonstrate how participants make judgments about their own and others' deontic rights "to set rules concerning what should be done" (Stevanovic & Peräkylä 2012: 298) and use them as resources in producing and interpreting social actions (Stevanovic 2011; Stevanovic & Peräkylä 2012). According to Stevanovic (2011: 4), a participant's *deontic status* is "regarded as the deontic rights that a certain person has irrespective of whether she momentarily claims these rights or not," whereas a participant's *deontic stance* concerns the moment-by-moment expression of deontic rights through the design of turns-at-talk. In a recent article on action formation and ascription, Heritage (2013: 569–70) suggested that the incongruence between the deontic stance indexed by one's utterance and the underlying deontic status can shape how the action performed with that utterance is understood by its recipient. Along similar lines, the present chapter explores how an incongruence between one's deontic stance and status provides resources for recipients' action ascription through an examination of sequences in which family members decide what to purchase while grocery shopping. In this setting, the father and the children of a family are regularly treated by the participants (both themselves and other family members) as having a weaker deontic status than the mother. Sometimes, however, the father and the children index a deontic stance in their utterance that is not consistent with the weaker deontic status ordinarily associated with them. We show that this incongruence between deontic stance and status exhibited by the fathers' or the children's utterance provides resources for the mother to respond to them in such a way as to display her inference about, or interpretation of, the action performed by the father's or the children's prior utterance.

The data used for this study come from interactions among family members while grocery shopping at a supermarket. An important feature of family members' purchase behavior at a supermarket is that they make "joint" decisions (Stevanovic 2012) on what to buy. In other words, the decision-making process, through interactions among family members, is a key feature of their purchase behavior (Keller & Ruus 2014). As will be discussed in detail below, when the family members initiate a decision-making sequence, they use one of the following two grammatical formats: (i) a noun phrase (hereafter NP) containing the name of (the category of) the product *without* being accompanied by a predicate, such as a verb (e.g., *Tamago?* "Eggs?"); (ii) an NP containing the name of (the category of) the product, accompanied by a predicate (e.g., *Tamago kau?* "Shall we buy eggs?"). An example of an utterance in format (i) is found in line 3 of Excerpt 9.1 below, while an utterance in format (ii) is exemplified in line 5 of Excerpt 9.2.

Excerpt 9.1 2014-06-01-1 13:08: Eggs

```
03 DAD: -> tamago
           Eggs
((Two lines omitted))
06 MOM:    soo tamago kawana
           so  egg    have.to.buy
           That's right, ((we)) should buy eggs.
```

Excerpt 9.2 2014-06-01-1 05:28: Garlic sprouts

```
05 DAD: -> ninniku no mee    iran
           garlic LK sprout not.need
           Don't ((we)) need garlic sprouts?
06         (1.2)
07 MOM:    eh  mata  yaku  n
           huh again grill N
           Huh? Are ((you)) going to grill ((them)) again?
```

We will illustrate how the choice between these two turn formats affects action ascription displayed by the recipient's utterance produced in responsive position in the purchase decision-making sequences.

In addition, our study sheds light on an interactional resource that has been little discussed in CA research on action formation and ascription so far: the "roles" concerned with decision-making among family members. Previous research on consumer behavior revealed that, in the process of purchase decision-making within a social group, such as a family, members of the group allocate decision-making roles among themselves, such as the "initiator," the "influencer," and the "decider" (Webster & Wind 1972). We demonstrate how these roles are negotiated interactionally and how action ascription is affected by such roles during the course of purchase decision-making sequences.

The remainder of this chapter is organized as follows. Section 9.2 briefly discusses relevant previous literature and other background contexts of this study. After introducing our data in Section 9.3, we report our findings in Section 9.4. Section 9.5 discusses the implications of our findings, while Section 9.6 provides some concluding remarks.

9.2 Background

Action formation and ascription are becoming an increasingly important area of research in CA (Couper-Kuhlen & Selting 2017; Enfield & Sidnell 2017; Levinson 2013; Seuren 2018). Several studies on directive actions – requests, proposals, suggestions, invitations, and so on – found that the relative distribution of deontic rights between interlocutors plays an important role in constructing such actions (Stevanovic 2011; Stevanovic & Peräkylä 2012). For instance, Stevanovic and Peräkylä (2012) found that, within the context of joint decision-making about future events, proposals are used when their final decision is contingent on the recipent's approval, while assertions that present future plans simply as future facts are used when there are no such contingencies.

As discussed above, an array of interactional resources employed in constructing a sequence-initiating action in specific interactional contexts can allow recipients to interpret the meaning of the first action. One such resource is the relationship between one's deontic status and stance, as suggested by Heritage (2013). If there is an incongruent relationship between the deontic status that is assumed to be conferred upon a speaker through past interactions and the deontic stance indexed through the design of his/her utterance, the recipient is motivated to infer why such incongruence is observed.

Recent CA studies have begun to pay serious attention to the details of interactional negotiations taking place among consumers (De Stefani 2013, 2014, forthcoming; Laurier 2008). In his analysis of couples' purchase decision-making process at a supermarket, De Stefani (2013) illustrates how the members of each couple verbally and nonverbally negotiate to initiate and close a decision-making sequence regarding each of the products that they consider for purchase. In another study, De Stefani (2014) describes practices by which co-shoppers categorize material objects in a supermarket as *potentially purchasable items* for them. One practice he identifies is a sequence-initiating utterance consisting of a stand-alone NP, which he shows is interpreted by co-shoppers as making a proposal for purchase (2014: 283). Our study contributes to this body of CA research on purchase decision-making by examining in detail how family members make decisions on what to buy through their interactions while grocery shopping.

9.3 Data

The supermarket where we collected our data is located in a suburban town in western Japan. The participants are three families (referred to in this chapter as Families A, B, and C), each consisting of parents (mother and father) and their young children around the ages of 5 to 8, who agreed to be video-recorded during their grocery shopping. Two researchers used hand-held video cameras to record the shopping behaviors of each family as they navigated the aisles of the supermarket, with one researcher walking in front of the family and the other behind them. Approximately 80 minutes of data were recorded. None of the families had prepared a shopping list in advance. Therefore, impulse buying, or unplanned decision-making to buy products, is the default mode of their shopping behavior.

As discussed above, we identified two types of grammatical formats used in sequence-initiating turns: an NP without a predicate (e.g., a verb) and an NP accompanied by a predicate. For convenience, we will call the former Type 1 and the latter Type 2. Types 1 and 2 may be produced either with rising intonation or without.[1] The NP contained in these turn formats may be a product/brand name (e.g., "Tropicana" for orange juice), the name of a good (e.g., "orange juice"), or the name of a category of goods (e.g., "beverages"). We collected a total of eighty-three utterances produced with either the Type 1 or Type 2 format. Of these, fifty-two utterances (63 percent) fall under Type 1, while thirty-one utterances (37 percent) fall under Type 2.

We will now examine in detail the decision-making sequences initiated with these two grammatical formats and show how the choice between them is consequential for action ascription by their recipients.

9.4 Analysis

9.4.1 *Type 1: [NP without Predicate]*

Type 1 utterances contain an NP without a predicate. This format tends to be used when family members find a product to which the other members have paid no attention. In Excerpt 9.3, which is an extended version of Excerpt 9.1

[1] We have found no systematic relationship between the turn-final intonation and the action implemented by that turn within the same turn format. We use the notation "(+?)" to indicate that the turn in question may or may not be produced with rising intonation.

above, the father glances at eggs during the silence in line 2. Then, he produces an utterance consisting only of an NP, *tamago* ("eggs") in line 3.[2]

Excerpt 9.3 2014-06-01-1 13:08 Family A: Eggs (CHI = child, DAD = father, MOM = mother)

```
01 Child:        ya da yakuruto mo:.
                 no CP Yakult also
                 "No, ((I want)) Yakult, too!"
02               (       1.2     )+Δ(          0.9       #)
   fat                             Δgazes at eggs section—,,,>
                 >>walks forward slowly—————————————————>
   fig                                                   #fig.9.1
03 Father: ->    t≠$amago
                 "Eggs"
   fat           ,≠gazes at his left->
                  -$turns left————>
04               (0.7) # (2.3)
   fat           ————————>
                 ————————>
   Fig                  #fig.9.2
```

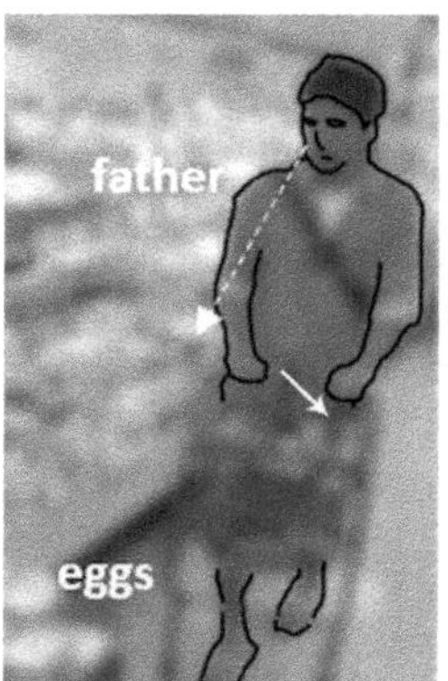

Figure 9.1 Family moves forward slowly as a pack

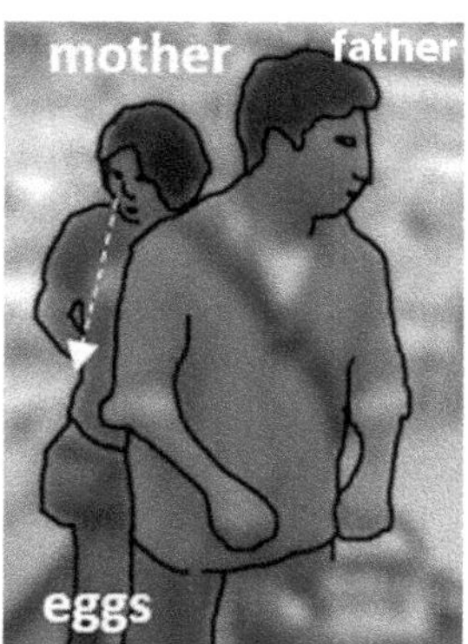

Figure 9.2 Father mentions eggs and looks away

```
05 Child:        dono  yaku&ru*to? [mama
                 which Yakult       mom
                 "Which  Yakult, mom?"
                                   [
```

[2] See the Notes on Abbreviations for an explanation of the abbreviations used in the interlinear glosses in the transcripts. The double parentheses used in the English translation are those elements that are not explicitly mentioned in the Japanese original.

```
06 Mother: ->                        [soo tamago kawana
                                      so  egg   have.to.buy
                                     "That's right, ((we)) should buy eggs."
   fat          ------------------------------------------------>
                --------&turns right----------------------------->
   mot                    *gazes at egg section------------------>
07 Father:      kaoo
                "Let's buy ((them))."
08 Mother:      demo konna      takkai      tamago nante (          )
                but  like.this expensive   egg    QT
                "But how expensive these eggs are!"
```

In line 1, the child expresses her desire to buy Yakult (a probiotic drink sold widely in Japan), which receives no response from her parents. In line 3, the father initiates a new sequence with *tamago*. When the father produces this utterance, he is in front of the mother as they move forward slowly as a pack (Figure 9.1; the mother is not seen in this figure as she is walking immediately behind the father). It appears on the video that the eggs are not visible from where the mother is when the father mentions them in line 3. In addition, the mother's line of vision is directed toward other products located in a different direction than the eggs. Thus, one possible description of the action performed by the father in line 3 is *environmental noticing* – noticing an object located in, or an event taking place in, the participants' environmental surroundings (Sacks 1992: 90). An environmental noticing solicits the recipients' attention to the "just-noticed" objects. Here, the father does not stop walking and actually passes the egg section when he utters *tamago* in line 3. He appears to do so to allow the mother behind him to move a few steps forward to where she can see the eggs. He thus establishes the physical configuration in which the mother can respond to his sequence-initiating action.

The problem of action ascription on the recipient's part becomes relevant at this point. If the father's action in line 3 is environmental noticing, then the appropriate response would be to take part in noticing (Schegloff 2007: 74) by uttering "oh," "yeah," and the like. However, as Kidwell and Zimmerman (2007) demonstrate, establishing joint attention between participants may lead to launching other sorts of action-sequences. Indeed, what the mother does in response contains something more than sharing the father's noticing: rather than simply claiming to take part in noticing, she produces the token *soo* ("That reminds me"), which is used here to mark recollection of something triggered by what the prior speaker has just said, and declares the need to purchase eggs (*tamago kawana* "((We)) should buy eggs"). We argue that, by declaring the need to buy eggs in response to the father's utterance, the mother ascribes to his Type

1 utterance the action of *nominating* a product for purchase consideration as well as noticing it. By "nominating," we mean that speakers pick out a particular product from their material surroundings and ask another person to consider it, while displaying little, if any, inclination toward the outcome of decision-making.

Note here that the father's utterance in line 3 does not display strong deontic rights for himself toward purchasing the eggs because it does not contain a predicate (e.g., a verb) that explicitly mentions what should be done with the eggs. His physical conduct also contributes to displaying this stance. As if moving out of the configuration where the issue of purchasing eggs would be discussed with the mother, the father organizes his conduct in such a way as to just mention the eggs in passing and look away from them quickly (lines 3–4; Figure 9.2). Thus, he shows his stance that he will not participate in the purchase decision-making *per se*. In contrast, when the mother says *kawana* ("should buy"), her utterance displays her stance that she is the person who can make the decision to buy eggs. As the expression of deontic modality "should buy" indicates, the mother makes her judgment as if there is no room for negotiation. More importantly, the father's and the mother's expressions of their deontic stances are *not* independent from one another, but are mutually coordinated and interdependent. That is, in the sequence-initiating turn, the father not only does not claim his deontic rights strongly to make a decision but also positions his interlocutor – the mother – as having deontic rights within the context of purchase decision-making, whereas the mother registers this positioning and behaves in accordance with it in the responsive turn. Therefore, the father and the mother collaboratively establish a deontic gradient (Stevanovic 2013) realized through the grammatical constructions of their turns-at-talk.

Children can also take the role of initiating a decision-making sequence by producing a Type 1 utterance. In Excerpt 9.4, the child notices eggs in front of him and then utters *mama tamago* ("Mom, eggs") in line 1.

Excerpt 9.4 2014-06-01-3 12:52 Family C: Eggs (CHI = child, MOM = mother)

```
01 Child: -> #mama          tamago.
              mother         eggs
             "Mom, eggs."
   chi       >>walks forward—>
   mom       gazes at drinks-,,,
   fig        #fig.9.3
02            (      0.2       )
   chi        ————————————————>
   mom        ,gazes at eggs——>
```

```
03 Mother:   tamago:? (.)<tamago> ka:
             Eggs         eggs     FP
             "E:ggs? (.) <Eggs> We:ll."
   chi       ————————————————————>
   mom       ————————————————————>
             ((The child and the mother pass the eggs' section #))
   fig                                                    #fig.9.4
```

Figure 9.3 Mother's gaze is brought to the eggs

Figure 9.4 Mother passes the egg section without saying anything

The child in this excerpt reinforces the efficacy of the *noticing* aspect of a Type 1 utterance by using the address term *mama* "Mom," thereby drawing the attention of the mother, who is looking in the direction of the drinks section located to the left of the egg section (Figure 9.3). This succeeds in bringing the mother's gaze to the eggs at the end of the child's turn in line 1. As we argued above, the environmental noticing here can be described as a "double-barreled" action in the sense that it not only makes it relevant for the recipient to share the noticing, but also initiates a decision-making sequence. The mother in this excerpt starts considering a purchase of eggs in line 3, first with a questioning repeat (*tamago:?*) and then with the NP + question particle *ka* produced with flat intonation (*tamago ka:*), a format often used for a self-addressed question embodying the act of contemplating in a monologue. In effect, she announces that it is her exclusive role to make a purchase decision and that her child will not be included in the decision-making process. This analysis is supported by the mother's subsequent conduct. Instead of conveying her final decision to the child, she passes by the egg section without saying anything (Figure 9.4).

The next excerpt shows a case in which a mother uses the Type 1 format. The way mothers use Type 1 utterances differs from how fathers or children use them. Mothers tend to use Type 1 utterances in situations where the products that they refer to are not present in the immediate surroundings. As shown in Excerpt 9.5 below, when a mother uses a Type 1 utterance, it is recurrently observed that the father and children begin to search the surrounding environment, locate the product mentioned by the mother, and change the course of their movement toward that product.

Excerpt 9.5 2014-06-01-2 10:34: Family B: Juice (CHI = child, DAD = father, MOM = mother)

```
((Father gazes at side dishes and says that they do not need side dishes))
01 MOM: -> juusu: ((Mother looks in the direction where juices are located))
           juice
           Juice
02 DAD: -> juusu (0.2) hai
           juice       yes
           Juice (0.2) Okay
((The father changes the course of his movement and heads toward the
juice section))
```

When the mother utters *juusu:* ("Juice") in line 1, she and the other family members are at some distance from the shelves where juices are stacked. The father responds by first repeating the product name mentioned by the mother and then producing an acceptance token *hai* ("Okay"). Immediately following these utterances in line 2, the father (and the children) start walking towards the juice section. Here, what the father does in response to the mother's mention of a product name is quite different from the responsive actions produced by the mothers in the previous two excerpts. By producing an acceptance token and starting to walk towards where the product is located, the father shows *compliance* rather than engaging in joint decision-making. That is, the father organizes his conduct so as to display his understanding that the purchase decision has already been made by the time the mother produces the sequence-initiating utterance. This in effect ascribes to the mother's Type 1 utterance the action of giving a *directive* to obtain the product to be purchased, rather than nominating the product for purchase consideration. In our data, it is recurrently observed that Type 1 utterances used by mothers are understood as claiming a stronger deontic stance than when fathers and children use them.

So far, we have examined how different actions are ascribed to Type 1 utterances when they are used by different family members. In the remainder of this section, we describe in more detail how family members' orientations to one another's deontic rights affect action ascription by focusing on Type 1 utterances produced by fathers or children and examining how the sequences initiated by those utterances are organized.

The following case is similar to Excerpt 9.3. The father walks ahead of the mother and, as he walks by the fruit section, verbalizes his noticing with an utterance consisting of a stand-alone NP, *kudamono* ("fruit"). Just as in Excerpt 9.3, the mother in this excerpt appears to have paid no attention to the fruits when the father produces this utterance. Furthermore, like the father in Excerpt 9.3, the father in this excerpt continues walking as he produces his utterance in line 5. To be more precise, he begins to walk slowly at the very beginning of his utterance, as if to designedly exhibit his stance that he will not participate in the purchase decision-making *per se*.

Excerpt 9.6 2014-06-01-2 22:03: Family B: Fruit (CH1 = child 1, DAD = father, MOM = mother)

```
01 CH1:      ma:ma: (.) [(          )nacchatta= ((CH1's shoe appears to have
             come off.))
             mom                    have.become
             Mo::m, (.) I've (            )
02 DAD:                 [ku-
03 MOM:      =aa hai hai.  ((Waits for CH1))
              oh yes yes
              Oh okay.
04           (3.9)  ((CH1 puts on shoe and catches up with DAD and CH2.))
05 DAD: ->   △kudamo#no
              fruits
   dad       △begins to walk slowly———>
   mom       >>gazes at vegetable section->
   fig                #fig.9.5
```

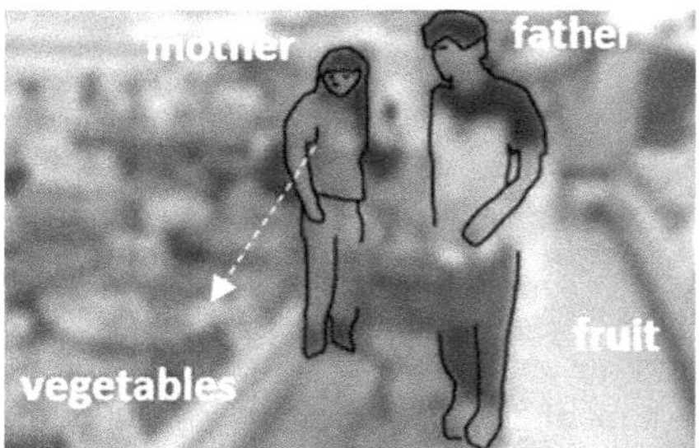

Figure 9.5 Mother gazes at vegetables

```
06           (1.2)
   fat       —>
   mot       —>
07 MOM: ->   $i#ranai=
              not.need
              ((We)) don't need ((them)).
   dad       ——————————————>
   mom       $gazes at fruit section->
   fig         #fig.9.6
```

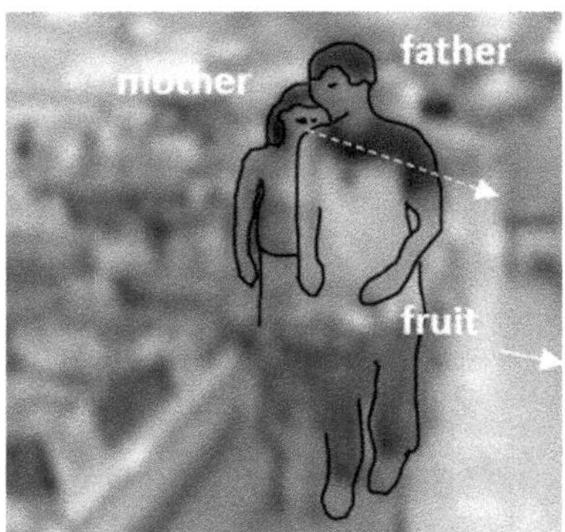

Figure 9.6 Mother directs her gaze toward the fruit section

```
08 DAD:     =iran?
             not.need
             ((We)) don't need ((them))?
   dad      ——>
   mom      ——>
09 MOM:     un
            No
   dad      ->
   mom      ->
10          (0.1)$&(      0.4       )
   dad      ————————————————————————>
   mom      ——$&looks forward->
11 DAd:     konna       mon?
            like.this thing
            Is this all?
```

In line 7, the mother responds to the father's utterance by declaring that there is no need to buy fruits. Her response contains two actions; while she responds to the *environmental noticing* implemented by the father's utterance by directing her gaze towards the fruits, she also responds to the *nomination* of fruits for purchase consideration by making a final decision. When she makes the decision not to purchase fruits, she does not explain why they do not need fruits. The way the mother constructs her turn displays her stance that no account is necessary for her declaration.

If we regard a rejection of this sort as a dispreferred response, then the mother's response may be seen as somewhat puzzling since it lacks any features (accounts, mitigations, etc.) that are often associated with how dispreferred second pair parts are produced (Schegloff 2007: 63–7). It is true that her response comes after a 1.2 second gap (line 6), yet this delay appears to be caused by the mother's body configuration when the first pair part was produced by the father. That is, since the mother had been paying attention to products other than fruits, she could not respond immediately. To be more precise, she is gazing at vegetables when the father utters *kudamono* ("fruit") in line 5 (Figure 9.5), and continues examining the vegetables during the following 1.2-second silence (line 6). Then, she twists her head, directs her gaze toward the fruit section (Figure 9.6), and says *iranai* "((We)) don't need ((them))" (line 7). Therefore, the delay in line 6 is likely not a feature of a dispreferred response. While the father's first pair part turn does not embody a claim of strong deontic rights over purchase decision-making, the mother's second pair part turn *does* display her stance that she has the right to decide whether to buy the product. This display of a deontic gradient (Stevanovic 2013) of influential power in making a purchase decision, embodied by the mother's turn, may explain why her turn does not contain any features associated with dispreferred actions. That is, as the father presents himself as a person who has weaker right to impact the decision-making, the mother can decide not to buy the product without any hesitation or account.

In Excerpt 9.7, the father mentions *moyashi* ("bean sprouts") in line 1 as he, the mother, and the child approach the section where bean sprouts are stacked.

Excerpt 9.7 2014-06-01-2 20:37 (Family B: Bean sprouts) (DAD = father)

```
01 DAD:-> moyashi
          bean.sprouts
          Bean sprouts
02      -> ((Mother looks at bean sprouts))
03      -> ((Mother, Father, and Child walk past bean sprouts))
```

In response to the father's Type 1 utterance in line 1, the mother twists her head and looks at the bean sprouts in line 2. Unlike the mothers in the previous fragments, however, the mother in this excerpt produces no verbal response and the three family members walk past the bean sprouts without adding them to the shopping basket. Here, the mother's conduct can be described as responding to the *noticing* embodied by the father's utterance with her glance at the bean sprouts (line 2), while turning down the *nomination* made by the father's utterance by continuing to walk past the bean sprouts (line 3).

So far, we have been examining cases of Type 1 utterances that contain a stand-alone NP in them. In our data, we identified a closely-related turn format consisiting of an NP followed by the topic particle *wa*.[3] From a structural point of view, [NP + *wa* (+?)] can be described as the first component of the topic-comment structure, such as *Tomato wa akai* ("Tomatoes are red"), where

[3] According to previous studies (e.g., Kuno 1973), the particle *wa* serves to present the preceding NP as the topic of the sentence, or as having a contrastive relationship with another NP. Takagi (2001: 190), based on her analysis on caregiver–child interaction, argues that [NP + *wa*] turn format is sensitive both to the "initial-ness" in the sequence it initiates and to the "embedded-ness" of the sequence it initiates within the activity already underway.

[NP + *wa*] (e.g., *tomato* + *wa*) provides the topic and the subsequent predicate (e.g., *akai* ["red"]) provides the comment. Note that, like Type 1 utterances containing stand-alone NPs, utterances in the form of [NP + *wa* (+?)] do not contain a predicate. Indeed, as we will show below, utterances in the form of [NP + *wa* (+?)] work quite similarly to utterances containing stand-alone NPs within the context of purchase decision-making. We thus regard [NP + *wa* (+?)] as a subcategory of the Type 1 format.

Excerpt 9.8 presents a case of an utterance in the form of [NP + *wa* (+?)] produced by a father to initiate a decision-making sequence. Here, the father approaches the shelf of frozen foods.

Excerpt 9.8 2014-06-01-2 22:42 (Family B: Frozen foods) (DAD = father, MOM = mother)

```
01 DAD: -> reetoo shokuhin wa?
          frozen food     TP
          Frozen foods wa?
02        (1.0) ((Mother turns her gaze to the frozen foods.))
03 MOM: -> ↑wa: i:ran::
           TP  not.need
          wa are not needed.
04 DAD:   iran?
          not.need
          Not needed?
05 MOM:   un
          No
06        (4.1)
07 DAD:   ja   konna     mon?
          then like.this thing
          Then, is this all?
08 MOM:   ↑un!
          Yep!
```

The sequence-initiating utterance in line 1 consists of an NP, *reetoo shokuhin* ("frozen food"), followed by the topic particle *wa*. In line 3, the mother repeats *wa* and then provides a predicate, *i:ran::* ("are not needed"), which completes the topic-comment structure initiated by the father's utterance. This turn format shares common features with those turns consisting of a stand-alone NP in that the actions performed by utterances in this turn format are "double-barreled." The mother in Excerpt 9.8 responds to the noticing aspect of the turn by bringing her gaze toward the product mentioned (line 2), and subsequently responds to the nominating aspect of the turn by declaring that the product need not be purchased (line 3). While we acknowledge the possibility that the presence or absence of the particle *wa* could have some important consequences for how these utterances work interactionally, at least as far as our data are concerned, we did not find any significant differences between the [stand-alone NP] format and the [NP + *wa*] format. We thus treat these two formats as subtypes of essentially the same format for noticing and nominating a product for purchase consideration.

In this subsection, we have described how Type 1 utterances produced by fathers or children are responded to by mothers and shown that mothers treat these utterances as both registering a noticing and nominating a product for purchase consideration. This action ascription is deeply embedded in the physical environment inside the supermarket, as well as the ongoing activity they are engaged in (i.e., grocery shopping). To bring attention to an item or a product in as "semiotically rich" an environment (De Stefani 2013) as a supermarket is an accountable matter in the sense that, of all the items and products displayed in the participants' surroundings, why they choose to bring attention to a particular one becomes an issue. This accountability, in combination with the deontic gradient between participants discussed above, explains why utterances presenting the name of (the category of) a product are not merely understood as registering noticing,[4] but also as performing an action relevant to the ongoing activity of grocery shopping, i.e., *nominating* a product for purchase consideration. In other words, the fact that the father or the child

[4] There are cases in which registering a noticing is the main action performed by a sequence-initiating turn. In such cases, fathers or children regularly design their utterances so that justification for their noticing is provided explicitly. In Excerpt 9.9, the father finds *Awaji*-grown onions. *Awaji* refers to an island known as a place where onions are grown as specialty products.

Excerpt 9.9 2014-06-01-1 04:53 (Family A: Awaji-grown onions) (DAD = father, MOM = mother)

```
01 DAD: -> mite (0.4) awaji san  no tamanegi ((Points at onions))
           look       Awaji grown LK onion
           Look. (0.4) Awaji-grown onions.
02         (0.7)
03 MOM: -> honma ya (0.2) sakki no [yatsu ya
           really CP      earlier LK thing FP
           Oh yeah. (0.2) It ((is what I saw)) a minute ago.
04 DAD:                            [<su>goi na
                                     amazing FP
                                    <A>mazing
```

First, to establish joint attention toward the onions, the father uses the directive *mite* ("look"), thereby formulating his utterance as registering a noticing explicitly. Then, in the subsequent part of his utterance, the father registers the noteworthiness of the object being mentioned by including the origin of the product, which is a well-known area for specialty onions. Thus, he provides justification for his noticing. The way the mother responds to the father's sequence-initiating action supports this observation. Her response, *honma ya* ("oh yeah," lit. "That's true"), displays her agreement with the noteworthiness of the onions registered by the father. Here, rather than treating the father's sequence-initiating action as a double-barreled action combining a noticing and nominating a product for purchase, the mother only responds to it as a noticing.

chose to bring attention to a specific item or product is understood by reference to the ongoing activity of grocery shopping, and is treated as initiating a decision-making sequence. Initiating a decision-making sequence puts the father or the child in a position to display their stance toward how he or she will be involved (or not) in the subsequent process of decision-making. The stance displayed by their turn is that they do not have a strong inclination about the outcome of decision-making. Grammatical constructions (and the accompanying embodied conduct) are employed as resources to exhibit this stance toward the decision-making process.

Before we conclude this subsection, let us make one more observation. Fathers or children rarely – if ever – resist mothers' decisions not to buy the products they nominate. For instance, in Excerpt 9.7 above, the decision-making sequence ends with the mother's (nonverbal) rejection in the responsive position, and no (verbal) response from the father follows. In the cases where the sequence is expanded after the mother's rejection, the post-expansion (Schegloff 2007) usually takes the form of a confirmation request sequence that is brought to closure as soon as the mother provides confirmation (see Excerpt 9.6, lines 8–9; Excerpt 9.8, lines 4–5).[5] We did not find any cases where the mother's rejection is followed by extended post-expansion sequences initiated by the father or the children in which the mother's decision is overtly contested. This observation provides further empirical support for the existence of the deontic gradient of influential power in decision-making between the mother and the father/children. That is, by designating themselves as not being involved in making the final decision as to whether to buy the product in question, fathers and children present their up-front stance that they will not resist or disagree with mothers' decisions.

9.4.2 *Division of Labor Concerning Purchase Decision-Making*

We have argued that fathers' or children's sequence-initiating turns that lack a predicate show their deontic stance that they are not in a position to make a purchase decision. The notion of the role of a "buying center" (Webster & Wind 1972) may be relevant here. A buying center is a unit consisting of group members who play various roles concerning purchase decision-making, such as the initiator (the person who initiates a decision-making process about a particular item or product), the influencer (the person who influences the outcome of decision-making), and the decider (the person who makes the final decision). By initiating a decision-making sequence using the turn formats that

[5] When mothers accept nominations, post-expansions tend to take different forms since additional interactional moves may be needed to implement their purchase behavior. For example, see Excerpt 9.3, lines 7–8.

do not contain an explicit mention of a predicate, fathers and children appear to play the role of the initiator of a decision-making process while avoiding presenting themselves as the decider. Mothers, on the other hand, play the role of the decider by uttering a predicate, which was missing in the fathers' or children's sequence-initiating turns. We argue here that there is a division of labor among family members in purchase decision-making. Family members, as members of a buying center, are assigned different roles and contribute differently to the decision-making process. Needless to say, these roles are locally negotiated. Family members constantly display their roles concerning purchase decision-making by exhibiting their deontic stance. Action ascription from the responsive position in a decision-making sequence is shaped in part by the roles assigned to the participants. That is, different actions are ascribed to sequence-initiating turns produced in the same utterance format depending on who initiates the sequence and who responds to it.

The environmental contexts in this supermarket afford this division of labor. Family members allocate their attention independently of one another to search for and pick up products effectively from their surroundings. In that sense, the father and children, as members of the family, play an important role during the shopping process, even if they may not have the right to make a final decision.

9.4.3 Type 2: [NP + Predicate]

Unlike Type 1, Type 2 not only presents an NP designating a product of interest, but also a predicate (e.g., a verb) concerning what to do with the product designated by the NP. In other words, while Type 1 is a lexical or phrasal construction, Type 2 is a sentential (or clausal) construction. In this subsection, we focus on Type 2 utterances produced by fathers and children to investigate how mothers ascribe different actions to these utterances as compared to when fathers and children produce Type 1 utterances.

Excerpt 9.10 (extended version of Excerpt 9.2) illustrates how an utterance in Type 2 is employed by a father to initiate a decision-making sequence. In line 5, the father produces the utterance *ninniku no mee iran* ("Don't ((we)) need garlic sprouts?"), which consists of an NP (*ninniku no me* ["garlic sprouts"]) and a negatively formatted verb (*iran* ["don't need"]).

Excerpt 9.10 2014-06-01-1 05:28 (Family A: Garlic sprouts) (DAD = father, MOM = mother, CHI = child)

```
01 DAD:  °aa° (0.4) kono hen  wa?    ((Points at a shelf))
          oh         this area TP
         °Oh° (0.4) ((How about)) this area?
```

02 **MOM:** **(** **)** **((Turns to Father while murmuring something))**
03 **CHI:** **nameko ya tte.**
nameko.mushroom CP QT
((It)) says nameko mushrooms.
04 **(1.8)** **((Father touches a package of garlic sprouts.))**
05 **DAD: -> ninniku no mee iran**
garlic LK sprout not.need
Don't ((we)) need garlic sprouts?
06 **(1.2)**
07 **MOM: -> eh mata yaku n**
huh again grill N
Huh? Are ((you)) going to grill ((them)) again?
08 **DAD:** **un:**
Yeah
09 **(1.0)**
10 **CHI:** **iru:?**
need
Do ((we)) need ((them))?
11 **(3.7)** **((Father continues to touch the package of garlic sprouts))**
12 **CHI:** **[iru:?**
need
Do ((we)) need ((them))?"
13 **DAD:** **[se- (.) sekkaku da kara ikko ((Hands a package to CHI))**
rare.chance CP because 1.piece
((It))'s too good an opportunity to miss, so ((we'll buy)) one."

Several observations can be made about the father's utterance in line 5. First and foremost, it includes a predicate (*iran* ["don't need"]) that is directly relevant to purchase decision-making; i.e., one of needing (or not) the product in question. In other words, unlike Type 1 utterances used by fathers, the father in this excerpt shows his deontic stance that he is in a position to say something about whether or not to purchase the garlic sprouts. Type 1 utterances discussed above are used to nominate products for consideration, but do not contain elements referring to any aspects of the decision to be made. Thus, Type 2 utterances contrast with Type 1 utterances with regard to the deontic stance they index in that the former contain elements that indicate the speaker's involvement in the subsequent decision-making.[6]

This does not mean that the father claims a strong deontic right using a Type 2 utterance. In fact, fathers carefully calibrate their stance on the deontic gradient vis-à-vis the mother by employing various resources to display their understanding that they have a weaker deontic right than the mother, even

[6] Compared with Type 1 utterances used by fathers and children (forty-three cases found in our data), Type 2 utterances used by fathers and children occur less frequently – thirteen cases, which is less than one third as often. This skewed distribution may reflect the fathers' and children's understanding that their default or primary role in the decision-making process is that of the initiator, and not of either the influencer or the decider.

when they claim that they are in a position to say something related to decision-making. For instance, in Excerpt 9.10 above, the father uses a negatively formatted verb, which makes his utterance "prefer" a negative answer.[7] By doing so, the father shows his understanding that the recipient might not be willing to accept his sequence-initiating action. There are no observable details in the interaction that would lead the father to anticipate an upcoming rejection by the mother. We argue that the negatively formatted verb displays the father's orientation to his weaker deontic status, even though the inclusion of a predicate in his sequence-initiating turn exhibits a stronger deontic stance than that expressed by the turn designs fathers ordinarily employ. This incongruence between the father's deontic stance, displayed through his turn design, and the deontic status ordinarily associated with him, motivates the mother to make an inference as to why her husband has opted to design his turn the way he did.

The mother's response in line 7 clearly illustrates how the incongruence between deontic stance and status noted above leads the recipient to make an inference in the responsive position. Here, the mother says *eh mata yaku n* ("huh? Are ((you)) going to grill ((them)) again?"),[8] which exhibits her inference that the father's utterance is based on his personal desire. Namely, even if the father may ordinarily be considered not to have the deontic right to make a purchase decision about products for family use, he may well be regarded as possessing the right to make a move for purchasing a product for his personal use. In this sense, the mother treats the father's action as making a *proposal* which displays his stance toward buying garlic sprouts.

Attributing the speaker's personal desire to an initiating turn in a decision-making sequence is also observed in Excerpt 9.11. In this excerpt, the mother in line 3 treats the father's utterance in line 1 as expressing his personal desire to buy the product he mentioned.

Excerpt 9.11 2014-06-01-3 18:20 (Family C: Cheese) (DAD = father, MOM = mother)

(The family members have been looking for a type of cheese that the mother wanted to purchase. They scanned the dairy section to no avail. The mother begins to leave the dairy section.)

```
01 DAD: -> e (.) hutuuni    kore: akan      no
           eh   as.normal  this  not.good  QP
           Huh? (.) Is thi:s one not good enough?
```

[7] In our data, we find seven out of thirteen cases where Type 2 utterances employed by fathers or children are either negatively formatted or somehow softened in terms of their deontic claims.

[8] The interjection *eh* in turn-initial position may indicate that the stance her husband had taken departs from her *a priori* expectation (Hayashi 2009).

```
          ((Father touches a package of cheese.))
02        (3.1)
          ((Mother turns back to the dairy section and looks at the cheese))
03 MOM: -> sore? (0.8) sore hoshii n?
          it         it   want  QP
          That one? (0.8) ((Do you)) want that one?
04        (1.0)
05 MOM:   taberu? zettai
          eat     absolutely
          ((Are you)) sure ((you are going)) to eat ((it))?
```

In line 1, the father produces an utterance with a predicate and, by doing so, indicates a deontic stance that he is in a position to say something about whether to purchase the cheese in question. Here, the father deploys a grammatically negative predicate (*akan* "not good"), thereby displaying his orientation to the possibility of an upcoming rejection by the mother.[9] We argue, as we did with the father's utterance in the previous excerpt, that the father in this excerpt orients to the fact that his utterance displays a deontic stance that is incongruous with the deontic status ordinarily associated with him. This incongruence leads the mother to make an inference as to what motivates the father to opt to design his turn the way he did. Thus, in response to the father's utterance, the mother asks, *sore? (0.8) sore hoshii n?* ("That one? (0.8) ((Do you)) want that one?") in line 3. She displays her inference that what motivated the father to claim his deontic rights by producing a predicate in the sequence-initial position is his desire to purchase the cheese for personal consumption.[10] She then seeks confirmation from the father that he will consume the cheese (line 5). By doing so, the mother in effect displays her action ascription concerning the father's prior utterance. That is, she treats the father's utterance as making a *proposal* to purchase the cheese, and based on that action ascription, she checks to see if a condition for agreeing to the proposal is met. This type of account solicitation by the mother is also observed in line 7 of Excerpt 9.10 (*eh mata yaku n* ("huh? Are ((you)) going to grill ((them)) again?"). The fact that an account is pursued when the fathers make a proposal supports our claim that a weaker deontic status is ordinarily conferred up fathers.

Sometimes, fathers or children exhibit their personal desire to buy a product in the turn design of their sequence-initiating action and thereby forestall

[9] Note that since the mother is beginning to leave the cheese section, the likelihood of an upcoming rejection can be regarded as quite high. We thank an anonymous reviewer for bringing this point to our attention.

[10] When the mother pursues a response from the father in line 5, she also uses this inference as a resource to construct her question.

mothers' inference. For instance, in Excerpt 9.12, a child is holding a chocolate candy when she asks her mother for permission to buy it (line 1).

Excerpt 9.12 2014-06-01-1 15:16 (Family A: Snack) (MOM = mother, CHI = child)

01 **CHI: -> mama chokobooru katte ii?((holding a chocolate candy))**
mom chocoball buy can
Mom can ((I)) buy Chocoball ((=chocolate candy))?
02 **(0.3)**
03 **MOM: °un°**
yes
°Yes°
04 **(0.2)**
05 **CHI: ii?**
OK
Is it okay?
06 **MOM: °ii yo°**
OK FP
°It's okay.°

The design of the child's utterance in line 1 encodes her personal desire to purchase the product mentioned. This is achieved by invoking the [mother–child] membership categories (Sacks 1972) and casting herself as a child. First, the child addresses her recipient as *mama* ("mom"), thereby invoking the [mother] category. Second, she asks her mother for permission to purchase *Chocoball*, a chocolate candy which is arguably a product for children. This act of asking her mother for permission to buy a product for children is bound to the [child] category. With these features of her turn design, the child encodes her personal desire to purchase the product in question. Thus, the mother, as a recipient, does not have to infer why her child has used a Type 2 utterance to express a stronger deontic stance than usual. Indeed, unlike the mothers' responses in Excerpts 9.10 and 9.11, the mother in this excerpt simply grants her child permission to buy the candy in line 3. Note here that, although the inclusion of a predicate in the child's utterance in line 1 expresses a stronger deontic stance than the deontic status often associated with children, the child does display her careful calibration of her stance on the deontic gradient vis-à-vis her mother. That is, while the child claims her deontic right to say something about the purchase of the product in question based on her personal desire, she leaves the final decision to her mother by framing her utterance as a request for permission. And, by granting the child permission, the mother in turn displays her action ascription concerning the child's utterance, that is, that the child has made a *proposal* to purchase the product in question within the activity of purchase decision-making for which she, the mother, plays the role of the decider.

In this subsection, we described how utterances in the [NP + predicate] format used by fathers or children exhibit incongruence between the deontic stance indexed by the turn design and the deontic status ordinarily associated with those participants. We then argued that such incongruence motivates mothers to make an inference as to why the fathers or children opted to design their turns the way they did. Mothers often ascribe to these utterances the action of making a proposal to purchase the product in question based on the speakers' personal interest in it and respond to them as such.

9.5 Discussion

We found that when fathers or children initiate a decision-making process, they frequently use an abbreviated utterance format: [name of (the category of) the product (+?)] (e.g., *Tamago?* ["Eggs?"]). Mothers ascribe to utterances in this format "double-barreled" actions: *environmental noticing* and *nominating* products for purchase consideration. This action ascription is displayed by mothers' subsequent conduct; i.e., first by bringing their attention to the object of the fathers' or children's noticing, and then by producing a response in which mothers make their own decision as to whether to purchase the product or not. Mothers produce a predicate (e.g., *Kau* ["((We'll)) buy ((it))"], *Iranai* ["((We)) don't need ((it))"]) indicating their decision regarding the purchase of the product mentioned by fathers or children. By treating preceding utterances as simply *nominating* products and by responding to them with a declaration of their own decision, mothers claim their deontic rights.

On the other hand, when fathers or children produce an utterance in a sentential format (e.g., *Tamago kawanai*? ["Why don't ((we)) buy eggs?"]), mothers ascribe to it a kind of *proposal* and attribute the fathers' or children's desire to purchase the product to it (e.g., by saying "Do you want eggs?"). As these patterns show, family members constantly negotiate their deontic rights to make a purchase decision by coordinating the utterance format and the corresponding action ascription.

A possible account for the differential action ascription of the lexical/phrasal format vs, the sentential format from the responsive position might be that some predicates (such as verbs to *buy*, *need*, *have*, etc.) operate as indicators of the speakers' deontic rights since they concern making purchase decisions. To put it another way, mothers have deontic rights to produce predicates without the need to provide any account for using them. In cases where fathers or children utter predicates, recipients are motivated to find out why they claim a deontic right.

Through detailed examinations of purchase decision-making processes, we also described how family members effectively organize a mundane, everyday activity (i.e., grocery shopping at the supermarket). Despite the fact that purchase decision-making is always embedded within concrete physical and social contexts, traditional consumer behavior research has rarely investigated real-time decision-making processes in "environmentally rich" situations. In our study, we identified practices through which family members solve interactional problems *in situ* to successfully organize decision-making processes in an environment where a vast array of products are stacked and displayed around the participants. First, we showed that an interactional move to establish joint orientation toward a product may also operate as an initiating action of a decision-making sequence. Second, by using an abbreviated utterance form while continuing to walk or temporarily suspending walking, members can select items efficiently as they navigate through the aisles of the supermarket. The Type 1 turn format suits the participants' practical concerns. Given that the basic mode of their physical activity is walking around, shortened utterance forms are convenient in effectively bringing others' attention to particular items in their surroundings.[11] Mothers' responses in the second position of a sequence also embody their orientation toward making the sequence minimal. In many cases, mothers' responsive turns are produced with lexical and phrasal constructions (see Excerpts 9.6 and 9.8) or no verbal response at all (see Excerpt 9.7). Moreover, as discussed earlier, the Type 1 format rarely leads to an extended post-expansion where the mother's decision is contested by the father or children. Third, fathers and children who initiate a decision-making sequence not only display their weaker deontic stance, but also cast the mother as the person who has deontic rights to make a purchase decision. This is achieved by using grammatically abbreviated forms of utterances. Given that Type 1 utterances leave it up to their recipients to utter a predicate indicating their purchase decision, these utterances embody their speakers' weaker deontic stance while casting the recipients as possessing deontic rights over purchase decisions. In other words, fathers and children appear to try to reduce contingencies concerning purchase decision-making by exhibiting their stance that they will not resist whatever decision the mothers subsequently make. Our analysis thus elucidated the reflexive relationship between the structural properties of interactions and the members' practical and interactional achievement of their ongoing activities.[12]

[11] This point resonates with the findings of Sorjonen and Raevaara (2014), who demonstrate that a customer's usage of a phrasal format to make a request in convenience stores is deeply tied to the arrangements of the store's physical settings.

[12] One might wonder if this division of roles depends on who prepares everyday meals within the family. That is, if it is the father that ordinarily prepares meals in a particular family, he may be regarded as possessing deontic rights over purchase decisions. Although this possibility is

Space constraints did not allow us to analyze the participants' bodily conduct in a systematic manner. Data suggest that the speaker's bodily conduct and its relationship to the surrounding physical environment play an important role in producing and recognizing actions performed in purchase decision-making. Fathers or children, for instance, sometimes touch the package of a product while producing a Type 2 utterance. When fathers or children who initiate decision-making sequences are physically close to the product in question, their utterances and bodily conduct are often understood as showing commitment to purchasing the product. The precise role of bodily conduct in purchase decision-making remains to be explored.

9.6 Conclusions

This paper argued that the deontic stances realized through the choice of grammatical formats used in initiating decision-making sequences were important, both in terms of action formation and ascription. Types 1 and 2 have differentiated characteristics in terms of the deontic stance they display. While Type 1 shows a weaker deontic stance regarding the purchase decision, Type 2 claims the speaker's deontic rights (i.e., the right to say something about purchase decision-making).

As Couper-Kuhlen and Selting (2017: 211) argue, action ascription is intrinsically inferential. Hence, identifying a practice by which the inference of a recipient of a social action (cf. Deppermann 2018) becomes a matter of practical concern for the participants is important for investigating action ascription in talk-in-interaction. We have argued that incongruence between the deontic status that fathers or children are ordinarily associated with and the deontic stance they display through their choice of turn format (and other embodied conduct) creates an opportunity space (i.e., the second position in a decision-making sequence) for mothers to make an inference. Fathers and children constantly display a weaker deontic stance relative to mothers and show their understanding that that is their basic or primary mode of participation in the purchase decision-making activity. They sometimes choose the Type 2 format and present themselves as people who can say something about the decision-making. In such situations, mothers can see a mismatch between their deontic status and stance. Mothers are normatively expected to provide an adequate response since they are in the second position of an adjacency pair sequence. In order to provide a second pair part turn and move the decision-making sequence forward, mothers are motivated to infer why

plausible when we consider the current situation of division of household duties within Japanese families, further empirical research is needed in order to verify this point.

fathers and children have shown incongruence between their deontic status and stance.

It should also be noted that Type 1 utterance are differentially treated when produced by fathers/children vs. mothers. This suggest that how an action is ascribed may be shaped by roles concerning purchase decision-making in this particular social context. That is, whether the role of the producer of a Type 1 utterance is the initiator, the influencer, or the decider affects how the utterance is understood and responded to. CA research on action formation and ascription has sought to describe a wide array of interactional properties or resources that are enlisted for action formation and ascription. Our analysis has revealed another interactional resource – roles in purchase decision-making – can play an important part in action ascription.

Acknowledgments

We are grateful to Arnulf Deppermann, Michael Haugh, and two anonymous reviewers for their constructive criticism and helpful feedback on earlier drafts of our article. A version of this work was presented at the 25th Japanese/Korean Linguistics Conference held at the University of Hawai'i, Manoa on October 12–14, 2017. This work was supported by JSPS KAKENHI Grant Numbers 15K17144, 20K01883.

Notes on Abbreviations

Abbreviations used for the interlinear glosses in the transcripts:

CP = copula
FP = final particle
INJ = interjection
LK = nominal-linking particle
N = nominalizer
QP = question particle
QT = quotative particle
TP = topic particle

REFERENCES

Couper-Kuhlen, E. & Selting, M. (2017). *Interactional Linguistics: An Introduction to Language in Social Interaction*. Cambridge: Cambridge University Press.

Deppermann, A. (2018). Inferential practices in social interaction: A conversationanalytic account. *Open Linguistics*, 4(1), 1–37.

De Stefani, E. (2013). The collaborative organisation of next actions in a semiotically rich environment: Shopping as a couple. In P. Haddington, L. Mondada & M.

Nevile, eds., *Interaction and Mobility: Language and the Body in Motion*. Berlin: De Gruyter, pp. 123–51.
(2014). Establishing joint orientation towards commercial objects in a self-service store: How practices of categorisation matter. In M. Nevile, P. Haddington, T. Heinemann & M. Rauniomaa, eds., *Interacting with Objects: Language, Materiality, and Social Activity*. Amsterdam: John Benjamins, pp. 271–94.
(forthcoming). Approaching the counter: Situated decision-making of couples shopping in a supermarket. In B. A. Fox, L. Mondada & M.-L. Sorjonen, eds., *Encounters at the counter: Language, embodiment and material objects in shops*. Cambridge: Cambridge University Press.
Enfield, N. J. & Sidnell, J. (2017). *The Concept of Action*. Cambridge: Cambridge University Press.
Hayashi, M. (2009). Marking a "noticing of departure" in talk: Eh-prefaced turns in Japanese conversation. *Journal of Pragmatics*, 41(10), 2100–29.
Heritage, J. (2013). Action formation and its epistemic (and other) backgrounds. *Discourse Studies*, 15, 551–78.
Keller, M. & Ruus, R. (2014). Pre-schoolers, parents and supermarkets: Co-shopping as a social practice. *International Journal of Consumer Studies*, 38(1), 119–26.
Kidwell, M. & Zimmerman, D. H. (2007). Joint attention as action. *Journal of Pragmatics*, 39(3), 592–611.
Kuno, S. (1973). *The Structure of the Japanese language, Vol. 3*. Cambridge, MA: MIT Press.
Laurier, E. (2008). Drinking up endings: Conversational resources of the café. *Language & Communication*, 28(2), 165–81.
Levinson, S. C. (2013). Action formation and ascription. In J. Sidnell & T. Stivers, eds., *Handbook of Conversation Analysis*. Chichester: Wiley-Blackwell, pp. 103–30.
Sacks, H. (1972). An initial investigation of the usability of conversational data for doing sociology. In D. Sudnow, ed., *Studies in Social Interaction*. New York, NY: The Free Press, pp. 31–74.
(1992). *Lectures on Conversation, Volume 2*. Oxford: Basil Blackwell.
Schegloff, E. A. (2007). *Sequence Organization in Interaction: A Primer in Conversation Analysis*. Cambridge: Cambridge University Press.
Seuren, L. M. (2018). Assessing answers: Action ascription in third position. *Research on Language and Social Interaction*, 51(1), 33–51.
Sorjonen, M.-L. & Raevaara, L. (2014). On the grammatical form of requests at the convenience store: Requesting as embodied action. In P. Drew & E. Couper-Kuhlen, eds., *Requesting in Social Interaction*. Amsterdam: John Benjamins, pp. 243–68.
Stevanovic, M. (2011). Participants' deontic rights and action formation: The case of declarative requests for action. *Interaction and Linguistic Structures (InLiSt)*, 52, 1–37.
(2012). Establishing joint decisions in a dyad. *Discourse Studies*, 14(6), 779–803.
(2013). Deontic rights in interaction: A conversation analytic study on authority and cooperation. Dissertation, University of Helsinki.

Stevanovic, M. & Peräkylä, A. (2012). Deontic authority in interaction: The right to announce, propose, and decide. *Research on Language and Social Interaction*, 45(3), 297–321.

Takagi, T. (2001). Sequence management in Japanese child-adult interactions. Dissertation, University of California, Santa Barbara.

Webster, F. E. & Wind, Y. (1972). *Organizational Buying Behavior*. New York, NY: Prentice Hall.

10 Action Ascription and Action Assessment

Ya-*Suffixed Answers to Questions in Mandarin Conversation*

Yaxin Wu and Guodong Yu

10.1 Introduction

It is generally acknowledged in Conversation Analysis (hereafter CA) that people are doing social actions when talking to each other (Schegloff 1996a). What is even more fascinating is that interlocutors can successfully deliver and construe actions so that the progressivity of interactions can be smoothly achieved (Levinson 2013). CA research has demonstrated that people employ specific resources to perform an action. These resources may be syntactic, lexical, prosodic, or gestural in terms of composition, and are sensitive to their location within a turn constructional unit (hereafter TCU), turn, and sequence in terms of position (Heritage 2010). What makes action formation and action ascription more complicated is that a TCU may implement more than one action; furthermore, a primary action may be coupled with a secondary action. Specifically, a primary action is the action that places constraints on its response while a secondary action, which does "not change the nature of the sequential action type now due," is usually a display of the speaker's emotional, epistemic or deontic status etc. (Levinson 2013: 107). The primary action is an interactionally required action, while the secondary action is a parasitic one with its own interactional consequence. The secondary action is merely a modification or an enrichment of the primary action.

A complete understanding of an action involves not only its action type (primary action) but also its action property (secondary action) or "collateral effects" (Sidnell & Enfield 2014). In the responsive turn, the speaker displays both his/her attribution of the primary action and his/her assessment of the epiphenomenal properties of that action through different turn constructional components. Therefore, when a responsive turn is designed, what is woven into the turn includes not only practices doing social actions but also practices doing attitudes (emotional, moral, epistemic, deontic, etc.). The understanding of the former (i.e., primary action) is termed as action ascription (Levinson 2013), while the comprehension of the latter (i.e., secondary action) is called action assessment in the present study.

This research focuses on a particular parasitic action performed by the TCU-end particle *ya* (呀) attached to answers in question–answer sequences in Mandarin conversations. The particle *ya* investigated in this study is a practice to indicate the preceding questioning is construed as being inapposite, inappropriate or problematic. It shows the *ya* speaker's attitude toward the questioning he/she answers. The focus of the present study is action assessment, which is parasitic on or adheres to action ascription understood as "the assignment of an action to a turn as revealed by the response of a next speaker" (Levinson 2013: 104). Correspondingly, action assessment is understood as a display of the emotional, moral, epistemic, or deontic attitude toward the action ascribed. Action ascription and action assessment are joint contributions with different components of a TCU. For the present study, the answer as one component of a TCU ascribes the previous turn as a questioning, and the TCU-end particle *ya* tints the questioning with a sense of being inappropriate, inapposite, or problematic.

In talk-in-interaction, interlocuters deliver actions by means of composing linguistic or nonlinguistic resources into TCUs and construe actions by decomposing relevant TCUs into different constituting practices. Focusing on the TCU-end particle *ya* in answers to questioning, we aim to demonstrate the joint contributions made by the answer *per se* and the TCU-end particle *ya* for the action ascription to and action assessment of the interrogative as an inapposite questioning, which is hearably different from a mere answering when *ya* is not attached to the end of the answer. Since it is comparatively straightforward for an answer to ascribe the previous turn as a questioning, our focus will be on the second component, namely, the particle *ya* suffixed to answers. The goal of the present study is to unravel the grounds for assessing a questioning as inapposite/inappropriate when an answer ends with the particle *ya*.

10.2 When Inquiries Are Inappropriate

Questioning is a practice for interactants to seek information or confirmation from one another. As the first pair part of an adjacency pair (Heritage 1984a; Schegloff 2007), a questioning makes an answer as its second pair part conditionally relevant. However, when a questioning or inquiry is treated as inappropriate or problematic, either the questioner or the answerer can use communicative resources or practices to make the problematicity or inappositeness in questioning salient or even bring it to the surface of interaction.

In Mandarin, the particle "*a*" as a variant of *ya* (Chao 1968) can be attached to the end of question-word questions (similar to the wh-questions in English) to "mark either the matter addressed by the question, or the question itself, as in some way problematic from the *a* speaker's point of view" (Wu 2004: 172).

For instance, when an *a* is attached to question-word questions, disjunctive questions, or V-not-V questions,[1] the *a* speaker marks "the matter addressed by the question as problematic" (2004: 153) or "the very launching of the question as problematic" (2004: 164).

Excerpt 10.1 CS Party

```
01 W:     ta  hai          jianchai        ou↑
          3sg in-addition work-part-time PRT
          He also has a part-time job.
02 C:     [zhe  ge zeme kai
           this C  how  open
          [How do (I) open this?
03 W:     [hhh     san   tian zai    taida,      san   tian zuo ji        <hh
           (laugh) three day  at (University) three day  do (prostitute)
           (laugh)
           [hh Three days at Taiwan University, and three days as a
          pros(titute)-<hh'
04 L:     hhhhhhh [hhhh
          (laugh)
          hhhhhhh [hhhh
05 C: ->           [zhe  yao     zeme kai   a¿
                    this require how open PRT
                   [How can (I) open this A¿
```

Wu (2004: 155[19])

In this example, C is trying to open a bottle of water while the others are engaged in telling a joke. In line 2, C makes a request by questioning the method of opening the bottle (Wu 2004: 156), and C constructs this turn in a question-word question format (Li & Thompson 1981) without adding the particle *a* to the end of the question. This question/request does not receive a response from the other participants, who are engaged in their joke telling, though C still cannot open the bottle after several tries. Then C redoes her question/request in turn 5 in a slightly upgraded version (i.e., the addition of *yao*, 'require, need to' in line 5), and this turn is suffixed with the particle *a*. *A* at this sequential position helps its speaker C to express the stance that "the unavailability of the remedy being requested is unexpected and problematic" (Wu 2004: 156) or the "matter being addressed by the question as problematic" (2004: 153).

The problematicity or inappropriateness of a question could also be pointed out by the question recipient or the answerer. When a questioning is deemed as inappropriate, either because the sought-for information has been covered in the previous conversation (Wu & Heritage 2017) or the questioning itself steps into the questioner's own epistemic territory (Heritage & Raymond 2012;

[1] This stands for the "verb-not-verb" question in Mandarin, like "go-not-go" or "eat-not-eat."

Schegloff 1996a), the recipient could adopt conversational practices to problematize the questioning or to display its inappositeness. The particle *oh* in oh-prefaced responses to questions in English is one of such devices that interactants could employ to indicate that a question is "problematic in terms of its relevance, presuppositions, or context" (Heritage 1998: 291).

Excerpt 10.2 (Heritage: 01:18:2) (JAN = Jan, IVY = Ivy)

```
01 JAN:     .t okay now that' s roas:''' chickn isn' it. Th[at] =
02 IVY:                                                     [It-] =
03 JAN:     =[roasting chick' n<]
04 IVY:     =[it  h  a s   bee:n] cooked.
05          (.)
06 IVY:     It' s been co[oked.
07 JAN:                  [Iz ↑BEEN cooked.=
08 IVY: ->  =Oh yes.
09 JAN:     oh well thaz good....
```

Heritage (1998: 297[7])

In the above example, Ivy has explicitly conveyed twice the cooking state of the chicken respectively in lines 4 and 6 ("it has been cooked"), but Jan still requests confirmation about the cooking state of the chicken in line 7. It is observable to both the participants and conversation analysts that the answer to the inquiry has been given twice in the immediately preceding turns to the inquiry. Rationally people do not ask questions whose answers have been already given. So, it is unnecessary or inapposite for Jan to initiate the confirmation-seeking inquiry in line 7, which is responded with an oh-prefaced confirmation. Here *oh* is a practice to indicate the answerer's assessment of the inquiry as inapposite.

Like *oh*-prefaced responses to inquiries, the particle *ya* in Mandarin could also be used by the answerer to indicate to the questioner that his or her question in the adjacently previous turn is problematic or to assess the question as inappropriate. In our data, *ya* occurring at the end of a TCU, along with the other components preceding it, constitutes a complete intonation contour and syntactic structure and executes a recognizable social action, though the deletion of *ya* does not change the syntactic structure or the semantic meaning of the TCU which it suffixes.

Excerpt 10.3 2015/Liu Le:1 (LIU = Liu, HAO = Hao)

```
81 LIU: -> mǎi xīn  shǒujī    méi?
           buy new  cellphone not?
           Have you bought a new cell phone or not?
82         (0.8)
83 HAO: -> mǎi le  ya.  °zhè gè  jiu  shì°.
           buy PFV PRT. this CL  just be.
           I have bought one YA. The one I am using now is the new one.
```

In Excerpt 10.3, line 81 and the first TCU in line 83 constitute a questioning/answer adjacency pair, and the answer "I have bought one" ("*mǎi le*") is suffixed by a grammatically redundant *ya*. In addition to providing a type-conforming second pair part and ascribing line 81 as a question, what communicative function does *ya* perform?

10.3 *Ya* in Mandarin

Mandarin is a particle-rich language. Particles in Mandarin have been given different labels, such as, *Zhuci* (helping words) (Lü & Zhu 1953), *Yuqi ci* (mood words) (Wang 1955), sentence-final particles (Li & Thompson 1981), utterance particles (Luke 1990), and so on. No matter what label researchers adopt in their studies, particles in Mandarin are unstressed and have the neutral tone.[2]

Taking the grammatical functions of particles into consideration, we could divide the particles in Mandarin into two categories, namely, the constituent particles and the nonconstituent particles. The constituent particles are an essential or indispensable component of the syntactic structure which ends with them, and deleting the particles changes the syntactic structure and the semantic meaning of the TCU itself. For instance, TCU-end particle "*ma*" in Excerpt 10.4 is a constituent of the interrogative suffixed by it. This particle cannot be deleted, otherwise the syntactic structure is changed from an interrogative into a declarative, and the social action that it executes is changed from a question to a request or a command in Mandarin.

Excerpt 10.4

nǐ qù ma?	**nǐ qu.**
You go PRT?	You go.
Will you go?	*You go.*

The nonconstituent particles are not grammatically and semantically required components of the TCU to which these particles suffix, and the

[2] Six sentence-final particles along with their pragmatic functions are summarized as follows (Li & Thompson 1981: 238):

le	'Currently Relevant State'
ne	'Response to Expectation'
ba	'Solicit Agreement'
ou	'Friendly Warning'
a/ya	'Reduce Forcefulness'
ma	'Question'

deletion of them does not change the syntactic structure and the truth-conditional meaning of the utterance or TCU itself. For example:

Excerpt 10.5 Li & Thompson (1981: 315)

```
(a) chī -  fàn!
    eat -  food
    Eat!
(b) chī -  fàn   a/ya
    eat -  food  RF
    Eat, OK?!
```

Li & Thompson (1981:315[254])

A/Ya in Excerpt 10.5 is a nonconstituent particle, because grammatically speaking the deletion of *a/ya* does not change the syntactic structure of the imperative which is suffixed by *a/ya*. No matter whether the TCU ends with *a/ya*, the overall syntactic structure of the TCU is nevertheless an imperative, and the social action that it carries out is a directive. In the meantime, the addition of *a/ya* to the imperative does not modify its semantic meaning.

Generally speaking, nonconstituent particles relate to communicative contexts in various ways, but normally do not determine the action of the sentence/utterance to which they are suffixed; instead what they do is to indicate how an utterance "is to be taken by the hearer" (Li & Thompson 1981: 317). Specifically, *a/ya* performs the "function of reducing the forcefulness of the message conveyed by the sentence; it is glossed as "reduced forcefulness" (Li & Thompson 1981: 313). Chao (1968) specifies that *a/ya* can occur at the end of confirmative questions, commands, impatient statements, and warnings. The pragmatic function of *a/ya* is to make the listed actions less forceful, or more endearing, or less belligerent than the ones without *a/ya* at the end of the sentence. For instance, in Excerpt 10.5, (b) is friendlier than (a) as a command. One can imagine (a) "being used by a marine sergeant addressing the recruits in a mess hall," while for (b) one can imagine "a context in which a concerned parent is urging his/her child to eat" (Li & Thompson 1981:315).

Being different from the above observation of the functions of nonconstituent particles, the addition of these particles to a TCU may change the social action performed by the TCU from one type to another, implement extra social actions besides the one done by the TCU, or divulge the speaker's attitudinal stance on the preceding action responded to or the action implemented. More specifically, in the present study, we claim that adding a nonconstituent particle *ya* to an answer helps the answerer to indirectly point out to the questioner that the questioning is inapposite or problematic in some sense. Assessing an interrogative as a problematic questioning is realized by adding the particle *ya* to the answer. Compared to explicitly pointing out the inappropriateness of a questioning, the suffixation of the particle *ya* to the answer is off-record, and thus is comparatively soft in force, since it maintains the progressivity of the questioning–answer sequence without causing any hiatus and does not bring the inappropriateness onto the surface of communication.

10.4 Data and Research Method

This research adopts conversation analysis (Drew 2005) as its research method, and the phenomenon under investigation is part of a research project on turn-final particles in Mandarin conversations. The particle *ya* may occur in various sequential positions, one of which is the final position of an answer to a question.

The data for this study were collected by the Discourse & Interaction Group (DIG), Shanxi University, P.R. China. The corpus consists of 20 hours of audio-recordings of daily conversations in Mandarin, in which 102 examples of TCU-end *ya* in answers to questioning are identified. All the questions are employed to request information or confirmation. These examples are transcribed in accordance with the Jeffersonian transcription system (Jefferson 2004; Hepburn & Bolden 2017). The bottom-up data-driven method of conversation analysis is used to probe into the interactional details and particulars of the examples to reveal the practices used by members of society to implement, ascribe, and assess social actions.

10.5 TCU-End Particle *Ya* in Answers to Questioning: A Practice to Assess the Questioning as Inapposite

Interactants are not expected to tell each other what is known to them (Sacks 1987), thus it is understandable that interactants do not hope to be asked about information which is shared between them. When interactants are in a relation of epistemic symmetry concerning a piece of information (Heritage 2012), then there is no need for either of them to ask the other for that piece of information. If the questioning does happen, then the co-interactant could resort to conversational practices to tell or give a hint to the questioner that the questioning is inapposite.

When speakers respond with *ya*-suffixed answers to questions they challenge the presupposition in which the question grounds. With a *ya*-suffixed answer, question recipients assert that it is inconceivable that the questioner has based on such a presupposition to raise the question. The question should not have been asked due to its unsound presupposition. From the question recipient's perspective, the problem of the presupposition lies in the questioner's epistemic access and moral challenges (Stivers, Mondada & Steensig 2011). In some cases, the presupposition by which the question is triggered is not in alignment with the questioner's epistemic access, which is the common ground (Clark 1996) between the interlocuters; in other cases, the question presupposes the temporary missing of certain aspect of morality of the question recipient. Due to the above reasons, the presupposition of "aska-blility" of the question is contested (Stivers 2011), which puts the legitimacy of the questioning into doubt.

10.5.1 Treating Sought-for Information as Already Known

When a question concerns something which has been explicitly or implicitly mentioned in the present conversation or even right in the adjacently preceding turn to the questioning itself, then the question is treated as inappropriate by the answerer. Since the sought-for information is already given by the co-interactant, and this information or knowledge falls into the shared epistemic territory between them (Heritage 2013a, 2013b), there is simply no need for the question to be raised at all unless an account (Raymond & Stivers 2016) is provided by the questioner. Facing a question whose answer has just been given in the previous part of the conversation, the answerer in Mandarin could use the nonconstituent particle *ya* to signal to the questioner that the questioning is inappropriate.

Excerpt 10.6 2015/Liu Le:1 (HAO = Hao, LIU = Liu)

77 **HAO:** **jìu shi me:. wǒ hái chóu de, wǒ shuō shì-**
even be PRT. I even worry NOM, I say be-
78 **.hh méi diànhuà hàomǎ, $yī gè dōu méi yǒu$.**
.hh not telephone number, one CL even not have
It is so. I have been worried about that, I mean, I don't have telephone numbers now, not even one number.
79 **(.)**
80 **LIU:** **en:::=**
Uhu
Uhu.
81 **HAO: ->** **=dōu hé- huàn le shǒujī, dōu, dōu méi la.**
even with change PFV cellphone, all, all lost CRS
I have changed a cellphone. All the telephone numbers are lost.
82 **nà gè shǒujī huài la, dōu kāi bù liǎo jī.**
that CL cellphone broke CRS, even turn-on not able machine.
The previous one broke down, and it cannot even be turned on.
83 **LIU: ->** **mǎi xīn shǒujī méi?**
buy new cellphone not?
Have you bought a new cell phone or not?
84 **(0.8)**
85 **HAO: ->** **mǎi le ya. °zhè gè jìu shì°.=**
buy PFV PRT. this CL just be.
I have bought one YA. The one I am using now is the new one.
86 **LIU:** **=nǐ yǐqián shǒujī bú bèifèn ya,**
you previous cellphone not back-up PRT,

87 **nǐ méi yǒu nà zhǒng yúnpán ya:.**
you not have that kind cloud-drive PRT:.
Haven't you backed up your previous cellphone? Don't you have that kind of cloud-drive?

In this example, Liu calls Hao to keep in touch (Drew & Chilton 2000), and before this excerpt they found out that both of them had lost the telephone numbers on their respective cellphones. In lines 77–8, Hao expresses her anxiety about her failure in transferring telephone numbers onto her new phone, and an extreme case formulation *yīgè dōu méi yǒu* (Pomerantz 1986) is used in her troubles-telling, literally not having even one number on her phone. In lines 81–2, Hao details that her previous cellphone broke down and it could not even be switched on, so the broken one has been replaced (*hùan le shǒujī*), but she still does not have any phone numbers on this newly used phone. After Hao's troubles-telling sequence, the recipient Liu initiates an inquiry sequence in line 83, asking about whether Hao has bought a new phone. This question is grounded in the presupposition that Hao replaced her broken cellphone with an old phone which still works instead of a newly bought one, although what Hao said in lines 81 may be interpreted as she has replaced the broken phone with either an old but usable one or a newly bought one, although it is unusual for ordinary people to have an extra phone. After the inquiry, the second pair part does not come out immediately; instead, there occurs a 0.8-second silence. This silence could be a harbinger of a forthcoming disaffiliative response (Stivers 2008) or a sign of Hao's confusion. What comes after this significant silence is an answer suffixed with the particle *ya*, (*mǎi le ya*), namely, "I have bought a new one YA." *Ya* at this sequential position is not a necessary element both grammatically and semantically. This seemingly redundant *ya* indicates to its recipient Liu that she has the epistemic access to the answer of the question, so her question should not have been asked. The particle *ya* is a practice to assess the inquiry as inapposite. The second TCU in line 85 further supports her assessment, implying that the current call would have been impossible if she didn't buy a new phone. Liu's response in lines 86–7 could be understood as an acceptance of Hao's action assessment, since she does not deny the assessment. This practice of TCU-end *ya* indicating the inappositeness of the question is comparatively soft, because it is done simply by adding a nonconstituent particle to the type-conforming answer. Otherwise, Hao could interrupt the contiguity of the interaction by pointing out in line 85 that the answer had just been given or why Liu asks that again at this sequential position.

The presupposition of the question claimed as problematic by the answerer via the particle *ya* can be traced back either to the previous part of the current conversation or to the past conversations between the interlocuters. As shown in the above example, the questioner may have the epistemic access to the presupposition of the question from the preceding part of the current conversation. In the following example, the questioner bases her questioning on an inappropriate presupposition due to her forgetting her epistemic access to the answer from their past conversations.

Excerpt 10.7 2017/YSH: ZHR (QI = Qi, LI= Li)

```
01 QI:    wéi:
          hello:
          Hello.
02        (0.9)
03 LI:    āi:  gàn má  ne?
          yes: do what PRT?
          Yes, and what are you doing?
04 QI:    .hh āi ya, gāng gěi  nà  gè háizi  bǔ     wán    kè,
          .hh INT,  just give that CL child make-up finish lessons,
05        huí  sùshè  la.
          back  dorm  PRT.
          AIYA, just finished tutoring that child after his class, and I am
          back to the dorm now.
06        (0.9)
07 LI:    jīntiān bǔ      de  shá,
          today  make-up NOM what?
          What did you teach him today?
08 QI:    .h jīntiān:  bǔ     le  yī  fèn shùxué juàn,
          .h today: make-up CRS one CL  math   exam-paper,
09        hái      jiǎng lē  yī  fèn          yǔwén  juàn.
          further teach CRS one CL            Chinese exam-paper.
          Today I taught him a math exam paper, and a Chinese exam paper.
10        (0.5)
11 LI:-> >xiànzài zhèi háizi< jǐ        niánjí  la?
           now     this child< how-many grade  PRT?
           In which grade is he now?
12 QI:-> .h liù niánjí ya, wǒ gēn  nǐ shuō guò  da.
          .h six  grade  PRT, I  with  you say once PRT.
          Year Six YA, I told you once.
13        (0.8)
14 LI:    °ēn ° wàng  le  (0.5) lìu niánjí.
          uhm  forget CRS       six grade
          uhm. I forgot it.  Year Six.
15        (1.3)
16 QI:    ēn:
          uhm.
```

In line 3 the caller Li asks the called Qi what she is involved with. In her answer to Li's inquiry, Qi uses the person reference "that child" to refer to the student she just finished tutoring. Compared with "a child," "that child" is a recognitional person reference (Schegloff 1996a), which displays that Qi might have mentioned this child to Li in their past conversations and Qi assumes that Li can recognize this child. In line 11 Li asks Qi about the grade that the child is in now. This question evidences the child has been recognized by Li. Meanwhile, it also shows that Li does not have the epistemic access to the grade the child is in now. The adverbial "*now*" and the turn-final particle *la* in Li's question design convey that Qi has tutored the child for quite some time and Li might know which grade the child was in in the past but could not calculate which grade the child is in now due to the exact time when Qi told him about that last time. The particle *ya* suffixed to Qi's answer in line 12 assesses Li's question as inapposite and contests the askability of the question assuming the questioner Li has the epistemic access to the answer. This assumption is plainly supported by the second TCU of the turn, namely, Qi had already told Li about the grade of the child, so it is inconceivable for Li to presuppose that he didn't know it and raise the question. The second TCU is an account for the secondary action of the first TCU implemented by the particle *ya*, namely assessing the preceding questioning as inapposite. The account rationalizes her assessment.

10.5.2 Treating a Question as Challenging the Recipient's Morality

Similar to "of course" in English as the response to inquiry (confirmation-/ disconfirmation-seeking) (Stivers 2011), the particle *ya* suffixed to answers assesses the preceding question as problematic for the question and may sometimes challenge the morality of the question recipient. When the presupposition of the question is against the questioner's own claimed knowledge, the question becomes unaskable (Stivers 2011) and is heard as challenging the morality of the question recipient.

Excerpt 10.8 ZMY (ZHU = Zhu, LU = Lu)

01 **ZHU:** **wǒ yī tiān zuì duō de shíhou dǎ sì fèn gōng,**
I one day most abundant NOM time do four CL work,
The maximum is that I do four part-time jobs one day.

02 **LU:** **kěndìng cānguǎn, wǒ néng xiǎngdào de=**
definite restaurant, I can think-of NOM
definitely restaurants, I can think of.

03 **ZHU:** **=méi dǎ guò cānguǎn'er. en, wǒ yī qù le,**
not do once restaurant. uhm, I once go PFT,
I had not worked at a restaurant. uhm, when I arrived there,

04 **péngyou jiū gàosù wǒ, dǎ shénme dōu bù néng dǎ cānguǎn'er.**
friend then tell me, do what even not able work resurgent.
my friend told me, no matter where you work, you cannot work at a restaurant.

05 **wǒ shuō wéishénme=**
I say why
and I asked why.
06 LU: **=cānguǎn'er yǒu xiǎofèi,**
restaurant have tips,
you get tips at restaurants.
07 ZHU: **en duì, yīnwei dǎ cānguǎn huì bǎ nǐde zìxìnxīn**
uhm right, because work restaurant will BA your confidence
08 **<dǎ méi le>.**
work not PFT.
uhm right, because working at a restaurant will make you lose your confidence.
09 **dànshi dǎ le suǒyǒu de gōng,**
but do PFT all NOM work,
but I did various kinds of part-time jobs,
10 **bùguǎn shì jiāo zhōngwén na,**
No-matter be teach Chinese PRT,
no matter it was teaching Chinese NA,
11 **jiāo wǔdǎo a, jiāo tàijíquán na,**
teach dance PRT, teach shadow-boxing PRT,
teaching dance A, teaching shadow boxing NA,
12 **gěi rénjia dǎsǎo wèishēng a,**
give them clean sanitation PRT,
or house cleaning A,
13 **hái shì zuò dàiwèi ya = dào xīěrdùn fàndiàn gěi dàiwèi ya,**
or be do usher PRT go Hilton restaurant give usher PRT,
or ushering at Hilton restaurant YA,
14 **hái shì zuò: jīntiān jiào bǎoān ba,**
or be do today call security-guard PRT,
or security guard
15 **gěi yī gè [dàde diànnǎo gōngsī.**
give one CL big computer company.
at a big computer company.
16 LU: **[nǐ zuò bǎoān?**
you do security-guard?
you worked as security guard?
17 ZHU: **duì.**
right.
((11 lines omitted))
29 LU: -> **nǐ jiāo tàijíquán, nǐ huì ma?**
you teach shadow-boxing, you know PRT?
you taught shadow boxing, but do you know how to do it?
30 ZHU:-> **wǒ huì ya. Guòqù wángkūn lǎoshī (.) shuō**
I can PRT. past name teacher (.) say
oh, I can YA. in the past Teacher Wang Kun said
31 **nǐmen gēchàng yǎnyuán dōu yào liàn qì ,**
you singer actors all should exercise breathing
all the singer actors should exercise breathing,
32 **nà nǐmen jiùyào xué zhègè: : tàijíquán ,**
then you need learn this:: shadow-boxing,
so you need to learn shadow-boxing.

33 **tā jiù qīnzì jiāo , ā: a:**
he then himself teach, PRT PRT
then he himself taught us shadow-boxing.
34 **>ránhòu<wǒ jiù xué , xué wán le yǐhòu ne ,**
then I just learn, learn end PFT after PRT,
and I learned it with him. after I finished learning it,
35 **wǒ dào le měiguó yǐhòu ,**
I arrived PFT America after,
and when I was in America,
36 **rénjiā shuō , éi , nǐmen zhōngguó yǒu gè jiào shénmē shénmē**
others say, PRT, you China have Cl call what what
people there asked me whether there was something called
37 **shénme tàijíquán ? wǒ shuō wǒ huì .**
what shadow-boxing? I say I can.
shadow-boxing in China. I said yes and I could play it.
38 **ránhòu jiù kāishǐ jiāo , jiāo xiān jiāo yīnyuè xuéyuàn de .**
then right-away start teach,teach first teach music school NOM.
After that, I started to teach shadow-boxing, and taught the school of music firstly.

This excerpt is from a TV interview program, Lu is the interviewer and Zhu is the interviewee. Zhu is talking about her experience when she immigrated to the USA. From lines 8 to 14 Zhu lists the part-time jobs she took when she was in the USA, one of which is teaching shadow-boxing (line 11). But in line 29 the interviewer Lu shows her doubt about whether Zhu can play shadow-boxing. As a response to Lu's questioning, Zhu designs her answer with an affirmation ending with the particle *ya* (line 30), since Zhu has mentioned that teaching shadow-boxing was one of her part-time jobs when she was in America in line 11. Having the ability to do something is the prerequisite for teaching it. Therefore, teaching shadow-boxing presupposes having the ability to play shadow-boxing; that is, by saying that she had taught shadow-boxing, Zhu implicitly conveys that she has the ability to play shadow-boxing. In line 29, the first TCU shows the interviewer Lu hearing Zhu tell her that she taught shadow-boxing in the previous part of the conversation. Knowing this, Lu still asks the question about whether Zhu has the ability to play shadow-boxing. So, Lu's question presupposes that Zhu may have taught shadow-boxing without actually really knowing how to do it. This presupposition clearly contests the morality of the question recipient. Thus, the interviewer's questioning about Zhu's ability to play shadow-boxing in line 29 is inapposite due to its untenable presupposition. In the responsive turn, the particle *ya* is attached to the end of the answer indicating the inappositeness of the questioning. On the one hand, making a negative assessment of the questioning is a disaffiliative response, which usually requires an account; on the other hand, the question can also be regarded as a known-answer question, which makes an account conditionally relevant

(Raymond & Stivers 2016). Then the second TCU of the responsive turn (lines 30–8) is the account, which legitimizes the negative assessment made by the first TCU about the preceding questioning and normatively fulfills the interactional task required by the preceding known-answer question as well.

In our social life, people of a particular category should do what they are normatively assumed to do in a particular period of time at a particular place. Otherwise, their professional morality will be judged negatively. For instance, from Monday to Friday, students should study in classrooms or libraries during the working day. Likewise, teachers should teach in classrooms during their teaching hours and should work in their office during their office hours. Failure to do so will be considered as dereliction of duty to various degrees. So, people usually do what they are required to do during a specific period of time at a specific place in line with their membership category (Sacks 1992). In the following example, the particle *ya* is attached to the answer to assess the question it responds to as inapposite due to the inconceivable presupposition that challenges the answerer's professional morality.

Excerpt 10.9 2015/LL:5 (ZH = Zh, XI = Xi)

```
07 ZH:    .hhgàn má   de  ne.
          .hhdo  what CRS PRT.
          What are you doing now?
08        (0.9)
09 XI:->  wǒ-, zài sùshè:: ne.
          I-,  at  dorm::  PRT.
          I am at my dorm.
10        (1.3)
11 ZH:->  nǐ  zěnme méi qù xuéxí ne:,
          you why   not go study PRT:,
          why didn't you go to study?
12        (1.0)
13 XI:->  >xuéxí ya, zài sùshè xuéxí ne  me<
          study PRT, at  dorm  study PRT PRT<
          I am studying YA, studying at my dorm. NE ME
14        (0.5)
15 Zh:    o::, zài sùshè xuéxí ne::. nǐ  zěnme méi qù- méi qù bàngōngshì ne::.
          oh::,at dorm  study PRT::.you why  not go- not go office     PRT::.
          Oh, study at your dorm. Why didn't you go to your office?
16        (1.2)
17 Xi:    āi::: tch, nà  dì'er tài lěng,
          INT   tch that place too cold.
          AI, tch, that place is too cold.
```

This is a telephone conversation between Zh and her boyfriend Xi. In line 7, Zh asks Xi what he is doing. Xi does not inform Zh of what he is engaged in;

instead, he tells her his whereabouts, that is, he is at his dorm. Then there is a 1.3-second gap in line 10 before Zh's turn, which possibly projects a disaffiliation to Xi's staying at his dorm or the unexpectedness of Xi's location at that time of the day. Knowing Xi is in his dorm, Zh asks another question about the reason why Xi is not studying at that moment. It is clear from this question that Zh has taken "Xi is not studying now in his dorm" as the presupposition of her question, and this presupposition is not conveyed by Xi but inferred by Zh. This inference may come from the general idea that dorms are usually not the proper place to study in or that people usually do not study in their dorms. This presupposition is defeasible, because although the dorm is not a typical place for studying, this does not necessarily mean that staying in a dorm makes studying impossible. This presupposition overlooks Xi's morality of doing what his membership category requires him to do. Simply speaking, people usually do what they are expected to do. This is the natural scene of our social life (cf. Garfinkel 1964). In line 13, instead of providing an explanation of why he is not studying, Xi not only disaffirms Zh's presupposition but also shows his negative assessment of the question by using the TCU-final particle *ya*. Furthermore, he also corrects Zh's problematic presupposition in the second TCU and assesses Zh's presupposition as unreasonable or illegitimate, again by using the TCU-final double particles *ne me* (Yu, Wu & Drew 2019).

People are responsible not only for what they are expected to do but also for what they are expected to know. This is called epistemic responsibility; namely, people have rights and obligations to know what they are expected to know. This is part of the morality of knowledge, and people are held accountable when they fail to fulfill their epistemic responsibility (Stivers, Mondada & Steensig 2011).

Excerpt 10.10 2017/RXY:Friends:04:40 (GAO = Gao, CUI = Cui)

```
91 GAO:     āi, wǒ gǎnjué nèi shá, xiàmén yě bù cuò, tch.
            PRT, I feel that what, place-name too not bad,
            You know what, I think Xiamen is a good place.
92          nà kuài dìfāng gǎnjué jiù shì-
            that piece place feel even be-
93          tāmēn búshì yǒu rén qù le ma,
            they not-be have people go CRS PRT.
            I feel that place is-, many people have been there.
94 CUI:     ēn.
            uhu
            Uhu.
95 GAO: ->  zhào de nà xiē zhàopiān dōu tǐng měi de,
            take NOM that CL photo all very beautiful NOM,
            All the photos taken there are very beautiful.
96          jìu shì nà zhǒng-yǒu gè dìfāng jiào shá? gǔlàngyǔ, tīng gùo méi?
            just be that CL- have CL place name what? name, hear PFV not?
```

There is a place, and what is its name? Gulangyu, have you heard about it?

97 **CUI: -> kěndìng tīng guò ya, zhè néng méi tīng guò? hāhāhāhā**
definitely hear PFV PRT, this able not hear PRV? hahahaha
Of course I have definitely heard about it YA. How can one not have heard about it? hahahah

98 **GAO: wǒ gǎnjué nà biān tǐng hǎo de, aí, zán yǒu jīhuì kěyǐ qù.**
I feel that side very good NOM, INT, we have chance may go.
I think that place is very good, and we can go there for a visit when we have opportunity.

Gao and Cui, who are two postgraduates, are talking about some domestic travel destinations, and in lines 91–3, Gao introduces one specific place Xiamen, which is a coastal city in the south of China, and she knows that some people around them have recently been there. In response to this informing, Cui gives a continuer in line 94, and Gao continues her telling in line 95–6. She first positively assesses the photos taken by those who have just visited Xiamen, and then she introduces one particular scenic spot in Xiamen through word search (Kitzinger 2013, Schegloff, Jefferson & Sacks 1977), which suggests Gao is not familiar with this place. Gulangyu is a well-known resort in China. It is common for ordinary people, especially for people with higher education, to know this place. In other words, people with higher education, such as postgraduates, are regarded as having the epistemic responsibility to know this place. But Gao's question in line 96 presupposes that Cui might not know this place. This presupposition challenges Cui's morality of knowledge. In responding to Gao's question, Cui designs her answer not only with an affirmation *tīng guò* (I have heard about it) but also enhances her affirmation with the adverb *kěndìng* (definitely) and displays her negative stance toward the question with the TCU-ending particle *ya*. In this responsive turn, the second TCU in the syntactic form of a rhetorical question and the laughter after it further demonstrate the illegitimacy and inconceivability of the presupposition of the question. The inappositeness of the presupposition lies in its challenge to the question recipient's morality of knowledge.

10.5.3 Deviant Case of the TCU-End Ya

The above observation shows that the particle *ya* suffixed to an answer to a question is a practice to assess the preceding question as inapposite. As has been illustrated, the inappropriateness of the questions is caused by their inconceivable presuppositions, which either neglects the questioner's own epistemic access to the answer or puts the answerer's morality into doubt. This function of the particle *ya* is also evidenced in deviant cases when the questioner neither has the epistemic access to the answer of the question nor challenges the morality of the answerer.

Excerpt 10.11 2015/LYF:6 (YAN = Yan, Li = Li)

110 **YAN:** **wǒ shuō nà nǐ huíqù dǎsuàn gàn má a?**
I say then you go back plan do-what PRT?
What you plan to do when you go back?

111 **LI:** **jìxù zuò zhè gè hángyè ya.**
continue do this CL profession PRT.
Continue to be in the present profession YA.

112 **(2.4)**

113 **YAN:** **nǐ xiànzài zuò shá hángyè wǒ dōu bù zhīdào.**
you now do what profession I even not know.
I don't know what profession you are in at present.

114 **LI:** **jìu shì huán- huán píng.**
just be environment- environment assessment
Just environment assessment.

Yan and Li are former classmates and now work in different cities, and this is a telephone conversation between them. Before this excerpt, Li has told Yan that he is going to quit the present job and go back to his hometown. In line 110, Yan asks Li what profession he is going to take when he goes back to his hometown. Yan presupposes through the question that what Li will do will be different from what he is currently doing. In answering the question with the indexical expression "the present profession," Li presupposes, in turn, that Yan knows what Li is currently doing. The nonconstituent particle *ya* is used at the end of the answer. After this answer, instead of an information receipt, there is a long gap in line 112, which frequently projects a disaffiliative response (Schegloff 2007). In line 113 Yan denies Li's presupposition displayed in his answer, claiming that he does not even know what profession Li carries out at present. Meanwhile, this turn is hearably defensive. Yan's denial of Li's presupposition in the declarative syntactic format works both as a repair-initiation and a defense against Li's negative assessment of the question. The defense attributes Li's turn as offensive. The offense is caused by the unfavorable assessment of the question practiced by the TCU-end particle *ya*. If the particle *ya* had not been attached to Li's answer, Yan would have designed his turn in an interrogative format (such as "What is your current profession?"). The difference between choosing an interrogative or a declarative as a repair-initiator in this particular sequential position is that the former is not hearably defensive whereas the latter is. The use of *ya* is treated as unwarranted by the questioner denying the question is inapposite and claiming he or she has been unfavorably assessed. This type of deviant case offers additional evidence of the interactional function played by the particle *ya* in this sequential position.

When the use of *ya* is itself treated as inapposite, the sequence pattern runs like this: questioning – answer ending with *ya* – questioner's denial of the inappositeness of the question.

10.6 Discussion

As Schegloff (1996b: 5) claims "Talk is constructed and is attended by its recipients for the action or actions it may be doing." The major aim of Conversation Analysis is to find out practices members of society use to deliver and interpret actions in interactions (Drew 2005). Social actions can be easily carried out and understood by members of society but are hard for conversation analysts to describe. As there is no inventory of action labels, it is not always simple to name an action using an existing term, such as request, invitation, or offer. What makes the issue more complex is that one TCU may do multiple actions on the one hand and "main jobs" and "secondary jobs" on the other hand (Levinson 2013: 107). While the assignment of a description to the main job done by a TCU is termed as action ascription, the attribution of a description to the secondary job done by the same TCU is named action assessment in the present study. The latter is parasitic on the former. Action ascription is pair type-based, and action assessment is affectivity-based (Reber 2012); that is to say, action ascription is an assignment of action types to prior actions by current actions (cf. Deppermann & Haugh, Chapter 1 in this volume), while action assessment is an assignment of affects to the prior turn by the current turn. Our talk is sometimes, if not always, affect-laden. Linguistic, paralinguistic, or even nonlinguistic resources are used to deliver various affects. The particle *ya* suffixed to the answer in a question–answer sequence is such a practice to express the annoyance of the speaker, which in turn assesses the prior question as unaskable or problematic. If the assessment is warranted, the talk will progress (Excerpts 10.6, 10.8, 10.9, and 10.10) or the questioner acknowledges the assessment in the third position (Excerpt 10.7). Otherwise, if the assessment is unwarranted, the questioner retorts with repair-initiation (Excerpt 10.11). All of this proves that the affect (annoyance) expressed by *ya* is recognized by the questioner and intersubjectivity is achieved between the interlocuters. The particle *ya* is both a practice to deliver the affect of being annoyed in terms of action formation and a practice to assess the prior questioning as problematic in terms of action assessment in the meantime. Due to the negatively valanced affect the particle *ya* suggests, the *ya*-suffixed answer is hearably disaffiliative. An account frequently follows the answer to legitimize the disaffiliation.

10.7 Conclusion

Action formation and action ascription are the major themes of conversation analysis. Attention has been paid mainly to practices implementing primary actions or doing main jobs. Less attention has been paid to practices implementing secondary actions or expressing affectivity. Similarly, when action ascription is concerned, the action type of the prior turn is assigned by the action type of the current turn; for example, an answer ascribes its prior action as an inquiry. Little research has been done on what can be interpreted about the prior turn from the secondary action carried out by the responsive turn. Following Levinson (2013), the present study discriminates between action formation (primary action) and affect formation (secondary action), and between action ascription and action assessment. The particle *ya* suffixed to an answer is both a practice expressing the affect of annoyance and a practice to assess the prior questioning as problematic in Mandarin conversation. Particles in different languages may be major resources of affect formation and action assessment.

Acknowledgments

This research is funded by the Ministry of Education of the People's Republic of China (A Conversational Analysis of Turn-Final Particles in Mandarin, 19YJA740063). We deeply appreciate the editors' and reviewers' comments on the earlier drafts and their revision advices.

Notes on Glossing Conventions

BA the *ba* marker in the *ba* construction
CL classifier
CRS currently relevant state
INT interjection
NOM nominalizer
PFV perfective
PRT particle
RF reduce forcefulness (*a/ya*)

REFERENCES

Chao, Y. (1968). *A Grammar of Spoken Chinese*. Los Angeles, CA: University of California Press.
Clark, H. (1996). *Using Language*. Cambridge: Cambridge University Press.
Curl, T. S. & Drew, P. (2008). Contingency and action: A comparison of two forms of requesting. *Research on Language and Social Interaction*, 41 (2), 129–53.

Drew, P. (2005). Conversation analysis. In K. Fitch & R. Robert, eds., *Handbook of Language and Social Interaction*. Mahwah, NJ: Lawrence Erlbaum, pp. 71–102.
Drew, P. & Chilton, K. (2000). Calling just to keep in touchy: Regular and habitualised telephone calls as an environment for small talk. In J. Coupland, ed., *Small Talk*. London: Pearson Education, pp. 137–62.
Drew, P. & Couper-Kuhlen, E. (2014). *Requesting in Social Interaction*. Amsterdam: John Benjamins.
Garfinkel, H. (1964). Studies of the routine grounds of everyday activities. *Social Problems*, 11(3), 225–50.
Hepburn, A. & Bolden, G. (2017). *Transcribing for Social Research*. London: Sage.
Heritage, J. (1984a). *Garfinkel and Ethnomethodology*. Cambridge: Polity Press.
(1984b). A change-of-state token and aspects of its sequential placement. In J. M. Atkinson & J. Heritage, eds., *Structures of Social Action: Studies in Conversation Analysis*. Cambridge: Cambridge University Press, pp. 299–345.
(1998). Oh-prefaced responses to inquiry. *Language in Society*, 27, 291–334.
(2010). Conversation analysis: Practices and methods. In D. Silverman, ed., *Qualitative Research: Theory, Method and Practice*, 3rd ed. London: Sage, pp. 208–30.
(2012). Epistemics in action: Action formation and territories of knowledge. *Research on Language & and Social Interaction*, 45(1), 1–29.
(2013a). Action formation and its epistemic (and other) backgrounds. *Discourse Studies*, 15(5), 551–78.
(2013b). Epistemics in conversation. In J. Sidnell & T. Stivers, eds., *Handbook of Conversation Analysis*. Chichester: Wiley-Blackwell, pp. 370–94.
Heritage, J. & Raymond, G. (2012). Navigating epistemic landscapes: Acquiescence, agency and resistance in responses to polar questions. In J. P. De Ruiter, ed. *Questions: Formal, Functional and Interactional Perspectives*. Cambridge: Cambridge University Press, pp. 179–92.
Heritage, J. & Sefi, S. (1992). Dilemmas of advice: Aspects of the delivery and reception of advice in interactions between health visitors and first time mothers. In P. Drew & J. Heritage, eds., *Talk at Work*. Cambridge: Cambridge University Press, pp. 359–419.
Jefferson, G. (2004). Glossary of transcript symbols with an introduction. In G. A. Lerner, ed. *Conversation Analysis: Studies from the First Generation*. Amsterdam: John Benjamins, pp. 13–31.
Kitzinger, C. (2013). Repair. In J. Sidnell & T. Stivers, eds., *Handbook of Conversation Analysis*. Chichester: Wiley-Blackwell, pp. 229–56.
Levinson, S. C. (2013). Action formation and ascription. In J. Sidnell & T. Stivers, eds., *Handbook of Conversation Analysis*. Chichester: Wiley-Blackwell, pp. 103–30.
Li, C. & Thompson, S. A. (1981). *Mandarin Chinese: A Functional Reference Grammar*. Los Angeles, CA: University of California Press.
Luke, K. K. (1990). *Utterance Particles in Cantonese Conversation*. Amsterdam: John Benjamins.
Lü, S. X. & Zhu, D. X. (1953). *Yufa Xiuci Jianhua* (Talks on Grammar and Rhetoric). Beijing: Zhonguo Qingnian.
Pomerantz, A. (1986). Extreme case formulations: A way of legitimizing claims. *Human Studies*, 9, 219–29.

Pomerantz, A. & Heritage, J. (2013). Preference. In J. Sidnell & T. Stivers, eds., *Handbook of Conversation Analysis*. Chichester: Wiley-Blackwell, pp. 210–28.

Raymond, C. W. & Stivers, T. (2016). The omnirelevance of accountability: Off-record account solicitations. In J. D. Robinson, ed. *Accountability in Social Interaction*. Oxford: Oxford University Press, pp. 321–54.

Raymond, G. (2003). Grammatical and social organization: Yes/no interrogatives and the structure of responding. *American Sociological Review*, 68(6), 939–67.

Reber, E. (2012). *Affectivity in Interaction: Sound Objects in English*. Amsterdam: John Benjamins.

Sacks, H. (1987). On the preferences for agreement and contiguity in sequences in conversation. In G. Button & J. Lee, eds., *Talk and Social Organization*. Clevedon: Multilingual Matters, pp. 54–69.

(1992). *Lectures on Conversation*. 2 vols. Oxford: Blackwell.

Sacks, H., Schegloff, E. A. & Jefferson, G. (1974). A simplest systematics for the organization of turn-taking for conversation. *Language*, 50(4), 696–735.

Schegloff, E. A. (1996a). Some practices for referring to persons in talk-in-interaction: A partial sketch of a systematics. In B. Fox, ed., *Studies in Anaphora*. Amsterdam: John Benjamins, pp. 437–85.

(1996b). Issues of relevance for discourse analysis: contingency in action, interaction and co-participant context. In E. H. Hovy and D. Scott, eds., Computational and Conversational Discourse: Burning Issues – An Interdisciplinary Account. Heidelberg: Springer Verlag, pp. 3–38.

(2007). *Sequence Organization in Interaction: A Primer in Conversation Analysis*. Cambridge: Cambridge University Press.

Schegloff, E. A., Jefferson, G. & Sacks, H. (1977). The preference for self-correction in the organization of repair in conversation. *Language*, 53(2), 361–82.

Shaw, C., Potter, J. & Hepburn, A. (2015). Advice-implicative actions: Using interrogatives and assessments to deliver advice in mundane conversation. *Discourse Studies*, 17(3), 317–42.

Sidnell, J. & Enfield, N. J. (2014). The ontology of action, in interaction. In N. Enfield, P. Kockelman & J. Sidnell, eds., *Cambridge Handbook of Linguistic Anthropology*. Cambridge: Cambridge University Press, pp. 423–46.

Stivers, T. (2008). Stance, alignment, and affiliation during storytelling: When nodding is a token of affiliation. *Research on Language and Social Interaction*, 41(1), 31–57.

(2011). Morality and question design: "Of course" as contesting a presupposition of askability. In T. Stivers, L. Mondada & J. Steensig, eds., *The Morality of Knowledge in Conversation*. Cambridge: Cambridge University Press, pp. 82–106.

Stivers, T., Mondada, L. & Steensig, J. (2011). Knowledge, morality and affiliation in social interaction. In T. Stivers, L. Mondada & J. Steensig, eds., *The Morality of Knowledge in Conversation*. Cambridge: Cambridge University Press, pp. 3–26.

Wang, L. (1955). *Zhongguo Xiandai Yufa* (A Modern Grammar of Chinese). Beijing: Zhonghua.

Wu, R. J. R. (2004). *Stance in Talk: A Conversation Analysis of Mandarin Final Particles*. Amsterdam: John Benjamins.

Wu, R. J. R. & Heritage, J. (2017). Particles and epistemics: Convergences and divergences between English and Mandarin. In G. Raymond, G. H. Lerner & J. Heritage, eds., *Enabling Human Conduct*. Amsterdam: John Benjamins. pp. 273–97.

Yu, G., Wu, Y. & Drew, P. (2019). Couples bickering: Disaffiliation and discord in Chinese conversation. *Discourse Studies*, 21(4), 458–80.

11 Actions and Identities in Emergency Calls
The Case of Thanking

Tom Koole and Lotte van Burgsteden

11.1 Introduction

In their pioneering work on emergency calls, Whalen and Zimmerman (1987) analysed emergency reports of callers to emergency call-centres as requests for help based on the observation that call-takers respond to them by either granting or denying help. This analysis was subsequently complicated when Bergmann (1993) observed that call-takers may not only grant help but also thank the caller and thereby treat the caller's emergency report as more than only a request. Bergmann related this to two different caller identities, that of the 'Nutznießer' or 'beneficiary', a caller who calls the emergency services for an emergency (s)he herself suffers from, and that of the 'Wohltäter', 'do-gooder' or 'benefactor', a caller who "altruistically provide[s]" the service of "having brought a problem of public safety to official attention" (Heritage & Clayman 2010: 83). A few decades later, Raymond and Zimmerman (2016) showed how in emergency calls, troubles in the alignment of participants' identities (i.e., who is benefactor and who is beneficiary) and troubles in the completion of participants' projects (i.e., whether the outcome pursued by the caller or call-taker is an outcome the other is willing to cooperate in providing) play a role in how calls get closed. Call-takers may for instance pursue a 'thanks' from callers when this expression of gratitude is absent and relevant, moving toward a mutually ratified call closure.

Bergmann's and Raymond and Zimmerman's analysis made it clear how much participant identities and actions are two sides of the same coin. By thanking the caller, the call-taker treats the caller as benefactor and at the same time treats his or her incident report as providing a service rather than only making a request (Bergmann 1993). Or in situations where call-takers pursue a 'thank-you', which gets followed by a 'thank-you' from the caller, both caller and call-taker orient to the call-taker as being the service benefactor (Raymond & Zimmerman 2016). Call-takers may also refrain from thanking or pursuing a 'thank-you' from the caller as a way to let go of any effort to align with the caller as either beneficiary or benefactor, treating the caller's project as one with 'ulterior motives' (Raymond & Zimmerman 2016).

With their focus on responsive actions as determining the character of the responded-to action, the analyses of Whalen and Zimmerman's (1987), Bergmann and Raymond and Zimmerman are examples of Mead's (1934) earlier analysis that participants' responsive actions determine the meaning of the speaker's contributions: granting help or thanking in response to an emergency report ascribes particular action statuses to that report, respectively that of making a request or offering a service. Several decades later, this has led Levinson (2013) to the notion of action ascription. The analyses of Whalen and Zimmerman, Bergmann, and Raymond and Zimmerman also resonate with the analyses Couper-Kuhlen (2014) and Clayman and Heritage (2014) made of interactional sequences in which future actions are arranged. They concluded that requests can be characterised and are recognised by participants as having the requester as beneficiary of the future action.

Our present analysis of emergency calls in the Netherlands pursues this theoretical interest in the relation between participant identities and action ascription. It confirms both Whalen and Zimmerman analysis of the incident report as a request for help and Bergmann analysis of call-takers' 'thank-yous' in response to third-party callers. Our analysis lends support to Raymond and Zimmerman (2016) claim that ascribing action status to the caller's information delivery, along with ascribing caller identity, is a process that does not hinge only on whether the caller presents himself initially as being involved in the reported incident, or as being a witness of the emergency (s)he calls for. As Clayman and Heritage (2014) mention, some complexities of action ascription regarding offers and requests have to do with contextual features of the interaction itself, "including the identities and other social characteristics that participants attribute to one another" (p. 58). Our analysis will show that the caller 'identities' (Bergmann 1993; Zimmerman 1998) of beneficiary versus benefactor are not brought about only by the way in which the caller initially reports the emergency. The interaction in between the caller's initial incident report and the closing of an emergency call may produce a context in which third-party callers (callers witnessing an incident) may be treated as having made a request, while first-party callers (callers involved in an incident) may be treated as having offered a service. We thereby take the same view as, amongst others, Raymond and Zimmerman (2016), Bucholtz and Hall (2005), and Antaki and Widdicombe (1998) that identity is something that emerges in "the fine detail of everyday interaction" (Antaki & Widdicombe 1998: 1) rather than being "a stable structure located primarily in the individual psyche or in fixed social categories" (Bucholtz & Hall 2005: 586).

11.2 Data and Method

This research draws upon a corpus of 441 recorded telephone calls to an emergency call-centre in the Netherlands, made in the year 2010. We have used conversation analysis (CA) as a research method that aims to describe and clarify the methods or techniques that ordinary speakers use and rely on as participants in social interaction (Atkinson & Heritage 1984). For the present investigation of action formation and action ascription, we used the methods of CA to determine the means (Garfinkel 1967: 'methods') that caller and call-takers use to establish the action status of the caller's turns. CA methods involve making transcriptions of the calls according to the conventions designed by Gail Jefferson (2004). Then we made 'collections' of caller and call-taker 'thank-yous'. When instances of particular phenomena are gathered into a collection, researchers can start describing interactional practices or phenomena in terms of their generic properties, departing from the particularities of a single case (Sidnell 2013). This description involved an analysis that focuses on turn design (lexical choice, grammatical format, prosody) and sequential placement (what does this turn respond to) of the 'thank-you' turns, resulting in the regularities presented here.

11.3 Action Ascription and Identities in Emergency Calls

As Levinson (2013) amongst others has shown, Schegloff's (2007) action formation problem is not only a question of what makes a turn recognisable to others as a particular action, but also an issue of how others in responding to that turn display their understanding and thereby ascribe action status to it. In the context of emergency calls, when a caller states something like '*My car is on fire*', the call-taker may regard this utterance as a request (Whalen & Zimmerman 1987; Zimmerman 1984), namely a request for help from the fire brigade. When a call-taker promises to send help, (s)he indeed treats the utterance of the caller as a request thereby co-determining the action the utterance of the caller performs.

Zimmerman (1998) speaks of two different types of identities that participants seem to treat as relevant in emergency calls: 'discourse identities' and 'situated identities'. Discourse identities are "integral to the moment-by-moment organization of the interaction" (Zimmerman 1998: 90). For particular types of interaction, such as emergency calls, different discourse identities may become relevant in particular segments, such as story teller/recipient and questioner/answerer. In our data, for example, we see that third-party callers (callers witnessing an incident) design their incident report overwhelmingly as a report, thereby not assuming the discourse identity of 'requester', while the first-party callers (callers involved in an incident) may design their report either as a report or as a request for assistance. Situated identities on the other hand, originate in specific kinds of situations, where in emergency calls these situated identities are 'citizen-complainant' and 'call-taker' (Zimmerman 1998). Raymond and Zimmerman (2007, 2016) speak of the situated identities of *service seeker* (the beneficiary of the service) and of *service provider* (the benefactor of the service) and argue that callers are pre-aligned as service seekers and call-takers as service providers. We see orientations to these identities in Excerpt 11.1, in which the caller thanks the call-taker who has informed the caller that help is sent. Here, the caller has reported that he believes he is having a heart attack and thus has self-identified as the beneficiary of the emergency service:

Excerpt 11.1 T10 (CTA = Call-taker, CAL = Caller)

```
52 CTA:    oké, (.) nou >we hebben in ieder geval een ziekenauto alvast<
           okay (.) well in any case we have already notified an ambulance
53         eh (.) gewaarschuwd en eh >er komt nu hulp uw kant op.<
           and eh help is coming your way now.
54 CAL: -> dankuwel.
           thank you.
55 CTA:    ja?
           yes?
56 CAL:    ja.
           yes.
57 CTA:    oké=
           okay=
58 CAL:    =doeg
           =bye
```

The call-taker has previously indicated that she will also send the police, which the 'in any case' (line 52) in her turn seems to be dealing with, indicating that an ambulance is being sent in addition to some other emergency service. When the caller subsequently thanks the call-taker (line 54) he re-establishes himself as a service beneficiary.

This is different when the *call-taker* expresses appreciation by thanking the caller at the closing of the call. This can be the case when the caller has called as a witness of an incident in which (s)he was not personally involved. In these cases, the call-taker, then, can be portrayed as the beneficiary of the emergency report. By calling the emergency centre these callers may be said to make a request on behalf of someone else, but the thanking behaviour of both caller and call-taker treats the call not as *requesting* a service but as *providing* one (Bergmann 1993).

An example of explicitly thanking the caller for reporting the incident is shown in Excerpt 11.2, where the caller calls about an accident she has witnessed in which two cars are involved. As is shown in the excerpt, the call-taker decides to send help and thanks the caller (line 54):

Excerpt 11.2 Multidisciplinary reports – 1100919 (CTA = Call-taker, CAL = Caller)

```
49 CTA:   op- d- ambulance is onder↑weg
          at- th- ambulance is on its ↑way
50        politie(sterkte) is ook aange- aangestuurd.
          police(strength) has also been dispatched.
51        (0.8)
52 CAL:   o[ké
          okay
53 CTA:    [ja?=
            yes?=
54     -> =>bedankt voor het bellen.<
            thanks for calling.
55 CAL:   [jo
           Yo
56 CTA:   [daag.
           bye.
```

In response to the call-taker's announcement that help is underway (lines 49–50), the caller in line 52 produces an acknowledgement but not a thank-you. In contrast, it is the call-taker who produces a token of gratitude with 'Thanks for calling' (line 54), with which he explicitly indicates that he is thanking the caller for calling the emergency centre. The caller does not explicitly state something in the manner of 'You're welcome' but uses the more implicit form 'Yo'. In this extract, then, both the call-taker and the caller orient to the caller as someone who called about the problems of someone else (i.e., not a service beneficiary), and thereby they orient to the caller's incident report as offering a service rather than requesting one.

We found the practice of thanking in response to granting a request to be much more frequent in our emergency call data than Floyd et al. (2018) found to be the case in mundane request sequences. While Floyd et al. (2018) found a maximum of 15 percent of granted requests being responded to with a 'thank-you' (in British English and Italian), in our emergency call data thanking seems to be the default option: around 80 percent of the calls ended with either the caller or the call-taker thanking the other. Among the deviant cases were instances that ended in conflicts between caller and call-taker (cf. Raymond & Zimmerman 2016) and cases where the caller was in a serious physical condition.

In general, the closing sequences in emergency calls where the *caller* expresses gratitude can roughly be represented as follows:

CTA	promise of sending help
CAL	optional receipt + expression of gratitude
CTA	optional (variant of) 'you're welcome' (e.g., 'all right'; 'yes PRT' ['ja hoor'])
CTA	'goodbyes'
CAL	'goodbyes'

On the other hand, the closing sequences in emergency calls where a *call-taker* expresses gratitude can roughly be represented as follows:

CTA	promise of sending help
CAL	optional receipt
CTA	expression of gratitude
CAL	optional (variant of) 'you're welcome' (e.g., 'all right'; 'yes PRT' ['ja hoor'])
CTA	'goodbyes'
CAl	'goodbyes'

11.4 Analysis

11.4.1 Call-Taker's Locally Occasioned Thanking

In Excerpts 11.1 and 11.2 above we have shown an instance of the caller thanking the call-taker, thereby self-identifying as a 'beneficiary' making a 'request' (Whalen & Zimmerman 1987), and an instance of the call-taker thanking the caller thereby identifying the caller as a 'benefactor' offering a 'service'. In general, our data show instances of what Mosegaard Hansen (2016: 699) has called 'unilateral thanking' with either the caller or the call-taker being the only party to thank the other.

Our data however also show instances where the call-taker designs his thanks to the caller as locally occasioned rather than related to the identity of the caller as 'benefactor'. Compare the call-takers' thanking turns in Excerpts 11.3 and 11.4.

Excerpt 11.3 Monodisciplinary reports – 1100804 (CTA = Call-taker, CAL = Caller)

```
62 CAL:    [dus ik heb geen idee.
             so I have no idea.
63 CTA:    [nou we komen toch even met spoed ↑kijken
             well we will come urgently anyway
```

64 **en ik stuur [gelijk politie even mee ↑hoo:r?**
and I will send the police along as well PRT
65 CAL: **[ja lijkt me handig**
yes seems convenient to me
66 **(0.3)**
67 **↓ja (.) is goed.**
yes (.) is fine.
68 CTA: -> **dankje↑we:l (.) daa::g.**
thank you (.) bye.
69 CAL: **ja (.) ↓daa:g**
yes (.) bye

Excerpt 11.4 Multidisciplinary reports – 1070118-3 (CTA = Call-taker, CAL = Caller)

11 CTA: **we gaan erheen hoor**
we are going there PRT
12 CAL: **↑ja o[ké**
↑yes okay
13 CTA: **[wat is uw telefoonnummer, >nul dertig tweeënzestig**
What is your phone number, >zero thirty sixty-two
14 **↓vier<=**
↓four<=
15 **=wat is uw ↓naa:m**
=what's your ↓na:me
16 CAL: **eh ter apel.**
eh Ter Apel.
17 CTA: **<te:r A:pel>=**
<te:r A:pel>=
18 -> **=danku↑wel**
=thank you
19 CAL: **ja?**
yes?
20 CTA: **joe daag.**
yo bye.

In Excerpt 11.3, the call-taker produces his thanking turn (line 68) in response to the caller's acknowledgement (line 67) of the announcement that help will be sent and subsequently the call-taker proceeds to closing the call by initiating a greeting sequence (line 68: 'bye'). As Wakin and Zimmerman (1999) observed, the call-taker's promising of assistance initiates the pre-closing sequence in emergency calls: when the purpose of the call has been achieved, nothing more has to be discussed. In Excerpt 11.4 in contrast, we see that the call-taker's thanking turn (lines 17–18) is placed and designed differently. Sequentially, it follows the caller's answer to the call-taker's query for the caller's name and thereby constitutes a third position receipt (Schegloff 2007), and in the design of the turn, the thanking follows the acknowledgement (by repetition) of the answer. Thus, in contrast with Excerpt 11.3, both the sequential placement and the design of the call-taker's thanking turn in Excerpt 11.4 make it understandable as acknowledging the caller's answer rather than as thanking the caller for making the call and treating him as a benefactor.

Also in Excerpt 11.5 we see the thanking turn placed and designed as responding in third position to the just provided telephone number.

Excerpt 11.5 Multidisciplinary reports – 1070118-Z (CTA = Call-taker, CAL = Caller)

08 **CTA:** **[o:ké wij komen die kant op=**
okay we are coming your way
09 **CAL:** **[(en-)**
(and-)
10 **CTA:** **=m-mag ik uw telefoonnummer nog even note↑ren**
c- could I take your telephone number
11 **CAL:** **eh**
eh
12 **(0.5)**
13 **↑nul dertig twee- eh >twee drie vier vijf zes zeven ze↓ven<=**
zero thirty two- eh >two three four five six seven seven<
14 **CTA: -> =oké >danku↑wel<**
okay thank you
15 **CAL:** **jo**
Yo
16 **CTA:** **>ja hoor<**
yes PRT

In line 10 the call-taker asks for the telephone number of the caller, who supplies an answer in line 13, to which the call-taker responds by acknowledging the answer with 'okay' and 'thank you'. The placement, in third position once more, and the conjunction with 'okay' produce a plausible understanding of 'thank you' as responding to the just prior answer.

We see a similar structure in Excerpt 11.6 where the caller is an employee of a party centre in which a customer fell ill:

Excerpt 11.6 Monodisciplinary reports – 1101216 (CTA = Call-taker, CAL = Caller)

106 **CTA:** **↓goed (.) u zorgt voor opvang bij de ingang?**
↓fine (.) you will take care of reception at the entrance?
107 **(0.8)**
108 **CAL:** **wij zorgen voor opvang=**
we will take care of reception
109 **=ja dat- u kunt hier vlak voor rijden=daar is een hele grote ingang-**
yes that- you can drive right in front=there is a really big entry-

110 **hele grote entree.**
really big entrance.
111 **CTA: goed als u regelt dat er iemand ↓staat=**
alright if you arrange that somebody will be there=
112 **-> =↑pri↓ma (.) danku↑wel**
fine thank you
113 **CAL: ja: ik zal d'r zelf in ieder geval ↓staan**
yes I will be there myself in any case
114 **CTA: >ja hoor ↓daag<**
yes PRT ↓bye

The call-taker makes a request to the caller to wait for the emergency services (line 106), after which the caller complies with this request (line 108) and subsequently provides a description of where the ambulance can go to (line 109–10). Then, once more in third position, the call-taker acknowledges the caller's compliance, assesses it ('fine' line 112), and thanks him (line 112). As was the case in the examples provided above, the design of the thanking in conjunction with the assessments of the caller's compliance and its sequential placement following the caller's response produce a plausible understanding as thanking the caller for arranging someone at the entrance rather than thanking him for reporting the incident.

We have just shown that call-takers' 'thank-yous' to callers in the closing section of the call are placed and designed to display the target of the thanking. When referring to 'design' here, we are speaking in terms of the turn elements that precede the thanking. Call-takers may thank callers for making the call and thus treat the caller as a benefactor who provides a service to the call-centre, or they may thank the caller for an action performed immediately prior to the thanking such as answering a question or complying with a request. The distinction that Houtkoop (1987) and Clayman and Heritage (2014) make between proposals, respectively requests, for immediate action versus action in some future, can possibly be adopted here in terms of 'distal' 'thank-yous' that refer to the caller's distant initial incident report as opposed to 'proximal' 'thank-yous' that refer to an action in the immediately prior turn. Yet the fact that these thankings are all done after the call-taker has announced that help is underway and therewith the call has entered its closing stage (Wakin & Zimmerman 1999) is a feature of placement that renders them potentially ambiguous between thanking the caller for calling and thanking for a just prior action, this in spite of the other sequential and design features of these thankings. This means that these 'thank-yous' may be heard as dealing with something that happened in the local environment, rather than 'solely' dealing with the global environment where call-takers' expressions of gratitude are about the caller's provision of a service to the emergency centre.

11.4.2 Treating Third-Party Callers as Beneficiaries

A call-taker's identification of a caller as either a beneficiary or a benefactor and their actions as respectively requesting a service or offering one, does not necessarily coincide with the caller's identification as first-party caller (i.e., a participant in the emergency incident) or third-party caller (i.e., a witness of the incident). Excerpt 11.7 provides an example where the caller explicitly identifies as a witness and yet is not thanked as a benefactor at the end of the call.

Excerpt 11.7 Monodisciplinary reports, ambulance – 1100707 (CTA = Call-taker, CAL = Caller)

01 **CTA: ambulance↑dienst**
ambulance service
02 **CAL: ↓ja ↓dag u SPREEKT met een GETUIGE,**
yes hello this is a witness speaking
03 **IK ZAG NET- D'R WERD HIER EEN KINDJE AANGEREEJE?**
I just saw- a little child was run over here
04 **CTA: ja,=**
yes,=
05 **CAL: =KINDJE ZIT NU WEL OP SCHOOT BIJ D'R MOEDER,=**
child is sitting on the lap of her mother now,
06 **=MAAR D'R MOET WEL- D'R MOET WEL IEMAND KO:MEN WANT**
but someone has to- someone has to come because
07 **D'R KOMT BLOED UIT D'R MO:ND?**
there is blood coming out of her mouth?
08 **CTA: en waar ↑is dat,**
and where ↑is that
09 **CAL: EH IN TUBBERGEN OP DE DORPSWEG (.) TER HOOGTE VAN DE KRUIDVAT.**
eh in Tubbergen in the Dorpsweg (.) near the Kruidvat.*

((lines 10 to 77 omitted))

78 **CAL: ze heeft wat pijn in d'r knie:,**
she has some pain in her knee
79 **CTA: ja ze zit bij jullie binnen op de- in de kruidvat?**
yes she is inside with you at the- in the Kruidvat?
80 **CAL: ze zit in de WINKE:L,op [een stoel.**
she is in the shop (.) on a chair.
81 **CTA: [oké.(.) ↓goed nou we komen even kijken (.) ja?**
okay.(.) fine well we will come look PRT yes?
82 **CAL: =ja? goed hoor [tot zo=**
=yes? fine PRT see you soon
83 **CTA: [pri↑ma**
fine
84 **↓daag**
↓bye

* Dutch drugstore chain

In line 2 the caller identifies herself explicitly as 'a witness', in other words as a benefactor of the emergency service and not a beneficiary. Her position as third-party caller is further established by her reference to the child as 'a little child', a form of person reference that denies prior acquaintance, and by later in the call asking another bystander for the age of the child (not in transcript). At the same time, she makes an explicit request or demand that 'someone should come'. Also, the greater volume of her voice in lines 2–9 is hearable as being emotionally involved in the incident. This ambiguity between witness and involvement, which is understandable when witnessing tragic events such as this one involving a child, is reflected in the way the call is concluded.

From lines 8 to 80 call-taker and caller conduct the 'interrogative series' (Whalen & Zimmerman 1987) in which the call-taker asks the caller for further information, and this is concluded in line 81 when the call-taker announces that help will be dispatched. As we have seen in, for example, Excerpt 11.1, this is the position in which a beneficiary caller could thank the call-taker. Yet, the caller responds with 'fine' and 'see you soon' (line 82) but does not thank the call-taker for sending help. This shows her orientation to her 'status' of benefactor: she is offering the service of informing the emergency call-centre and is requesting a service of which she herself is not a beneficiary. As Raymond and Zimmerman (2016) have shown, in some cases call-takers treat the absence of the caller's thanks as *relevantly absent* by pursuing a 'thank you' from the caller. In this fragment, however, the call-taker does not treat the absence of the caller's thanking as relevantly absent, as he subsequently moves to the closing by greeting 'fine bye' (line 83 and 84), thereby letting pass the moment of expression of gratitude and turning to the moment of hanging up the phone. In other words, the call-taker accepts the caller's acting as non-beneficiary of the call-centre's service. Yet the call-taker does not treat the caller in the alternative identity of benefactor: he does not thank the caller for reporting the accident in which the child is involved. Thus, we see that neither participant thanks the other and thus they retain the ambiguity that we saw in the opening of the call with regard to the caller's identity and the action she performs as either a that of a witness benefactor who offers the service of informing the call-centre, or that of beneficiary who requests a service of the centre.

This is also the case in Excerpt 11.8, where a witness-caller seems to get 'too involved' in the incident she is calling for by repeatedly stating the urgency of the need for help. In this fragment a woman is calling the emergency centre for an accident with a boat. The caller was close to a river when an explosion occurred at a boat sailing in that river and a man fell off the boat (line 15). The caller and the other people near her are witnesses of the incident which she states in phrases such as 'we are standing too far away to see what is happening' (lines 15–16).

Excerpt 11.8 Multidisciplinary reports – 1090226 (CTA = Call-taker, CAL = Caller)

15 **CAL: en e:h d'r was een ↑man te water gegaan maar ja >we staan te ver weg**
and eh there was a man that fell in the water but yes we are standing too far away
16 **om te zien wat er ge↓beu:rt [dus misschien dat jullie iets kunnen doen<**
to see what is happening so maybe you could do something
17 **CTA: [en dat ad-**
and that ad-

((lines 18 to 42 about location and a possible fire on the boat omitted))

43 **CTA: maar u hoorde een [explosie op de boot?**
but you heard an explosion on the boat?
44 **CAL: [HIJ LOOPT WEL TE ZWAAIEN.**
he is PRT waving
45 **IK DENK dat je heel snel moet komen.**
I think that you really need to come fast.
46 ***CTA: j:a,***
ye:s,

((lines 47 to 52 on the distance between caller and the incident omitted))

53 **CTA: ja. (.) wij gaan- wij gaan e;H in ieder geval alarmeren mevrouw hoor.=**
yes. (.) we are going- we are eh going to dispatch in any case madam PRT
54 **CAL: =ja: zou ik maar gauw doen volgens mij is het niet goed daaro.**
yes I would do that rather quickly I don't think it's going well over there.
56 **CTA: Nee dat begrijp ik.**
no I understand that

((lines 56 to 75 about caller's telephone number omitted))

76 CTA: nou de: collega's die hebben de brandweer al gealarmeerd.
well the colleagues they have alarmed the fire brigade already
77 **CAL: o:ké.**
okay
78 **CTA: ja?**
yes?
79 **CAL: ik zie die man al zwaaien. ja [o:↑ké**
I already see that man waving. yes o:↑kay
80 **CTA: [o↑ké (.) ↓daa[g**
Okay (.) bye
81 **CAL: [↓doe:g**
bye

As in Excerpt 11.7, the call in Excerpt 11.8 runs off without either of the parties thanking the other. If the caller had been identified as the beneficiary of the call-centre's service, line 77, following the call-taker's announcement that help is underway would have been the place to thank the call-taker. Instead, the caller merely acknowledges the announcement (line 77: 'okay'), which shows an orientation to her identity as witness benefactor and to her report as a service to the call-centre. On the other hand, if the call-taker had identified the caller as a benefactor, he would have had the opportunity to thank the caller in response to her acknowledgement, notably in line 78, after the caller acknowledges the call-taker's promise of assistance. Instead, the call-taker acknowledges the caller's receipt of the dispatch announcement with "ja?" (*yes?*, line 78), thus initiating the closing of the call.

The absence of thanking in this call may be occasioned by an ambiguity regarding the identity of the caller, as happened in Excerpt 11.7. Although she explicitly identifies herself as not directly involved in the incident, she also produces request-like actions such as 'I think that you really need to come fast' (line 45) and 'I would do that rather quickly' (line 54). Requests cast the requester as a beneficiary rather than as someone offering the service of 'having brought a problem of public safety to official attention' (Heritage & Clayman 2010: 83).

These data show that the identification of the caller as beneficiary or as witness benefactor is an interactional process that does not stop after the caller's initial incident report and is not automatically tied to the extra-interactional status of the caller as witness of the incident. Raymond and Zimmerman (2016) also showed an instance where "thank you is neither produced nor missing" (p. 729), which had to do with problems posed by disjunctive projects: the call-taker treated the caller's project as one with "ulterior motives". In our data, we do not have situations in which these more 'substantial problems' as described by Raymond and Zimmerman arise, yet Excerpts 11.7 and 11.8 show that calls can be concluded without the participants having reached alignment on the callers' identities: these calls are concluded with the callers acting as benefactors and the call-takers treating them as beneficiaries.

11.4.3 Thanking a Beneficiary

In opposition to Excerpt 11.7 and 11.8 where witness callers do not receive 'thank-yous' from the call-takers, our data also show cases where callers who are directly involved in the reported incident are thanked by the call-taker. This is another example of how the identities of the callers and the actions ascribed to them result from interactional contingencies rather than from their 'objective' relation to the reported incident.

One such contingency is when the caller hands over the telephone to another participant, who on the one hand is more directly involved in the incident than the first caller and thus seems to qualify even more as a beneficiary, but who on the other hand collaborates with the call-taker to come to a 'solution' for the incident at hand, and even more importantly as an interactional contingency, who in spite of being a potential beneficiary is *not* the one who made or makes a request for help.

In Excerpt 11.9 a woman has called for a fire alarm that went off while people were roofing. Prior to the excerpt the caller has answered the call-taker's questions partly after consulting people near her. In line 47 one of the roofers has taken over the telephone and introduces himself.

Excerpt 11.9 Monodisciplinary reports, fire brigade – 1111114 (CTA = Call-taker, CAL = Caller)

47 **CAL:** **hai met ger↑rie**
hi this is Ger↑rie
48 **CTA:** **hoi: met de meldkamer brandweer.**
hi this is the emergency room fire brigade.
49 **CAL:** **e:h ze zijn aan 't e::h (.) 't dak aan 't e:h reguleren?**
eh they are e::h (.) fixing the roof?
50 **CTA:** **ja,**
yes,
51 **(0.4)**
52 **CAL:** **[e:n-**
and-
53 **CTA:** **[maar is daar nu brand of is d'r niks aan de hand.=**
but is there a fire right now or is nothing going on.=
54 **CAL:** **=↓nee °d'r is°- (.) d'r is voorlopig nog niks aan de hand.**
=↓no °there is°- (.) there is nothing going on for now.
55 **CTA:** **dus u heeft geen brandweer nodig.**
so you don't need the fire brigade.
56 **CAL:** **nee.**
no.
57 **CTA:** **oké. (.) dus (.) ik eh (.) hoef niemand te sturen.=**
okay. (.) so (.) I eh (.) don't need to send someone.=
58 **CAL:** **=>nee nee< dankuwel.**
=>no no< thank you.

((lines 59 to 63 omitted))

64 **CTA:** **kunt u mij honderd procent zeker zeggen dat >er niks aan de hand is**
can you tell me with one hundred per cent certainty that there is nothing wrong
65 **of moet ik nog even iemand voor de nacontrole sturen,<**
or shall I still send someone for the follow-up inspection,<
66 **CAL:** **e:::h ik ga et zelf even nalopen en eh**
e:::h I will just go check it myself and eh
67 **(0.5)**
68 **CTA:** **ik eh- ik >vind 't toch-< ik eh- ik stuur even iemand in ieder geval**
I eh-I still think- I eh-I will just send someone in any case

69 **even voor de nacontro[le dat dat-**
just for the follow-up inspection so that-
70 **CAL:** **[ja: da's ↑pri↓ma**
ye:s that's fine
71 **CTA:** **ja?**
yes?
72 **CAL:** **ja.=**
yes.=
73 **CTA:** **=o↑ké**
=o↑kay
74 **(0.3)**
75 **->** **be↓[dankt**
thanks
76 **CAL:** **[oké [↓daag**
okay ↓bye
77 **CTA:** **[↓daa:g**
↓bye:

Caller Gerrie engages in the interrogative series with the call-taker by answering the call-taker's questions but is not the one who issued the initial incident report and requested help. Indeed, he denies (lines 56, 58) that help is needed, and when the call-taker insists that she will send someone 'for the follow-up inspection' (line 69) the caller accepts this service (line 70: 'yes that's fine') rather than thanking the call-taker for it. In this context the call-taker ends the call with thanking the caller (line 75), which seems to target the collaboration with caller Gerrie and the information provided by him and thus does not treat him as a beneficiary.

This is also the case in Excerpt 11.10. This call was made by someone who was waiting for a bus that turned out to be partly on fire. While she calls, the bus is standing at the bus stop and cannot go any further. This seems to identify the bus driver as involved in the incident and as a potential beneficiary of help when the telephone is handed to him and he introduces himself to the call-taker in line 51.

Excerpt 11.10 Monodisciplinary reports, fire brigade – 1111027 (CTA = Call-taker, CAL = Caller)

51 **CAL:** **↓ja (.) met jansen spreekt u.**
↓yes (.) this is Jansen speaking.
52 **CTA:** **dag meneer u spreekt met michel vaus=**
hello sir this is Michel Vaus=
53 **=meldkamer ↑brand↓weer (.)**
=emergency room fire brigade (.)
54 **eh ik begrijp dat uw bus in brand heeft gestaan?**
eh I understand that your bus was on fire?
55 **CAL:** **ja.**
yes.

56 **CTA: en e:hm is die bu- is die brand uit?**
and e:hm is that bu- is that fire out?
57 **CAL: e:h voor zover ik nu zien kan is die uit.**
e:h as far as I can see right now it's out.
58 **CTA: wilt u voor de [zekerheid-**
would you just to be sure-
59 **CAL: ['k heb em aan de onder-**
[I have on the bottom-
60 **(0.3)**
61 **ja 'k heb geen kleppen opengetrok↑ken (.)**
yes I did not open any valves (.)
62 **'k heb alle spanning d'r af gehaald=**
I have switched off the electricity=
63 **='k heb em onderuit eh gespoten?**
=I have sprayed it eh from beneath?
64 **CTA: ja,**
yes
65 **CAL: en zoals 'k et nu zie d'r rookt nog boven?**
and as I can see it now there's still smoke on top?
66 **nou wordt al minder**
well it's becoming less already
67 **CTA: de personen zijn uit de bus?**
the passengers are out of the bus?
68 **CAL: ↓ja iedereen is uit de bus.=**
↓yes everyone is out of the bus.=
69 **CTA: =oké wat ik wil <doen>=**
=okay what I want to do=
70 **=ik stuur de brandweer toch even ter plaatse voor een nacontrole**
=I will send the fire brigade anyway for a follow-up inspection
71 **als eh u dat eh prima [vindt**
if you are okay with that
72 **CAL: [ja. (.) ja. heel graag.**
yes. (.) yes. please.
73 **CTA: ja?**
yes?
74 **CAL: ik heb e:h centraalpost ook al eh gemeld?=**
I e:h also reported it to central command?
75 **CTA: =oké fantastisch? (.) [e::h**
okay great? (.) e::h
76 **CAL: [dus die zullen ook wel contact opnemen**
maar een-
so they will also contact you but an-
77 **eh ik sta bij halte 'centrum' in sittard=**
eh I am at bus stop 'Centre' in Sittard=
78 **CTA: =oké nou eh de brandweer eh alarmeer ik (.) en eh die komen**
even ter plaatse.
=okay well eh I will alarm the fire brigade (.) and eh they will
come to the scene
79 **CAL: o:°ké.° (.) [prima**
o:kay. (.) fine

80 **CTA: ->** **[hartstikke bedankt hoor.**
thank you very much PRT.
81 **CAL:** **jo. (.) tot uw dienst.**
yo. (.) at your service.
82 **CTA:** **↓daag**
↓bye
83 **CAL:** **↓daag**
↓bye

Like the caller in Excerpt 11.9, the bus driver engages with the call-taker in a question-answer series but does not produce a request for help, and indeed seems to hint on several occasions (line 57, lines 61–3) that help is not needed anymore. When the call-taker proposes to send help he requests the bus driver's agreement (line 71), another indication that the driver is not treated as having requested assistance, and when the call-taker finally confirms the dispatch of the fire brigade (line 78), the bus driver acknowledges and accepts this but does not thank the call-taker although his 'please' (line 72) does express appreciation. Instead, as in Excerpt 11.9, the call-taker thanks the caller who also portrays himself as having provided a service by responding to the call-taker's thanking with 'at your service' (line 81).

Although the roofer in Excerpt 11.9 and the bus driver in Excerpt 11.10 can be seen as beneficiaries of the fire brigade dispatches to their respective incidents, the call-takers, by thanking them in these two calls, ascribe to the activities of these callers the status of providing a service rather than receiving one, aligned with the callers' absence of thankings for the dispatching of help. Here, perhaps even more strongly than in other examples, we see that the identification of a caller as requesting or providing a service is contingent upon the local interactional context rather than on the context of the incident.

11.5 Conclusion

In this paper we have focused on *action formation* and *action ascription* in emergency calls. In particular we have investigated how callers and call-takers use 'thank-yous' in the closing section of the call to ascribe identities to the caller and action statuses to the caller's incident report. As Levinson (2013) notes, the notions of action formation and action ascription are a puzzle as "direct empirical investigations under the rubric of 'action formation' or 'recognition' are few and far between" (p. 105). Our contribution to solving the puzzle was triggered in the first place by the work of Whalen and Zimmerman (1987), who showed that call-takers by granting or denying emergency assistance and the caller by thanking the call-taker, treat the emergency report as a request for help and the caller as a beneficiary of the assistance. In the second place, this study has built upon the work of Bergmann

(1993), who showed that when call-takers thank the caller, they treat the caller as a benefactor who offers the service of reporting an emergency in which he or she has no stake. This study has also built on Raymond and Zimmerman's (2016) analysis, which has shown how call-takers' and callers' misaligned identities (i.e., who is beneficiary and who is benefactor) and disjunctive projects play a role in how calls come to be closed.

Our study of thanking in Dutch emergency calls supports the studies by Whalen and Zimmerman and Bergmann, but also shows, in line with Raymond and Zimmerman, how action formation and action ascription are subject to local interactional contingencies much more than to institutional identities. Bergmann's addition to the findings of Whalen and Zimmerman was to show that callers are not always treated as beneficiaries making requests, but may also be treated as benefactors offering a service. He labelled these two different identities the 'Nutznießer' (beneficiary) and the 'Wohltäter' (benefactor), the latter of which is characterised by Heritage and Clayman (2010: 83) as someone who 'altruistically provide[s]' the service of "having brought a problem of public safety to official attention". The present study is again an addition to these studies by showing that caller identities of beneficiary or benefactor, and the corresponding actions of 'making a request' and 'offering a service', are ascribed as a result of a series of interactional contingencies that develop in the course of the call.

We have shown that for a caller to be treated as a benefactor it is not enough to present him/herself in the incident report as a witness or bystander. The pre-alignment of call-takers as service providers and callers as service seekers (Raymond & Zimmerman 2007, 2016) may be complicated by the design of the caller's incident report – we see that both first-party and third-party callers often design their incident reports *not* as service-seeking requests – as well as by contingencies in the course of the call, such as the caller's displayed emotional involvement, that may make the call-taker treat the caller as a beneficiary and the report as a request. Also, callers who may be 'objectively' and institutionally identified as beneficiaries, since they are involved in the incident and have potentially suffered from it, may be treated as benefactors. This occurs, for example, when this 'objective beneficiary' is not the person who called the emergency room and is not the one who issued the request for assistance. Along these lines, we have seen that the pre-alignment of the caller as a service seeker and that of the call-taker as a service provider endure throughout calls to the emergency centre, but what complicates this matter is that the situated identities of beneficiary and benefactor emerge within the call due to particular contingencies occurring in the course of the call.

Our findings support those of Curl and Drew (2008) and Rossi (2015) on the formation of requests in English and Italian. These studies found that the design of request turns is oriented to local contingencies rather than to interaction-external contingencies such as power relations. In our study we have moved in the opposite direction by showing that similarly designed turns can be treated both as requesting and as offering a service. The contingencies that are responsible for these treatments are not located in the requesting or offering turn alone, but are produced in the course of the interaction.

The analyses by Couper-Kuhlen (2014) and Clayman and Heritage (2014) of the role of the benefactive status in action formation can help us to specify the difference between the actions of requesting and service delivery in our data. Couper-Kuhlen and Clayman and Heritage argue that turns are treated as requests when the speaker is the beneficiary of the proposed action, while they are treated as offers when the turn's recipient is the beneficiary. In our data we see that an incident report can indeed be treated as a 'request' when the caller is the beneficiary of the requested assistance. Yet the other option we found, in which the reporting turn is treated as a service delivery, is not identical to the 'offers' in the analyses of Couper-Kuhlen and Clayman and Heritage. While in offers the recipient of the turn is the beneficiary of the proposed action, in the service deliveries in our data the call-taker is the beneficiary of the report but not of the proposed action of dispatching assistance. Thus, in ascribing to a turn the action of a service, the call-taker's orientation is not on benefactive status in relation to the proposed future action but on being the beneficiary of getting the incident reported.

In relation to questions raised in the introductory chapter of this volume (Deppermann & Haugh, Chapter 1 in this volume) our analysis has shown that the turns that perform action ascription can also be actions in their own right. Indeed, the 'thank-yous' that ascribe actions to the initial incident report in these emergency calls are at the same time part of the closing sequences (Schegloff & Sacks 1973) of the calls and are therewith consequential for the interactional unfolding of the call. The analysis also shows that action ascription need not proceed in the first turn following the turn in which the to-be-ascribed-action is performed. And importantly, action ascription is shown in this analysis as not only oriented to the design of the caller's incident report, even when the caller explicitly identifies as 'witness' of the incident (Excerpt 11.7, above) rather than as victim, but also to displays of more or less involvement on the part of the caller. In terms of Clayman and Heritage (2014) we could say that these displays add to and potentially alter the benefactive status of the caller. Perhaps we can even say that thereby the action of request or offer is not just ascribed to the caller's initial incident report, but to the entire activity of calling and reporting.

We were able to use thankings by caller or call-taker in the closing section of the emergency calls as the litmus test for establishing whether the caller's incident report was treated as a request or as a service. In contrast to requests being made in mundane interaction (Floyd et al. 2018), in emergency call data parties making a request are under the obligation to thank their benefactor while parties being offered a service likewise thank their benefactor. Thus, a 'thank-you' from the caller indicates that the call-taker has granted a prior request by the caller, while a 'thank-you' from the call-taker treats the caller as having offered a service. Indeed, as accountable actions (Garfinkel 1967) the 'thank-yous' are the methods whereby the participants themselves ascribe action status to the other's prior activities.

Acknowledgements

We thank the reviewers of this paper for their generous and helpful comments and we thank Iris van der Wal for her assistance in counting the number of 'thank-yous'.

REFERENCES

Antaki, C. & Widdicombe, S. (1998). Identity as an achievement and as a tool. In C. Antaki & S. Widdicombe, eds., *Identities in Talk.* London: Sage, pp. 1–14.

Atkinson, J. M. & Heritage, J. (1984). *Structures of Social Action: Studies in Conversation Analysis*, Cambridge: Cambridge University Press.

Bergmann, J. R. (1993). Alarmiertes Verstehen: Kommunikation in Feuerwehrnotrufen. In T. Jung & S. Mueller-Doohm, eds., *Wirklichkeit in Deutungprozess: Verstehen und Methoden in den Kultur- und Sozialwissenschaften*. Frankfurt am Main: Suhrkamp, pp. 287–328.

Bucholtz, M. & Hall, K. (2005). Identity and interaction: A sociocultural linguistic approach. *Discourse Studies*, 7(4–5), 585–614.

Clayman, S. & Heritage, J. (2014). Benefactors and beneficiaries: Benefactive status and stance in the management of offers and requests. In P. Drew & E. Couper-Kuhlen, eds., *Requesting in Social Interaction.* Amsterdam: John Benjamins, pp. 55–86.

Couper-Kuhlen, E. (2014). What does grammar tell us about action? *Pragmatics*, 24(3), 623–47.

Curl, T. S. & Drew, P. (2008). Contingency and action: A comparison of two forms of requesting. *Research on Language and Social Interaction*, 41(2), 129–53.

Floyd, S., Rossi, G., Baranova, J. et al. (2018). Universals and cultural diversity in the expression of gratitude. *Royal Society Open Science*, 5, 180391.

Garfinkel, H. (1967). *Studies in Ethnomethodology*. Englewood Cliffs, NJ: Prentice-Hall.

Heritage, J. & Clayman, S. (2010). *Talk in Action: Interactions, Identities and Institutions*. Chichester: Wiley-Blackwell.

Houtkoop-Steenstra, H. (1987). Establishing agreement. Dissertation, University of Amsterdam.

Jefferson, G. (2004). Glossary of transcript symbols with an introduction. In G. H. Lerner, ed., *Conversation Analysis: Studies from the First Generation.* Amsterdam: John Benjamins, pp. 13–31.

Lerner, G. (1996). On the "semi-permeable" character of grammatical units in conversation: Conditional entry into the turn space of another speaker. In E. Ochs, E. A. Schegloff & S. A. Thompson, eds., *Interaction and Grammar*. Cambridge: Cambridge University Press, pp. 238–76.

Levinson, S. C. (2013). Action formation and ascription. In T. Stivers & J. Sidnell, eds., *Handbook of Conversation Analysis*. Chichester: Wiley-Blackwell, pp. 103–30.

Mead, G. H. (1934). *Mind, Self, and Society*. Chicago, IL: University of Chicago Press.

Mosegaard Hansen, M.-B. M. (2016). Patterns of thanking in the closing section of UK service calls: Marking conversational macro-structure vs managing interpersonal relations. *Pragmatics and Society*, 7(4), 664–92.

Raymond, G. & Zimmerman, D. H. (2007). Rights and responsibilities in calls for help: the case of the Mountain Glade Fire. *Research on Language and Social Interaction*, 40(1), 33–61.

(2016). Closing matters: Alignment and mis-alignment in sequence and call closings in institutional interaction. *Discourse Studies*, 16(8), 716–36.

Rossi, G. (2015) The request system in Italian interaction. Dissertation, Radboud University, Nijmegen.

Schegloff, E. A. (2007). *Sequence Organization in Interaction: A Primer in Conversation Analysis*. Cambridge: Cambridge University Press.

Schegloff, E. A. & Sacks, H. (1973). Opening up closings. *Semiotica*, 8(4), 289–327.

Sidnell, J. (2013). Basic conversation analytic methods. In J. Sidnell & T. Stivers, eds., *Handbook of Conversation Analysis*. Chichester: Wiley-Blackwell, pp. 77–99.

Wakin, M. & Zimmerman, D. H. (1999). Reduction and specialization in emergency and directory assistance calls. *Research on Language and Social Interaction*, 32 (4), 409–37.

Whalen, M. R. & Zimmerman, D. H. (1987). Sequential and institutional contexts in calls for help. *Social Psychology Quarterly*, 50(2), 172–85.

(1990). Describing trouble: Practical epistemology in citizen calls to the police. *Language in Society*, 19, 465–92.

Whalen, J., Zimmerman, D. H. & Whalen, M. (1988). When words fail: A single case analysis. *Social Problems*, 35(4), 309–46.

Zimmerman, D. H. (1984). Talk and its occasion: the case of calling the police. In D. Schiffrin, ed., *Meaning, Form and Use in Context: Linguistic Applications*. Washington, DC: Georgetown University Press, pp. 210–28.

(1992). The interactional organization of calls for emergency assistance. In P. Drew & J. Heritage, eds., *Talk at Work: Interaction in Institutional Settings*. Cambridge: Cambridge University Press, pp. 418–69.

(1998). Identity, context and interaction. In C. Antaki & S. Widdicombe, eds., *Identities in Talk*. London: Sage, pp. 87–106.

Zimmerman, D. H. & Wakin, M. (1995). Thank you's and the management of closings in emergency calls. Paper presented at the Annual Meeting of the American Sociological Association, Washington DC.

Part III

Revisiting Action Ascription

12 Action and Accountability in Interaction

N. J. Enfield and Jack Sidnell

12.1 Introduction

We start with two axioms about the relation between language and action:

Axiom 1 *What we say (vocally and otherwise) and what we do by saying it are two different, yet related, things.* The same words (e.g., 'She's just starting') can have different import in different contexts (e.g., giving an account, defending somebody, noticing something). An analysis of action must determine the link between the specific practices used (i.e., words and grammatical constructions, prosody, contextual positioning, bodily conduct), and the action that these practices achieve in any instance of social interaction. This leads to the question: How does saying X count as doing Y?[1]

Axiom 2 An action, in interaction, is fully consummated only by its relation to the result it brings about, a central aspect of which is the response it engenders. Since action in interaction is action upon another person, what is effectively done by a move is only fully determined with reference to how that move is responded to (as long as that response is allowed through).[2] An analysis of action must incorporate both formulation and interpretation, and the relation of co-determination between the two. This leads to the question: How is saying X related to the appropriate response Z?[3]

These two axioms lead us to the central puzzle for the study of action in interaction. This is a puzzle of interpretation that participants constantly face: How does a person decide, on the basis of what someone is saying, what would be an appropriate response? One answer is that "in order to respond, a participant *must have ascribed some action* to a prior turn" (Couper-Kuhlen & Selting 2018: 231; our emphasis). On this account, interpreting a move as an action demands that we categorize the swatch of behavior 'as action X', sorting

[1] Axiom 1 is the starting point for speech act theory and much of the literature in philosophical pragmatics.

[2] The response has to be 'allowed through' if it is going to help determine what the prior action was. In third position repair, a speaker – post-response – often indicates they were not doing the thing the recipient has taken them to be doing (Schegloff 1992; Sidnell 2017). This supports our point, because it shows the power of the response to cast the prior as an action of a certain kind.

[3] Axiom 2 is the starting point for conversation analysis and much of the literature on social interaction.

the stream of interactional conduct into appropriate categories or bins, and *through that act of categorization* thus knowing what an appropriate response would be. This binning account of action presupposes a defined "inventory of action types" (Levinson 2013: 122).[4]

Some examples seem compatible with this view, suggesting that linguistic practices map onto social actions in straightforward ways. Take the exchanges in the following cases from a family dinner:

Excerpt 12.1 (DAD = father, MOM = mother)

```
01 DAD:   an' may I have thuh -butter please.
02 MOM:   yes.=hh ((extending hand to pass butter))
```

Excerpt 12.2 (MOM = mother, DAD = father)

```
01 MOM:   °can I have the butter please,°
02 DAD:   sure. ((extending hand to pass butter))
```

Here, an identifiable linguistic structure is used in a way that is readily recognizable to us as analysts, and to the participants, as a request (see, e.g., Couper-Kuhlen 2014; Curl & Drew 2008). There are two kinds of evidence for this. One concerns internal composition: measurable features of the highlighted moves themselves. In these cases, we can identify a 'May/Can I have X please' yes/no question construction that is consistent across the cases. Second, there is the sequential status of the move. We can point to the uptake that each of these moves receives: the addressed parties immediately produce a verbal confirmation ('sure', 'yes') in response to the ostensive yes-no question, while at the same time producing a bodily action of passing the named/requested object.

On the basis of these features of position and composition, it is hard to imagine anybody hesitating to label the highlighted moves as requests. Nor is there any reason to think that the interactants had any doubt as to how they should respond (i.e., by fulfilling the request). But this cannot form the basis of a general account of action. Why not? Because the vast majority of moves in interaction are not recognizable like these textbook examples. Anyone who has attempted to work through a conversational transcript and exhaustively 'identify the action' in each line knows that it is a hopeless task. Many utterances resist description in terms of action types, while others admit of several descriptions. We contend that focusing primarily on such minimally ambiguous cases as in our examples of requests does more harm than good in the

[4] According to Levinson (2013), this list contains both actions labeled by 'vernacular metalinguistic terms' and analysts' technical terms.

study of interaction. Seemingly straightforward words-to-action mappings, such as mealtime requests, are a poor model for action. The truth is that most moves in interaction lack this clarity of design-to-action mapping.[5]

We argue that participants in interaction need not definitively formulate or categorize conduct in order to respond to it. On our view, interaction does not involve a kind of binning procedure in which the stream of conduct is sorted into discrete action types. Prior actions are frequently described in interaction ('Don't *tell* me what to do!', 'You already *asked* me that,' etc.) but even in such cases, there is no guarantee that the 'action' proposed by such a description accurately (or adequately, or exhaustively) describes what was done. Indeed, there are good reasons for supposing that it could not possibly do this, that no bit of conduct could be definitively described by a single description. Moreover, describing an action is inevitably itself an action and thus bound up within its own set of accountabilities.

Our approach to the puzzle of action in interaction can be summarized with reference to three proposals (see Enfield & Sidnell 2017):

Proposal 1 Every move is made up of a combination of independent features from all corners of the semiotic repertoire; all features potentially matter for the interpretation (and thus the construction) of action, and none necessarily signal specific actions. The task of figuring out how to respond in interaction requires us to view a person's conduct as means to some ends (i.e., as purposive, goal-directed behavior). This presupposes that people subprehend others' goals from their conduct.[6] The machinery of interaction is organized around recipients' flexible capacity to interpret conduct by viewing it as goal-directed and purposive: i.e., people's propensity to interpret controlled conduct as having been produced for a reason.[7] This is what people are doing when they ask – consciously or not – 'Why that now?' in the flow of

[5] To be clear, our critique is not a methodological one. The binning model is a widely held 'concept of action' which informs much scholarship into the organization of social interaction. Whether or not analysts go about binning actions in the course of their investigations, the binning idea constitutes an underlying, tacitly held conceptual model of the way interaction works. Because the binning model is so deeply held and so rooted in our language (through, e.g., metalinguistic vocabulary as well as the grammar of reported speech, see Silverstein 1979; Rumsey 1990), it is difficult to see past it or to conceptualize the phenomena of action in interaction in other ways (though there are exceptions: Schegloff has made similar points to ours, in his lectures for instance – see also Schegloff 2009 – and has often warned against basing an analysis on a presumed inventory of action types, suggesting instead that analysis should be primarily grounded in *practices*).

[6] We use the term *subprehension* (Enfield 2013: 222, n28) to refer to a tacit awareness of what is normatively or culturally possible next. When we subprehend a certain response in interaction, this means that we are not surprised that it has happened. But we do not necessarily want to say that we had actively *anticipated* or *expected* it to happen.

[7] This is why we ultimately don't accept the practions model of action (Schegloff 1992; Enfield 2013: 100): it assumes a fixed connection between 'set of practices X' and 'action Y'. That said, we recognize that many form–action associations are frequent and entrenched.

interaction (Schegloff & Sacks 1973). We do not mean that people are always mentalizing 'What is her reason?' We mean that, as Garfinkel (1952: 367) argued, we are guided by a sense of how people in general would likely interpret others' conduct in terms of its reasons.[8]

Proposal 2 An action cannot be identified and talked about without a description being chosen for that action, and any description is one among many possible; at the same time, responding to an action is not equivalent to describing it, nor does it entail that a description of it has been made at any level. There are two ways in which a move can be categorized in action terms. One is what it is called (or effectively called; i.e., how it can be described),[9] while the other is in the way an action is (appropriately) treated in response (drawing on the inferences of means-to-ends mapping). How we respond to an action and what we call it can be two quite different things.[10] So when, in response to one participant saying something, a recipient passes the butter, their passing the butter does not describe the prior action. Rather, it treats the prior move as requiring the passing of the butter. Crucially, it does not definitively characterize the initiating conduct as having been an instance of a particular action (e.g., as a request, complaint, command, instruction, or suggestion).[11] A definitive categorization of conduct into action types is not required for the orderly flow of interaction.

Proposal 3 *Alternate descriptions of action foreground different accountabilities* (Schegloff 1988; Sidnell 2017). *The verbal description of an action invokes a particular set of rights and duties for which those involved are treated as accountable, and therefore such description is specifically relevant to thematizing the accountability of participants; analysts must be careful as to whether they mean to be thematizing certain accountabilities and not others when they name actions in interaction.* Conduct in interaction is designed by reference to accountability (Heritage 1984; Robinson 2016; Sidnell 2017). Accountability harnesses the linguistic capacity for reflexive formulation; i.e., the fact that language can be used to say things about itself (Jakobson 1971[1957]). In order to hold someone accountable, you have to be able to say what they have done, and to do this you have to choose one way of describing or formulating their conduct as a type of (intentional) action (or by word-for-word report, e.g., 'She said, "She's just starting"'). Saying what a person has done is equivalent to saying what they are accountable for having done.

[8] Our semiotic account begins not with senders/speakers and thus not with intention, but with receivers/hearers and thus with interpretation. It is a recipient-driven system (Krebs & Dawkins 1984, Enfield 2013: 16–17).

[9] Overt labelling of actions by participants in interaction is not uncommon in cases of third position repair ('I wasn't criticizing, I was asking').

[10] The distinction between 'treating as' and 'describing as' may point to two ends of a continuum, with a possible middle ground. Consider the case (Sidnell 2017) in which person B's delivery truck is pointed in the wrong direction on a narrow one-way street. A: *You know this is one way right?* B: *I've got a permit so relax.* B's response seems to imply that A's turn was an accusation of sorts, but they do not call it anything or describe it as such. B does, however, implicate that A's initial turn was 'not relaxed', and in this way B is holding A accountable for a possible transgression.

[11] If for instance someone says 'this bread is dry' (thereby doing something describable as 'complaining'), another may respond by passing the butter.

The essence and upshot of these proposals that interaction can proceed without the use of explicit formulation was anticipated half a century ago by Harvey Sacks (1995: 517):

> [T]here's no room in the world to definitively propose formulations of activities, identifications, and settings. They are things that have got to be used with caution. And there may well be ways of allowing things to go on without their necessary invocation.

12.2 The Many Bits of Conduct That Make Up Actions

What alternative to a binning approach to action will account for the orderly organization of conduct in interaction? The following fragment from a conversation between a husband and wife having dinner allows us to illustrate our approach to this problem. Our observations will focus on the highlighted lines (3, 13):

Excerpt 12.3 Ravioli dinner (KIM = Kim, MAR = Mark)

```
Kim:     I don't like it.
         (35.0)
Mark:    Dennis came in today:=uh:m (0.2) tlk=He wrote this big
         letter tuh Ford,
         (1.4)
Mark:    Cuz his car's been in the shop ya know,
         (1.5)
Mark:    tlk for so long,
         (.)
Mark:    Took 'em like two weeks tuh fix his transmission.
         (0.3)
Mark:    (H[e had tuh ri-)/(he had uh ru-)
Kim:       [So he wrote a complaint?
         (2.0)
Mark:    .hh Mm hm?
         (4.0)
Mark:    ≠We:11, (0.5) he has like:eight hundred dollars in:
         (.) rental cars fer (.) two weeks.
         (0.4)
```

There has been a lapse (for 35 seconds) when Mark produces the talk at line 3, 'Dennis came in today:=uh:m (0.2)'. We might ask: '*What action* is Mark doing at line 3'? The problem with the question is that it is unconstrained and could be answered accurately in any number of ways.[12] We could say that he is

[12] This is because action ascription by labeling is an act of categorization, and categorization of the same objective entity can be made in a wide range of ways. This is true for any named phenomena. Take Fido: Is he a dog? A pet? A mammal? All are true descriptions.

'asserting that X'. We could equally well say that he is 'telling Kim X' or that he is 'proffering a topic'. Alternatively, we could say that he is 'making a bid to tell a story', and so on. We propose that a better question to ask is this: 'How can Kim appropriately respond to what Mark has done?' This question goes directly to what matters for these participants. It is the question that Kim has to answer. We suggest that in order for Kim to do this, she needs to look for clues in the design of Mark's move. This point is of course well known to analysts of talk in interaction, but we emphasize that her inspection of his turn need not be – and will seldom if ever be – aimed at categorizing *what action* has been produced. Her concern is how to appropriately respond.

Taking this as a starting point we can notice that Mark's turn refers to someone by name, thereby indicating that Kim should be able to recognize who he is talking about (Sacks & Schegloff 1979). Mark has, then, begun to talk about someone that both speaker and recipient know. Moreover, by saying that Dennis 'came in today', Mark has placed this person, whom both speaker and recipient know, in a setting consisting of a place indicated solely by 'came in' (likely Mark's workplace, drawing on Mark and Kim's common ground) and a time, 'today'. Such recognitional references to persons coupled with descriptions of settings are strongly associated with the beginnings of stories (Dingemanse, Rossi & Floyd 2017; Jefferson 1978; Rossano 2012; Sacks 1995; Sidnell 2010). This does not mean that a participant has to categorize the move as a 'story launching'. The key thing is that they need to respond to such reference–description couplings by showing themselves to be willing recipients (Stivers 2008).

So, Mark has talked in such a way as to suggest that he has something to tell Kim about a mutual acquaintance – something that he learned today. The reference–description coupling might well have been enough for Kim to be able to produce an appropriate aligning response which, had the turn reached completion at this point, might have been something like 'uh huh' (Schegloff 1982). However, Mark does not come to possible completion of this unit at 'today'. Instead he produces 'uhm' latched to 'today' with no perceptible gap. In this way, Mark shows that the unit of talk so far produced is to be continued. Particles such as English 'uhm' in a position like this often have as their basic function 'turn-holding'.[13] Here, Kim can gather that Mark has more to say and thus that this part of the talk is merely a beginning to something more extensive. At the same time, disfluencies such as this one regularly elicit the gaze of a nongazing recipient (Goodwin 1979; Rossano 2012).

[13] See the discussion of 'appositionals' in Sacks, Schegloff and Jefferson (1974: 719; cf. also Clark & Fox-Tree 2002; Walker 2012).

How then does Kim respond? Her glance to Mark is timed to coincide with just that moment when he is continuing without actually speaking. With a quick glance Kim can show Mark that she recognizes a boundary in the talk has been reached but that the talk will nevertheless continue. Moreover, by glancing while not talking (and thus not initiating repair), Kim conveys that she has recognized the person referred to by the name 'Dennis'.

We might say that Kim's glance responds to Mark's talk not as a speech act of asserting but as the beginning of a larger project, the telling of a story. Does her response entail that she has made a specific 'action ascription'? Rather than say that Kim has at some level decided 'This is a story launching', a simpler account is that by responding with a glance, and with no talk of her own, Kim aligns with the activity Mark has initiated, an activity in which she will serve as recipient and he as teller. There is no evidence that Kim has categorized Mark's turn (by ascription or recognition or in some other way) as anything specific at all, whether it be 'story launching' or 'announcement' or 'topic bid' or something else. All she has had to do is produce an appropriate response. At the very least, this is a more parsimonious account than a binning-style, action categorization account. Under both accounts, the appropriate response must be selected. In our account, there is no intermediate level of action labeling.

Any analysis of action must account for how and why Kim produces the response she produces – in other words, why she treats Mark's move in a certain way – and it is not clear that we need to do more than that. Naming the action – e.g., as 'launching a story' – is not only more than is needed, it also adds something that demonstrably isn't there; it adds that Mark is specifically accountable for just that action (and correspondingly it implies that he is not accountable for the alternative – but not offered – descriptions of what he was doing).

Let us further develop this argument as we turn to the next line of interest. After his first mention of Dennis coming in today, Mark continues, saying that Dennis wrote to Ford, because of how long his car was in the shop. Then Kim says:

line 13 Kim 'So he wrote a complaint?'

With 'So he wrote a complaint?' Kim formulates the upshot of what Mark has been saying by glossing in speech act terms the action that Dennis was engaged in by writing 'a big letter', as Mark put it. Naming the action Dennis was engaged in provides a strong demonstration of understanding of what Mark has been saying, because it requires Kim to piece together the bits of information so far provided. This can be seen as furthering the work of alignment that Kim began with the glance discussed earlier. A demonstration of understanding shows not just that she has acted as a recipient but that she has understood.

Different kinds of responses are made relevant at different points within the project Mark is engaged in. So in line 3, the talk 'Dennis came in today:=uh:m (0.2)' only made a display of alignment relevant from Kim. At that point, little else had been revealed to which she might respond. Here, however, with more of the story, Kim can respond more substantially, showing both a willingness to continue aligning as the story's recipient and some of the fruits of that alignment. With 'So he wrote a complaint?' Kim displays an understanding of what has so far been said.

An action is constructed from components, and some actions are leaner than others. For instance, Kim's glance consists solely of a head/gaze reorientation and momentary suspension of her other bodily actions.[14] 'So he wrote a complaint?', on the other hand, is produced while she looks at her plate (where it landed after Mark's 'two weeks' – Kim gazing at Mark before that) and so does not actively employ gaze for her action. Rather the action here makes use of the linguistic resources of lexical semantics and grammar. 'So' shows the relation to the prior talk, marking what is said as an inference from the evidence Mark has provided (Raymond 2004). The rest of the turn draws on English semantics to name the action that Dennis was engaged in. In Peircean terms, this is a representational interpretant of Mark's statement in lines 3–4 (Enfield 2013; Kockelman 2005). Notice that although the grammatical construction is declarative, Kim can be interpreted as doing questioning here. In line 15 Mark confirms with 'Mm hm?' Declarative utterances like this are routinely treated as seeking answer-type responses where they concern matters in the recipient's epistemic domain (Heritage 2012). Mark knows better than Kim what Dennis was doing in writing the big letter and thus her turn is treated as seeking confirmation.

By our account, the orderliness of interaction does not depend on the capacity of participants to take a particular bit of conduct (e.g., the utterance 'That's a really nice jacket') and assign it to some particular action category – e.g., 'compliment' (Levinson 2013: 103). For a binning account to be correct, there must be an inventory of actions just as there is a defined set of phonemes in a language. Each token bit of conduct goes into an appropriate pre-existing action type category. The binning approach also suggests that it would be reasonable to ask how many actions there are. But to ask how many actions there are is like asking how many sentences there are. Here lies the key to our account: action is generated out of constituent elements of context and code

[14] This points to an important conceptual problem with the binning approach. On a binning account, Kim's glance must, of course, be binned. But as what? If the machinery of action requires binning each possible action into one bin from the inventory, then how do we deal with very lean 'actions' such as one constituted merely by a shift in a participant's gaze? Or more problematic: What about silence, e.g., after a request? Or a greeting? Is this also to be binned? If not, are we thereby committed to saying that it is not (an) action?

that we already need in order to infer utterance meanings, and to produce appropriate responses. There is no need to add another level, conscious or otherwise, at which action categorization is done. Indeed, our approach predicts that it would seldom be easy to label an action, while it will usually be straightforward to know what an appropriate next move would be. These two things are not the same. Our point is that interactants can know how to respond quite reliably by working up from turn components and finding a token solution, and not by having to assign the whole turn to an action category.

12.3 To Name an Action Is to Thematize Participants' Accountability

We have argued that an interactant is able to produce an appropriate response to another's move in interaction by building a token understanding of what a person is doing by what they are saying, based on features of the move's design and positioning. We have further suggested that there is no analytical need to propose that interactants categorize actions by binning token moves as this or that action type. Now we want to argue that the explicit labeling of an action not only adds nothing that is needed, but adds something that is not needed: namely, a specific claim about the accountability at hand. To name an action is to cast a move under a description (as an alternative to other possible descriptions), and this is a way of thematizing specific things for which a participant is claimed to be accountable (Sidnell 2017).

Let us look at a case in which – unlike those in the last section – the participants are concerned with categorizing moves in the interaction by explicitly labeling them in action terms. Our point will be that these descriptions do not identify or define the actions, rather they make claims about others' conduct in order to thematize a specific accountability for the participants in question.

In the following excerpt from a family dinner, a father, a mother, and their daughter aged around 10 are having an evening meal at home in Southern California.

Excerpt 12.4 Field trip (DAD = Father, CIN = Cindy, MOM = Mother)

```
Dad: So Ci:n (0.2) tell me abou your day.
     (0.5)
Cin: Uh:: .h
Dad: Wha' dju (d) learn.
     (1.0)
Dad: [Oh^::H yeah we went to thuh- we went to uh: (.)
Cin: [Uh: m-
Cin: Claim Jumper.
Dad: Claim Jum[per oday.
Mom:           [>Uh huh<
```

Mom: May I have a roll [please,
Cin: [For uh field rip.=
Dad: =Sure.
Dad: An' may I have thuh -butter please.
Mom: Yes.=.hh (0.5)
(0.5)
Cin: Went to Claim Jumper for our field trip.=
Dad: Yiea:h, an'- an'- tell me about it.
(0.5)
Mom: Cindy wantuh roll,
(1.0)
Cin: Mm[:
Mom: [It's soft, it's good,
Dad: Come on,
Cin: Ye[ah.
Dad: [Describe this thing to me,
Cin: Uh:m_ .h It was fu:n?,
(0.3)
Dad: No.
(.)
Dad: You're gonna h(h)afta do uh lot [better than that.]
Mom: [Well she's-] she'll s
she's-
Dad: Hey[shh::
Mom: [Just starting. [°She's just starting.°
Dad: [Don't' defend 'er:,
Dad: [I wanna hear this from °her.°
Mom: [((mumble something at high pitch))
Mom: She'll do fine,
(0.5)
Cin: Uhm (2.0) what's this?,
(1-0)
Mom: Uh garbanzo bean.

We begin when the father selects his daughter to 'tell (him) about' her day (line 1). By using the phrase 'tell me about', the father is naming a kind of action: 'to tell someone about something'. With this, the father thematizes a normative set of practices that would constitute an instance of the named action. He is not describing an action that has taken place, rather he is directing the daughter to carry out the action he is describing. By a combination of factors, the daughter, as a participant in the joint activity of conversation at dinner, is now obliged to do something that could be defended as an action of the kind described. For one thing, she is the recipient of a directive, linguistically formatted in the imperative. For another, the family is engaged in a social activity – that of having an evening meal together – which by virtue of the cultural context, identifies this action, specifically with reference to what happened during the day leading up to the evening meal, as one that the daughter should recognize. And thirdly, he is her father, which has obvious implications for the power relationship between the two (e.g., such that the daughter is unlikely to be able to make the same directive to her father, or at least not in the same terms). So, with this line the father obliges the daughter to act in a certain way, thus prospectively holding her accountable for producing a swatch of conduct that defensibly fits his action description.

The father quickly follows up his directive 'Tell me about your day' with a question 'What'd you learn?' (line 4), narrowing the scope of what the daughter might say in her projected telling. After a second's silence the father continues to narrow the scope of what the daughter can do. With line 6 'Oh, yeah we went to uh', the father 'does remembering' of what the daughter was going to do that day, transposing himself as subject of this remembering. Before he produces the name of the place the daughter was going, she completes his turn (line 8), saying 'Claim Jumper', a restaurant that she visited on a class excursion that day.[15]

At this point, the mother inserts a request for a roll, immediately followed by the father's request for butter (see Excerpt 12.1 above), and then the daughter picks up the topic, saying 'Went to Claim Jumper for our field trip' (line 17). What is the daughter doing with this assertion? It could be that she is fulfilling the obligation that the father gave her by saying 'Tell me about your day' in line 1. The father immediately discounts this possibility by saying 'Yeah and tell me about it' in line 18, reacting to the assertion ('yeah') and then reissuing the directive 'tell me about it'. Again, there is brief talk relating to passing rolls, and the father resumes with 'Describe this thing to me' (line 26). He has now reiterated his directive using two action descriptions: 'tell me about it' and 'describe it to me'. By doing so, he is showing that nothing the daughter has produced so far is accepted as an instance of an action fitting the description. These descriptions are not merely seeking to categorize the daughter's talk, but are being used in the context of holding her accountable for the appropriateness and effectiveness of her conduct.

The daughter then moves from making an objective assertion about what happened to taking an evaluative stance, stating 'Um it was fun?' in line 27. There are two notable aspects of her turn design here. First is the interjection *um* (Clark & Fox Tree 2002; Schegloff 2010). While interjections such as *um* and *uh* appear in many sequential contexts, this one resembles those cases in which such a form is used to preface an estimate or a guess. And although she is producing a subjective assessment of her own experience, it is nevertheless delivered as a 'guess.' Thus another notable aspect is the try-marking – a

[15] https://en.wikipedia.org/wiki/Claim_Jumper.

distinctive type of pitch rise in turn-final position, typically used for mobilizing a confirmation of recognition from the talk's recipient (Sacks & Schegloff 1979) – on 'fun'. She is not only stating that it was fun, but she is at that moment mobilizing a response from the father (Stivers & Rossano 2010). A try-marker usually adds an implicit question, canonically occurring on a recognitional reference such as a name. The name assumes 'you know who/what/where I'm talking about', and the try-marker adds a question – 'Can you confirm that you recognize this reference?' – thereby making a confirming response relevant next. Line 27 – 'Um it was fun? – differs from the canonical pattern in lacking a recognitional reference. Here, the try-marking appears to convey, together with the 'estimating' *um*, 'Is this adequate?'.

But the projected action of 'telling someone about something' normatively requires a multi-unit turn, and this is what the daughter will be held accountable for. The daughter at this point has used a single TCU, one hearable as asking for confirmation that she is doing, or has done, the required thing. Giving evidence in support of the idea that the try-marker is asking a yes-no question, the father's first move (line 29) is to say 'No', responding to the implicit question in the try-marker. This is followed up by a strong rebuke in line 31: 'You're going to have to do a lot better than that'. This is a clear case in which a person is held accountable for their conduct in terms of its failure to fit with a verbal description of the desired behavior in action terms.[16]

To summarize, the father's rebuke makes sense if we interpret the daughter as offering 'Um it was fun?' as a possible instance of 'telling someone about something'. The daughter is held to account for her failure to produce an action of the described kind. This shows the power of an explicit action description and, one way such actions descriptions are used in social interaction (for others see Sidnell 2017).

What happens next gives further support to this view. The mother says 'she's just starting' (beginning in overlap in line 32, and emerging in lines 33 and 35). This proposes an alternative action description of the daughter's turn from the father's original in line 1. By characterizing 'Um it was fun?' as 'just starting', the mother offers a charitable interpretation, allowing that the daughter is in fact embarking on producing an action of just the requested kind.[17] If indeed the daughter is just starting, then the father's rebuke in line 31 is not justified. What can we say about the mother's action here?

[16] Joint action entails mutual commitment, and this commitment has a moral dimension: if one person fails to keep up their part of the commitment, the other is entitled to 'rebuke' them (Gilbert 1992). In Gilbert's example of going for a walk together, if one person walks faster than the other and draws ahead, the first person may be entitled to say something like 'I can't keep up, you are going to have to slow down!' Conversation is joint action in this sense (Clark 1996; Enfield 2017).

[17] The mother's line 'She's just starting' also suggests an analysis by which the daughter's try-marking checks the recipient's understanding with minimal disruption to the progress of her

There are two ways of answering. The father helps us with one way, by naming the mother's action (line 36), attempting to hold her accountable for what she has just done: 'Don't *defend* her'. Was the mother defending the daughter? A binning analysis would suggest that there is a correct answer to this question, but on our view this question is not about defining action but about thematizing accountability. This is necessarily selective. Which is the right formulation to select? We might say, as the father does, that the mother was defending the daughter. Or we might say that she was rebuking the father for an uncharitable interpretation of the daughter's move 'Um it was fun?' Indeed, the father's choice of the word 'defend' may imply that she had been under 'attack' from the father (an interesting collateral effect of the father's word choice).

But of course what the father *calls* the action does not tell us what the mother was doing. Our point is that by calling it something, he is making a claim to what the mother can be held accountable for having done. This is what analysts are doing when they bin moves as nameable actions. Sometimes this may be justified (see the 'requests' in Section 12.2), but there is seldom any basis for doing so – or for doing so in a way that claims to be definitive/exhaustive. In the last section, we concentrated on moves that have straightforward responses but that are not straightforwardly nameable, and do not imply straightforward accountability.

It is impossible to say, definitively, what singular action 'She's just starting' implements. Whatever action it accomplishes is bound up with the details of its context. No description can ever do more than gloss it. It is useful however to consider what the options are. Searle (1969), for instance, seems committed to describing it as an assertion (of belief). Schegloff (1996) might advise a 'praction' analysis in which a collection of like cases is brought together in order to reveal a contingent mapping between composition, position, and function.[18] Levinson might conclude that whatever action this implements, it will be included in an inventory or 'bag' of actions. Our own account insists that there are always alternate possibilities. There could have been other analyses than that which 'Don't defend her' implies. There is no single, unequivocal, definitive analysis for the father to arrive at. Rather, he chooses the analysis – that the mother was 'defending' the daughter in lines 32–35 – which fits his purposes. While this may seem obvious, it raises a less obvious challenge for analysts: What are *our* purposes, such that we may decide what aspects of a participant's accountability to thematize?

telling. Try-marking can elicit recipient responses within a single TCU and before it reaches possible completion (see Sidnell 2010).

18 On 'practions' in action analysis, see Enfield (2013: 100).

12.4 Conclusion

The conceptual problem of action in interaction has long exercised philosophers of language, and action is increasingly viewed in conversation analysis as a domain of order alongside turn-taking, repair, and sequence organization. To define and understand action in interaction, a valid account must both (1) handle the empirical particulars of the languages and cultures of any given data, and (2) explain how those local particulars are instances of a species-wide domain of order, with predictions for how variation in human interaction is constrained.[19] In conclusion, we want to comment on the implications of our account of (1), which has been the focus of this paper, for our account of (2).[20]

One path to a universal theory of action begins with some global macro categories for actions, which any action will be an instance of. The psychologist Michael Tomasello (2008) proposes three macro actions in interaction, grounded in empirical findings of comparative behavioral psychology. These actions are requesting (to secure another's help for meeting your own goals), helping (to provide your help for meeting another's goals), and sharing (for meeting common goals, and for the cohesion of social relationships). Tomasello argues that these macro actions require distinct social motivations and underlying cognitive capacities that are both universal and unique in our species. He leaves implicit how these three categories are instantiated by token actions of the kind we have discussed here.

The philosopher John Searle (1969, 2010) takes a different approach. He establishes macro categories of action based on four distinct types of mental state, which he takes as prior: assertives (corresponding to beliefs), directives (corresponding to desires), commissives (corresponding to intentions), and expressives (corresponding to feelings). From basic intentional states (Searle 1983), grounded in individual human cognition, Searle derives general communicative actions.[21]

These two theories offer an exhaustive inventory of action types, or action elements, that are proposed to exist universally. They do not link the macro action categories to actions at the more specific level of token cases in data from conversation. By contrast, accounts of action that begin with conversational data work with categories of action that are much more specific in nature, and greater in number, than the macro action categories suggested by

[19] See Sidnell (2009), Sidnell and Enfield (2012), Dingemanse and Floyd (2014), Enfield (2017).

[20] On action in relation to human diversity, see Part III of Enfield and Sidnell (2017).

[21] Searle has a fifth type of speech act – the declarative – that is not based on a basic psychological state, unless perhaps imagining (see Searle 2010).

Tomasello and Searle (see, e.g., Levinson 2013, 2017; Schegloff 1996, 1997[22]). Our view is that no distinct set of action types, whether general or specific, is necessary or sufficient for thinking about action in interaction. We acknowledge that existing approaches have important virtues, methodological and otherwise. Action labels serve a useful role in analysis, and in scholarly communication. We have argued that a binning analysis – sorting the stream of conduct into discrete action types – has a role, but this role does not provide a general account for action in interaction. Categorization of actions is relevant to a categorizer's goal of thematizing accountability (see our examples 'Tell me about your day', 'She's just starting', and 'Don't defend her'). This insight requires that we attend to the reflexive quality of language, something that Linguistic Anthropology has dealt with more than Conversation Analysis. Accountability is a glue that holds interaction together. For a theory of action to be built on that idea, we need to acknowledge that participants work on the assumption that people are pursuing goals, and they seek to ascribe reasons behind others' behavior that make sense in terms of those likely goals.

If there are no types of action independent from the observed tokens of goal-directed conduct, then is it possible to compare actions across cultures? One way to study action comparatively is to focus on the social problems that people need to solve (Schegloff 2006; Sidnell & Enfield 2012). Some of those are likely to be universal, such as initiating repair (Dingemanse et al. 2015) or recruiting others' assistance (Floyd, Rossi & Enfield 2020), and others are likely to be culture-specific. These problems in need of interactional solutions are not, of course, actions themselves, rather they are the ends that means are contrived to meet. Actions are not problems that need solving. They are the means-for-ends solutions to those problems. From an interpreter's perspective, the task is to work from the means – the practices used – to the infer the ends. In addition, actions are bound up with the uptakes that they elicit, and that in turn help consummate actions, given that action in interaction is, ultimately and necessarily, distributed and collaborative in nature (Enfield & Kockelman 2017).

We conclude that participants in interaction do not need to recognize action types or categories in order to respond appropriately. Other theories that have addressed the problem of action ascription seem to assume that such ascription involves assigning each bit of conduct to an action type category, essentially a process of labeling. Our view is that when participants are analyzing moves in the

[22] While Schegloff (2006) makes several proposals as to what is likely to universally underlie the organization of human interaction, he does not claim that any specific actions, or general action types, are universal, or otherwise serve as a universal comparative framework for understanding action in human interaction. What Schegloff lists are universal problems that people need to solve in interaction (the turn-taking problem, the repair problem, etc.) – i.e., interactional *ends* that people universally need to devise means for.

flow of interaction they are not labeling or otherwise identifying actions, rather they are considering the details of turns-at-talk, under the assumption that the speaker's conduct is purposive and goal-directed, for their relevance in deciding what to do next and how to do it. And all of such details are potentially relevant to what someone will be understood to be doing. Action category labels are convenient heuristics but they are ultimately neither necessary nor sufficient. Category labels cannot substitute for practice-based analysis of situated social action.

Acknowledgments

This is a significantly revised version of an article originally published in *Discourse Studies* 19(5) under the title, "On the concept of action in the study of interaction."

REFERENCES

Clark, H. (1996). *Using Language*. Cambridge: Cambridge University Press.

Clark, H. & Fox Tree, J. (2002). Using uh and um in spontaneous speaking. *Cognition*, 84, 73–111.

Couper-Kuhlen, E. (2014). What does grammar tell us about action? *Pragmatics*, 24(3), 623–47.

Couper-Kuhlen, E. & Selting, M. (2018). *Interactional Linguistics: An Introduction to Language in Social Interaction*. Cambridge: Cambridge University Press.

Curl, T. & Drew, P. (2008). Contingency and action: A comparison of two forms of requesting. *Research on Language and Social Interaction*, 41, 129–53.

Dingemanse, M. & Floyd, S. (2014). Conversation across cultures. In N. Enfield, P. Kockelman & J. Sidnell, eds., *Cambridge Handbook of Linguistic Anthropology*. Cambridge: Cambridge University Press, pp. 447–80.

Dingemanse, M., Roberts, S. G., Baranova, J. et al. (2015). Universal principles in the repair of communication problems. *PLOS ONE* 10(9), e013610.

Dingemanse, M., Rossi, G. & Floyd, S. (2017). Place reference in story beginnings: A cross-linguistic study of narrative and interactional affordances. *Language in Society*, 46(2), 129–58.

Enfield, N. J. (2013). *Relationship Thinking: Agency, Enchrony, and Human Sociality*. New York, NY: Oxford University Press.

(2017). *How We Talk: The Inner Workings of Conversation*, New York, NY: Basic Books.

Enfield, N. J. & Kockelman, P., eds. (2017). *Distributed Agency*. New York, NY: Oxford University Press.

Enfield, N. J. & Sidnell, J. (2017). *The Concept of Action*. Cambridge: Cambridge University Press.

Floyd, S., Rossi, G. & Enfield, N. J., eds. (2020). *Getting Others to Do Things: A Pragmatic Typology of Recruitments*. Berlin: Language Science Press.

Garfinkel, H. (1952). *The Perception of the Other: A Study in Social Order*. Harvard, MA: Harvard University Press.

Gilbert, M. (1992). *On Social Facts*. Princeton, NJ: Princeton University Press.
Goodwin, C. (1979). The interactive construction of a sentence in natural conversation. In G. Psathas, ed., *Everyday Language: Studies in Ethnomethodology*. New York, NY: Irvington Publishers, pp. 97–121.
Heritage, J. (1984). *Garfinkel and Ethnomethodology*. Cambridge: Polity Press.
(2012). Epistemics in action: Action formation and territories of knowledge. *Research on Language and Social Interaction*, 45(1), 1–29.
Jakobson, R. ([1957]1971). Shifters, verbals categories, and the Russian verb. In R. Jakobson, ed., *Selected Writings II: Word and Language*. The Hague: Mouton, pp. 130–47.
Jefferson, G. (1978). Sequential aspects of storytelling in conversation. In J. Schenkein, ed., *Studies in the Organization of Conversational Interaction*. New York, NY: Academic Press, pp. 219–48.
Kockelman, P. (2005). The semiotic stance. *Semiotica*, 157(1–4), 233–304.
Krebs, J. & Dawkins, R. (1984). Animal signals: Mind-reading and manipulation. In J. Krebs and N. Davies, eds., *Behavioural Ecology: An Evolutionary Approach*, 2nd ed. London: Blackwell, pp. 380–405.
Levinson, S. (2013). Action formation and ascription. In J. Sidnell & T. Stivers, eds., *Handbook of Conversation Analysis*. Chichester: Wiley-Blackwell, pp. 103–30.
(2017). Speech acts. In Y. Huang, ed., *The Oxford Handbook of Pragmatics*. New York, NY: Oxford University Press, pp. 199–216.
Raymond, G. (2004). Prompting action: The stand-alone "so" in sequences of talk-in-interaction. *Research on Language and Social Interaction*, 37(2), 185–218.
Robinson, J. D. (2016). Accountability in social interaction. In J. D. Robinson, ed., *Accountability in Social Interaction*. Oxford: Oxford University Press, pp. 1–44.
Rossano, F. (2012). *Gaze behaviour in face-to-face interaction*. Dissertation, Radboud University, Nijmegen.
Rumsey, A. (1990). Wording, meaning, and linguistic ideology. *American Anthropologist*, 92(2), 346–61.
Sacks, H. (1995). *Lectures on Conversation, Volume 1*. Oxford: Basil Blackwell.
Sacks, H. & Schegloff, E. A. (1979). Two preferences in the organization of reference to persons and their interaction. In G. Psathas, ed., *Everyday Language: Studies in Ethnomethodology*. New York, NY: Irvington, pp. 15–21.
Sacks, H., Schegloff, E. A. & Jefferson, G. (1974). A simplest systematics for the organization of turn-taking for conversation. *Language*, 50(4), 696–735.
Schegloff, E. A. (1982). Discourse as an interactional achievement: Some uses of "uh huh" and other things that come between sentences. In D. Tannen, ed., *Analysing Discourse: Text and Talk*. Washington, DC: Georgetown University Press, pp. 71–93.
(1988). Description in the social sciences I: Talk-in-interaction. *IPRA Papers in Pragmatics*, 2(1–2), 1–24.
(1992). Repair after next turn: The last structurally provided defense of intersubjectivity in conversation. *American Journal of Sociology*, 97(5), 1295–345.
(1996). Confirming allusions: Toward an empirical account of action. *American Journal of Sociology*, 102(1), 161–216.
(1997). Practices and actions: Boundary cases of other-initiated repair. *Discourse Processes*, 23(3), 499–545.

(2006). Interaction: The infrastructure for social institutions, the natural ecological niche for language, and the arena in which culture is enacted. In N. J. Enfield & S. C. Levinson, eds., *Roots of Human Sociality: Culture, Cognition, and Interaction*. Oxford: Berg, pp. 70–96.

(2009). Prolegomena to the analysis of action(s) in talk-in-interaction. Paper presented at LISO, University of California Santa Barbara.

(2010). Some other u(h)ms. *Discourse Processes*, 47(2), 130–74.

Schegloff, E. A. & Sacks, H. (1973). Opening up closings. *Semiotica*, 8(4), 289–327.

Searle, J. (1969). *Speech Acts: An Essay in the Philosophy of Language*. Cambridge: Cambridge University Press.

(1983). *Intentionality: An Essay in the Philosophy of Mind*. Cambridge: Cambridge University Press.

(2010). *Making the Social World*. Oxford: Oxford University Press.

Sidnell, J. (2009). Comparative perspectives in conversation analysis. In J. Sidnell, ed., *Conversation Analysis: Comparative Perspectives*. Cambridge: Cambridge University Press, pp. 3–33.

(2010). *Conversation Analysis: An Introduction*. Oxford: Wiley-Blackwell.

(2017). Action in interaction is conduct under a description. *Language in Society*, 46 (3), 313–37.

Sidnell, J. & Enfield, N. J. (2012). Language diversity and social action: a third locus of linguistic relativity. *Current Anthropology*, 53(3), 302–33.

Silverstein, M. (1979). Language structure and linguistic ideology. In P. Clyne, W. Hanks & C. Hofbauer, eds., *The Elements: A Parasession on Linguistic Units and Levels*. Chicago, IL: Chicago Linguistic Society, pp. 193–247.

Stivers, T. (2008). Stance, alignment, and affiliation during storytelling: When nodding is a token of affiliation. *Research on Language and Social Interaction*, 41(1), 31–57.

Stivers, T. & Rossano, F. (2010). Mobilizing response. *Research on Language and Social Interaction*, 43(1), 3–31.

Tomasello, M. (2008). *Origins of Human Communication*. Cambridge, MA: MIT Press.

Walker, G. (2012). Coordination and interpretation of vocal and visible resources: 'Trail-off' conjunctions. *Language and Speech*, 55(1), 141–63.

13 The Multiple Accountabilities of Action

John Heritage

13.1 Introduction

I want to begin my commentary on the issues raised by this excellent collection of papers by recalling that it was John Searle who, a little over fifty years ago, clearly stated the problem with which this volume (and many others) is occupied.[1] How is it possible, he asked,

> that when a speaker stands before a hearer and emits an acoustic blast such remarkable things occur as: the speaker means something; the sounds he emits mean something; the hearer understands what is meant; the speaker makes a statement, asks a question, or gives an order? (1969: 3)

In the interim, the language sciences have made major strides in many areas that clearly contribute to the solution of Searle's problem: prosody, lexis, syntax, multimodality and others. Yet the problem of action formation and ascription has remained stubbornly unsettled and unsolved.

Searle's initiatives sparked a boom in the study of speech acts that lasted a full decade before foundering "without the most fundamental issues being resolved at all" (Levinson 2017: 200). In retrospect, speech act theory set up its motivating problems in a fashion that was doomed to failure. It focused on the 'big actions' – requests, offers, promises etc. – using the accepted linguistic practice of the period: a focus on isolated sentences invented by the analyst, considered quite out of context, and through a lens of 'top-down' conditionalities that gave little access to what actual speakers might be using to make sense of actual utterances. Many of the problems were diagnosed by Levinson (1981, 1983) in a trenchant critique of several primary assumptions emerging in the Labovian version of a speech act theory of discourse (Labov 1972; Labov & Fanshel 1977): (i) the notion that there are specific speech acts performed in speaking; (ii) that determinate utterance units can be mapped on to determinate actions; (iii) that there are specifiable procedures that map the utterance units to the

[1] I would like to thank the editors, Arnulf Deppermann and Michael Haugh, as well as Steve Clayman, Paul Drew and Chase Raymond for their insightful comments on this paper.

speech acts; and (iv) that rules of interactional sequencing stated over speech act types regulate the organization of interaction (Levinson 1981: 473–4). At most, these assumptions might apply to formal ceremonies such as weddings, or highly regulated encounters such as classrooms in which the I-R-E sequence (Sinclair & Coulthard 1975) is rigorously administered (Drew and Heritage 1992: 13–15). For other kinds of interactions, however, they could gain no traction. Levinson had no difficulty in demolishing all of them, though by this time, most of the major players were abandoning the field.

As the papers in this volume attest though, there has been a revival of interest in these issues, and a renewal in the perception of their significance. A good deal of this renewal has come about through the efforts of conversation analysts. For CA, the domain of social action – the pivotal and definitive topic of the field – could hardly be abandoned or its problematics brushed aside. However, CA stood apart from speech act theory and rejected a linguistic methodology that enumerated action types *a priori* and then administered them 'top-down', taking some version of an 'etic-cum-emic' stance towards the data (Schegloff 1988, 1992a). Speech act theory, while lacking a conception of sequence, focused almost entirely on actions normally occurring first in a sequence (requests, offers etc.). However, CA offered few contributions in this domain, viewing first actions through the lens of second actions – one important 'proof procedure' (Sacks, Schegloff & Jefferson 1974; but see Wootton 1989 for a broader view) for the practical characterization of first actions. The result was a significant gap at the very heart of CA – the analysis of 'first actions' that set sequences in motion. For while second actions might give strong clues about the first actions to which they respond, they cannot be entirely definitive (Drew, Chapter 3 in this volume; Goodwin & Goodwin 1987; Heritage & Atkinson 1984; Schegloff 1996a), nor can they yield insight into how first actions were recognizable, and recognized, in the first place. As Levinson (2013: 105) observed, any study in sequence organization "relies crucially on an identification of, e.g., a first turn and its second" but this identification had largely been ad hoc and based on commonsense knowledge. Thus, the approach could be characterized as a 'loose hermeneutics' and even as the "soft underbelly" of CA (2013).

The present volume offers a wide variety of considerations which I think can move the issue of action ascription forward. These include discussions of action ascription as a temporal process, analysis of the role of sequential context in the construal of turns at talk, and of the role of activity contexts, investigations of the internal structure of turns and micro-sequences; work on the construal of 'long sequences'; the role of social status and role, and the role and significance of overt action descriptions, among many others. I am optimistic about developments in this area, though I do not believe the path will be easy.

13.2 The DNA of Accountability

The fundamental mechanism of social accountability in interaction, as very many of the contributors to this volume stress, is to be found in sequences (Robinson 2016). An especially striking feature of a number of contributions to the present volume is their embrace of what might be termed the 'three-step model of intersubjectivity'. This is founded in the following two notions: (i) a second turn response to a prior communicates, if only indirectly and inferentially, an ascription of the prior action that allows a first speaker to see whether (or how) they were understood; and (ii) a third turn from the first speaker is necessary for the second speaker to see whether the understanding conveyed in Turn 2 was appropriate. 'Turn 3' is thus the point at which an intersubjectively shared understanding of 'Turn 1' is first available and, just as important, is *known to be shared and accountably so* by the participants (Heritage 1984; Schegloff 1992b). Arundale is, I think, correct in observing that, with minor exceptions, each and every next turn at talk is subject to this three-step consolidation of action ascription. Thus, rather like a tracked vehicle, an ongoing process of intersubjective consolidation – an incarnate 'running index' (Heritage 1988) of the state of the talk – is continuously and unavoidably extruded through turns at talk. This is the DNA of social accountability in action.

It follows from this that each turn at talk, which we will label T_0, is managing several forms of engagement:

(1) Most immediately, it responds to the immediately prior turn at talk T_{-1}, displaying an understanding of it, and (except in the case of repair initiation) moving the action implemented in the sequence one step forward.
(2) As part of that response, it also addresses the understanding of the turn preceding T_{-1} (i.e., T_{-2}) that was conveyed in T_{-1}, confirming, adjusting or correcting that understanding, or merely, 'letting it pass'.
(3) As an action in its own right, it sets the terms for the next action T_{+1}, and thus sets the context within which that next action will be grasped.

As we know, however, 'intersubjective understanding' is not the explicit project of sequences. Rather the actions that compose sequences are accountable in their own right as actions and as competent understandings of what has gone before. In this context then, every turn embodies both an action ascription of the prior turn, and an action in its own right, and as Deppermann and Kaiser, Drew, and Haugh (all in this volume) variously insist, doubly accountable in terms of the understanding it exhibits and the action that it implements.

Arundale (Chapter 2 in this volume) cites an example from Schegloff (1992b) which is a classical illustration of this double accountability:

Excerpt 13.1 Schegloff (1992b: 1321)

```
1 Marty:  Loes, do you have a calendar,
2 Loes:   Yeah ((reaches for her desk calendar))
3 Marty:  Do you have one that hangs on the wall?
4 Loes:   Oh, you want one.
5 Marty:  Yeah
```

The responsive action (line 2) that moves to grant line 1's request, is corrected by a second request (line 3), whereupon Loes (line 4) articulates the understanding that Marty's line 1 was intended as an effort to take possession of a calendar, rather than merely to consult one. This 'display of understanding' simultaneously conveys a revised understanding of line 1, while also covertly accounting for the previous misunderstanding. Accountability in the two fundamental senses of understanding and action are seamlessly interwoven here.

Schegloff and Sacks (1973) introduced this theme of accountability into CA through the famous question 'Why that now?' This question was understood as emic in character: a domain of accountability that the participants sorted out for themselves. Enfield and Sidnell (Chapter 12 in this volume) add the following to this inventory: "How does a person decide, on the basis of what someone is saying, what would be an appropriate response?", or as Haugh (Chapter 4 in this volume) puts it, "Why that next?" Things start to get rather slippery at this point. "Why that now?" is, at bottom, a question about action ascription-in-context, whereas "Why that next?" concerns the meaning and social appropriateness of next turns. While these two elements are conjoined, they may be far from coterminous.

13.3 Bins and Their Discontents

Earlier versions of speech act theory seemed to presuppose a finite set of candidate actions, and there is a significant demolition of this notion in Enfield and Sidnell's chapter. First, there is the notion that action ascription could possibly involve assigning a sample of talk to an *a priori* action label selected, presumably, from a collection of others of this sort. Though it may have seemed credible in the 1970s, this notion now seems implausible to say the least. Indeed, it seems a relic of an era in which speech act assignment was construed as simple and definite, in which actions were not 'layered' (Raymond & Stivers 2016; Rossi 2018), and were not characterized in terms of family resemblances (Rosch 1978): approximations that have central and peripheral exemplars and, for this very reason, can be elaborated by context (see Raymond 2019 for a recent discussion). If the collection of candidate actions is composed of approximate contents comprising much overlap and entanglement, how much value can we assign to any kind of 'binning' process? Enfield and Sidnell (Chapter 12 in this volume) refer to the hopeless and, I would add, dizzying experience of going through a transcript and attaching action labels to every turn, noting that "many utterances resist description in terms of action types while others admit of several descriptions." To which one can only add, 'Amen.'

Enfield and Sidnell are also surely correct in drawing a distinction between describing an action and responding to it. As they note, describing an action in the here-and-now is always also a 'move' in the here-and-now (cf. Drew 2003; Garfinkel & Sacks 1970), and as Deppermann and Kaiser (Chapter 6 in this volume; see also Clayman & Fox 2017) observe, it is also quite common for it to be an adversarial one, as indeed it is in Enfield and Sidnell's "Field Trip" example (Chapter 12 in this volume). The same issue applies, perhaps *a fortiori*, in attributions of strategy as Helmer's contribution (Chapter 7 in this volume) ably demonstrates.

With all this said, I would be reluctant to abandon action categories as resources in the construal of intersubjective understanding. Each culture, indeed each language, possesses a storehouse of vernacular action categories that are widely used especially in reported speech and appear to be generally recognizable and recognized in an 'I know it when I see it' kind of way (Wierzbicka 1987). Sequence organization is organized, at least approximately, by reference to these categories, and they can hardly be dissolved into features of reference, stance, deontics, epistemics and the like even though these latter may be highly significant features of action design.

I also think there are increasing grounds for optimism about the action ascription problem. Both 'bottom-up' resources arising from within the turn, and 'top-down' resources from outside the turn *per se*, are objects of increasing investigation, and it is becoming clear, I think, that both kinds of resources are simultaneously involved in action ascription. However, the processes through which they 'mesh' together are presently unknown and under-studied. It should also be recognized from the outset that the distinctions considered here are abstractions and are not likely to be real for the participants. It should also be recognized their interplay in concrete occasions of conduct – presently unknown – is likely to be complex and reticulated.

In what follows, I will briefly review some of the resources for action ascription in terms of bottom-up (turn-internal) and top-down (turn-external) characteristics, beginning with bottom-up resources.

13.4 Bottom-Up Resources

There is a long tradition of studies within CA documenting that speakers can anticipate turn completion. This embraces research on overlap (Jefferson 1973, 1983, 1986, 2004; Sacks, Schegloff & Jefferson 1974; Schegloff 1996b, 2000; Vatanen 2018), and collaborative completions (Lerner 1996, 2004) among other phenomena (see De Ruiter, Mitterer & Enfield 2006). These studies focused for the most part on the completion of the linguistic units that make up turns at talk – 'locutionary acts' in the older vocabulary (but see also Ford & Thompson 1996). Their upshot is brilliantly summarized in a set of observations attributed to an unpublished paper by Raymond and Lerner:

> When one initiates a turn at talk, the unfolding turn-so-far will project roughly what it will take to complete it. Moreover, the continuing moment-by-moment unfolding of a turn will be inspected for the progressive realization (suspension, deflection, or abandonment) of what has been projected so far. The hallmark of this realization is found in such material elements as the pace of the talk, the adjacent placement of syntactically next words and the intonation contour that carries the talk. Moreover there are circumstances in which the forward progress of a speaking turn can be delayed or sped up or even abandoned, and a set of practices by which such disturbances to the normal or normative progress of a speaking turn toward possible completion are implemented; and these practices can furnish the resources for recipient action as well. In this sense the projectability of a speaker's turn at talk constitutes a proximate normative structure within which a range of other organizational contingencies are coordinated and managed – including the timing and design of action by others; it is precisely this progressively realized structure that makes any deflections in its locally projected course a site of action, a recognizable form of action, and a site of action and interpretation by others. (quoted in Szczepek Reed & Raymond 2013: 4)

However, a recent and important development is the view stressed by Levinson and his colleagues that action ascription is a highly time-sensitive process. In particular, recent neurolinguistic evidence suggests that respondents start to fashion responses some time before the preceding turn to which they are responding is complete (Bögels, Casillas & Levinson 2018; Bögels, Magyari & Levinson 2015; Gisladottir, Bögels & Levinson 2018). These observations evidence the significance of expectation and prediction in the ascription of actions if fitted responses are to be produced within the modal 200 milliseconds that elapse between the end of a current turn and the beginning of the next (Bögels, Kendrick & Levinson 2019; see also Jefferson 1989). In turn, these findings suggest that turns are likely 'front-loaded' with action ascription relevant resources, and that we should be looking at turn-initial, or near turn-initial, position to find critical resources that a hearer can use. If sequential and other top-down resources set broad parameters for next actions, it is the bottom-up resources of turn design that

Table 13.1 *Distinctive dimensions of proposals, offers, requests and suggestions*

Dimension	Agent of future action	Beneficiary of future action
Proposal	Self & other	Self & other
Offer	Self	Other
Request	Other	Self
Suggestion	Other	Other

Couper-Kuhlen (2014: 634)

enable their realization and ascription. What, however, are the resources involved?

13.4.1 Grammar

In a compelling paper, Couper-Kuhlen (2014) developed a schema of distinctive dimensions of four major kinds of speech acts, represented in schematic form in Table 1. Each of these classes of actions can be realized through a variety of distinctive turn formats. While these formats can themselves often realize more than one type of action, thus necessitating the use of other resources to narrow the action projection involved, it is also the case that these formats can also be projected from quite early in the turn. An example from Paul Drew (Chapter 3 in this volume) can serve to illustrate this.

Excerpt 13.2 NB VII (Power tools: 82–91) (MAR = Margy, EDN = Edna)

```
Mar:   = W'l haftuh do tha[t more] o[:ften.]
Edn:                      [.hhhhh]  [Wul w]hy don't we:uh-m:=
Edn:   =Why don't I take you'n Mo:m up there tuh: Coco's.someday
       fer lu:nch.We'll go, bkuzz up there tu[h,
Mar:                                         [k Goo:d.
Edn:   Ha:h?
Mar:   That's a good deal. .hh-.hh=
Edn:   =Eh I'll take you bo:th [up
Mar:                           [No:::: wil all go Dutch.=
Mar:   =B't [let's do  that.]
```

Here, as Drew notes, Edna's action is reformatted from a suggestion (line 2) to an invitation (line 3): a transformation which is available to analysts and participants in the first three words of the turn and its revision (see Drew, Chapter 3 in this volume; Drew, Walker & Ogden 2013). Here we may say that the respondent (Margy) will already be possessed of an action 'lemma' long before the emergence of the main body of the utterance, and a 'lemma' of the response may also already be in process. It is possible that many of the main classes of 'large actions' in English are discriminable and projectable from early in the turn, though considerable research will be needed to secure these possibilities, especially for agglutinative languages (e.g., Korean and Japanese) which rely less on word order.

Similar considerations can arise with actions defined by relative epistemic positioning (Heritage 2012). Almost any action begun with the word *you* is quite likely to project a turn that will use declarative syntax to a K+ recipient, thus being understood as questioning:

Excerpt 13.3 NB II:2:10(R)

```
Nan:   I [jst uh,h for'd iz mai:i stick it in th'onvelope'n
Emm:     [°Mm:°
       (0.4)
Nan:   send it all on up to im en .hhh[hhh
Emm:                                  [Yih know wher'e is the:n,
       (0.8)
Nan:   I have never had any of it retu:rned Emma,h
Emm:   Oh::.
Nan:   At a:ll, so: [I jist assoom
```

In a similar vein, quotative frames reliably project hearsay or reported speech that will be understood to be 'questioning' when directed to a K+ recipient:

Excerpt 13.4 Rah:12:4:ST

```
Jen:   =[Okay then I w]'z askin='er en she says yer
       working tomorrow ez well.
Ida:   Yes I'm s'pose to be tihmorrow yes,
Jen:   O[h:::.
Ida:    [Yeh,
```

All in all, as Couper-Kuhlen's pioneering work has shown, grammar provides plenty of resources for action ascription, many of them emerging early enough in turns to function as resources for the early formation of response. That grammar is a robust contributor to the process is also attested by the growing corpora of cross-linguistic research on, for example, requests (Drew & Couper-Kuhlen 2014; Floyd, Rossi & Enfield 2020; Rossi in press). These grammatical elements will function as partial (that is, nonapodictic) resources within a complex and developing matrix of attributive resources.

'Binning' notions also hardly address the shading of actions that can be managed through different linguistic realizations of their pragmatic 'core'. I take this to be a part of Drew's account of the micro-politics of action, and it is also front and center in Couper-Kuhlen and Thompson's account of advice-giving sequences (Chapter 8 in this volume). This shading is also to be found in Wu and Yu's account in this volume of *ya*-suffixed answers to questions. While the main line of the action may lie in the 'answer', the *ya* suffix is certainly highly significant. I cannot speak to the issue in Mandarin, but near relatives of this kind of coloring, for example *oh*-prefacing in English (Wu 2004; Wu & Heritage 2018) are frequently to be found in direct reported speech, and this is likely an index of their significance to recipients, interlocutors and overhearers.

13.4.2 Lexicon

Of course, as Enfield and Sidnell (Chapter 12 in this volume) also observe, many of the turns making up a conversation are not the 'big first actions' that speech act theory was designed to address. But here, too, there is hope. Many turn-initial objects and activities give quite reliable indications of the action to come, though primarily through narrowing the possibilities rather than any one-to-one projection. For example, the word *well* in the context of responses to questions reliably predicts upcoming aspects of action that are of extreme relevance to recipients who must fashion a response. First, it predicts that the response is likely to be dispreferred (Davidson 1984). *Well*-prefaced responses to questions are a little more than nine times more likely when the response is dispreferred, by comparison with responses that are not (OR:9.2 [$p < .001$; 95% confidence interval 4.1–20.6]) (Heritage 2015: 93; Kendrick & Torreira 2015). The reliability of this index makes it readily useful to pre-empt dispreferred responses at the time they are begun, as some of Davidson's examples demonstrated.

Second, *well* also predicts that responses to questions will be expanded to two or more turn constructional units (cf. Schegloff & Lerner 2009). These expanded units are also approximately nine times more likely to be prefaced by *well*, than not (OR: 9.3 [$p < 001$; 95% confidence interval 4.1–21.4]) (Heritage 2015: 93). This can give important information about actions-in-progress. Consider the following excerpt:

Excerpt 13.5 Heritage 2:4

```
E:   And we were wondering if there's anything we can do to help
M:   [Well that's]
E:   [I mean ] can we do any shopping for her or
     something like tha:t?
     (0.7)
M:   Well that's most ki:nd Edgerton .hhh At the ↑moment
     no:. Because we've still got two bo:ys at home.
```

Here Edgerton's offer of help is appreciated with the response *Well that's most ki:nd Edgerton*. Without the *well* preface, the response could be understood as an *acceptance* of the offer. However, with the *well* preface, the recipient can anticipate that the response is not yet done at the first turn constructional unit boundary, and that the first unit is indeed likely to be an *appreciation* that is designedly prefatory to a *refusal* of the offer.

This projection of turn-expansion is deployed frequently in narrative responses to questions, as in the following case from a medical encounter. Here the *well*-prefaced initiation of a response to the doctor's question, rapidly followed by the introduction of a past time reference (line 2), makes it all but certain that a narrative will follow:

Excerpt 13.6 Sore throat (DOC = doctor, PAT = patient)

```
 1  Doc:    An' what can we do for ya today.
 2          ˙hh Well I was here on September=h <twenty third>
 3          because I had <bronchial> (.) >an' I< was put on
 4          zi:throma[x.
 5  Doc:             [Mm hm,
 6  Pat:    ˙hh thuh following: Tuesday Wednesday I had such a
 7          sore throat I could hardly swallo[w
 8  Doc:                                     [Mm [hm,
 9  Pat:                                         [ hh I came
10          i:n fo:r a culture an' it was negativ[e.
11  Doc:                                         [(n)Okay,
12  Pat:    ˙hhhhhh it wa- started on this si:de it went ta both
13          si:des (an') >I can hardly swallow< thuh culture was
14          negative.
15  Doc:    [Mm hm,
16  Pat:    [˙hh So I been takin' i:buprofin (.) using
17          sa:lt=h ˙h zinc lozengers ˙hh an' it won't go away
18          from this side.
19  Doc:    (n)[Oka:y,
20  Pat:       [It gets really sore in this side an'
21          then its feels like its up in to my ear.
22  Doc:    Okay,
23          (.)
24  Doc:    [Okay,
25  Pat:    [˙h An' that's why I'm here today. 'Cause its been
26          (.) long.
27  Doc:    O:kay,
28  Doc:    >˙hh< Well that sounds like a pretty good history
```

In addition to *well*, almost all these narratives begin with a reference to past time (e.g., line 2 above), which is also a reliable indication of a narrative initiation and make their way towards the patient's present situation (Heritage

& Clayman 2010: 109–15; Robinson & Heritage 2005). In an unpublished study, it was found that some 57 percent of them are *well*-prefaced (Heritage and Robinson, n.d.). In the case above, it is noticeable that as the patient moves towards the present at line 16, the doctor shifts from a fairly consistent use of *Mm Hm* as a continuer, to the shift-implicative *Okay* (Beach 1993; Betz et al. 2021) with rising intonation (Guthrie 1997; Heritage & Clayman 2010), all of these indicating a willingness to begin questioning (which occurs at line 28), while also permitting narrative continuation. Here, then, the narrative is clearly indexed from the outset, the doctor's responses are fitted to the progress of the narrative, and a clean exit from it is accomplished. *Well* is undoubtedly not the only turn-initial particle that projects the possibility of certain social actions, while making others less likely. It is likely that turn-initial resources of these kinds may also serve to enable early action ascription in agglutinative languages such as Japanese and Korean as well (Hayashi 2004a, 2004b; Heritage & Sorjonen 2018; Kim 1999; Kim & Kuroshima 2013). At the same time, since TCU-final affixes play a significant role in these languages, and at least some enable 'incremental transformability' (Iwasaki 2009; Tanaka 2000) across the progress of a turn, only more work across a range of such languages will clarify the nature of their 'early' action projection resources (Tanaka 1999; see Couper-Kuhlen & Selting 2018: 42–7 for discussion), 'top-down' resources (see below) may make a larger contribution in action projection in languages such as these.

13.4.3 Beyond Language: Prosody and Gaze

Final rising intonation is often held to be a significant resource in discriminating questions from other actions involving declarative syntax. While this generalization does not hold up well with, for example, English polar questions (Couper-Kuhlen 2012; Geluykens 1988; Levinson 2013; Stivers 2010, among many others), it does for Romance languages like Italian that do not use interrogative syntax or morphology to distinguish polar questions from declarative counterparts (Rossi in press; see also Raymond 2015). On the other hand, there is good evidence that beginning an utterance with elevated pitch can project new topic beginnings (Couper-Kuhlen 2001, 2004). Moreover, elevated pitch at turn-beginnings can discriminate questions designed to invite agreement with an evaluation from more straightforwardly information-seeking questions (Sicoli, Stivers, Enfield & Levinson 2014). Prosodic elements such as elevated pitch can co-occur with other resources that index a similar conclusion. For example, high onset starts and turn-initial *well* independently predict topic shifts (Heritage 2015: 95–6), thus increasing likelihood in the projection of the upcoming action. In the following example, a teasing sequence about Beth's dancing skills is interdicted by Mom (line 7):

Excerpt 13.7 Virginia: 474–480

```
VIR:    She's good. 'Cuz pa- (0.8) Paul taught 'er how.
        (1.0)
VIR:    Paul danc[es good.
PRU:             [>Oh I thought you were the one that [taught her how.<
WES:                                                  [Oh 'e did?
        (.)
MOM:    ˙hhh ↑Well that's something_else. (0.3) ↑I_don't_think that
        you should be going to the parties that Beth goe:s to. She is
        eighteen years old.An' you are fou:rtee:n, darlin'
```

Here, the two early-occurring components guide recipients to the likelihood that Mom's re-entry into the conversation will also involve initiating a new topic.

Stress patterns can also furnish resources for action ascription. In the 1974 film *The Conversation*, an investigator using a rifle microphone picks up a fragment of conversation in which a male speaker tells a female: "He'd *kill* us if he had the chance." The investigator understands this to be a warning. Later in the film, the fragment reappears with a crucial change in stress: "He'd kill *us* if he had the chance," and the investigator understands the utterance as a justification for an intended murder. In a paper on prosody, Schegloff (1998) identifies similar uses of stress that contribute to the recognition of an utterance as a compliment, and also to the subsequent declination of the compliment as well. This use of what is often referred to as 'contrastive stress' (Bolinger 1961; see also Höhle 1992) has been shown to be implicated in, and therefore relevant to, the formation and ascription of a wide range of social actions in interaction (e.g., Couper-Kuhlen 1984; Ogden 2006; Raymond 2017, 2019; Stivers 2005).

While prosodic patterns may not readily map onto specific actions or action types (Couper-Kuhlen 2009; Walker 2014), they may contribute in a more generalized way. For example, final rising intonation is quite strongly associated with requesting new information, but it is also associated with continuative uses for words like *yes* and *okay*, which are more generally deployed to communicate agreement or acceptance. And it is also associated with the practice of 'try-marking' (Sacks & Schegloff 1979) in which the speaker is trying to solicit a display of recognition from the recipient and, finally, with summoning the attention of a recipient (Heritage 2013a: 567–9). In all these cases, final rising intonation has a response-mobilizing property (Stivers & Rossano 2010) which functions across all these action environments, adding definition to signals that are otherwise elaborated in a multiplicity of distinctive ways.

It is also the case that speaker behaviors at turn beginning and pre-beginning (Deppermann 2013; Deppermann & Schmidt 2021; Kaukomaa, Peräkylä &

Ruusuvuori 2013, 2014; Kendrick & Torreira 2015; Schegloff 1996b) can also forecast the kind of action to come. For example, Kendrick and Holler (2017: 26; see also Robinson 2020) have demonstrated that, in the context of responses to questions, "The vast majority of dispreferred responses are produced with gaze aversion, whereas only a minority of preferred ones are." This suggests that gaze aversion at turn-beginnings is a reliable indicator of upcoming dispreferred responses and, in fact there is good evidence that recipient gaze aversion at turn-beginnings can prompt transition space repair by questioners, who find that the question as put may be problematic. As Kendrick and Holler (2017: 26) conclude, "the first visible moments of response furnish crucial resources for early action recognition."

Other research on gaze has focused on its role in sequence organization. Working from the hypothesis that speakers work to avoid mutual gaze during a lapse in talking, Rossano (2012, 2013) showed that mutual gaze withdrawal at possible sequence closure was strongly associated with actual sequence closure. This effect was enhanced if the speaker who initiated the sequence was the first to withdraw gaze. Though these findings are subject to some cultural variation (Rossano, Brown & Levinson 2009), it is certainly likely that mutual gaze withdrawal generally projects that the next turn at talk will *not* be a continuation of the preceding sequence, thus ruling out turns that might otherwise have been anticipated.

13.4.4 Multiple Actions within the Utterance

One of Charles Goodwin's greatest legacies lies in his recognition that the utterance is not only a carrier of social action, but also, and in and of itself, a site within which multiple social actions are occurring. Whereas spoken language is housed in turns that require the avoidance of overlap for acoustical reasons, gestures and body behavior, by contrast, can arise before turns begin and be reflexively involved in micro-adjustments across spoken turns, facilitating early action ascription and response (Goodwin 2017; Mondada 2021). Goodwin and the whole field of multimodal investigation which has flourished in his wake established the significant role that these 'within utterance' actions play in the constitution and ascription of action. For example, in 'Concurrent operations on talk', a paper focused on assessment sequences, Charles and Candy Goodwin (1987) examined the interplay between speakers *within* assessment turns. Examining utterances like 'It wz s::so: goo:d', they observe that the sentence is divided between a first part referencing the assessable, and a second part concerned with the assessment action itself. In the second part, there is noticeable segmental lengthening beginning with the intensifier 's::so:' and they argue that "This raises the possibility that by attending to the pre-positioned intensifier recipients of sentences of the type now being examined might be able to align themselves to the emerging talk as an assessment before the assessment term itself is actually produced" (Goodwin & Goodwin 1987: 23). The intensifier is a segment of an assessment activity that is now recognizable ahead of time. One important result is that a recipient becomes able to join in assessing the assessable simultaneously with the primary assessor.

Excerpt 13.8 G:50:03:45 (DIA = Dianne, CLA = Clacia)

```
Dianne:   Jeff made en asparagus pie
          it wz s[: : s::so: goo:d.
Clacia:          [I love it.
```

Goodwin & Goodwin (1987: 24)

Overall, the initial description of the asparagus pie, and the initial movement into what will turn out to be an assessment and coupled with body behavior (not described here), enables the recipient, Clacia, not only to grasp that an assessment is in progress but also its valence, and to provide an agreeing assessment (though from an 'external' epistemic stance, since she did not eat the actual pie). Though it was not focused on action ascription *per se*, Goodwin's work provides innumerable examples of the ways in which the recognizability of actions are managed through activities that are interior to the utterance, and has been a trail-blazing stimulus for research documenting the micro-management of first and second actions in tandem with one another (Deppermann & Schmidt 2021; Deppermann & Streeck 2018; Mondada 2014, 2018, 2021; Streeck et al. 2011).

13.5 Top-Down Resources

Once we begin to look outside the turn, a wide variety of other resources for action ascription come into view. Many of these 'external' contextual resources are also highly front-loaded and offer presumptive action ascriptions that kick in before the action proper is even begun. Pre-eminent among these resources is sequence organization itself.

13.5.1 Sequence

Sequence organization is undoubtedly the paramount resource for action ascription in human action. Any consideration of the predictive role of sequencing in action ascription has to begin with adjacency pairs (Schegloff 2007), where first pair parts (greetings, questions etc.) establish the normative conditional relevance of specific types of second pair parts (Schegloff & Sacks 1973). 'Classical' adjacency pairs such as greetings are very strongly associated with next turn responses, if only because of the negative accountability of nonresponse (Heritage 1984, 1988). The same is broadly true of questions where, aided by the phenomenon of implicature, a surprisingly large degree of latitude in reply construction may manifest itself. The following example, though invented, is instructive:

Excerpt 13.9 Levinson (1983: 102)

```
A:    Where's Bill?
B:    There's a yellow VW outside Sue's house.
```

While, at a literal level, B does not answer A's question, a recipient may infer that Bill in fact possesses a yellow VW and can find in that inference an answer to the question, albeit an indirect one.

In many, perhaps most, question-answer sequences, the apparatus of cohesion (Drew 2013; Halliday & Hasan 1976; Raymond, Clift & Heritage 2021) is a central aspect of finding that a response to a question is in fact an answer to it.

Excerpt 13.10 Heritage: 1:6

```
MrsH:   O:keh-eh Oh he i:s coming back t' [morrow i[s he?
Edg:                                      ['t!     [He'll
        be back again tomorrow I would think about mid
        da:y so if you: you could pho:ne throu:gh, (0.5)
        uh this ti:me tomorrow? could you?
```

Excerpt 13.11 NB: 13 (EMM = Emma, LOT = Lottie)

```
Emm:    .hhhh Is there any place around here that u-has
        those Lottie do yih know
Lot:    A::krun's I think's the only place
        that [I know
Emm:         [Go:d that's right Akrun's
```

In Excerpt 13.10, practices of cohesion – for example – the repeat of *he*, *back*, and the preservation of the question's future orientation in the response turn consolidate the conclusion that lines 2–3 are designed to answer the question in line 1. Similarly, in Excerpt 13.11, the naming of a 'place' (*Akrun's*) at line 3, and its characterization as the *only place* (and with the 'for what' left unexpressed) similarly assures that the response will be understood as 'answering' the question at lines 1–2.

By the same token, the absence of cohesion between turns can serve to indicate various kinds of non-answer responses. Thus in Excerpt 13.12, a response to the question at line 6 could not normally be treated as an 'answer' when it begins with *I vote*! (line 7):

Excerpt 13.12 NB:II:1:256076 (EMM = Emma, LOT = Lottie)

```
Emm:        yihknow ah u-she gets ↓awful depressed over these
            things ↓yihknow she's rea:l (0.2) p'litical mi:nded 'n,
            (0.3)
Lot:        Ye:ah:
Emm:        wo[r k- ]
Lot:   ->     [She a] Democra:t?
Emm:   ->   .t.hhhh I vote eether wa:y.h
            (.)
Lot:        Yeah,
Emm:        .hmhh.t.h I didn'git tuh vote I decline'tuh state this
            ti:me when I registered so: I jst uh,h didn'git tuh vote
            fer pre:s'dent so:
```

Similarly, in the following case, the patient's response at line 3, though apparently addressed to a 'locational' issue, is grossly misfitted to the question, and instead serves to launch a narrative. The patient addresses the question in lines 7–8, but only as an aside after the narrative is fully launched (Stivers & Heritage 2001):

Excerpt 13.13 MidWest 3.4 (Cov = doctor, PAT = patient)

```
DOC: -> Whe[re was her cancer.
PAT:       [( -)
PAT: -> .hhh Well:- she lived in Arizona an:'- she::
        wouldn't go tuh doctor much. She only went
        to uh chiropracter. (h[u-)
DOC:                          [Mm[hm,
PAT:                             [An:d she had(:)/('t)
        like- in her stomach somewhere I guess but (.)
        thuh- even- that guy had told her tuh go (into)
        uh medical doctor.
DOC:    Mm hm,
```

Cohesion, or its absence, in tense and/or aspect across turns is also a resource for meaning making (Raymond 2020), as in the following excerpt:

Excerpt 13.14 MidWest 3.4: 229–235

```
DOC:     Do you have brothers 'n sisters?
PAT:     Ah there was eight in our family. hh
DOC:     How many are there now:.
         (.)
PAT:     Ah: seven.
         (.)
DOC:     What happened t'thuh one who died,=
```

Here the shift in tense from the doctor's present tense (line 1) to the patient's past perfect response (line 2) was not lost on the doctor who immediately (line 3) pursues the issue that the response intimates.

And in Excerpt 13.15, practices of cohesion – specifically the repetition of *the difference is* (line 3) – are resources through which this the interviewee – UK mineworkers' leader, Arthur Scargill – attempts to convey that he is 'answering' the question, though the attentive listener is rapidly disabused of this expectation during the rest of the IE's turn (Clayman 2001; Clayman & Heritage 2002):

Excerpt 13.15 WAO: 3/13/79: Arthur Scargill

```
IR: ->  .hhh er What's the difference between your marxism
        and Mister McGarhey's communism.
AS: ->  er The difference is_that it's the press that constantly
        call me a ma:rxist when I do not, (.) and never have (.)
        er er_given that description of myself....
```

All in all, it seems reasonable to conclude that, in the context of 'tight' adjacency pairs such as Q–A sequences, practices of cohesion operate early in responses to cement the conclusion that an appropriately fitted response is in the works.

13.5.2 Activities

Reaching beyond the sequence as a resource for action ascription, we can also consider that a considerable amount of talk is produced as part of what Gail Jefferson (1980a, 1988) called 'big packages', for example, storytelling, troubles telling etc. Many kinds of cooperative action including, for example, food preparation (Mondada 2014a; Rossi 2018; Thompson, Raymond & Fox 2020) and museum guidance (Mondada 2011, 2013, 2017, see also Mondada 2014b) are similarly organized. That participants organize their conduct in relation to these 'packages' was elegantly shown in a paper by Schegloff (2011), who observes that interactants may end an activity by reusing some of the words with which they started it. Mondada (Chapter 5 in this volume) offers a beautiful case study showing that across languages and cultures the practice of sampling the taste of cheese culminates in an evaluation which, if positive, will be understood to constitute the selection of the cheese for purchase. These evaluations can be very minimal – a *yes* or a nod will do. Here, an activity that is focused from the outset on an eventual economic transaction enables an apparently minimal action to serve as the vehicle to communicate a decision.

In story telling too, an outcome, its valence and sometimes the stance to be taken towards the protagonists is made available to recipients through the story preface (Couper-Kuhlen & Selting 2018; Mandelbaum 2013; Sacks 1974). This permits recipients to track the story components across their course and to respond appropriately at the story conclusion. Although some of the resources involved are clearly sequential, they are understood and operated on in terms of the adumbrated goal of the storyteller as it is managed within story time and across the temporal parameters of the telling.

13.5.3 Institutions

According to Drew and Heritage (1992: 22), institutional interaction is characterized by (i) restricted goal orientations, (ii) special constraints on what will be treated as allowable contributions to the business at hand, and (iii) inferential frameworks and procedures that are specific to particular institutional contexts. It will be obvious that each of these characteristics greatly simplifies the task of action ascription.

Sometimes a particular 'slot' will strongly overdetermine the understanding of a wide variety of talk that is produced to fill it. For example, openings in primary care (Robinson 1998, 2006) are characterized by a moment in which the doctor invites the patient to present their reason for the visit. This may be done using a variety of resources:

Varieties of primary care openings
What can I do for you today?
What's the problem?
How can I help?
What's up?
What's going on?
How are you?
You are here today because ...
Where does it hurt? (Korean [Park 2014])

The Korean opening is highly ritualized in that it is deployed regardless of whether the doctor has grounds to believe the patient is in pain, and nonetheless functions effectively. In the anglophone world, a problem presentation may be solicited be a wide variety of questions, some of which are listed above. In other cases, clinicians may exploit ambiguities in 'how are you' questions (Robinson 2006: 39–40), which may be treated by the patient either as the occasion to present a concern or, alternatively, as an occasion for a normative response, e.g., *Fine*. In the latter context, sequences such as a following may ensue:

Excerpt 13.16 P3:105.17 (DOC = doctor, PAT = patient)

```
Doc:    How'r ya feelin' today
Pat:    .hh Uh pretty goo:d.
Doc:    Bu::t, hh
Pat:    But my leg's been botherin' me here f' prob'ly
        'bout the past four weeks,
```

Here, the doctor's simple addition of the conjunction *but* to the patient's downgraded self-assessment *pretty good* (line 2) (Jefferson 1980b) effectively functions as a third position repair (Schegloff 1992b), and is sufficient to convey that the patient's response is incomplete, and to invite him to expand his response by presenting his problem.

The institutionalized overall trajectory of task-focused interactions in primary care may serve as the common ground (Clark 1996) on which patients and their doctors may move on from one phase of the medical visit to another (Heritage & Maynard 2006; Robinson 2003). For example, Robinson and Stivers (2001) have documented completely wordless transitions from the history-taking to the physical examination stage of medical visits. In such cases, a variety of multimodal resources are pressed into service to achieve this outcome, but this could not be achieved without a joint orientation to the overall structure of the visit and the place of this moment in the interaction within it.

Institutional relationships are not set in stone, however. As Bergmann (1993) was the first to observe (see also Raymond & Zimmerman 2016), callers to emergency services may present themselves either as *offering* help (by notifying the agencies about problematic circumstances), or as *seeking* help. As Koole and van Burgsteden show in their chapter (Chapter 11 in this volume) about calls to Dutch emergency services, the expression of thanks is a key element in this determination as an intersubjective and public matter. Here the outcome – most often late in the call – about who expresses thanks to whom can reach back over the whole call, retrospectively coloring the meaning of all its component actions.

The argument of this section has been that institutional contexts, expressed in the activities that make up goal-directed encounters, and the sequences that implement those activities substantially contribute to the likelihood of particular types of social actions and, correspondingly, to their appropriate ascription. These contributions are reinforced with a further component that is not confined in any way to institutional contexts, and it is to this component – personal statuses and rights – that we finally turn.

13.5.4 Personal Statuses and Rights

It is an unquestionable fact that persons bring a variety of statuses and rights to social interaction (Ervin-Tripp 1981). While these are by no means indefeasible or incontestable, and while they may require acknowledgment and validation within interactional contexts, they are nonetheless powerful and relevant sources of guidance in action ascription. Among a variety of such resources, epistemic (Heritage 2012; Kamio 1997; Labov & Fanshel 1977) and deontic rights (Stevanovic & Peräkylä 2012; Stevanovic & Svennevig 2015) have emerged as significant in action formation and ascription at many levels of detail. A central element in their functioning is the interplay between the stance taken up within an utterance and the underlying status and rights that the speaker has to take up such a stance. In general, speakers manage interaction so as to maintain congruence between the epistemic or deontic stance taken up in an utterance and their underlying rights to take such a stance. Thus, as Heritage (2012) has argued, any utterance that represents a state of affairs concerning which the speaker is deemed to be relatively unknowledgeable (K−) to a speaker who is believed to be knowledgeable (K+) will be understood as 'requesting information' ("questioning") regardless of its morphosyntactic or prosodic design. While this is a process that runs smoothly to the point of near invisibility, small glitches in congruency can be revealing of its operation. For example, in Excerpt 13.17 Sam and Kim work out with the same trainer on different days. Kim comes home after a training session and, a little later, the following ensues:

Excerpt 13.17 JH: FN (KIM = Kim, SAM = Sam) (Kim has just returned from a fitness class that she and Sam attend separately.)

```
Kim:    So you're going to Mary on Monday.
Sam:    Tuesday.
Kim:    No she's got a problem with Tuesday. She told me.
Sam:    Oh.
```

Here Sam, understanding himself to have primary rights to knowledge of his own schedule, responds to what he takes to be a question from Kim, supplying what he assumes is a correct answer. Kim then reveals her K+ status on this particular matter and accounts for it on the basis of very recent information she received from the trainer (line 3), which Sam then takes as new information and as a correction (line 4).

So also with deontics (Aikhenvald 2010; Sorjonen, Raevaara & Couper-Kuhlen 2017). As Heritage (2013a) noted, deontic incongruity can be exploited in imperative responses to surprising or exciting news, such as *Shut up!* or *Get out of here!* Similarly, parties who are moving towards closing an interaction may use imperatives to this end:

Excerpt 13.18 Schegloff and Sacks (1973: 313) (B has called to invite C, but C is going out to dinner.)

```
B:  ->  Yeah. Well get on your clothes and get out and collect
        some of that free food and we'll make it some other
        time Judy then.
C:      time Judy then.
B:      Bye bye
C:      Bye bye
```

Commenting on this case, Schegloff and Sacks (1973: 313) observe that

> While B's initial utterance in this excerpt might be grammatically characterized as an imperative or a command, and C's "Okay" as a submission or accession to it, in no sense but a technical syntactic one would those be anything but whimsical characterizations.

As Schegloff and Sacks go on to observe, the utterance is of course a proposal to close the call: an action grounded in the imperative's proposal to the recipient to engage in some other action than continuing the call, and the subsequent clause's proposal to meet some other time.

Hiramoto and Hayashi (Chapter 9 in this volume) provide a startlingly clear demonstration of a role-based division of deontic resources within a family group. As they progress through the aisles of a supermarket, family members name various potential purchases (e.g., eggs, juice), sometimes within a clause that frames the named object as 'suggested' or 'asked about'. However, while the mother's namings are generally treated as instructions to other family members to search and find particular products, namings by the other family members (whether with, or without the additional clausal features) are understood as suggestions that may result in a decision from the mother, or which may be ignored altogether. In these sequences, the D+ deontic status of the mother is inescapably inscribed into the interaction.

Similar observations can be made about benefactive utterances (Clayman & Heritage 2014). And, at the risk of banality, the contextual dependencies involved in 'knowing what to say next' on local statuses and rights is beyond enumeration. Taking a simple utterance in a call to the emergency services, *Someone just vandalized my car* (Wilson 1991), it is not difficult to permutate a wide variety of action ascriptions, as in Table 13.2.

Table 13.2 *"Someone just vandalized my car"*

Utterance	Context	Recipient action attribution	Fitted response
Someone just vandalized my car	Call to 911 Emergency	Request for assistance	We'll send someone out there.
Someone just vandalized my car	Call to doctor's office	Account for non-attendance	Do you want to reschedule your appointment?
Someone just vandalized my car	Call to friend	Complaint/Request for sympathy	That's terrible! When did it happen?
Someone just vandalized my car	Call to friend on day of exam	Request for a ride	Do you need a ride? I'll stop by and pick you up.

Wilson (1991); Heritage and Clayman (2010: 65)

There is a very large amount to research to be done on the relations between talk and the instantiation of roles and identities, and the mechanisms through which these relations are sustained and reproduced (Heritage 1988; Raymond 2019; see also the literature review in Heritage & Maynard 2021).

13.6 Beyond Ascription and beyond the Adjacency Pair

Although a great deal has been written about the significance of adjacency pairs, it may not do to exaggerate their empirical frequency. Conversations are far from being constructed exclusively from them (though they may 'chain' in various ways). Rather it may be better to consider sequential organization in terms of degrees of constraint. CA is built on the fundamental assumption of 'nextness': specifically, that a next turn should be built to be, and accountably will be, understood as fitted to the prior (Sacks 1987; Schegloff & Sacks 1973). Thus, we can think of much 'looser' forms of sequentiality than are embodied in the 'tight' sequential implicativeness of adjacency pairs. Not only does this allow us to conceptualize the sequential implicativeness of a turn as arranged along an 'analog' cline rather than 'digital' bipartite division (Stivers & Rossano 2010), but it also invites us to contemplate the various ways that participants can deploy cohesive practices to position individual turns as the accountable constituents of sequences. In Excerpt 13.19, the first five turns (lines 1–5) emerge in classical adjacency pair terms. Subsequently (line 6), Mum expands the sequence by producing a more elaborate description (*Garlic'n parsley*), perhaps demonstrating that she has bought the tablets that Lesley had advised, and this is confirmed by Lesley at line 7 with an additional query that links the tablets to 'Whole Food(s)':

Excerpt 13.19 Field 1:1:89–94 (LES = Lesley, MUM = mother)

```
1  Les:     Uh didyuh get yer garlic tablets.
2  Mum:     Yes I've got them,
3  Les:     Have yuh t- started tak[ing th'm
4  Mum:                            [I started taking th' m t' da:y
5  Les: -> Oh well do:n[e
6  Mum:                [Garlic'n parsley.
7  Les:    ↑THAT'S RI:ght.[BY hhoh-u-Whole Food?
8  Mum:                   [( )
9          (0.3)
10 Mum:    Whole Foo:ds ye[s,
11                        [YES well done,
12         (0.3)
13 Mum:    (          )
14         (0.6)
15 Les:    's I've got Katharine on: th'm too: now,
```

At line 10, Mum confirms 'Whole Foods' as the origin of the tablets, correcting Lesley's lax pronunciation (*Whole Food*) at line 7, and Lesley moves towards sequence closure at line 11 with a second version of her assessment at line 5 (*well done*). Subsequently, however, she reopens the topic with the announcement that she has her daughter (Katharine) *on: th'm too: now,* using the anaphoric reference (*them*) to connect this observation to the 'garlic tablets' of lines 1–11. In these data, we see a complex mixture of sequential and cohesive resources deployed in the achievement of a coherent conversational passage.

Given the default assumption is that a next turn will be fitted to the prior, it is not surprising that there are a large variety of turn-initial particles in most languages that function to lift or fine-tune that assumption (Heritage 2013b; Heritage & Sorjonen 2018). Though this cannot be the moment to develop this line of argument, the role of turn-initiality as a resource for projection should be noted (Schegloff 1996b), and indeed one of the earliest turn-initial objects to be identified in this context was *by the way* – a phrase designed to lift the expectation of fittedness for the next turn at talk (Schegloff & Sacks 1973).

Given that every next turn at talk is subject to the process of three-turn consolidation of action ascription, the process can narrow down the parameters of the problem very considerably even though the problem of intersubjectivity may not be 'solved'. At the same time, it can introduce a sequential 'micro-politics' of the kind that Drew writes about. In the following case, from a collection compiled by Gail Jefferson, where Joan has bought Linda's children some clothing for their dolls, the following ensues:

Excerpt 13.20 TCI(b):16:59:SO (LIN = Linda, JOA = Joan)

```
Linda:   Where did you get the clothes at.
Joan:    At uh Toy City,
Linda:   Were they on sa:le?=
Joan:    =Ah::, yeah.
Linda:   Ye:ah.
Joan:    I went with uh: :m (·) Fay one day...
```

Here Linda's (line 5) acknowledgment of Joan's reply to her question (line 4) does not convey that this response was 'news' to her as, for example, an *oh*-response would have. Rather it conveys that Linda may have expected this response. It further conveys the perspective that Joan is penny-pinching, even when buying gifts for a friend's children. In addition to routine third position responses in Q–A sequences, such as *oh* and *mm hm* indexing information transfer and response incompleteness respectively, there are responses such as *okay* which, as Seuren (2018) observes, can take up a deontic stance in relation to the information conveyed.

These simple third turns, though, are as nothing compared with the immense variegation of actions that can emerge through the operations of 'nextness' in talk structured by open sequentiality. In such contexts, each turn at talk can enable multiple 'nexts', and orderliness can only emerge in and through the multiplicity of indexical and reflexive processes of practical reasoning. This creates much greater complexity for the accountability of action, and its study.

13.7 Discussion

The notion of accountability was classically elucidated by Garfinkel (1967) in terms of two elements: the recognizability and intelligibility of actions, and their reasonableness under given circumstances. A foundational proposition of our field is that human action is entangled within an inescapable web of accountability, in which we are in Merleau-Ponty's phrase 'condemned to meaning' and, with that meaning, condemned to judgment. Goffman expressed this notion in "On face work" with his characterization of a 'line':

> Regardless of whether a person intends to take a line, he will find that he has done so in effect. The other participants will assume that he has more or less willfully taken a stand, so that if he is to deal with their response to him he must take into consideration the impression they have possibly formed of him. (Goffman 1955: 213)

Garfinkel made a similar observation a few years earlier:

> The big question is not whether actors understand each other or not. The fact is that they do understand each other, that they *will* understand each other, but the catch is that they will understand each other regardless of how they *would* be understood. (Garfinkel 1952: 357)

For Goffman, this accountability was primarily understood in 'ritual' and moral terms. To this, Garfinkel (1967) added the question of intelligibility, and it was this latter focus that became central to CA studies of turn-taking, repair, sequence organization and so on, and which enabled CA to transcend its Goffmanian roots. The conception of accountability offered in these statements and within CA more generally involves what might be termed an objective hermeneutics of accountability operating at the level of turns and sequences.

For some versions of social and linguistic theorizing, an apparatus of rules is thought of as a set of constraints imprisoning and corralling human action with little room for maneuver. It may, however, be more productive to view linguistic and interactional structures as something more like a playground climbing frame; a resource for 'climbing through', a means by which action can be fabricated in infinite variety. In their "Concurrent operations" paper, Charles and Candy Goodwin observe that

> The treatment that a bit of talk gets in a next utterance may be quite different from the way in which it was heard and dealt with as it was spoken; indeed, rather than presenting a naked analysis of the prior talk, next utterances characteristically transform that talk in some fashion – deal with it not in its own terms but rather in the way in which it is relevant to the projects of the subsequent speaker. (Goodwin & Goodwin 1987: 4)

The upshot of these observations is the open horizon of talk's accountability both in terms of sense-making and in the construction of action. 'Why that now?' and 'Why that next?' are both questions that function in retrospect, and it is the *anticipation* of that retrospect that, as both Goffman and Garfinkel recognized, conditions action formation and channels its emergent interactional pathways.

13.8 Conclusion

Given the specificity of turns at talk, in combination with the specificity of their sequential and social positioning, it is hard to resist the conclusion that, at the limit, every social action is singular and ineffable. Even the blandest of conversational contributions – the lowly *mm hm*s and *oh*s – may be subject to an essential singularity: one cannot step into the same river twice. I personally find it useful to think of an utterance as like a large and complex molecule with many modes of possible attachment to its contexts, and multiple ways through which it may be elaborated upon in next turn and beyond. This perspective induces a certain modesty about what we may be able to achieve in the analysis of action formation and ascription. But it should not induce hopelessness. Significant advances have been achieved in our understanding of action ascription and, though we are very far from our goals, they are achievable if we set them wisely.

REFERENCES

Aikhenvald, A. Y. (2010). *Imperatives and Commands*. Oxford: Oxford University Press.

Beach, W. A. (1993). Transitional regularities for casual "okay" usages. *Journal of Pragmatics*, 19, 325–52.

Bergmann, J. R. (1993). Alarmiertes Verstehen: Kommunikation in Feuerwehrnotrufen. In T. Jung & S. Mueller-Doohm, eds., *Wirklichkeit im Deutungsprozess: Verstehen und Methoden in den Kultur- und Sozialwissenschaften*. Frankfurt am Main: Suhrkamp, pp. 287–328.

Betz, E., Deppermann, A., Mondada, L. & Sorjonen, M.-L., eds. (2021). *OKAY across Languages: Toward a Comparative Approach to Its Use in Talk-in-Interaction*. Amsterdam: John Benjamins.

Bögels, S., Casillas, M. & Levinson, S. C. (2018). Planning versus comprehension in turn-taking: Fast responders show reduced anticipatory processing of the question. *Neuropsychologia*, 109, 295–310.

Bögels, S., Kendrick, K. & Levinson, S. C. (2019). Conversational expectations get revised as response latencies unfold. *Language, Cognition and Neuroscience*, 35 (6), 1–14.

Bögels, S., Magyari, L. & Levinson, S. C. (2015). Neural signatures of response planning occur midway through an incoming question in conversation. *Scientific Reports*, 5, 12881.

Bolinger, D. L. (1961). Contrastive accent and contrastive stress. *Language*, 37, 83–96.

Clark, H. (1996). *Using Language.* Cambridge: Cambridge University Press.

Clayman, S. E. (2001). Answers and evasions. *Language in Society,* 30, 403–42.

Clayman, S. E. & Fox, M. P. (2017). Hardballs and softballs: Modulating adversarialness in journalistic questioning. *Journal of Language and Politics,* 16, 20–40.

Clayman, S. E. & Heritage, J. (2002). *The News Interview: Journalists and Public Figures on the Air.* Cambridge: Cambridge University Press.

(2014). Benefactors and beneficiaries: Benefactive status and stance in the management of offers and requests. In P. Drew & E. Couper-Kuhlen, eds., *Requesting in Social Interaction.* Amsterdam: Benjamins, pp. 55–86.

Couper-Kuhlen, E. (1984). A new look at contrastive intonation. In R. J. Watts & U. Weidmann, eds., *Modes of Interpretation: Essays Presented to Ernst Leisi on the Occasion of his 65th Birthday*. Tübingen: Gunter Narr.

(2001). Interactional prosody: High onsets in reason-for-the-call turns. *Language in Society,* 30, 29–53.

(2004). Prosody and sequence organization in English conversation: The case of new beginnings. In E. Couper-Kuhlen & C. Ford, eds., *Sound Patterns in Interaction: Cross-Linguistic Studies from Conversation.* Amsterdam: John Benjamins, pp. 335–76.

(2009). A sequential approach to affect: The case of "disappointment." In M. Haakana, M. Laakso & J. Lindstrom, eds., *Talk in Interaction: Comparative Dimensions.* Helsinki: Suomalaisen Kirjallisuuden Seura (Finnish Literature Society), pp. 94–123.

(2012). Some truths and untruths about final intonation in conversational questions. In J.-P. De Ruiter, ed., *Questions: Formal, Functional and Interactional Perspectives*. Cambridge: Cambridge University Press, pp. 123–45.

(2014). What does grammar tell us about action? *Pragmatics*, 24(3), 623–47.

Couper-Kuhlen, E. & Selting, M. (2018). *Interactional Linguistics: Studying Language in Social Interaction*. Cambridge: Cambridge University Press.

Davidson, J. A. (1984). Subsequent versions of invitations, offers, requests, and proposals dealing with potential or actual rejection. In J. M. Atkinson & J. Heritage, eds., *Structures of Social Action: Studies in Conversation Analysis.* Cambridge: Cambridge University Press, pp. 102–28.

De Ruiter, J.-P., Mitterer, J. P. & Enfield, N. J. (2006). Projecting the end of a speaker's turn: A cognitive cornerstone of conversation. *Language*, 82, 515–35.

Deppermann, A. (2013). Turn-design at turn-beginnings: Multimodal resources to deal with tasks of turn-construction in German. *Journal of Pragmatics*, 46, 91–121.

Deppermann, A. & Schmidt, A. (2021). Micro-sequential coordination in bodily early responses. *Discourse Processes* 58(4), 372–396, doi:10.1080/0163853X.2020.1842630.

Deppermann, A. & Streeck, J., eds. (2018). *Time in Embodied Interaction: Synchronicity and Sequentiality of Multimodal Resources*. Amsterdam: John Benjamins.

Drew, P. (2003). Comparative analysis of talk-in-interaction in different institutional settings: A sketch. In P. Glenn, C. Lebaron & J. Mandelbaum, eds., *Studies in Language and Social Interaction: In Honor of Robert Hopper*. Mahwah, NJ: Erlbaum, pp. 293–308.

(2013). Turn design. In J. Sidnell & T. Stivers, eds., *Handbook of Conversation Analysis*. Chichester: Wiley-Blackwell, pp. 131–49.

Drew, P. & Couper-Kuhlen, E. (2014). *Requesting in Social Interaction*. Amsterdam: John Benjamins.

Drew, P. & Heritage, J. (1992). Analyzing talk at work: An introduction. In P. Drew & J. Heritage, eds., *Talk at Work*. Cambridge: Cambridge University Press, pp. 3–65.

Drew, P., Walker, T. & Ogden, R. (2013). Self-repair and action construction. In M. Hayashi, G. Raymond & J. Sidnell, eds., *Conversational Repair and Human Understanding*. Cambridge: Cambridge University Press, pp. 71–94.

Ervin-Tripp, S. (1981). How to make and understand a request. In H. Parret, M. Sbisa & J. Verschueren, eds., *Possibilities and Limitations of Pragmatics*. Amsterdam: Benjamins, pp. 195–210.

Floyd, S., Rossi, G. & Enfield, N. J., eds. (2020). *Getting Others to Do Things: A Pragmatic Typology of Recruitments*. Berlin: Language Science Press.

Ford, C. E. & Thompson, S. A. (1996). Interactional units in conversation: syntactic, intonational and pragmatic resources for the management of turns. In E. Ochs, E. A. Schegloff & S. A. Thompson, eds., *Interaction and Grammar*. Cambridge: Cambridge University Press, pp. 134–84.

Garfinkel, H. (1952). The perception of the other: A study in social order. Dissertation, Harvard University, Cambridge, MA.

(1967). *Studies in Ethnomethodology*. Englewood Cliffs, NJ: Prentice-Hall.

Garfinkel, H. & Sacks, H. (1970). On formal structures of practical actions. In J. D. Mckinney & E. A. Tiryakian, eds., *Theoretical Sociology*. New York, NY: Appleton-Century Crofts, pp. 337–66.

Geluykens, R. (1988). On the myth of rising intonation in polar questions. *Journal of Pragmatics*, 12, 467–85.

Gisladottir, R. S., Bögels, S. & Levinson, S. C. (2018). Oscillatory brain responses reflect anticipation during comprehension of speech acts in spoken dialog. *Frontiers in Human Neuroscience*, 12, doi:10.3389/fnhum.2018.00034.

Goffman, E. (1955). On face work. *Psychiatry*, 18, 213–31.

Goodwin, C. & Goodwin, M. H. (1987). Concurrent operations on talk: Notes on the interactive organization of assessments. *IPrA Papers in Pragmatics*, 1, 1–54.

Guthrie, A. (1997). On the systematic deployment of okay and mmhmm in academic advising sessions. *Pragmatics*, 7, 397–415.

Halliday, M. A. K. & Hasan, R. (1976). *Cohesion in English*. London: Longman.

Hayashi, M. (2004a). Discourse within a sentence: An exploration of postpositions in Japanese as an interactional resource. *Language in Society*, 33, 343–76.
(2004b). Projection and grammar: Notes on the "action-projecting" use of the distal demonstrative *are* in Japanese. *Journal of Pragmatics*, 36, 1337–74.
Heritage, J. (1984). *Garfinkel and Ethnomethodology*. Cambridge: Polity Press.
(1988). Explanations as accounts: A conversation analytic perspective. In C. Antaki, ed., *Analysing Everyday Explanation: A Casebook of Methods*. London: Sage, pp. 127–44.
(2012). Epistemics in action: Action formation and territories of knowledge. *Research on Language and Social Interaction*, 45(1), 1–29.
(2013a). Action formation and its epistemic (and other) backgrounds. *Discourse Studies*, 15, 547–74.
(2013b). Turn-initial position and some of its occupants. *Journal of Pragmatics*, 57, 331–7.
(2015). *Well*-prefaced turns in English conversation: A conversation analytic perspective. *Journal of Pragmatics*, 88, 88–104.
Heritage, J. & Atkinson, J. M. (1984). Introduction. In J. M. Atkinson & J. Heritage, eds., *Structures of Social Action: Studies in Conversation Analysis*. Cambridge: Cambridge University Press, pp. 1–15.
Heritage, J. & Clayman, S. E. (2010). *Talk in Action: Interactions, Identities and Institutions*. Chichester: Wiley-Blackwell.
Heritage, J. & Maynard, D. W. (2006). Problems and prospects in the study of physician-patient interaction: 30 years of research. *Annual Review of Sociology*, 32, 351–74.
(2021). Harold Garfinkel and ethnomethodology's legacies: Introduction. In D. W. Maynard & J. Heritage, eds., *Harold Garfinkel: Praxis, Social Order and Ethnomethodology's Legacies*. Oxford: Oxford University Press.
Heritage, J. & Robinson, J. D. (n.d.). Expanded responses in primary care problem presentations. Unpublished Ms. UCLA Department of Sociology.
Heritage, J. & Sorjonen, M.-L., eds. (2018). *Between Turn and Sequence: Turn-Initial Particles across Languages*. Amsterdam: John Benjamins.
Höhle, T. N. (1992). Über Verum-Fokus im Deutschen. In J. Jacobs, ed., *Informationsstruktur und Grammatik*. Opladen: Westdeutscher Verlag, pp. 112–41.
Iwasaki, S. (2009). Initiating interactive turn spaces in Japanese conversation: Local projection and collaborative action. *Discourse Processes*, 46, 226–46.
Jefferson, G. (1973). A case of precision timing in ordinary conversation: Overlapped tag-positioned address terms in closing sequences. *Semiotica*, 9, 47–96.
(1980a). End of Grant Report on Conversations in which "Troubles" or "Anxieties" are Expressed (HR 4805/2). London: Social Science Research Council.
(1980b). On "trouble-premonitory" response to inquiry. *Sociological Inquiry*, 50, 153–85.
(1983). Two explorations of the organization of overlapping talk in conversation: "Notes on some orderlinesses of overlap onset" and "On a failed hypothesis: 'Conjunctionals' as overlap-vulnerable." Tilburg Papers in Language and Literature 28. Tilburg: University of Tilburg.
(1986). Notes on "latency" in overlap onset. *Human Studies*, 9, 153–83.

(1988). On the sequential organization of troubles-talk in ordinary conversation. *Social Problems*, 35(4), 418–41.

(1989). Preliminary notes on a possible metric which provides for a "standard maximum" silence of approximately one second in conversation. In D. Roger & P. Bull, eds., *Conversation: An Interdisciplinary Perspective.* Clevedon: Multilingual Matters, pp. 166–96.

(2004). A sketch of some orderly aspects of overlap in natural conversation. In G. Lerner, ed., *Conversation Analysis: Studies from the First Generation.* Amsterdam: John Benjamins, pp. 43–59.

Kamio, A. (1997). *Territory of Information.* Amsterdam: John Benjamins.

Kaukomaa, T., Peräkylä, A. & Ruusuvuori, J. (2013). Turn-opening smiles: Facial expression constructing emotional transition in conversation. *Journal of Pragmatics*, 55, 21–42.

(2014). Foreshadowing a problem: Turn-opening frowns in conversation. *Journal of Pragmatics*, 71, 132–47.

Kendrick, K. & Holler, J. (2017). Gaze direction signals response preference in conversation. *Research on Language and Social Interaction*, 50, 12–32.

Kendrick, K. & Torreira, F. (2015). The timing and construction of preference: A quantitative study. *Discourse Processes*, 52, 255–89.

Kim, H. R. S. & Kuroshima, S., eds. (2013). Turn beginnings in interaction: An introduction. *Journal of Pragmatics*, 57, 267–73.

Kim, K.-H. (1999). Phrasal unit boundaries and organization of turns and sequences in Korean conversation. *Human Studies*, 22, 425–46.

Labov, W. (1972). *Sociolinguistic Patterns*. Philadelphia, PA: University of Pennsylvania Press.

Labov, W. & Fanshel, D. (1977). *Therapeutic Discourse: Psychotherapy as Conversation.* New York, NY: Academic Press.

Lerner, G. (1996). On the "semi-permeable" character of grammatical units in conversation: Conditional entry into the turn-space of another speaker. In E. Ochs, E. A. Schegloff & S. Thompson, eds., *Interaction and Grammar.* Cambridge: Cambridge University Press, pp. 238–76.

(2004). Collaborative turn sequences. In G. Lerner, ed., *Conversation Analysis: Studies from the First Generation.* Amsterdam: John Benjamins, pp. 225–56.

Levinson, S. C. (1981). The essential inadequacies of speech act models of dialogue. In H. Parret, M. Sbisa & J. Verschueren, eds., *Possibilities and Limitations of Pragmatics.* Amsterdam: John Benjamins, pp. 473–92.

(1983). *Pragmatics.* Cambridge: Cambridge University Press.

(1992). Activity types and language. In P. Drew & J. Heritage, eds., *Talk at Work.* Cambridge: Cambridge University Press, pp. 66–100.

(2013). Action formation and ascription. In J. Sidnell & T. Stivers, eds., *Handbook of Conversation Analysis.* Boston, MA: Wiley-Blackwell, pp. 103–30.

(2017). Speech acts. In Y. Huang, ed., *Oxford Handbook of Pragmatics.* Oxford: Oxford University Press, pp. 199–216.

Mandelbaum, J. (2013). Storytelling in conversation. In J. Sidnell & T. Stivers, eds., *Handbook of Conversation Analysis.* New York: Wiley-Blackwell, pp. 492–508.

Mondada, L. (2011). The management of knowledge discrepancies and of epistemic changes in institutional interactions. In T. Stivers, L. Mondada & J. Steensig, eds., *The Morality of Knowledge in Conversation*. Cambridge: Cambridge University Press, pp. 27–57.

(2012). Garden lessons: Embodied action and joint attention in extended sequences. In H. Nasu & F. C. Waksler, eds., *Interaction and Everyday Life: Phenomenological and Ethnomethodological Essays in honor of George Psathas*. Plymouth: Lexington, pp. 279–96.

(2013). Displaying, contesting and negotiating epistemic authority in social interaction: Descriptions and questions in guided visits. *Discourse Studies*, 15, 597–626.

(2014a). Cooking instructions and the shaping of things in the kitchen. In M. Nevile, T. Heinemann, P. Haddington & M. Rauniomaa, eds., *Interacting with Objects: Language, Materiality, and Social Activity*, 199–226.

(2014b). The local constitution of multimodal resources for social interaction. *Journal of Pragmatics*, 65, 137–56.

(2017). Walking and talking together: Questions/answers and mobile participation in guided visits. *Social Science Information*, 56, 220–53.

(2018). Multiple temporalities of language and body in interaction: challenges for transcribing multimodality. *Research on Language and Social Interaction*, 51(1), 85–106.

(2021). How early can embodied responses be? Issues in time and sequentiality. *Discourse Processes*, 58(4), 397–418.

Ogden, R. (2006). Phonetics and social action in agreements and disagreements. *Journal of Pragmatics*, 38, 1752–75.

Park, Y. (2014). Openings in Korean primary care discourse: Where does it hurt? *Discourse and Cognition* 담화와인지, 21, 29–56.

Raymond, C. W. (2015). Questions and responses in Spanish monolingual and Spanish–English bilingual conversation. *Language & Communication*, 42, 50–68.

(2017). Indexing a contrast: The do-construction in English conversation. *Journal of Pragmatics*, 118, 22–37.

(2019). Intersubjectivity, normativity and grammar. *Social Psychology Quarterly*, 82, 182–204.

(2020). Tense and aspect in sequences of action. Unpublished manuscript, University of Colorado.

Raymond, C. W., Clift, R. & Heritage, J. (2021). Reference without anaphora: On agency through grammar. *Journal of Linguistics*, doi:10.1515/ling-2021-0058.

Raymond, C. W. & Stivers, T. (2016). Off-record account solicitations. In J. D. Robinson, ed., *Accountability in Social Interaction.* Oxford: Oxford University Press, pp. 321–53.

Raymond, G. & Zimmerman, D. H. (2016). Closing matters: Alignment and misalignment in sequence and call closings in institutional interaction. *Discourse Studies*, 18(6), 716–36.

Robinson, J. D. (1998). Getting down to business: Talk, gaze, and body orientation during openings of doctor–patient consultations. *Human Communication Research*, 25, 97–123.

(2003). An interactional structure of medical activities during acute visits and its implications for patients' participation. *Health Communication*, 15, 27–57.

(2006). Soliciting patients' presenting concerns. In J. Heritage & D. Maynard, eds., *Communication in Medical Care: Interactions between Primary Care Physicians and Patients.* Cambridge: Cambridge University Press, pp. 22–47.

Robinson, J. D. ed. (2016). *Accountability in Social Interaction*. Oxford: Oxford University Press.

(2020). Revisiting preference organization in context: A qualitative and quantitative examination of responses to information seeking. *Research on Language and Social Interaction*, 53(2), 197–222.

Robinson, J. D. & Heritage, J. (2005). The structure of patients' presenting concerns: The completion relevance of current symptoms. *Social Science and Medicine*, 61, 481–93.

Robinson, J. D. & Stivers, T. (2001). Achieving activity transitions in primary-care encounters: From history taking to physical examination. *Human Communication Research*, 27, 253–98.

Rosch, E. (1978). Principles of categorization. In E. Rosch & B. Lloyd, eds., *Cognition and Categorization*. Hillsdale, NJ: Erlbaum, pp. 27–48.

Rossano, F. (2012). Gaze behavior in face-to-face interaction. Dissertation, Radboud University, Nijmegen.

(2013). Gaze in conversation. In J. Sidnell & T. Stivers, eds., *Handbook of Conversation Analysis*. Chichester: Wiley-Blackwell, pp. 308–29.

Rossano, F., Brown, P. & Levinson, S. C. (2009). Gaze, questioning and culture. In J. Sidnell, ed. *Conversation Analysis: Comparative Perspectives*. Cambridge: Cambridge University Press, pp. 187–249.

Rossi, G. (2018). Composite social actions: The case of factual declaratives in everyday interaction. *Research on Language and Social Interaction*, 51(4), 379–97.

(in press). *Systems of Social Action: The Case of Requesting in Italian*. Oxford: Oxford University Press.

Sacks, H. (1974). An analysis of the course of a joke's telling in conversation. In R. Bauman & J. Sherzer, eds., *Explorations in the Ethnography of Speaking*. Cambridge: Cambridge University Press, pp. 337–53.

(1987). On the preferences for agreement and contiguity in sequences in conversation. In G. Button & J. Lee, eds., *Talk and Social Organisation*. Clevedon: Multilingual Matters, 54–69.

Sacks, H. & Schegloff, E. A. (1979). Two preferences in the organization of reference to persons and their interaction. In G. Psathas, ed., *Everyday Language: Studies in Ethnomethodology*. New York, NY: Irvington, pp. 15–21.

Sacks, H., Schegloff, E. A. & Jefferson, G. (1974). A simplest systematics for the organization of turn-taking for conversation. *Language*, 50(4), 696–735.

Schegloff, E. A. (1988). Presequences and indirection: Applying speech act theory to ordinary conversation. *Journal of Pragmatics*, 12, 55–62.

(1992a). To Searle on conversation: A note in return. In H. Parret & J. Verschueren, eds., *(On) Searle On Conversation*. Amsterdam: John Benjamins, pp. 113–28.

(1992b). Repair after next turn: The last structurally provided defense of intersubjectivity in conversation. *American Journal of Sociology*, 97(5), 1295–345.

(1996a). Confirming allusions: Toward an empirical account of action. *American Journal of Sociology*, 102(1), 161–216.

(1996b). Turn organization: One intersection of grammar and interaction. In E. Ochs, S. Thompson & E. Schegloff, eds., *Interaction and Grammar*. Cambridge: Cambridge University Press, pp. 52–133.

(1998). Reflections on studying prosody in talk-in-interaction. *Language and Speech*, 41, 235–63.

(2000). Overlapping talk and the organization of turn-taking for conversation. *Language in Society*, 29, 1–63.

(2007). *Sequence Organization in Interaction: A Primer in Conversation Analysis.* Cambridge: Cambridge University Press.

(2011). Word repeats as unit ends. *Discourse Studies*, 13, 367–80.

Schegloff, E. A. & Lerner, G. H. (2009). Beginning to respond: *Well*-prefaced responses to *wh*-questions. *Research on Language and Social Interaction*, 42, 91–115.

Schegloff, E. A. & Sacks, H. (1973). Opening up closings. *Semiotica*, 8(4), 289–327.

Searle, J. R. (1969). *Speech Acts: An Essay in the Philosophy of Language.* Cambridge: Cambridge University Press.

Seuren, L. M. 2018. Assessing answers: Action ascription in third position. *Research on Language and Social Interaction*, 5(1), 33–51.

Sicoli, M. A., Stivers, T., Enfield, N. J. & Levinson, S. C. (2015). Marked initial pitch in questions signals marked communicative function. *Language and Speech*, 58, 204–23.

Sinclair, J. & Coulthard, M. (1975). *Towards an Analysis of Discourse.* London: Oxford University Press.

Sorjonen, M.-L., Raevaara, L. & Couper-Kuhlen, E., eds. (2017). *Imperative Turns at Talk: the Design of Directives in Action.* Amsterdam: John Benjamins.

Stevanovic, M. & Peräkylä, A. (2012). Deontic authority in interaction: The right to announce, propose, and decide. *Research on Language and Social Interaction*, 45 (3), 297–321.

Stevanovic, M. & Svennevig, J. (2015). Introduction: Epistemics and deontics in conversational directives. *Journal of Pragmatics*, 78, 1–6.

Stivers, T. (2005). Modified repeats: One method for asserting primary rights from second position. *Research on Language and Social Interaction*, 38, 131–58.

(2010). An overview of the question–response system in American English. *Journal of Pragmatics*, 42, 2772–81.

Stivers, T. & Heritage, J. (2001). Breaking the sequential mold: Answering "more than the question" during medical history taking. *Text*, 21, 151–85.

Stivers, T. & Rossano, F. (2010). Mobilizing response. *Research on Language and Social Interaction*, 43(1), 3–31.

Streeck, J., Goodwin, C. & Lebaron, C., eds. (2011). *Embodied Interaction: Language and Body in the Material World.* Cambridge: Cambridge University Press.

Szczepek Reed, B. & Raymond, G. (2013). The question of units for language, action and interaction. In B. Szczepek Reed & G. Raymond, eds., *Units of Talk – Units of Action*. Amsterdam: John Benjamins, 1–10.

Tanaka, H. (1999). Grammar and social interaction in Japanese and Anglo-American English: The display of context, social identity and social relation. *Human Studies*, 22, 363–95.

(2000). Turn projection in Japanese talk-in-interaction. *Research on Language and Social Interaction*, 33, 1–38.

Thompson, S. A., Raymond, C. W. & Fox, B. A. (2020). The grammar of proposals for joint activities. *International Linguistics*, doi:10.1075/il.20011.tho.

Vatanen, A. (2018). Responding in early overlap: Recognitional onsets in assertion sequences. *Research on Language and Social Interaction*, 51(2), 107–26.
Walker, T. (2014). Form ≠ function: The independence of prosody and action. *Research on Language and Social Interaction*, 47(1), 1–16.
Wierzbicka, A. (1987). *English Speech Acts: A Semantic Dictionary,* Cambridge, MA: Academic Press.
Wilson, T. P. (1991). Social structure and the sequential organization of interaction. In D. Boden & D. H. Zimmerman, eds., *Talk and Social Structure.* Cambridge: Polity, pp. 22–43.
Wootton, A. (1989). Remarks on the methodology of Conversation Analysis. In P. Bull & D. Roger, eds., *Conversation: An Interdisciplinary Approach.* Clevedon: Multilingual Matters, pp. 238–58.
Wu, R. J. R. (2004). *Stance in Talk: A Conversation Analysis of Mandarin Final Particles.* Amsterdam: John Benjamins.
Wu, R. J. R. & Heritage, J. (2018). Particles and epistemics: Convergences and divergences between English and Mandarin. In G. Raymond, G. H. Lerner & J. Heritage, eds., *Enabling Human Conduct: Naturalistic Studies of Talk-in-Interaction in Honor of Emanuel A. Schegloff.* Amsterdam: John Benjamins, pp. 273–98.

Appendix A Transcription Conventions (CA)

Source: Jefferson, G. (2004). Glossary of transcript symbols with an introduction. In G. Lerner (ed.), *Conversation Analysis: Studies from the First Generation*. Amsterdam: John Benjamins, pp. 13–31.

(.)	micro pause
(0.2)	timed pause
[ ]	beginning and end of overlapping speech
> <	faster pace of speech
< >	slower pace of the speech
( )	inaudible/incomprehensible stretch of speech
(( ))	contextual information
word	stressed word or syllable
↑	upstep in intonation
↓	downstep in intonation
CAPITALS	loud voice delivery
hum(h)our	interspersed laughter particles
=	latched speech
::	stretched sound
→	line of particular interest to the analysis

Appendix B Transcription Conventions (GAT2)

Source: Selting, M., Auer, P., Barth-Weingarten, D., Bergmann, J., Bergmann, P. et al. (2011). A system for transcribing talk-in-interaction: GAT 2. Translated and adapted for English by E. Couper-Kuhlen & D. Barth-Weingarten. *Gesprächsforschung* 12, 1–51, www.gespraechsforschung-online.de/en/2011.html.

[ ]	overlap and simultaneous talk
=	latching
(.)	micropause (shorter than 0.2 sec)
(2.85)	measured pause
geht_s	assimilation of words
:, ::, :::	segmental lengthening, according to duration
((laughs))	non-verbal vocal actions and events
akZENT	focal accent
akzEnt	secondary stress
?	pitch rising to high at end of intonation phrase
,	pitch rising to mid at end of intonation phrase
-	level pitch at end of intonation phrase
;	pitch falling to mid at end of intonation phrase
.	pitch falling to low at end of intonation phrase
<<p> >	piano, soft
<<f>	forte, loud
<<h> >	high pitch register
<<p> >	piano, soft
<<all> >	allegro, fast
°h	inbreath, according to duration
h°	outbreath, according to duration
<<creaky voice>>	commentaries regarding voice qualities with indication of scope
(solche)	assumed wording

Appendix C Conventions for Multimodal Transcription

Source: Mondada, L. (2018). Multiple temporalities of language and body in interaction: Challenges for transcribing multimodality. *Research on Language and Social Interaction*, 51(1), 85–106.

* *	Descriptions of embodied actions are delimited between two identical symbols
+ +	and synchronized with corresponding stretches of talk/silences.
*–>	The action described continues across subsequent lines
—>*	until the same symbol reoccurs.
>>	The action described begins before the beginning of the extract.
–>>	The action described continues after the end of the extract.
....	Preparation phase of an action.
—	Duration of the apex of an action
,,,,,	Retraction of an action
dri	Participant who performs the embodied action
fig	The exact moment at which a screen shot was taken is indicated
#	within a turn at talk or within silences.

Index

For EU product safety concerns, contact us at Calle de José Abascal, 56–1°, 28003 Madrid, Spain or eugpsr@cambridge.org.

www.ingramcontent.com/pod-product-compliance
Ingram Content Group UK Ltd.
Pitfield, Milton Keynes, MK11 3LW, UK
UKHW020400140625
459647UK00020B/2576

* 9 7 8 1 1 0 8 4 6 5 0 7 6 *